GREAT IDEAS FOR YOUR GARDEN

JANE COURTIER • ALISON R. FRANCIS
PETER McHOY • ANDREW MIKOLAJSKI

Select Editions

Authors: Jane Courtier, Alison R. Francis,
Peter McHoy, Andrew Mikolajski

First published in Canada in 2005 by
Select Editions
3918 Kitchener St
Burnaby BC Canada
V5C 3M2

Tel: 604-415-2444
Fax: 604-415-3444

A Marshall Edition
Conceived, edited, and designed by Marshall Editions
The Old Brewery, 6 Blundell Street, London N7 9BH, U.K.
www.quarto.com

ISBN 1-894905-77-6

1 3 5 7 9 10 8 6 4 2

Originated in Singapore by PICA
Printed and bound in China by Midas Printing Limited

Design for this edition: Red Alert Design
Copy-editing: Jane Chapman

CONTENTS

PART ONE:
DESIGN
SOLUTIONS

In gardening, as in other spheres, beauty is subjective. A garden with grass left long, an unstructured appearance, and some weeds left as food for the caterpillars of certain butterflies, is likely to please a wildlife enthusiast, but is certain to irritate a gardener whose tastes include neatly edged formal beds, and seasonal bedding plants set out in regimented rows. However, the gardener who prefers his or her garden simply to evolve may have equal contempt for a carefully structured garden with a strong formal design element. Whatever your gardening tastes, this section of the book reflects a variety of gardening styles, seeking to stimulate your imagination and offer exciting solutions that you can develop and adapt to your own individual taste.

ASSESSING YOUR NEEDS

Much can be achieved in a garden by careful design. Features have to be planned carefully, taking into account their impact on the overall look: you can't consider a patio or a pool in isolation—it has to work well with other elements that are fighting for attention.

Areas of paving or decking can be introduced and separate "rooms" created, each with their own features and focal points just waiting to be explored. Compartments can sometimes be introduced by planting hedges to divide the garden into distinct areas. Or a decorative trellis, painted an attractive and stylish color or covered with a climber, can achieve the desired effect without being too "heavy" visually, or depriving plants of light.

Low box hedges (*Buxus sempervirens* "Suffruticosa"), or low walls, raised beds, and even raised ponds, can be used to create compartments that have to be explored by walking around obstacles and through "entrances" without the garden looking cluttered or oppressive. Climbers and wall shrubs can often be used to make the most of vertical space and to hide fences.

Unusual solutions

This section of the book also addresses the issues of small gardens, and smaller areas cordoned off within large gardens. In these gardens, choosing plants and making the most of space is a critical business. Gardeners blessed with a large or rambling plot can indulge a fancy for a plant that is perhaps spectacular for a brief moment and boring for the rest of the year, or indulge in color-themed borders because there are always other parts of the garden to hold interest once a particular bed or border has passed its best. But in a smaller "room," every plant has to work hard to justify its inclusion, which usually means it must be attractive over a long period, or at least have several "high points" during the season, with perhaps spring flowers and fall color or berries.

In a suburban garden there are usually garden fences or walls within eyeshot whichever way you turn, the house will dominate certain views, and often neighboring properties shatter any illusion of a rural retreat. For these reasons a more structured approach is often a better choice, and careful design is needed to create focal points in the right places, and above all create a sense of unity that to some extent compensates for other restraints.

1
PAVING
AND DECKING

The garden floor and especially the patio surface should be attractive as well as practical. Many patios and paths are constructed of plain paving slabs and can look boring as well as commonplace. With just a little thought, and often only a modest budget, it is possible to give your garden real style as well as a stronger sense of design simply by choosing an appropriate material and pattern for your paving or decking. The options shown in this chapter provide only a taste of the possibilities, so spend a little time exploring your local stores and sending for catalogs – it's worth the effort.

CREATING A DESIGN

If you do not know where to begin when it comes to planning your garden, copy a rough outline of the space on to graph paper, then use tracing paper overlays to experiment with various designs. You are more likely to come up with something pleasing if you mark a square grid over the basic outline. Dividing it up into rectangles is a practical option, then you can make beds, borders, and paths follow this plan if you desire a formal outline. You can also subdivide your larger squares into smaller units to provide a more flexible design.

DESIGN BASICS

Nonplant features such as paving, trellises, raised beds, ponds, and paths are called "hard landscaping." Hard landscaping provides the skeleton of the design: it gives the garden its shape and structure; its esthetic qualities, its color and appeal, will come from the plants, or "soft landscaping." Attaining a balance between these two elements is the key to good design. Newly constructed gardens often look harsh until the plants have matured.

Initially, you should not spend too much time working out detailed planting plans for beds and borders; merely seek to establish the effect you want to create with your chosen plants. Visualize borders packed with plants, with growth tumbling over straight edges to soften the effect.

MARKING OUT
A garden hose provides a useful tool for marking out the outline of a new feature, perhaps for paving or decking, within the garden.

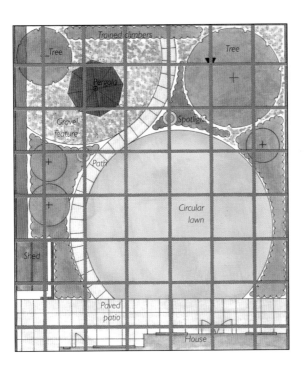

PLANNING AHEAD
Careful and imaginative
planning can enliven a simple,
square-shaped garden.

TIPS

Think carefully about
the type of surfaces
you want in your
garden. Gravel blends
harmoniously with
plants and bricks.
Bricks and clay pavers
are "warm" and
seldom detract from
the plants, while
concrete paving slabs
are "colder" and suit
more formal areas of
paving such as a patio.

MAKING PLANS

It is always worth making lists of
desired features. Unless you manage
to incorporate most of your essential
features, you'll probably be
frustrated in the long term. Be
practical and don't set your aims too
high. Budget is also a consideration.

■ Vary the angle of your features to
create a more interesting vista. Paths,
for example, can zigzag through the
garden at a 45 degree angle.

■ If your budget is small, create a
garden plan that you can execute in
stages, over months or even years.
You can begin with a patio, build a
pond the following year, and maybe
add an arbor or trellis work with
climbers. If you have them all
planned from the beginning,
throughout the different stages, your
garden will still look well designed
with all your features well integrated.

■ If you are seeking a softer effect,
incorporate flowing curves rather
than acute angles. Draw a series of
circles on your plan and use circular
beds, circular areas of paving
(see pp. 24–25), even a circular lawn.
Use arcs to link the curves of circular
features to create a flowing design.

■ It is especially important to have
an overall plan in sight before you
start to construct paths, walls, and
raised beds: these are labor-intensive
features to build and difficult and
expensive to adapt afterward.

■ Before starting construction work,
try to mark out your plan with pegs
and string. View it from different
angles, if possible from an upstairs
window to gain an aerial view. It's
surprising how different things
appear once transferred from
paper to garden.

ESSENTIAL TOOLS

A selection of basic, good-quality tools is essential if you are doing any type of construction work in the garden, such as paving, decking, or erecting a trellis. It is usually easier and cheaper to rent specialized equipment, such as a plate compactor (for vibrating pavers), which you are not likely to use often.

CONSTRUCTION KIT

The following basic tools should be a part of any gardener's armory and will be particularly useful for preparing the site prior to laying paving or decking. To ensure that your tools perform well and last a long time, it is important that they are properly maintained. Always clean your tools after using them.

■ **Rake** A rake is used for leveling the soil surface.

■ **Garden hose** A garden hose is useful for marking out informal and irregular shapes in the garden.

■ **Spade** A spade is essential for marking out and digging the site.

■ **Straightedge** A straight plank of wood is useful for marking out straight lines, checking the level of paving slabs and bricks, and for tamping down when laying concrete.

■ **Builder's level** A traditional tool for establishing the level of any garden feature, such as slabs and pavers.

■ **Measure** A simple tape measure is important for measuring the dimensions of features in your garden.

GARDEN RAKE

BUILDER'S LEVEL

STRAIGHTEDGE

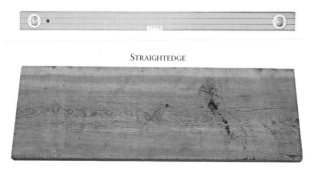

■ **Wheelbarrow**
Essential for transporting plants and heavy items, clearing debris, and moving earth. If you are transporting very heavy loads or working on rough ground, a model with a ball wheel is easier to push than a solid wheel version.

WHEELBARROW

■ **Mallet** A wooden mallet is useful for tamping pavers, bricks, and paving slabs into position.

■ **Builder's trowel** A hand trowel is essential for mixing small quantities of mortar and for cementing mortar around slabs, bricks, and pavers.

■ **Pointing tool** A useful tool for giving a neat finish to pavers, slabs, and brickwork, pointing tools seal the mortar joints and help provide protection against weather damage.

■ **Hammer** A hammer is necessary for nailing decking and constructing frames for concrete.

■ **Screwdriver** A screwdriver is useful for fixing screws into decking.

■ **Electric drill** An electric drill with a selection of drill bits is essential for decking, wooden arbors, and temporary frames for laying concrete and slabs.

■ **Brush** A firm brush is necessary for brushing off sand and excess mortar from newly laid paving.

■ **Builder's square** A square is necessary for checking the angles of frames and corners for paved areas.

Warning

• Wear the correct safety gear when using heavy or powered equipment in the garden. Tools powered by the main electrical supply should be fitted with a circuit breaker.

• Keep tools with sharp edges away from children.

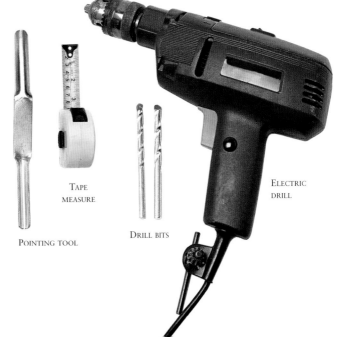

POINTING TOOL

TAPE MEASURE

DRILL BITS

ELECTRIC DRILL

PAVING STYLES

Designed to be functional, paving comes in so many materials, shapes, and imaginative designs, that there is no excuse for any paved area to look boring or mundane. While concrete paving slabs are the most popular material for patios, pavers and bricks are sometimes more appropriate. There is also a wide range of premolded concrete paving that is designed to look like small pavers and which is much quicker and easier to lay.

PLAIN OR COLORED

■ **Plain patterns** If you prefer plain patterns that don't detract from the surrounding plants, there are plenty of slabs with riven or stonelike finishes. Rectangular rather than square slabs look more interesting, even if laid in simple staggered rows.

■ **Color and size** Uniformly colored slabs can add warmth to a patio, but be wary of bright colors. Add interest by using slabs of different sizes to make a pleasing pattern rather than mixing different colors.

■ **Small slabs** Small areas often look best paved with small slabs, which give the illusion of a denser, larger expanse of paving despite the restricted space.

PLACE TO PAUSE
Irregular-shaped pavers in a staggered, circular pattern are effective in a small space.

CREATING ILLUSIONS

Natural stone slabs always look good but are expensive. For a cheaper alternative, look for good-quality concrete slabs that have been designed to simulate stone. Break up the design by leaving planting gaps between some of the slabs. Weathered stone pavers can create a natural look and include stippled, scored, and pebbled textures.

If you want to create the illusion of bricks and pavers while actually using concrete paving slabs, choose from the wide range of premolded slabs designed to simulate pavers. They won't have the same effect as the real thing, but are worthwhile for being fast to lay and low in cost.

NATURAL-STONE EFFECT SLABS

PREMOLDED PAVING SLABS

SHAPE AND TEXTURE

Consider the texture, color, and style when selecting your paving materials, choosing those that reflect the mood of your garden and its setting. Terra-cotta tiles look good in a fine, formal setting, while rough-edged secondhand bricks are more suited to a rural environment or cottage garden.

PLAYING WITH SHAPES

Laying slabs in straight, unstaggered rows is not a good idea for large areas of paving, and can look monotonous in a small patio setting. The exception is a formal paved area, where symmetry can emphasize the sense of formality and unity.

SLABS WITH INSETS

Flat areas can be given definition by artificially setting paving materials at different levels to form a series of shallow steps at irregular angles.

Bricks are particularly good for providing variation in shape and design in a small area. A variety of textures can be created using stones, pebbles, gravel, and wood.

ABSTRACT MOSAIC
Rough stone cobbles
arranged in a cartwheel-
patterned mosaic offer
the opportunity to
experiment with texture,
direction, and color.

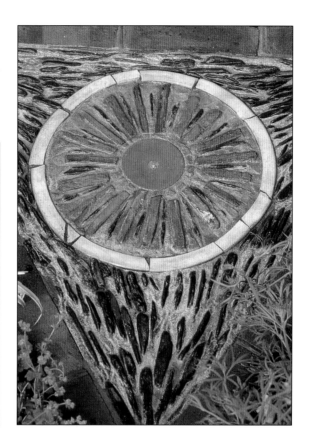

TEXTURE

• To bring out the
surface textures of
natural stone paving,
do not be too keen to
mortar the joints flush
with the surface.

• Try to blend the
features in your garden
with the surroundings.
Smooth, flat surfaces
will work best in a
modern urban garden,
while natural, rough-
cut textures suit an
informal rural setting.

EXPERIMENTING WITH SHAPES

■ **Mosaics** Small, modern gardens
are excellent for experimenting with
original and abstract designs. A
geometric, hard-edged layout can
provide a framework for colorful and
original mosaics of differently shaped
stones, such as the one shown above.

■ **Circular formations** Some
manufacturers offer a selection of
slabs in various sizes, which when
put together form a circle (see pp.
24–25). It is well worth considering
this style of paving if you have only a
very small area in which to create an
impact. If backed by a curved raised
bed, or arranged around a specimen
plant, this style can provide a strong
focal point.

■ **Mixing shapes** Mixing rectangular
paving with circular slabs demands
skill if the design is to work well.
A variety of loose paving materials
can be used for infilling between
both rectangular and circular slabs.

■ **Hexagonal paving** Requiring
careful positioning, hexagonal paving
can look out of place in an informal
setting and is best used where you
want to create a modern image.
While it is a simple task to make
a straight edge with special half
slabs, it is also possible to design the
paved area so that plants fill in
the irregular edge. It is easier to buy
these from the manufacturer than
to try to cut them yourself.

BRICKS AND PAVERS

Valued for their warm and earthy appearance, bricks used as
paving for patios and paths can be useful if you want these to
match garden walls or your house. By using the same kind of brick,
you can create a sense of unity that suggests a well-planned garden.
Similar in size to bricks, clay and concrete pavers provide hardwearing
and flexible surfaces and are ideal for small or confined areas such
as driveways. Granite "setts," or hand-hewn stones, can also be used
in a small garden to create a traditional "cobbled" effect or for
patterned and mosaic-style paving.

COORDINATION IN BRICK

Brick paving brings an informal touch to the
garden. Like clay and concrete pavers, bricks can
be laid in many patterns (see pp. 22–23), on edge
as well as face-up. The mortar can also contribute
to the design: use pale mortar to emphasize the
paving pattern, otherwise add a colorant to make
the mortar joints more conspicuous.

BRICKS OR CLAY PAVERS

Superficially, bricks
and clay pavers look
similar – both are
made from baked clay,
have similar coloring,
and from a distance
seem to have similar
dimensions. Bricks are,
however, thicker and
need to be mortared
together, which means
an additional job and
can radically change
the visual appearance
of the paving. Pavers,
by contrast, are butt-
joined and firmly
secured simply by
bedding on sand
and vibrating the
pavers with a plate
compactor.

COTTAGE PATH
A narrow brick path in
straight lines blends easily
with the surrounding
flower beds.

CONCRETE PAVERS

Clay and concrete pavers are made to fit together without mortared joints. They are usually bedded on a base of sand over consolidated hardcore, then locked together by more sand being vibrated between the joints. This method of laying on sand has led to the term "flexible paving," since the pavers are not set in concrete and can be lifted and relaid if necessary. If properly laid, pavers are an ideal, hardwearing option for driveways.

Clay pavers can be laid in a variety of patterns and are small enough to make a path or area of paving look well proportioned in even a small garden. Additionally, staggered and cut pavers look less obtrusive than paving slabs where changes of direction are required. Clay pavers blend well with brick features. Concrete pavers are available in a wide range of colors and shapes and are excellent for paving a small area. However, although a color range sounds attractive, using too many together is not a good idea.

■ **Setts and cobbles** Hand-hewn granite setts are useful for small areas of paving but can be expensive. Small rectangular concrete blocks with a similar effect, and sometimes described as "cobbles," are more readily available. Both are ideal for creating fans and circle patterns.

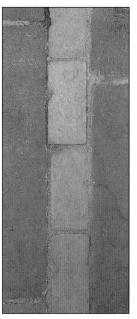

BRICK INSETS PROVIDE A SUBTLE ADDITION TO A PAVING FEATURE

PAVED PATIO
Clay pavers in a herringbone pattern integrate well with a garden wall, brick pillar, and terra-cotta containers.

LAYING PAVING SLABS

Paving slabs are heavy to handle but reasonably quick and easy to lay. They come in many shapes, sizes, and finishes, making them popular for patios and pathways. For very light use you can simply bed them on sand, provided the soil beneath is firmly consolidated, but whenever possible it is wise to prepare a proper foundation and bed your paving on mortar. Make sure that you have all the necessary tools to hand before you start (see pp. 12–13 for the tools you need).

PREPARING THE GROUND

1 As a starting point for your paving, use string and pegs to mark out the area to be paved. Check that the corners are at right angles using a builder's square. Excavate the area to allow for 2 in (5 cm) of compacted hardcore and 2 in (5 cm) of sand and ballast, plus the depth of the slabs and mortar. Dig down to firm subsoil, then tamp down with a thick piece of wood. Using a straightedge and builder's level, insert marking pegs in a grid at 6-ft (2-m) intervals as level guides.

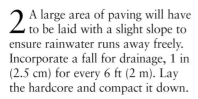

2 A large area of paving will have to be laid with a slight slope to ensure rainwater runs away freely. Incorporate a fall for drainage, 1 in (2.5 cm) for every 6 ft (2 m). Lay the hardcore and compact it down.

3 Apply 3 in (8 cm) of sand and gravel (ballast). This should be firmly compacted down to a depth of 2 in (5 cm). Level the sand and gravel by tamping with a straightedge to produce a smooth surface.

POSITIONING THE SLABS

1 Start laying the slabs at a clearly defined edge. Using a trowel, cover the sand with a solid base of mortar. Lower the slab and firm into position. Other methods for laying mortar include putting a blob of mortar on each corner and in the center of the slab, or laying mortar around the edges with a cross of mortar through the center ("box and cross" method). However, water can seep into the gaps and freeze, causing problems in winter.

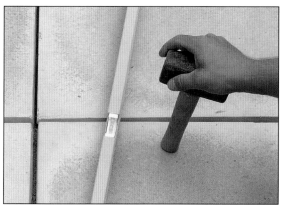

2 Tap down the slab with the handle of your mallet until it is level with the neighboring slabs. Check the evenness with a long builder's level to ensure the paving is laid without uneven edges or hollows where surface water could collect. Remember to slope the paving to allow for drainage.

3 Some slabs are designed to butt up without mortaring, but others require a mortar joint. Use spacers (you can cut these from scrap wood) to ensure that the slabs are an even distance apart. Once the bedding mortar has set, fill in the gaps between the paving using a pointing tool. You can make the mortar flush with the paving or recess it slightly with a pointing tool. Wipe off any mortar from the surface of the slabs before it dries.

LAYING PAVERS

Clay and concrete pavers are usually bedded on sand. Provided the base has been carefully prepared, they will be perfectly stable and able to withstand the same use and wear as paving slabs, and are particularly suited to driveways. Sand vibrated between the pavers helps to lock them together, while a firmly mortared restraining edge to the area ensures stability.

PREPARATION

■ Prepare the ground carefully by excavating the area and consolidating the base. You will need to allow for 2 in (5 cm) of hardcore or sand and gravel mix, 2 in (5 cm) of sharp sand, and the thickness of the pavers.

■ It is important to have a firm edge to hold the paving, so mortar the edge pavers into position if there is not already a firm edge such as a house wall or a raised bed. Do not mortar between the edging pavers,

otherwise they won't match the other pavers, which are butt joined.

■ Once the edge is firm, lay and compact the hardcore or sand and gravel mix, using a plate compactor.

■ Lay 2 in (5 cm) of sharp sand, then level this by using a board with notches cut at each end to the depth of the pavers. By placing the notched end over the edges you can obtain a smooth, level surface for laying.

1 Lay the paving in your chosen pattern. Lay a small area at a time, making sure the pavers butt up to each other. Brush sharp sand over the pavers, then continue with the next section. When the whole area has been laid, brush in more sharp sand.

2 Vibrate the sand between the joints, using a plate compactor. This will bed the sand between the pavers efficiently. Brush more sharp sand over to fill the spaces created by vibration, then vibrate again. Repeat until the paving is firmly locked into place.

PAVING PATTERNS

Brick pavers can be laid in several ways to create attractive patterns. The herringbone pattern requires bricks to be cut to fit at the margins of the area, where the pattern should be edged with a row of pavers positioned head to tail. Box-shaped patterns, such as basketweave, wattleweave, and interlocking boxes, do not require any cutting at the edges and so might be a more practical option if you are laying pavers for the first time.

INSPECTION COVERS

Gardens have to be constructed around objects such as drain inspection covers. To mask an inspection cover, buy one of the special metal trays designed to be put in the space occupied by the flush cover. These have a tray deep enough to take pavers, producing a flush finish with the surrounding paving.

HERRINGBONE
PATTERN BRICK
PAVERS

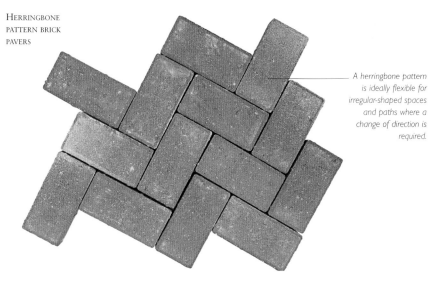

A herringbone pattern is ideally flexible for irregular-shaped spaces and paths where a change of direction is required.

INTERLOCKING BOXES

BASKETWEAVE

PAVING IN CIRCLES

Although difficult to integrate into a small space, circular patterns are worth the effort. A small circular patio can make an interesting visual feature, and introducing circular paved areas in other parts of the garden can be extremely eye-catching. Circular lawns are an alternative option and can be used to complement circular paving and other circular features. If you do not have space for complete circles, curved bays and semi-circular features are also effective.

THINKING IN CIRCLES

In the garden, curved and round features look better together rather than combined with straight-edged flower beds and paths. If your garden is long, try building a small, curved patio at the top end and framing it with a curved trellis to create a strong focal point. Curved pathways are another possibility, but they should be broad and sweeping rather than tight – generous curves are easier to negotiate with garden equipment as well as to construct.

Paving can be curved around a central feature, such as a flower bed or specimen plant. To avoid the feature looking like a bullseye, the paving can be spaced to reflect the curves without circling it entirely.

It can be difficult to link circular features with more angular elements. Wherever you need to integrate curved and straight lines, consider gravel or stones as combining materials.

MAKING AN ENTRANCE
A circular standing area at the entrance to your door can be a welcoming gesture, as well as provide a strong design element.

SECRET CIRCLES

Paved sitting areas do not have to be situated close to the house. Even in a compact or crowded garden it is possible to create a small secluded area. Try paving a small circle away from the house and surround it with tall-growing flowers and shrubs. Include fragrant blooms or foliage for an even more pleasing experience. A round table and curved benches or chairs can also help to emphasize the circular design. Garden centers and stores sell a wide range of paving stones and flagstones that have been specially designed for paving in circles.

FORWARD PLANNING

Many people build their circular patios too small for outdoor eating and entertaining. While initially the diameter may look large, the surface area may be smaller than you expect once garden furniture is in position. Think carefully about how you plan to use your patio before marking it out. Position any garden furniture you're likely to use, to ensure that your patio will be practical as well as attractive.

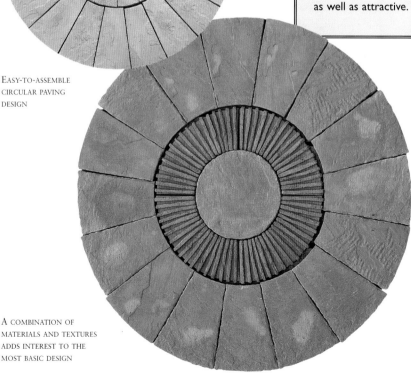

EASY-TO-ASSEMBLE CIRCULAR PAVING DESIGN

A COMBINATION OF MATERIALS AND TEXTURES ADDS INTEREST TO THE MOST BASIC DESIGN

PAVING ALTERNATIVES

Carefully chosen paving materials can provide a perfect foil for plants and can link a house and garden. There is a wealth of materials available; however, it is best to limit yourself to using just a few to gain the most effective results, especially in a small garden where it is easy to crowd the space.

MATERIAL CHOICE

No matter how small your choice of paving material, and how well it works in a particular setting, it is always worth considering enhancing the effect by mixing it with other materials. Old railroad ties can look surprisingly good blended with bricks, while paving slabs and bricks set in gravel can look really special.

QUARRY TILES

■ **Loose materials** Gravel (see pp. 50–55 for more detail), grit, pea shingle, and wood chips are excellent materials for combining with pathways, patios, and border areas.

■ **Pebbles** Decorative and practical, pebbles and large stones can be used to decorate surface areas that are not necessarily intended to be walked on.

■ **Slate** Crushed slate stones can be arranged in various ways, including simulating a dry riverbed to form a feature in the garden.

COGS AND COILS
Metal washers make an original loose material for bordering shrubs and paths.

TILES

Tiles are a good alternative to paving slabs. Ideal for linking outside and inside areas such as patios and conservatories, quarry tiles have a smooth, attractive appearance and are frostproof. Alternatively, terracotta tiles are excellent for a formal look. Unfortunately, they are porous and prone to frost damage. Tiles are brittle and should be laid on a concrete subbase. They should be soaked in water before laying, so that they do not absorb too much moisture from the mortar.

SPECIAL EFFECTS

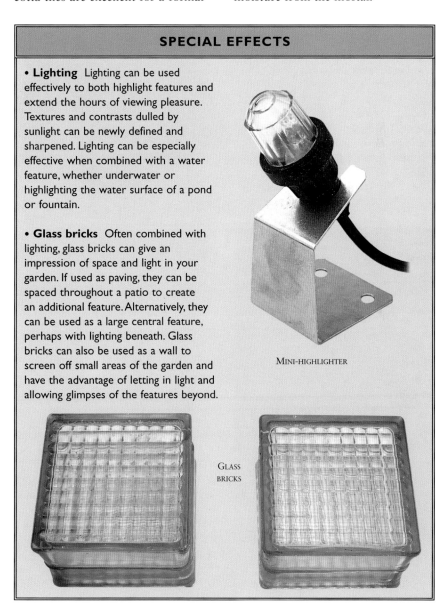

• **Lighting** Lighting can be used effectively to both highlight features and extend the hours of viewing pleasure. Textures and contrasts dulled by sunlight can be newly defined and sharpened. Lighting can be especially effective when combined with a water feature, whether underwater or highlighting the water surface of a pond or fountain.

• **Glass bricks** Often combined with lighting, glass bricks can give an impression of space and light in your garden. If used as paving, they can be spaced throughout a patio to create an additional feature. Alternatively, they can be used as a large central feature, perhaps with lighting beneath. Glass bricks can also be used as a wall to screen off small areas of the garden and have the advantage of letting in light and allowing glimpses of the features beyond.

MINI-HIGHLIGHTER

GLASS BRICKS

CHANGING LEVELS

Gardens that incorporate changes of level will always be more visually interesting than those that are completely flat. Creating different levels can add so much more character and allow features and focal points to be seen from more than one angle.

ADDING INTEREST

Modest level changes can be accommodated even where space is limited. A tiny backyard could be improved by building some shallow steps and a short path leading to a raised flower bed. The overall height difference might be minimal, but it can add an extra dimension to the garden that would have been lacking if left flat and level. Fortunately, changes in height do not have to be drastic to be

PRECAST
CORNER PIECE

effective, and even a level change of as little as 6–12 in (15–30 cm) can be all that is required in a small garden. It is enough to add variety and give a sense of anticipation as you explore the garden.

■ **Steps** Introducing a few steps that extend the path in a straight line can serve to emphasize the smallness of the garden. Try turning the path as you raise the level. This simple device can be very effective in a small space. Specially precast corner pieces can make turning corners easier.

■ **Patios** A slightly raised patio can provide a change of level and offer a slightly elevated position from which to view the garden. Patios can also be lowered to create a sunken patio. Sunken patios are particularly effective if trailing plants are added around the rim. They can also be combined with containers either on or around the patio.

STEPPING UP
These curved steps give the impression of space as well as suggesting unseen treasures beyond the lushness of the border plants.

ELEVATED FEATURES

■ **Raised beds** Break up the monotony of a large patio area with a permanently raised bed. This can be planted with trailing plants, shrubs, and climbers to introduce both height and color. It will also allow you to use soil that is different from the soil in the rest of your garden, thereby allowing you to grow different plants.

■ **Raised ponds** An alternative to a raised bed in an area of paving is a mini raised pond. However small, this feature will create maximum impact, particularly if it is decorated with containers around the edges and a small fountain in the center.

RAISED INTEREST
A raised water feature with a broad brick edging can provide a cool place to sit on a warm summer evening.

TRAILING PLANTS FOR RAISED BEDS

Make the most of raised beds by using plants that will tumble over the edge to clothe the walls. Be sure to include upright plants in your planting scheme to provide vertical growth.

Aubrieta
Aurinia saxatilis
Bidens ferulifolia
Convolvulus sabatius
Fuchsia spp. (cascading varieties)
Genista lydia Broom
Hedera Ivy (small-leaved)
Pelargonium peltatum Ivy-leaf geranium
Penstimon newberryi Mountain pride
Petunia Surfinia series
Sutera cordata
Thunbergia alata Black-eyed susan
Tropaeolum (some varieties)
Verbena hybrida

USING WOOD

Wood is one of the warmest and most natural materials to use in the garden. It can easily be included in your small garden design, either mixed with other materials or as timber decking to cover large areas. Old railroad ties can look surprisingly tasteful when blended with bricks and pavers, while decking panels provide a natural alternative to paving slabs.

TYPES OF SURFACES

■ **Decking panels** Timber decking (see p. 32) can be purchased as readymade panels that can either be joined together to make an area of decking or used individually as large steppingstones or platforms for containers. Decking panels come in a variety of patterns and colors and can be stained to match any garden.

■ **Timber rings** Cross sections cut from the trunk of a tree make ideal steppingstones for a path, especially in woodland areas or among shrubs. They can be combined with bark chippings and gravel.

■ **Wood chips** Chippings from tree bark make an ideal surface for a garden path either on their own or combined with timber rings.

■ **Railroad ties** Old railroad ties impregnated with bitumen make a long-lasting material for imaginative pathways. They come ready aged and blend easily with plants, shrubs, gravel, wood chips, and brick.

SLEEPER STEPS
Old railroad ties provide a softer, more natural look that combines well with border shrubs for paths and steps.

WOODEN PLATFORMS

Decking provides a wonderful opportunity to raise the viewpoint. Elevating the sitting area by 2 ft (60 cm) will give the impression of a viewing platform among the vegetation if you plant the surrounding area densely using lush plants. Low-level decks may lack some of the impact of raised decks, but you can make up for this by using a strong design with materials that frame and emphasize the timber. A strong colored stain can also add extra interest.

BOARDWALK
Decking platform can be used effectively as boardwalks and simple bridges.

AT THE WATER'S EDGE

• Decking can look very good in combination with water and is a low-maintenance way of providing an elevated seating area close to the water's edge. Use decking squares to edge a pool or pond, as they can hide unsightly liner material.

• Take care when staining wood near water, as it can harm plants and fish.

• Prevent pondside decking from becoming slippery by covering it with fine grade chicken wire nailed in place.

RAISED DECKING PROVIDES WATERSIDE SEATING

RAISED DECKING

An area of decking can add an extra touch of style to your garden and offers a softer-looking alternative to stone or brick paving. Versatile and easy to maintain, timber decking naturally blends with plants and shrubs and can be stained a variety of colors to contrast or complement the style of your garden. Decks can be made of preassembled panels or lengths of ordinary wooden planking. All timber should be treated with a wood preservative prior to construction.

SIMPLE RAISED DECKING

Decking is a simple job that most people can tackle. It is essential to have free air circulation beneath the boards and no direct contact between the decking and the soil.

■ Measure out the area to be decked, using string. Check that any corners form right angles.

■ Lay the wooden joists parallel to each other within the marked area, evenly spaced. Mark out 6 in (15 cm) around each joist to determine the width of the trenches that will take the supports. Dig the trenches 1 in (2.5 cm) deeper than the height of the concrete blocks.

MATERIALS AND TOOLS YOU WILL NEED

MATERIALS
(Note that quantities will depend on the extent of your decking.)
• Planks of wood
• Wooden joists 4 in x 4 in (10 cm x 10 cm) thickness
• Fascia boards for edging
• Sand
• Concrete walling blocks
• Metal angle brackets
• Screws and wallboard anchors

TOOLS
Spade, builder's level, builder's square, mallet, electric drill, and drill bits.

1 Line the base of each trench with sand and bed down to a level of 2 in (5 cm). Place the concrete blocks on the sand and tread down to stand proud of the soil by 1 in (2.5 cm).

2 Roughly lay the joists on the blocks and check the level using a builder's level. Backfill around the blocks with earth and firm down so that the blocks are flush with the ground.

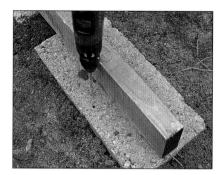

3 Center the joists in position across the concrete blocks. Mark out the brackets, four for each concrete block, to secure the blocks to the joists.

4 Drill screw holes into the concrete blocks and wooden joists. Insert wallboard anchors into the holes in the blocks, then screw down the brackets.

5 Fix the first plank across all the joists so that it is flush with the ends. Drill two holes per joist, drilling about 2 in (5 cm) into the joist. Screw the plank into place.

6 Position all the planks across the joists, leaving ⅕-in (5-mm) gap for expansion. Screw each plank down. Finally, fix on fascia boards around the edges with nails.

CONSTRUCTION TIPS

To create a paved area that looks good and remains hardwearing, certain basic techniques should be followed when cutting your paving material and mixing mortar and concrete. Most basic paving can be easily done by hand without the use of specialized equipment.

CUTTING BRICKS, SLABS, AND PAVERS

The easiest way to cut bricks, slabs, and pavers cleanly to size to fill in edges and corners is to rent a hydraulic block splitter.

If you have just a few blocks to cut, this can be done by hand. Rest the slab on a bed of sand. Mark a pencil line on both sides of the slab and use the blade of a large chisel and a club hammer to score a groove. Gradually deepen the groove by going over it with the hammer and chisel. Place the slab on a length of timber, aligning the groove with the timber edge. A gentle tap with the hammer should break the slab cleanly.

MIXING CONCRETE AND MORTAR

If you require a lot of concrete or mortar, rent a concrete mixer. Small quantities are easily mixed by hand. To make concrete for a path or paving area, mix one part cement with two parts sharp sand and three parts aggregate. Avoid laying concrete if the temperature is close to freezing or above 86°F (30°C). To make bedding mortar for paving slabs, mix one part cement with five parts sharp sand.

CLUB
HAMMER

MORTAR
TROWEL

PAVING TIPS

• Before excavating any area, locate underground utilities, such as gas pipes, water, electricity, television, and telephone cables, to avoid damaging them. Inspection covers must be left unobstructed.

• Surfaces that butt up directly to a house wall must finish 6 in (15 cm) below any dampproof course and incorporate a slight drainage slope to take water away from the house foundation. Gravel and shingle can be used around house walls for drainage.

• Do not walk on paving for at least 24 hours after laying. Ideally you should let the paving settle for 48 hours. Work out ways of keeping people and traffic off the area.

2
TRELLISES
AND SCREENS

Trellises and screens are invaluable features because they allow the gardener to use vertical growing space. They can be used to mask unattractive views beyond the garden, offer a degree of privacy if overlooked, and break up the internal design of the garden to provide interest. They are also useful for disguising damaged or discolored sections of a wall or fence.

A trellis is useful as a complement to the structure to which it is attached as well as providing support for climbing plants. Trellises can be decorative as well as functional: they can provide a focal point if painted; they can be combined with container plants; or they can be used to frame an ornament or a pleasing group of plants.

CREATING DIVISIONS

One way of creating interest in your garden is to divide it into several smaller areas; each of these "rooms" can be styled individually, with a single-color planting scheme or a themed design. Equally, if your garden is overlooked or exposed to traffic or unsightly objects, you may simply wish to create an inner "room" for privacy.

OUTDOOR ROOMS

Internal dividers in the garden may be made from a variety of materials, such as wattle, bamboo, or wooden trellis. By strategically positioning a single panel to divide an area, or by arranging several panels at angles to each other, you can create separate compartments. If you prefer greenery to timber, use the panel as a support for climbing and rambling plants. A trellis tends to be the most popular divider because its open weave does not look too oppressive and still allows light into the garden. Whether or not you decide to clothe your divider with plants, it is a good idea to introduce small "windows" through which tempting glimpses of other parts of the garden can be viewed. This simple device also lets in light through solid or close-weave panels and is particularly useful in small gardens because it creates the illusion of a larger plot beyond.

WATTLE SCREEN
A screen made from tightly bound reeds forms a textured backdrop to the bold, white blooms of a patio rose.

STYLE TIP

A stark but striking effect can be achieved by painting a screen or divider black and leaving it unplanted. The panel becomes a strong, structural feature that creates a dramatic silhouette against the skyline and planting.

SCREENS

Urban gardens, in particular, often find themselves overlooked, exposed to traffic, or their view obscured by an ugly building. If you want to shield your garden from the outside world, consider putting up a screen. Ranging from plain wooden fence or trellis panels to specially commissioned pieces in steel or ironwork that complement the architecture of your house, freestanding screens are a simple but effective solution.

If your current borders are not tall enough to maintain privacy, try fixing a trellis extension to the top to create height.

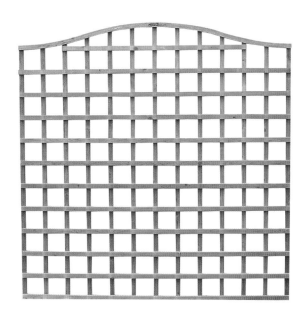

CONTOURED TRELLIS PANEL

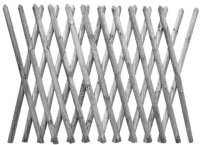

EXPANDING TRELLIS EXTENSION

PERFECTLY PRESERVED

Timber trelliswork needs to be treated regularly with a wood preservative. The wide range of colors available makes it possible for screens and dividers to blend in with a garden design. Light, bright colors are ideal for visually "lifting" a dull corner, while darker shades provide a sympathetic backdrop for bold planting schemes and focal points.

SECRET PLACES

If your garden is so overlooked that it's difficult to provide privacy by normal screening, consider introducing an arbor, summerhouse, or pergola that will offer the seclusion you seek. With careful positioning, your haven will become an attractive focal point as well as providing a sense of hidden secrecy that is sometimes so elusive in urban gardens.

PRIVATE RETREATS

In terms of garden design, the principle of a retreat is the same, whether you choose an elaborate summerhouse or a small gazebo. Placed in a prominent position, the structure will provide a vantage point for pleasing views of the garden and will create a trompe-l'oeil effect, which will help to broaden the perspective of the garden. Planting around your arbor or summerhouse will help to emphasize the sense of secluded privacy.

■ **Arbor** Usually a fully or partly enclosed garden structure, an arbor does not have to be big to be beautiful, just large enough to seat two or three people. Arbors are often constructed from trellis panels, which may not appear to offer much privacy, but once they have been covered with climbers they are transformed into secluded corners.

■ **Gazebo** Gazebos tend to be open-sided structures and are often used to house a statue, ornament, or an elaborate container. They are equally good as resting places, when fitted with a bench or garden seats. If placed in a corner of the garden that catches the evening sun, they make a welcome respite from a hard day's work in the city.

■ **Green walls** If you want a more naturalistic feel to your garden retreat, train evergreen conifers and hedging to form the "walls." Place a simple stone or wooden bench within for seating, and introduce some shade-loving plants that will thrive in a cool corner. By adding a small water feature, you can enhance the tranquil mood of this area with the soothing sound of water.

QUIET CORNER
A white trelliswork gazebo provides an elegant setting for this striking container display and offers a quiet corner for contemplation.

Climbing plants can be trained across roof struts

TIMBER PERGOLA

Base of pillar decorated by planted up containers

Once it has been covered in climbing plants, a pergola provides a secluded place to sit

SECLUDED SCENTS

Gazebos and pergolas provide an ideal place over which to grow fragrant climbers, such as roses, star or Chilean jasmines, and honeysuckles. The concentrated fragrance of the plants surrounding you on both sides, and possibly tumbling down in front and behind, will often linger in the still air, especially on long, summer evenings.

KEEPING IN STYLE

Choose a hideaway that suits the style of your garden; for example, a classical, white ironwork gazebo suits a formal garden, while a mock Japanese teahouse would look at home in an oriental-style garden. It is perfectly acceptable to borrow a particular style, even if the rest of your garden does not exactly follow that particular image. What matters is whether it looks "right" in a particular situation.

ORNAMENTAL STATUE OF BUDDHA

USING TRELLIS

Many attractive trellis features can be made from panels available from large garden centers or by mail order. It is worth obtaining a catalog first, so that you can study the range of products at home in your garden before making a decision. If you intend to use the trellis as a plant support, it needs to be more substantial than one that is used as a purely decorative feature, so don't skimp on quality just because you won't be able to see much of the trellis once it is planted.

PUTTING UP A SCREEN

Strong supporting posts are the key to a successful trellis screen to stop it blowing over in strong wind. Anchor each post in the ground with a post spike (shown here) or in a hole, which should be at least 2 ft (60 cm) deep. Place broken brick or rubble in the base of the hole so that the bottom of the post does not stand on the soil.

POST SPIKES

Metal post spikes can be set in concrete or simply driven directly into the ground. Their main advantage is that you can use shorter posts because the spike forms the post below ground level.

It is essential that post spikes are driven into the ground vertically, so check this frequently as you proceed. Depending on the type of spike, the post is held in place by tightened bolts or by teeth in the spike that "bite" into the timber.

POST SPIKE

1 Clear the area of any surface debris then push the post spike into position. Cap it with a dolly, and hammer gently into the ground just as far as the casing. Transfer the dolly to the top of the post to protect the timber from damage and to drive the post in evenly.

2 Hammer the post into the spike, and use a builder's level to check that it is vertical. If you are driving a post directly into a hole in the ground, fill around it with hardcore or rubble to keep it upright while you pour in concrete, packing it down to fill any air pockets.

3 Holding the panel perpendicular to the post, hammer long nails at the top and bottom of the trellis through the vertical batten and into the post. Use a builder's level to check that the panel is horizontal, adjusting if necessary, before securing with additional nails at regular intervals down the length of the screen.

4 If the top of your post is not pointed, fix a plain or decorative cap that will shed water and prevent the post from rotting. Apply a second coat of plant-friendly preservative or wood stain (see p. 37).

5 Allow the newly stained screen to dry for a few days before adding plants (see pp. 42–43). Remember to set climbing plants at an angle of 45° to the base of the panel.

LIVING SCREENS

Gardens with strong, modern designs benefit from the often harsh bold lines of screening devices; however, more subtle designs are better suited to the softened lines provided by mantles of evergreen and variegated foliage or colorful and often fragrant flowers trained over a screen or along the length of a bare expanse of wall or fencing.

FRAMEWORKS FOR PLANTS

■ **Obelisks and wigwams** Made from trellis panels or tightly bound hazel sticks, in a range of different heights, obelisks and wigwams provide the architectural bones of a screen designed to be clothed with climbing plants. They are most effective when arranged in a group; in gardens with limited growing space, pyramidal shapes trained with green foliage can be used to mimic trees.

■ **Palisading** Areas within a garden can be screened with a white-painted picket fence, which looks striking and takes the eye away from the view beyond without looking as obtrusive as a solid fence or wall. For seasonal summer variety, try planting golden hop at its base (see p. 88) to cloak it in a curtain of gold.

■ **Decorative hedges** There are plenty of small, hedging plants that make colorful living screens. Hollies, barberries, and cotoneasters all offer variegated foliage and brightly colored fruits. Roses such as *Rosa rugosa* offer year-round interest and their prickly habit is an effective deterrent to unwelcome visitors.

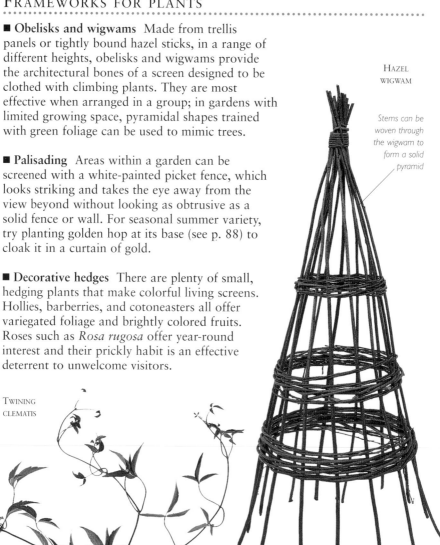

HAZEL
WIGWAM

Stems can be woven through the wigwam to form a solid pyramid

TWINING
CLEMATIS

■ **Trellis** Although a stained or painted trellis panel can be used to provide a distinctive vertical element in its own right, perhaps as a screen or division, once planted with a climbing plant (see right) it will provide a vertical curtain of growth; for planting suggestions see pages 83–93. A semievergreen honeysuckle provides some cover throughout the year, but reaches its peak in summer when the fragrant flowers are at their best. You may prefer to use leaf-shedding climbers that will expose more of the garden beyond the screen during the winter, or you could even train annual climbers to provide summer cover and color, leaving the trellis easier to preserve in winter.

■ **Trees** Try planting a row of willows and train them as they grow so they form a lattice pattern. After a few years you will have an unusual and attractive screen that will look good covered in foliage in summer and make an attractive feature when the stems are bare in winter.

You could try taking this idea a stage further and try planting young willows in a circle – with a gap for the entrance – interweaving them to form the walls and roof of a living arbor. Add interest by planting scented honeysuckle or clematis around the base to scramble through the summer canopy and provide an unusual focal point.

1 Dig a planting hole about 18 in (45 cm) from the base of the screen. By placing the plant in the hole at an angle of 45°, you will be able to train the shoots on to the lowest part of the screen.

2 Using garden canes, train the shoots in a fanned-out arrangement. Attach the shoots to the canes using garden twine, tied loosely, or wire ties. Remember to adjust the ties regularly as the plant grows.

CURTAINS OF FOLIAGE

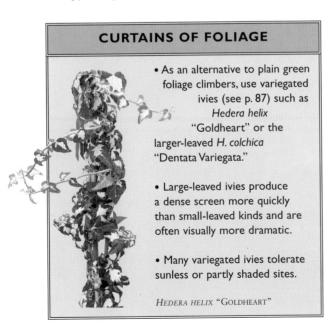

• As an alternative to plain green foliage climbers, use variegated ivies (see p. 87) such as *Hedera helix* "Goldheart" or the larger-leaved *H. colchica* "Dentata Variegata."

• Large-leaved ivies produce a dense screen more quickly than small-leaved kinds and are often visually more dramatic.

• Many variegated ivies tolerate sunless or partly shaded sites.

HEDERA HELIX "GOLDHEART"

SCREENING BOUNDARIES

One of the drawbacks of most small gardens is the close proximity of the boundary. Large, bare walls and plain panel fences tend to focus the eye on the confines of the garden, but with a little thought they can be easily transformed to provide additional planting areas and greater privacy, introducing another dimension to an outdoor "room."

CONCEALING DULL BOUNDARIES

The boundaries of many new gardens consist of an unbroken and unimaginative expanse of plain, high wooden fencing panels that make the area within appear even smaller and more enclosed than it really is. Equally, a bare expanse of brick can be overimposing in a small space.

■ **Using color** Unbroken expanses of fencing can be painted or stained a darker color so that the eye is drawn to other, more interesting features in the garden. Stick to natural shades and avoid light or bright colors that will become a focus.

■ **Using shapes** Rather than a fence of uniform height, alternate taller panels with shorter panels topped perhaps with a trellis extension over which climbing plants can be trained.

■ **Using plants** Attach trellis panels to a bare expanse of wall or fence and train climbers up it. Alternatively, plant tall, fast-growing plants and shrubs in front of it to add interest.

DRAWING THE EYE
A boldly planted basket positioned above head height creates a new dimension, drawing the eye away from the confines of a small garden.

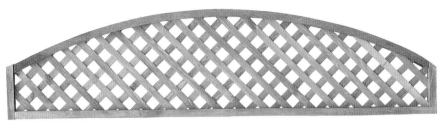

ARCHED WOODEN TRELLIS EXTENSION

PLAIN WOODEN TRELLIS EXTENSION

ADDING HEIGHT

If the boundaries of your garden are too low to block out an unsightly view beyond, the obvious solution is to increase the height in a style that is in keeping with the surroundings.

■ **Trellis extensions** Available in a range of shapes and styles, trellis extension panels are designed to be attached to the top of a low wall or fence to create extra height. As a support for climbers they will offer total privacy; however, painted in a color that matches the mood of your garden they can become a feature in their own right, allowing glimpses of the view beyond and letting in light.

If you find that a trellis strip fitted to a low brick wall looks out of place, render the wall and apply masonry paint for a more pleasing harmony.

■ **Wall troughs** A novel way of raising the height of a low wall is to fix lightweight planting troughs at intervals along the top. These can be planted up with small box hedges, conifers, or low-growing evergreen shrubs. For extra color you may want to use the troughs for cheerful arrangements of seasonal flowers.

■ **Arches** An arch can be added to the top of a low boundary fence or wall to create extra privacy and add interest and height. You can choose from a wide range of preformed metal arches or simply construct your own out of timber. The sides of the arch can be cloaked in climbers planted at the base of the wall and the height can be used for hanging eye-catching baskets.

TIMBER MAINTENANCE

Timber structures need to be treated regularly with a coating of preservative, but this type of maintenance can be difficult to carry out on fences clad with climbers. To expose the fence for treatment, prune the plants back hard after about three years (this must depend on whether the plant will tolerate this kind of treatment), or try to temporarily disentangle the plant.

CLEMATIS

TRELLIS ALTERNATIVES

When choosing a screen or divider, think creatively about what styles will best suit your garden and its surroundings, and bear in mind that your choice of materials may be limited by what you can easily obtain locally. If you have an aptitude for carpentry, all kinds of possibilities are open to you.

KEEPING IN STYLE

Despite its usefulness, trellis can become overused in a small garden. Here are just some of the many alternatives you might like to try.

■ **Rustic style** If you have a country garden, a wattle screen, lattice-work trellis made from unshaped timbers, and rustic fencing will add interest and atmosphere to the rural setting.

■ **Bamboo** If you have a Japanese-style garden, screens and dividers of dried bamboo canes will look entirely in keeping with the surroundings. You could consider combining these with a living screen of tall bamboos, but remember that some of these can form very dense clumps that will become overdominant in a small garden.

■ **Fruit trees** When space is at a premium you may want to consider using fruit trees that will do double duty as dividers. A series of cordon or double cordon fruit trees trained on horticultural wire stretched between upright posts, for example, makes an effective divider and will provide a tasty crop of fruit for your kitchen table.

BAMBOO BACKDROP FOR AN ORIENTAL-STYLE DISPLAY

■ **Metal** A decorative screen can be a feature in its own right. Sheets of corrugated iron or painted metal cut into strong, architectural shapes are popular in modern garden design.

■ **Artistic license** The severe restrictions of some small city gardens and courtyards often cramp the scope of a garden design, but with a little creative talent you can use illusions to mask them. Paint a trompe-l'oeil topiary or gazebo if you don't have the space for the real thing.

BRIGHT IDEA
The reflected light from this tile-effect aluminum screen brightens up a dull corner.

OVERHEAD SCREENING

PLEACHED TREES

A densely woven overhead screen can be formed by pleaching, or weaving, the branches of trees. As it can take several years before the screen is established, it is best to use three- to four-year-old trees. A similar effect can be achieved with espalier and fan-trained fruit trees planted against a fence or wall. This is a pleasing – and fruitful – way to add interest to a plain boundary (see pp. 42–43).

TRELLIS TIPS

Once you have decided to create an inner room or divisions within your garden, you need to find the right trellis, screen, or fence. If you intend to decorate the divider with climbing foliage or hanging containers, remember to equip yourself with the right fixings, supports, and preservatives too, to be sure of a secure and long-lasting feature.

CHOOSING TRELLIS

■ **Where to buy** Trellis panels are available at most garden centers and home improvement stores, but if you are looking for a specific style or more ornate panel, you may need to go to a specialist. Most fencing companies advertised in gardening magazines will be able to send you an illustrated catalog, and some of them will also offer a custom-made service, if you need panels made to your own specification. Make sure the trellis has been pretreated with a preservative.

■ **Styles** Trellis panels have either a rectangular or diagonal pattern of battens. If you intend to cover the panel with climbers, opt for a robust, preferably square pattern where the battens are not too close together. The wider spacing will make annual climbers easier to remove at the end of the season and will allow for the thickening stems of woody climbers. It will also make it easier to add a new coat of preservative every few years.

GARDEN
TWINE

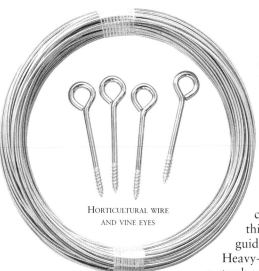

PLANT SUPPORTS

Young climbing plants will need to be attached securely to the lower batten of a trellis or wire until they are well established. Garden twine tied in a figure eight between the stem and the support will prevent any chafing; once the stems have thickened, use plastic ring ties to guide the plant up the support. Heavy-duty horticultural wire makes a sturdy support for climbing plants.

HORTICULTURAL WIRE
AND VINE EYES

3
INSTEAD OF GRASS

For many gardeners, a lawn is the central feature around which the rest of the garden revolves. For others it is a chore, demanding regular mowing, weeding, and feeding, not to mention edge-trimming. If you fall into the second category, there are plenty of alternatives to grass, ranging from plants such as thyme, chamomile, and even clover, to hard surfaces such as gravel. Each alternative will create a different atmosphere, so you should be able to find something suitable. Naturally, some of the options are less labor-intensive than others to maintain, so take that into account... as well as what looks good.

USING GRAVEL

Gravel is an amazingly versatile and interesting textural material that provides a practical and esthetically pleasing alternative to grass. It is relatively inexpensive, quick and simple to lay in even the most awkward layouts, and comes in many different colors and sizes, each with its own characteristic texture.

FULLY FUNCTIONAL

The true value of gravel is that it is more than just another paving material. It can be used as a hard landscaping surface in its own right, as a pleasing mulch through which you can grow a wide range of plants, as an infill between other paving materials, or as a low-maintenance alternative to grass lawns.

■ **Small spaces** Gravel is an ideal surface for a small area if you want something less formal than paving. It lends itself easily to designs that include both straight edges and

curves and complements container plantings in courtyard gardens. If you find gravel less comfortable than paving to walk on, just inset some steppingstones (see p. 59).

■ **Low maintenance** Grass lawns can be very demanding to maintain. They need regular feeding and watering and in summer may need mowing at least twice a week. One labor-saving alternative to grass is to replace it with gravel. What is more, you don't have to lift the whole lawn to use gravel. If, like so many

USING YOUR SENSES

When choosing gravel, consider the sight, sound, and feel of the material. Try laying a small area with your chosen gravel first (especially if it is going to be used in a prominent area of the garden) to make sure that you are happy with the color and texture. Some large gravels feel hard and uncomfortable underfoot; finer gravels tend to be kicked around easily; and some gravels are noisy to walk on.

SELECTION OF GRAVEL

gardeners, you feel that grass is an essential part of your garden design, just try replacing it with gravel in areas where it does not grow well, such as close to a fence, in a very shady position, or in awkward corners and along the edge of raised beds or walls where it is difficult to mow.

■ **Mulch** Colored gravel or pea shingle can be used as a surface instead of bare soil, and your garden will almost certainly look better for it. For example, the appearance of a bed of dark green, dwarf conifers surrounded by bare soil can be transformed by applying a thick layer of colored gravel; with the addition of a small ornament or larger pebbles and rocks it can become a focal point in your garden.

CANTERBURY SPAR

PEA SHINGLE

COLOR AND TEXTURE
A collage of colored gravels, natural stone slabs, and cobbles, interspersed with a grouping of alpine plants, adds interest to a dull corner.

GRAVEL LANDSCAPES

From pea shingle and sandstone chippings to slate, cobbles, and granite boulders, loose stones are too valuable to be treated as just another paving material. Make the most of their versatility by using them to "paint" a landscape or focal point in your garden. Experiment with mixing stones of different colors and sizes.

IMITATING NATURE

With a little creative flair, the wide range of colors, sizes, and textures of gravel can be used to create a stylish "picture." Soft sweeps of color punctuated with strategically placed rocks or cobbles suit abstract designs, while striking geometric shapes, outlined in edging, enhance formal designs and make ideal courtyard centerpieces. If you would like to try more than one theme, divide your garden into "rooms" (see pp. 36–37) and create a themed "mini-garden" in each.

PEBBLES

■ **Alpine scene** Pockets of gravel nestling between large rocks or boulders re-create a rocky outcrop in which many alpine plants will thrive. Mound-forming thrifts *(Armeria)*, crevice-dwelling saxifrages, and sun-loving rock roses *(Helianthemum)* are naturally adapted to growing in sandy or graveled conditions. It is easy to plant through gravel (see pp. 56–57); small informal drifts of compact plants often look more effective than isolated plants.

COBBLES

■ **Seashore** Using pea shingle, or a natural-colored gravel sprinkled with seashells, you can re-create a small pebble beach in your garden. Add some driftwood for effect and plant with coastal favorites, such as seaside asters *(Erigeron)*, livingstone daisies *(Dorotheanthus)*, tufted sedge *(Carex)*, eryngiums, and tamarisk.

BLUE SLATE

■ **Desert plain** Cacti and other succulents look their best in a graveled or stony area that mimics the dry, flat landscape of their native habitat. For best effect, space plants at a distance from each other and set them out individually rather than in groupings. Add one or two strong architectural plants such as hardy yuccas and the evergreen *Euphorbia myrsinites* as focal points.

■ **Running water** Versatile and easy to lay, gravel is an ideal material for free-form designs with soft, flowing lines and can mimic running water with great effect. Using a soft blue, small-grade gravel or smooth-sided slate, you can create the impression of a running stream weaving its path through small, informal drifts of woodland or wildflower plantings. Larger pebbles or cobbles placed at intervals along the stream can interrupt the direction of the flow to create interest and produce a more naturalistic effect.

RUNNING DRY
A broad "watercourse" created from varying sizes of natural blue slate makes an unusual path that leads visitors through the garden.

LAYING A GRAVEL BED

Gravel is quick and easy to lay, but you'll need a firm edge to contain it and reduce the risk of it being kicked onto surrounding beds. If you're laying a rectangular bed, perhaps to replace an existing lawn, use concrete edging blocks or slabs. For a softer, more "cottage garden" appearance, as here, edge the gravel with bricks or clay pavers.

MARKING OUT

If you are replacing an existing lawn, place your edging along the edges and mark the area of grass to be removed with a halfmoon edger. Use a garden hose to mark out an informal area, as shown below. Cut the grass around the perimeter with a halfmoon edger – a spade will produce a slightly curved cut.

ADDING INTEREST
An informal graveled area is decorated with an island bed, gravel plantings, and containers brimming with seasonal flowers.

■ **Cutting and digging** Slice away the grass where the edging is to be placed, excavating a sufficient depth to allow for the thickness of the edging plus at least 1 in (2.5 cm) to allow for hardcore and mortar to provide a firm base. Make sure that the hardcore is compacted and level.

■ **Mortar the edging** Lay the edging on blobs of mortar for stability and firm down with your foot. Use a builder's level to check that the finished edging is flat and even.

EXCAVATING AND ADDING GRAVEL

There are two different ways of preparing a gravel bed, each of which is equally satisfactory. Once the soil has been removed from the site, you can either add a layer of hardcore prior to the gravel, or the site can be covered in a weed-suppressing mulch.

■ **Remove the soil** Once the edging mortar has set and the edging is stable and secure, remove all the grass in the area that is to be graveled as well as 2 in (5 cm) of soil if you are going to add a black plastic mulch. If you propose to lay hardcore you will need to remove 5 in (10 cm) of soil and add a path weed killer to reduce the risk of deep-rooted perennial weeds penetrating the finished bed.

■ **Lay hardcore or mulching sheet** Lay heavy-duty plastic sheeting (see p. 57) over the whole area that is to be graveled, overlapping the lengths by about 2 in (5 cm). Alternatively, cover the entire area with 2 in (5 cm) of hardcore or rough-grade gravel.

■ **Add the gravel** Using a garden barrow, tip the surface gravel into position, ready for raking. As it is difficult to push a loaded barrow over laid gravel, start tipping at the end farthest from the point where you have access.

■ **Rake level** After tipping several wheelbarrow loads of gravel onto the prepared site, start to rake it level, topping up if required. Proceed gradually until the whole area has been evenly covered. Make sure the gravel is level with the edging – if it is piled up too high it will become scattered into the surrounding beds. You are now ready to start adding plants to your design.

PLANTS FOR GRAVEL

EVERGREEN	AROMATIC/FRAGRANT	FLOWERING
Carex flagellifera Sedge	**Artemisia ludoviciana** White sage	**Alchemilla mollis** Lady's mantle
Euphorbia amygdaloides "Rubra" Purple-leaved wood spurge	**Dianthus "La Bourboule"** Alpine pink	**Allium hollandicum** Ornamental onion
Ophiopogon planiscapus "Nigrescens" Lilyturf	**Origanum "Kent Beauty"** Origanum	**Papaver alpinum** Alpine poppy
Festuca glauca Blue fescue	**Rosmarinus spp.** Rosemary	**Persicaria vacciniifolia** Persicaria
Sedum acre Biting stonecrop	**Ruta graveolens 'Jackman's Blue'** Rue	**Saxifraga spp.** Saxifrage
Sempervivum tectorum Common houseleek	**Tanacetum argenteum** Tanacetum	**Sisyrinchium graminoides** Blue-eyed grass
Stachys byzantina Lamb's tongue	**Thymus spp.** Thyme	**Onopordum acanthium** Cotton thistle
		Verbascum olympicum Mullein

PLANTING IN GRAVEL

With such a wide choice of plants that will happily grow in gravel, there is no excuse for a large graveled area to look harsh, dull, and lifeless. Plants with aromatic foliage release their scent when brushed by passing feet; evergreen, mound- or rosette-forming plants dotted around the bed add year-round interest; bold, architectural plants make striking focal points; and the dainty flowers of alpine-dwelling plants offer delicate shades of color (see p. 55). Better still, the gravel acts as a mulch, keeping pernicious weeds at bay.

PLANTING DIRECTLY INTO GRAVEL

1 Using a trowel, clear the gravel to one side and dig out a planting hole through the level of hardcore. Set aside any soil removed from the hole.

2 Part-fill the hole with soil mix. It will be difficult to add fertilizers after planting, so add a slow-release or controlled-release fertilizer.

3 Gently slide the plant from its pot, tease out the roots, and place in the hole. Fill around the plant with soil and soil mix. Firm well and water.

4 Pull back the gravel around the crown of the plant. As gravel is free-draining, most plants won't mind if it piles up a little around the stems.

MULCHING AND PLANTING THROUGH PLASTIC

For a low-maintenance bed, the combination of plastic sheeting and a decorative layer of gravel is the perfect solution. A heavy-duty polyethylene liner or geotextile sheet makes an effective mulching barrier against persistent weeds and eliminates the time-consuming task of hand-weeding.

Geotextile allows water and air to reach the soil and plant roots, but excludes light which is essential to the germination of weed seeds. If you prefer, wood chippings, composted bark, leaf mold, or other loose materials may be used to provide a more attractive finish to the mulching barrier.

1 Remove any large stones, weeds, or debris from the ground and cover with a geotextile or black plastic mulching sheet. Allow an overlap of about 2 in (5 cm) where you have to add further lengths.

2 Using a knife or scissors, make two intersecting cuts in the mulching sheet, large enough for the rootball to pass through. Pull back the sheeting and make a planting hole with a trowel and line it with soil mix.

3 Gently slide the plant from its pot, tease out the roots, and pass the rootball through the sheeting and into the hole. Fill around the plant with soil and soil mix. Firm well and water.

4 Push the flaps of sheeting around the base of the plant. Add a layer of gravel or other decorative loose material, making a shallow depression around the neck of the plant.

Combining textures

Gardeners sometimes opt to cover an area with grass simply because they fear that a large expanse of paving or gravel might look dull and uninteresting. However, by using a combination of soft and hard landscaping materials as well as flowers and foliage, you can create stunning designs and patterns that will demand attention.

Mixing and merging materials

If you cover whole areas of your garden with a single material, such as paving or gravel alone, you will make the space look much smaller than it needs to. By mixing different materials, you can give your garden a strong sense of space and design and will find it easier to cope with irregular boundaries or difficult angles formed by awkward flower beds.

■ **Merging areas** If you want a paved area to merge gently into the garden rather than form an abrupt divide, gradually introduce an alternative surface such as gravel to act as a natural transition from one part of the garden to another. Position boulders or planted containers to add interest and color.

■ **Mixing hard and soft** Hard landscaping surfaces can dominate a design at the expense of soft planted surfaces. Don't rule out the inclusion of areas of grass, even if you want to introduce low-maintenance surfaces. Wood, grass, and gravel can happily coexist to form an interesting mixture of surfaces that can be skillfully enhanced by the careful positioning of a specimen plant.

■ **Soften hard edges** Allowing plants to tumble over the edges of borders will help to make the hard landscaping merge almost seamlessly with the surrounding.

■ **Infill with gravel** For variation, leave gaps between paving slabs and fill in with gravel.

SEAMLESS BLEND
A hard divide between a tiled patio and the rest of the garden is avoided by allowing paving tiles to flow into the graveled area alongside.

STEPPINGSTONES

Steppingstones serve a functional purpose by providing a way of getting from A to B in the garden. However, they are equally valuable as decoration and are very effective when used with other paving materials to add texture or color.

Available in a range of styles and materials, steppingstones can be used in many different ways. Brightly colored steppingstones threaded through a design will lead the eye around the garden, whereas plain, round stone slabs or timber decking tiles are a useful device to stop lawns from being worn down by shortcuts. Relieve a bare expanse of gravel with hexagonal paving slabs or small quarry tiles dotted in a wavy line, and look for precast pieces, such as oriental-style tiles, to enhance a themed garden. Timber rings set in a decorative mulch of loose woodchips work well as a woodland path, while a series of smooth-sided boulders give a naturalistic feel to a small garden stream or even a "dry" watercourse created from loose chippings (see p. 53).

PRECAST ORIENTAL-STYLE TILE

TIMBER DECKING TILE

TIMBER RING

KEEP IT SIMPLE

More is not necessarily always best when it comes to mixing different surfacing materials.

• Two or three different surfaces will look interesting without looking fussy, whereas four or five are likely to detract from the appeal of a simple design, especially in a small area.

• Avoid bright colors, which in any case become more muted as weathering takes place, and rely more on changes in surface texture.

TURTLE STEPPINGSTONE

ALTERNATIVE LAWNS

Fragrant lawns, which seldom need to be mowed, make appealing alternatives to grass lawns and are a low-maintenance alternative to hard landscaping. They are especially practical for small gardens in that many of the plants tend to be slow-growing and would take a long time to become established on a large expanse of ground.

FRAGRANCE AND FOLIAGE

There are many ground-covering plants that can be used to form a carpet of foliage that provides an interesting alternative to grass and create an ornamental feature to be viewed from other parts of the garden. Few of them, however, will tolerate being trodden on, making them unsuitable for play areas.

If the lawn is likely to be used regularly as a thoroughfare, try to minimize any possible damage through overuse by placing stepping-stones across the most commonly used routes (see p. 59). Another option is to consider introducing areas of alternative lawn around the edges of an existing grass lawn.

The effects of fragrant lawns of chamomiles, mints, or thymes can be best appreciated from a bench or seating area placed alongside the lawn from where you can reach down and gently crush the foliage to enjoy its subtle aroma.

TROUBLE-FREE LAWN
Planting an awkward corner with chamomile provides an aromatic carpet of green foliage and eliminates the problems of mowing.

CLOVER LAWN IN FLOWER

■ **Clover** Best known as a persistent weed in a grass lawn, clover provides attractive but hardwearing ground cover. Shamrock or white clover *(Trifolium repens)* is lush green, tough, very tolerant of wear, and does not mind being mowed.

■ **Chamomile** Roman chamomile *(Chamaemelum nobile)* is one of the most popular aromatic ground-covering plants that is used as an alternative to grass. This mat-forming plant bears white daisylike flowers in summer, and the apple scent of its bright green feathery leaves is released whenever the plant is crushed or trodden on. If you prefer to have a green carpet of lawn without any flowers, then choose the nonflowering lawn chamomile *(C. m.* "Treneague"). This low-growing variety puts down roots wherever its stems touch the ground.

■ **Corsican mint** The mat-forming Corsican mint *(Mentha requienii)* bears tiny purple flowers in summer and has round, bright green leaves that form an evergreen carpet. From a distance, the lawn has an almost mosslike appearance, but distinguishes itself by releasing

a wonderful mint fragrance when touched. Being fairly shallow-rooted, Corsican mint is not ideal for very dry situations, but needs good light.

■ **Thymes** Some hardwearing species such as *Thymus doerfleri* can be used as a living carpet that you can walk on; they release a delicious aroma when crushed. For just occasional use as a lawn, the mat-forming creeping or wild thyme *(Thymus serpyllum)* can serve a similar purpose to grass. It forms a ground-hugging green carpet of foliage and bears attractive pinkish purple flowers in summer. *T. s.* "Goldstream" planted as a lawn is valued for its light-green leaves with golden yellow variegation that makes a striking focal point. One drawback of using thymes is that they are a favorite plant for bees, and so are not suitable as lawns in homes with young children.

ROUTINE CARE

Most nongrass alternatives will not require regular mowing, but they will still need some routine care, chiefly hand-weeding. Unfortunately, the selective hormone lawn weed-killers, which are so successful in keeping grass lawns free of weeds, cannot be used on nongrass lawns; the chemicals will kill your chamomile or clover just as readily as they eliminate the dandelions and daisies in grass.

It is really important that you start with ground that is as weedfree as possible, and that you are prepared to carry out routine hand-weeding while the lawn plants become established. Once the plants have knitted together and covered the area, most weeds will be suppressed, and only occasional hand-weeding will be necessary.

USEFUL TO KNOW...

Once you have decided to replace your grass lawn or to introduce an area of soft landscaping into your garden design, you need to gather together the right equipment (see advice on pp. 12–13) and know where to look for the all-important materials.

BUYING GRAVEL

Shop around before buying gravel, and be prepared to spend time finding one that is just right for your proposed design. Many garden centers sell a range of colored gravels, and some have displays or catalogs showing the range that they stock or can obtain. Be sure to examine it both dry and wet, in sun and in shade, so that you can see its range of shades and surface textures.

Having decided on the type of gravel, you may wish to buy it in bags, or negotiate a special delivered price if you need a large quantity. Specialist stone and gravel suppliers will be able to deliver large quantities at a competitive price, but bear in mind that you will probably have to put in your own labor, moving the material by wheelbarrow from where the truck drops it off to the site where it is going to be used.

COLORED CHIPPINGS

BUYING LAWN PLANTS

Most garden centers stock pot-grown chamomile – choose the largest plants that you can afford so that your lawn establishes quickly. Most retail seed companies offer thymes and flowering chamomiles but you may have to contact an agricultural seed supplier to obtain clover seed.

ASSESSING QUANTITIES

Gravel and loose chippings sold in sacks, rather than by the cubic yard or meter, can be expensive. These sacks are ideal, however, if you just need to try out a small area to see whether it produces the desired effect.

Most suppliers will be able to advise you on how much material you will need for your project, so remember to take a note of the overall dimensions with you. If you are buying from a salvage yard, make sure that you buy enough materials to complete the job as you are unlikely to find the same or a matching material elsewhere.

To assess quantities for regular areas, multiply the length by the width by the depth; for more abstract shapes, draw the site to scale on graph paper. Multiply the total number of whole squares and those that are more than one-third full by the depth.

4
FOCAL POINTS

*No matter how carefully structured your overall design,
a garden needs highlights and focal points to arrest the
eye in particular places, to act as punctuation in the story
your garden is setting out to tell. Focal points can help to
take the eye to different parts of the garden in turn, so
that it's absorbed in segments rather than glanced at
quickly as a whole, and they help to take the eye inward
and away from the ever-present boundary fence or hedge.*

ORNAMENTS

Figures and statues can be used as focal or punctuation points around the garden. Choose figures that suit the surroundings and blend with the style of the garden. A classical bust may look inappropriate in a modern garden, while an abstract sculpture will look out of place in a country garden. Decide if your figure will look best in bold isolation, or whether it would be better half hidden by plants to give it an air of mystery.

CHOOSING SCULPTURE

Sculptural features can be striking or unobtrusive, traditional or abstract, depending on your personal taste and the look of your house and garden. In a small garden a small figure might be the only option because of lack of space. Provided the setting and background are appropriate, a small figure can have a big impact.

■ **Formal ornaments** Sculpted stone statues, particularly of classical Roman or Greek figures make an attractive centerpiece in a formal setting. Natural stone ornaments are expensive; however, most good garden centers stock a wide range of less costly reconstituted stone figures, which, with time, will mellow to blend with their surroundings. Formal statues are also ideal for combining with climbing plants, such as ivy.

CLASSICAL
BUST

SECURITY TIPS

• Don't put expensive ornaments in a prominent position where passersby can see them – they might disappear!

• Consider insuring expensive items.

• Small items are vulnerable to theft, so consider mortaring them to a plinth set into the ground.

■ **Abstract** An asymmetrical layout can be suitable for abstract figures. Abstract art is a popular option, but even an empty pot could be appropriate in the right setting.

■ **Wood** Sculptures and ornaments in wood as well as unusually shaped pieces of driftwood naturally blend well with most garden colors and textures. Animal and bird sculptures are popular motifs, as are carvings of the Buddha, and abstract figures.

CORRECT SITING

Consider using ornaments in areas of the garden where it is difficult to add impact with plants and flowers. Reconstituted stone figures can be used effectively to bring interest to dark and potentially boring corners in much the same way that you might use containers or specimen plants. Figures have the additional advantage of not needing sunlight or rain, and can potentially be sited in any position with minimal care and attention.

A classical layout with straight lines calls for a full stop, or something to punctuate junctions. Formal ornaments, such as a classical figure, a sundial, or a birdbath, are ideal for this purpose.

Take into account color as well as the detail and size of your figures. A pale color is best if you want your ornament to stand out as a focal point against a backdrop of green foliage. Do not be afraid to set a figure in a shrub border, especially among foliage shrubs, which can look rather predictable after a time.

SUNDIAL

STONE AND ROSES
In a small garden, a large ornament can sometimes be placed unobtrusively toward the back of a border, where it will seem less pretentious than it would positioned at the end of a path or patio.

FUN FEATURES

For some gardeners planning the garden is a serious business, and everything has to be done with a serious sense of design. However, gardening should also be fun, and if something frivolous appeals to you, then don't hesitate to use it. It is important to have a garden that is pleasing to you, and you will probably find that most of the visitors to your garden will share and enjoy your sense of humor too.

NOVELTY CONTAINERS

Small ornaments and novelty containers can be used very effectively to add interest to otherwise boring corners of the garden or to complement water features and plant borders. They are especially useful for livening up damp or dry areas of the garden where it is difficult to grow plants. Novelty containers can be purchased from many stores and garden centers. They have the advantage of already having been designed to take plants and should include drainage holes.

METAL FROG CONTAINER PLANTED WITH A DWARF CONIFER

Novelty containers do not have to be large or expensive to provide a pleasing focal point. Something small but with plenty of character, such as a container in the shape of an animal, bird, or fish, is ideal for a smaller space and introduces immediate interest. Novelty containers and ornaments in the shape of drinking animals or fish and amphibians can be combined with water features.

SMALL AND MOBILE

Small ornaments and containers have the advantage of being movable and can be repositioned periodically to change the look of your garden. This is especially useful if you want to bring containers of flowering plants to the fore as they come into season and move them to the back when they are past their best.

CHRYSANTHEMUMS IN PAINT POTS

CREATING A SCENE

The gardener can create interesting and sometimes amusing focal points with figurines.

Small ornaments in an open area of the garden are likely to have more impact if they form part of a group. Bird figurines, nestling on a gravel bed among the chamomile, have far more impact as a "family." Stone doves sculptured in a minimalistic style can be positioned on the lawn for a year-round effect. A grouping of decorative, colorful wooden "toadstools" is simple and unassuming, but attracts the eye to an area of the garden, such as the base of a tree, that you would almost certainly otherwise ignore. Groups of figures have the advantage of remaining mobile and versatile and can be moved or removed when you wish to change the features of your garden.

Most people either abhor or adore garden gnomes. However, they can be very striking if used to create a

CHESS GARDEN
A small corner of the garden can offer fun and entertainment in the shape of a permanent chessboard feature among the shrubs.

miniature scene and are much more effective in groups than as isolated, brightly painted little folk dotted around the garden. Place them among shrub borders or around water features for maximum impact.

Sculptures and models can also be linked to garden features for a pleasing and unexpected effect. For example, figures with buckets could be positioned by a water feature, or figures with garden implements could be sited on the grass or in the flower beds. Some gardeners prefer more original sculptures. Figures of dragons or crawling children can be positioned half-hidden among shrub borders and under trees, offering a pleasing surprise to visitors. Groups of colorful, sculptured stone mollusks can also be highly effective under trees and bushes.

ROCKY FEATURES

If positioned carefully, rocks can make an excellent focal point in a garden. Choose interesting and shapely rocks to create a feature that will arrest the eye immediately. It is surprising how easily a small group of stones can conjure up an alpine scree or how a few large beach pebbles can form a mini-seashore. Rocks are highly versatile and inexpensive and can be adapted to almost any shape, design, or area. They also combine well with loose materials such as gravel, stones, and wood chips.

ROCK STYLE

Rock gardens are generally more successful in large gardens, since they require a sloping site to be effective.

However, rocks and boulders are especially useful as focal points in dry or gravel gardens, or those planted with a Mediterranean theme. A cluster of rocks is likely to be visually more interesting than a single rock, and there is plenty of scope for artistic arrangements. A single large rock with sufficient height to arrest the eye from a distance can act as a focal point in a similar way to an ornament.

The rock will immediately take your eye across the garden and should command attention even in those bleak winter months when there is little else of color to appreciate. As large rocks are heavy and difficult to maneuver, positioning should be carefully planned.

Japanese Zen-style gardens also incorporate rocks extensively for their minimalist qualities. Boulders of various sizes can provide a suitable focus, especially when combined with a few plants and carefully raked gravel.

ASSORTED ROCKS
AND PEBBLES

ROCKY FOCUS
A few well-positioned rocks amid a gravel bed can form a pleasing, minimalistic feature in the garden.

USING GRAVEL

Gravel (see pp. 50–59) is versatile and easy to lay and is often used in the garden to form a natural transition between different surface materials such as paving and lawn.

If you have an expanse of gravel that seems to need a little something extra, try grouping together a few pebbles or stones or positioning a single boulder as a focal point.

A rock and gravel feature will also provide an attractive and unusual solution for a corner of the garden that is too shady for plants to thrive – it also has the advantage of requiring much less maintenance than a plant border.

Rocks and gravel always look harmonious, especially if you can partially bury the rocks so that they appear to project from the gravel rather than sit on the surface.

ROCKS AND WATER

Using a rock to break up the surface of a pond will add immeasurably to the visual impact. You could grow a bonsai tree, or perhaps some rock-hugging plant such as a houseleek *(Sempervivum)*, on the rock to make it look more like a miniature island. You will need to prepare a suitable base when the pond is being constructed, protecting the liner so that the rock does not puncture it.

Warning

• Always seek help to move rocks that are too heavy to handle alone.

• Plan ahead so that heavy rocks need to be moved as little as possible.

• Use levers and rollers to move rocks rather than attempt to lift them by muscle power alone.

• Mortar large, heavy rocks into position on a firm base, so they will not topple if someone leans on them.

GARDEN FURNITURE

Once you have created your perfect garden, you will want to spend plenty of time enjoying it. Take your garden furniture needs into consideration even at the planning stage: it may be possible to build a seat into the structure of the garden, combining it with an arbor or raised flower bed. When planning where the furniture will be positioned, consider how much space you will need. Remember that seating should be sited with relaxation in mind.

FURNITURE FOR ALL SEASONS

A cozy sitting area is a must in any garden and, if carefully positioned, will form an attractive focal point. Ideally, a sitting area should be designed as a permanent central feature, otherwise you will be left with an uninteresting void during those months when the furniture has been stored indoors.

There are many ways of providing attractive seating that can be left out all year to provide a year-round focus.

■ **Brick** Tables and benches built from brick can provide a durable and weatherproof year-round focal point on a patio. Simply add a few cushions in summer to give extra comfort for meals outdoors.

BRICK TABLE
In summer, cane chairs transform this striking brick table to make it the central feature of the garden, as well as a relaxing place to enjoy summer sunshine and outdoor entertaining.

■ **Wood** The natural colors and textures of timber seldom look out of place in any garden, and there are many interesting ways of adapting wood to make garden furniture.
To create a rustic-style seat, use some old railroad ties. The ties should be old and weathered and will blend with most garden materials.

■ **Metals** The sleek lines of steel and aluminum furniture suit a modern garden setting. Most metals can be left outside throughout the winter; however, ironwork must be painted.

■ **Color** Coordinate the colors of your furniture to match other garden features such as trellises or fences. The furniture will seem less obtrusive, especially in a small space.

CURVED GARDEN SEAT
A curved garden seat can make economical use of limited space, and is much cozier for couples to sit on than a straight bench.

HOT SEAT

If space is at a premium, adapt your built-in barbecue to double up as a garden seat. The metal barbecue equipment can be removed and a wooden seat and cushion slotted in to offer an extra seating option.

BRICK BARBECUE "SEAT"

When building your own barbecue, consider the following factors:

• Build your barbecue to fit a standard size grilling rack so that it can be replaced easily.

• Position a barbecue so that there is easy access to seating and to the house but far enough away to prevent cooking smells from penetrating indoors.

• Do not cramp a garden by siting the barbecue in the middle of a patio, especially as it may only be used seasonally.

• Build your barbecue from materials that blend easily with the surroundings.

• Do not build your barbecue directly under a tree or bush, which may be scorched if the heat becomes intense.

LIGHTING

Any garden feature can be enhanced by the creative use of lighting. Outdoor lights of all kinds are available that can be used to illuminate patios, ponds and other water features, secluded arbors, decking, glass bricks, and pathways. Some lighting can be floated or submerged in water. At night the effect of the lighting can be magnified, creating a dramatic spectacle. Lighting is especially useful if you wish to highlight a particular garden feature or to soften any harsh, rigid lines created by a wall or building.

SPOTLIGHTS

Artificial lighting is often both practical and attractive in courtyard or patio gardens. It can be used to cast the shadow of a tree or ornament against a brick wall, or to backlight a striking architectural plant. Lanterns are suitable for lighting pathways and patios.

Submersible globe lights can be used to underlight an interesting water feature or illuminate the fine spray of a fountain, while garden spotlights can shed light across the water surface of ponds and pools and deepen the reflection.

GARDEN
SPOTLIGHT

SUBMERSIBLE
GLOBE LIGHT

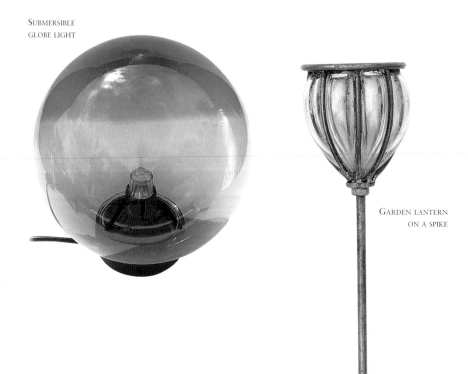

GARDEN LANTERN
ON A SPIKE

5
SMALL TREES, BIG IMPACT

If you have a small garden, or want to plant up a small "room" of a larger garden, it's very easy to make the error of planting only dwarf or compact plants. This means there is little to break up the garden, and the eye immediately focuses on the boundary. Every garden needs vertical elements to make it more three-dimensional and sometimes to help block out a less than pleasing view beyond. Small trees will help to make your garden seem more mature and more interesting. Small trees are also ideal for planting nearer to the house, so as not to block out light.

The trees outlined in this chapter are suitable for most small or medium-sized gardens. If you have space for just a few trees, you will find the following selection more than adequate.

MAPLE

The maples (genus *Acer*) will almost always demand admiring glances. Many, such as the paperbark maple, have beautiful peeling bark, dainty winged seeds or "keys," and glorious color in fall. Although maple trees are slow-growing, the keys may be produced at a relatively early age. Some maples may be grown in large containers.

VARIETIES

■ *Acer griseum* (Paperbark maple) Although it can be grown as a multistemmed tree similar to a large shrub, the paperbark maple will have maximum impact in a small garden if grown on a clear single trunk. The peeling cinnamon-colored bark of mature specimens looks good all year round but is especially attractive when it combines with the vivid red and orange foliage in fall. HEIGHT/SPREAD: 30 ft (10 m)

■ *Acer palmatum* "Atropurpureum" Ideal for a small garden, this Japanese maple combines an elegant shape with deep purple leaves that turn brilliant red in fall. Young specimens look more like shrubs, but with age most make beautiful small trees with a mound of dense foliage on a short trunk. HEIGHT/SPREAD: 20 ft (6 m)

GROWING HINTS

Maples prefer well-drained ground but will tolerate chalky soils. They can be grown in full sun or light shade and need shelter from strong winds, which may damage young leaves.

PAPERBARK MAPLE

JUNEBERRY

Although the juneberry, also known as shadbush or snowy mespilus (genus *Amelanchier*), is often raised as a shrub, it can also be grown as a small tree with a clear trunk. The stunning orange and red foliage in fall compensates for the relatively brief spring display of white flowers. In favorable summers, sweet berries may be borne.

VARIETIES

This is an undemanding tree that needs little routine care other than minimal pruning to remove any crossing, diseased, or damaged stems in late winter and early spring. The round or pear-shaped fruits produced on all species are attractive to birds and are edible when cooked.

■ *Amelanchier lamarckii*
This tree will make an impact in spring with its profusion of pure white flowers. The bronze leaves turn dark green in summer through to stunning orange-red in fall.
HEIGHT: 30 ft (10 m)
SPREAD: 40 ft (12 m)

■ *Amelanchier canadensis* (Shadbush)
This small, shrublike tree has mid-green leaves that mature to orange-red in fall. Its spikes of white spring flowers are followed by red fruit that mature to blue-black in late summer.
HEIGHT: 20 ft (6 m)
SPREAD: 10 ft (3 m)

■ *Amelanchier laevis*
(Allegheny serviceberry)
This spreading, shrubby tree has drooping spikes of white, spring flowers and bronze leaves that turn mid-green in summer.
HEIGHT/SPREAD: 25 ft (8 m)

JUNEBERRY

GROWING HINTS

Amelanchiers prefer lime-free soils with good drainage. Grow them in full sun if possible, although they will tolerate a site in partial shade.

Although juneberries enjoy rapid early growth, they do not reach their maximum height of 25 ft (8 m) for many years – which is good news for small gardens.

HAWTHORN

Compact and seldom outgrowing their welcome, thorny, deciduous hawthorns (genus *Crataegus*) deserve more recognition as garden trees. They put on a delightful display of flowers in late spring, and some varieties also yield bright fall berries. As they do not produce a large head, they make good specimen trees to plant in a lawn and are usually easy to mow around.

VARIETIES

■ *Crataegus laevigata*
(Midland hawthorn, May)
This rounded, thorny tree has white to pink flowers, which are followed by small, bright red fruit in fall. It also has a number of varieties that are prized for their attractive double flowers. Unfortunately, however, these double varieties do not produce a good display of fall berries.
　C. l. "Plena" is valued for its double white flowers that mature to pink.
　C. l. "Rosea Flore Pleno" bears clusters of double pink flowers.

MIDLAND HAWTHORN

C. l. "Paul's Scarlet," which is sometimes sold under its synonym C. l. "Coccinea Plena," has glossy dark green leaves and numerous clusters of double red flowers.
HEIGHT/SPREAD: 25 ft (8 m)

■ *Crataegus monogyna*
(Common hawthorn)
This hawthorn has dark green leaves and clusters of fragrant white spring flowers. The leaves and flowers of C. m. "Biflora" (Glastonbury thorn) may also emerge in mild winters.
HEIGHT: 30 ft (10 m)
SPREAD: 25 ft (8 m)

■ *Crataegus crus-galli*
(Cockspur thorn)
This American hawthorn has white flowers, followed by dark red berries and bright crimson fall foliage.
HEIGHT: 25 ft (8 m)
SPREAD: 30 ft (10 m)

GROWING HINTS

Hawthorns will thrive in almost any soil and although they perform best in full sun most will tolerate partial shade. They often remain compact for many years and need to be pruned only when branches are diseased, damaged, or crossing.

LABURNUM

No matter how many gardens possess a laburnum, the long cascading chains of yellow flowers of this small deciduous tree still manage to arrest the eye. Laburnums are easy to grow, reliable, and perform well, so don't let their popularity deter you from including one in your garden either as a specimen or to form a pergola. Remember that all parts of a laburnum including the seeds are toxic if eaten, so avoid growing this tree if you have a young family.

VARIETIES

■ *Laburnum* x *watereri* "Vossii"
This hybrid of common and Scotch laburnum is the most popular variety of laburnum. On a mature tree from late spring onward the branches are festooned with long drooping chains of yellow flowers, sometimes up to 2 ft (60 cm) long. As they open at about the same time as the leaves, the flowers are not concealed by the

GROWING HINTS

Laburnums will tolerate most soil types, and even grow on thin, chalky ground. They prefer full sun but will cope with light shade. Use one- or two-year old trees for training against walls and arches, tying in the branches to a frame while they are still supple.

foliage, and the spectacular display more than makes up for the slightly drab, gray-green foliage in summer. When produced, the dull brown seedpods often hang all summer, even after the seeds have been shed.
HEIGHT/SPREAD: 25 ft (8 m)

■ *Laburnum anagyroides*
(Common laburnum)
This spreading tree produces attractive soft, gray-green shoots and a profusion of yellow flowers in spring and summer.
HEIGHT/SPREAD: 25 ft (8 m)

■ *Laburnum alpinum* "Pendulum"
This cultivar is valued for its short-stemmed, weeping branches and slender spikes of bright yellow flowers.
HEIGHT/SPREAD: 6 ft (2 m)

LABURNUM X *WATERERI* "VOSSII"

MAGNOLIA

Grown for their large, exotic-looking blooms in mid-spring or early summer, magnolias form elegant showpieces in any garden and are bound to capture attention and admiration when allowed to spread unhindered. The flowers often emerge before the leaves and are a welcome sign that spring has arrived. Although they are slow-growing, magnolias eventually form imposing trees that are valuable as focal or punctuation points.

VARIETIES

■ *Magnolia x soulangeana*
Valued for its large, goblet-shaped flowers in shades of pure white, rose-pink, and red-purple this attractive tree will remain small for many years, but may eventually outgrow a very small garden. In exposed sites where the flowers may suffer wind damage, try training it against a wall. There are a number of color varieties.
  M. x s. "Rustica Rubra" has maroon flowers that are white inside.
  M. x s. "Lennei Alba" produces ivory-white flowers.
HEIGHT/SPREAD: 20 ft (6 m)

MAGNOLIA X SOULANGEANA

GROWING HINTS

Magnolias prefer to grow in fertile soil with good drainage, either in full sun or partial shade; they will tolerate chalk and clay but often give a poor performance. Bear in mind that the flowers may be damaged if frozen then thawed rapidly by direct early morning sun. Enrich dry sandy soils with organic matter before planting, and apply a layer of organic mulch in spring. Many magnolias take several years to reach their full height and although most will survive cramped conditions, they are better grown as specimens in lawns, where they can spread.

■ *Magnolia liliiflora* "Nigra"
This compact cultivar flowers from young, bearing dark purple-red flowers from early summer.
HEIGHT/SPREAD: 10 ft (3 m)

■ *Magnolia stellata* (Star magnolia)
The pretty star magnolia takes its name from its pure white sometimes pink-flushed star-shaped flowers. The leaves appear after the flowers and mature to yellow in fall.
HEIGHT: 10 ft (3 m)
SPREAD: 12 ft (4 m)

■ *Magnolia cylindrica*
This spreading tree has creamy-white cup-shaped flowers in spring.
HEIGHT/SPREAD: 15 ft (5 m)

CRAB APPLE

Ornamental crab apples (genus *Malus*) are round-headed deciduous trees that are widely grown for their fragrant blossoms in spring and small, colorful fruits in fall. Crab apples flower while young and grow quickly in their early years, yet they are unlikely to outgrow their space when mature, making them ideal specimens for a garden. The fruits are usually edible when cooked and often used to make a tasty jelly flavored with cloves.

VARIETIES

■ *Malus* x *purpurea*
This hybrid takes its name from the purple spring foliage and young wood, which provides interest into the summer. The purple-pink flowers are followed by deep red fruits.
HEIGHT: 22 ft (7 m)
SPREAD: 12 ft (4 m)

■ *Malus* "John Downie"
One of the best ornamental crab apples grown for its colorful red and orange fruit, "John Downie" also puts on a good spring display of pink buds opening to white blossoms.
HEIGHT: 30 ft (10 m)
SPREAD: 20 ft (6 m)

■ *Malus floribunda*
(Japanese crab apple)
Although this is one of the prettiest flowering trees when covered with blossoms in spring, the small yellow fruit are unspectacular. The flowers open rich rose but fade to pale pink.
HEIGHT/SPREAD: 30 ft (10 m)

■ *Malus* "White Cascade"
The white flowers of this weeping crab apple emerge from pink buds and are offset by dark green leaves. Small, greenish yellow fruits are borne in late summer.
HEIGHT/SPREAD: 15 ft (5 m)

ORNAMENTAL CRAB APPLES

GROWING HINTS

Ornamental crab apples will grow well in most soils except those prone to waterlogging. Most species, especially *Malus* x *purpurea*, do best in full sun, but will tolerate light shade. Carry out pruning during winter, removing any damaged, diseased, or crossing wood to maintain a balanced framework of branches. Check the fruit regularly for signs of apple scab that affects the leaves and fruits and spreads quickly. Remove all leaves and fruits marked with small dark brown patches or "scabs" and cut out diseased wood.

ORNAMENTAL CHERRY

Season after season of interest is guaranteed when you plant an
ornamental cherry (genus *Prunus*) in your garden: clusters of
dainty spring flowers in shades of pink are often followed by small,
decorative fruits, which are also enjoyed by visiting garden birds.
The tree rounds off its year with a grand finale of yellow, orange, and
flame foliage in fall. If your garden has room for just one specimen,
an ornamental cherry can be counted on to make a bold statement.

VARIETIES

■ *Prunus* "Amanogawa"
The semidouble shell pink flowers of
this pretty tree make a spectacular
spring show, only to be followed by
a colorful display of yellow and
orange foliage in fall. Its narrow,
pillarlike growth means that it will
not take up too much space in
your garden.
HEIGHT: 25 ft (8 m)
SPREAD: 12 ft (4 m)

■ *Prunus maackii*
(Manchurian cherry)
The Manchurian cherry is grown
chiefly for its peeling, yellow-brown
bark, and yellow fall foliage. In
spring it produces clusters of white
flowers, which are followed later
in the year by rounded, glossy
black fruits.
HEIGHT: 30 ft (10 m)
SPREAD: 25 ft (8 m)

JAPANESE CHERRY

GROWING HINTS

Flowering cherries like moist, fertile
soil with good drainage and a sunny
site. They are prone to several pests
and diseases, but an annual mulch of
organic matter in spring and regular
watering in dry summers should
boost their resistance.

■ *Prunus* "Kanzan"
Although not the most compact
of the flowering cherries, "Kanzan"
makes an ideal specimen in a lawn
and always attracts attention
when covered with its bright pink
flowers in spring. Although it is
unremarkable in summer, it excels
again in fall when the leaves turn
bronzy orange.
HEIGHT/SPREAD: 30 ft (10 m)

PEAR

Ornamental pear trees, valued for their silver or blue-gray foliage, make ideal specimens on lawns. If there is not enough space in your garden to accommodate one of the smaller ornamental varieties, try growing the common or wild pear *(Pyrus communis)*. This species can be trained as a cordon, fan, or espalier against a wall or even as a living screen or divider (see pp. 46–47) from which you can harvest a crop of tasty fruits.

VARIETIES

■ *Pyrus salicifolia* "Pendula"
This weeping, willow-leaved pear has unspectacular flowers and fruit, but its cascading branches covered in slender silver-gray foliage give it a distinctive shape that makes it a real focal point. It is one of the finest foliage trees for a small garden.
HEIGHT: 15 ft (5 m)
SPREAD: 12 ft (4 m)

PYRUS SALICIFOLIA "PENDULA"

GROWING HINTS

Pear trees will grow in most soils, but prefer a sunny site. To display their shape, plant pear trees in isolation in a lawn rather than crowded into a border. Although pear trees can grow tall, they are unlikely to outgrow their space for many years.

■ *Pyrus calleryana* "Chanticleer"
This ornamental pear has glossy dark green leaves that turn to red in fall. Sprays of white flowers appear in mid-spring, followed by small, brown fruits. Although it may grow tall, its narrow, conical shape makes it suitable for a small garden.
HEIGHT: 50 ft (15 m)
SPREAD: 20 ft (6 m)

■ *Pyrus communis* (Common pear)
The common pear, which produces white flowers and edible, greenish yellow fruit, can grow to a height of 50 ft (15 m), so try to choose cultivars that have been grafted on to quince rootstock, as this restricts the ultimate size of the tree.
P. c. "Beech Hill" is grown for its fiery red and orange foliage in fall.
HEIGHT: 30 ft (10 m)
SPREAD: 22 ft (7 m)

CHOOSING A TREE

Before choosing a tree, check that it will thrive within the temperature, rainfall, and humidity ranges that prevail on the planned site. Consider local factors such as exposure to wind, which may scorch foliage or cause distortion of the tree's canopy.

BUYING TREES

Garden centers usually carry a reasonable range of trees. Most of them will be happy to order a particular plant if it is not in stock. Alternatively, you can buy from mail-order suppliers who may sell bare-root rather than container-grown plants. There is no significant disadvantage in buying this type of plant provided that you plant during the dormant season between mid-fall and mid-spring. Young trees establish more quickly than older trees, but if you need immediate impact in your garden, look for a more mature specimen. This can usually be found at a specialist tree nursery, which will also have a range of "feathered" trees for growing against walls or for pleaching (see p. 47).

■ **Container-grown trees** Trees that dislike any disturbance to their roots are usually raised in containers. They can be bought and planted at any time of the year.

■ **Bare-root trees** Mostly deciduous trees are sold with soilless bare roots; they are raised in the ground and lifted when ready to be sold.

■ **Rootballed trees** Tall deciduous trees and most evergreens are sold with their rootball wrapped in hessian or netting to keep the ball in shape and to prevent the roots from drying out. The trees are raised in open ground prior to being lifted.

WHAT TO LOOK FOR

■ **Roots** Check that the roots are not coiled, overcrowded, or protruding from the drainage holes of the container. Reject any plants that are visibly damaged or diseased. When you try to remove the plant from its container, it should slide out easily and the soil should cling firmly to the rootball – this shows that the root system is established.

■ **Topgrowth** Check that the branches look healthy and show signs of vigorous growth. They should be well developed and balanced evenly around the stem. Rootball or bare-root trees in leaf are unlikely to survive transplanting.

CONTAINER-GROWN
TREE

*Well-established
root system*

6
USING VERTICAL SPACE

Making the most of vertical space is important whatever your garden size, as it adds interest, focus, and versatility. Plants will also help to clothe walls, fences, and screens, making them less obtrusive and adding color and interest to a dull expanse of brickwork.

Although most of us think first of climbers for this purpose, there is a wide selection of shrubs that can be grown against a wall or fence and which may be more appropriate if you just want to cover a height of about 6–8 ft (1.8–2.4 m). You can still grow climbers along a fence or boundary wall, however, if you train them horizontally. Be prepared to clip or prune back climbers and wall shrubs to keep them within bounds and to make sure that they don't cascade too far out into neighboring flower beds and borders, otherwise you will begin to lose valuable planting space in front of them.

CEANOTHUS

Popularly known as California lilacs (not to be confused with the true lilacs), ceanothus make ideal wall shrubs and can be trained and pruned to grow close to the wall. Some species will not tolerate a cold winter, so make sure you choose a variety suited to the climate in the area where you live. Some species flower early, others in fall, so by planting more than one kind you can lengthen the flowering season.

VARIETIES

■ *Ceanothus* "Autumnal Blue"
This evergreen variety has glossy leaves and large sprays of sky-blue flowers. In areas with severe winters, it is best grown against a sunny wall. All evergreen varieties need a light trim immediately after flowering.
HEIGHT/SPREAD: 10 ft (3 m)

■ *Ceanothus* "Perle Rose"
A deciduous variety with pale green leaves and sprays of unusually, pink flowers from midsummer to fall.
HEIGHT/SPREAD: 5 ft (1.5 m)

GROWING TIPS

Ceanothus like fertile soil with good drainage and dislike chalky soils. They perform best in full sun and need some shelter against strong, cold winds. If planted against a wall or fence some shade is inevitable for part of the day, but avoid sites in day-long shade. Remember that ceanothus can reach twice their expected height when trained against a wall and need pruning to stop them from sprawling.

■ *Ceanothus* "Gloire de Versailles"
A popular deciduous variety with powder-blue flowers in summer and fall. It is best pruned in early spring: trim back new shoots that are growing in the wrong place to within 3–4 in (8–10 cm) of the previous year's growth to ensure a good display of flowers.
HEIGHT/SPREAD: 5 ft (1.5 m)

■ *Ceanothus* x *veitchianus*
This tough, free-flowering evergreen produces deep blue flowers in late spring and early summer. With its small evergreen leaves and deeply impressed veins, the year-round interest of this variety makes it suitable for growing against a wall.
HEIGHT/SPREAD: 10 ft (3 m)

CEANOTHUS

CLEMATIS

A mong the most planted and best-loved climbers, clematis need no introduction. There are so many different kinds – evergreen or deciduous, vigorous or slow-growing, large- or small-flowered – that you are guaranteed to find one that suits your garden perfectly. You could have a whole collection of them! Clematis look attractive when trained on walls or a trellis or when allowed to scramble through trees.

VARIETIES

■ *Clematis montana*
If you need a vigorous clematis to help make a fence or brick wall more interesting, try the white-flowered *Clematis montana* or one of its many colorful cultivars. This spring-flowering species can reach a considerable height if it has a tall support, but can also be trained horizontally along a wall, where it will tumble down to produce a curtain of flowers.

■ *Clematis* "Bill Mackenzie"
Like other small-flowered climbers, C. "Bill Mackenzie" is often grown for its large, fluffy seedheads in fall, which follow on from the yellow bell-shaped flowers with distinctive red anthers that are produced from midsummer onward.

CLEMATIS "BILL MACKENZIE"

GROWING TIPS

Clematis do best in fertile, well-drained soil, but will tolerate chalky soils. Keep the flowering parts of the plant in full sun if possible, although the roots are best in shade. There is wide variation in height and vigor between the different species and varieties of clematis, so check a plant reference book or consult your supplier for the expected height and routine care of your chosen plant.

■ *Clematis* "Nelly Moser"
Large-flowered clematis with bold and beautiful blooms are less effective for clothing walls, but they are well worth considering for trellis screens and pergolas. They are especially valued for their twice-flowering habit: once in early summer and again in late summer.
  C. "Nelly Moser" is one of the most popular large-flowered, deciduous clematis. Its banded mauve flowers are paler in late summer and fade in full sun.

SPINDLE TREE

Often grown in open ground as a freestanding plant, this versatile evergreen shrub (genus *Euonymus*) will grow easily against a wall or fence, where its colorful foliage and fruits will brighten up a vertical space with year-round interest. A little light pruning of any protruding shoots is all that is needed to maintain the spindle tree's striking curtain of foliage.

VARIETIES

■ *Euonymus fortunei* cultivars
Although these rounded, evergreen shrubs are often seen as border or ground-cover shrubs, they can be trained to grow against a wall and will easily grow as high as 4–6 ft (1.2–1.8 m). Just cut out any long shoots that grow too far away from the wall, or trim the edge or top when it has reached its limit when the new growth has been produced in spring. You can even use the plant's scrambling and climbing tendencies to form a frame around a window or conceal an ugly drainpipe. Buy or make a suitable frame, then train the shoots to grow up it. Bear in mind that growth is relatively slow, so don't be too impatient. There are many variegated varieties available.

GROWING HINTS

This very tolerant and easy plant will grow well in most soils with good drainage, either in full sun or in partial shade. It will even do well in dry positions once it is established. Evergreen varieties need to be sheltered from cold, drying winds, and variegated cultivars need a site in full sun to enhance their foliage colors.

E. f. "Emerald 'n' Gold" has bright green leaves, edged in yellow and tinged pink in winter.
E. f. "Silver Queen" has dark green leaves with white margins that later turn to pink.
E. f. "Kewensis" has dark green leaves with pale green veins.
HEIGHT: 15 ft (5 m)
SPREAD: indefinite

■ *Euonymus japonicus*
(Japanese spindle)
This evergreen shrub can be grown as hedging, as a climbing shrub, or as a small tree, and is tolerant of coastal sites. It produces tiny, star-shaped flowers in summer, but is valued chiefly for its colorful foliage.
E. j. "Aureus" has dark green leaves, with a central yellow mark.
HEIGHT: 10 ft (3 m)
SPREAD: 6 ft (2 m)

SPINDLE TREE

IVY

Climbers don't come easier than ivy (genus *Hedera*). These versatile plants, which can be used as ground cover as well as climbers, are widely available and very easy to grow. They are also self-clinging, so you don't have to provide a support. Make the most of growing space in your garden by using ivies to cover walls; this makes the garden look more clothed and the walls less obtrusive.

VARIETIES

■ *Hedera helix* (Common ivy)
This fast-growing climber will create an instant curtain of foliage, but there are many variations to choose from, each varying in leaf shape, size, and coloring.

   H. h. "Glacier" is a variegated variety that is not too vigorous. It has gray-green leaves variegated with cream.

   H. h. "Buttercup" is a slow-growing variety with pale green leaves that turn yellow in full sun.

   H. h. "Atropurpurea" has dark green leaves that turn purple in cold weather.

   H. h. "Pedata" is an excellent ivy for cloaking walls. It is often commonly referred to as bird's foot ivy because of the shape of its leaves, which have a pronounced middle lobe that makes them look rather like a bird's foot.

HEDERA HELIX "BUTTERCUP"

■ *Hedera colchica* (Persian ivy, Bullock's heart ivy)
Large-leaved ivies such as *H. colchica* and its cultivars are ideal for quickly covering a wall and need regular pruning to be kept trim.

   H. c. "Dentata Variegata" has 6-in (15-cm) light green leaves, with gray-green mottling and cream margins.

   H. c. "Sulphur Heart" is similar to "Dentata Variegata" but grows more rapidly.

■ *Hedera hibernica* "Deltoidea"
The neat, heart-shaped leaves of the slow-growing *Hedera hibernica* "Deltoidea" are dark green with attractive veining. It forms a dense cloak on walls, fences, and trellises.

GROWING HINTS

Ivies grow in sun or dense shade, in almost any soil, and can simply be cut back if they outgrow their space with no long-term damage. They are so tough that they will survive in even the most unpromising places. Height and vigor depend on species and variety, so check with a plant reference guide or ask your supplier.

HOP

Best known for its drooping clusters of pale greenish-yellow summer flowers that are used in the production of beer, hops (genus *Humulus*) make attractive foliage climbers for a sunny fence or wall. The golden hop is one of those climbers that really grabs attention and its yellow curtain of foliage is ideal for bringing light to a dull, uninteresting corner of the garden.

VARIETIES

■ *Humulus lupulus* "Aureus"
(Golden hop)
Despite the fact that this attractive twining climber dies back in late fall, it is a popular plant. It is used to scramble through darker-leaved

shrubs or in an informal hedge will create some pleasing foliage combinations. In summer, the bristly stems bear drooping clusters of fragrant, golden yellow female flowers (or "hops"), which may be cut and used in dried flower arrangements. As the season progresses, however, the plant grows much larger and you may find that it swamps supporting plants. Bear in mind that when the plant dies back in fall, you will be left with a bare support until new shoots appear again in spring.

> ### GROWING HINTS
>
> Hops prefer well-drained soil and full sun, although they will tolerate partial shade. Provide a trellis or training wires if against a wall; use a large tripod, obelisk, or arch in borders.

GOLDEN HOP

JASMINE

The heady fragrance and dainty white flowers of jasmine (genus *Jasminum*) are a delicacy to be savored on long, summer evenings in the garden; trained over a pergola or an arbor, jasmine makes the perfect secret retreat. In contrast, winter jasmine needs to be placed in full view so that you can enjoy its colorful yellow flowers when it comes into its glory during winter.

VARIETIES

■ *Jasminum officinale*
(Common jasmine)
This vigorous, deciduous climber and its cultivars are grown for their strongly fragrant white flowers, which are produced from summer to early fall. In cool areas, they should be positioned in a sheltered site, in full sun and will suit a southwest facing wall.
   J. o. "Argenteovariegatum" has variegated gray-green leaves with cream margins.
   J. o. "Aureum" has yellow variegated leaves, which make an effective contrast when grown against the dark foliage of a hedge or conifer.
HEIGHT: 40 ft (12 m)

JASMINUM NUDIFLORUM

GROWING HINTS

Jasmines are easy to grow and will tolerate almost any soil with good drainage; they even cope well with impoverished conditions and can be planted in full sun or partial shade. Train the plant onto a tall support or training wires and it will quickly establish itself and climb unaided. If flowering is poor on a common jasmine, move it to a warmer site or less fertile soil. Prune winter jasmine annually, otherwise the new growth will grow over the older wood, making the plant look untidy.

■ *Jasminum nudiflorum*
(Winter jasmine)
A valuable addition to any garden, the winter jasmine makes a welcome display of bright yellow flowers set against dark green foliage at a time when there are few other flowers to bring color and cheer into the garden. Keep the plant upright and tidy by training it against a trellis or other support. Winter jasmine and firethorns make good companion wall shrubs, forming a colorful partnership as the jasmine's yellow flowers emerge at the same time as the orange and red firethorn berries.
HEIGHT/SPREAD: 10 ft (3 m)

HONEYSUCKLE

Climbing honeysuckles (genus *Lonicera*) are valued for their sweet fragrance and exotic-looking flowers. They can be grown on trellis panels, trained over pergolas, or scrambled through other plants. Honeysuckles are ideal for adding interest to an old tree stump or bare trunk and make attractive summer screens to divide up an area or conceal an unsightly object.

VARIETIES

■ *Lonicera periclymenum*
(Woodbine, Common honeysuckle)
Common honeysuckle is a vigorous climber that looks effective scrambled through an informal hedge or intertwined with clematis. By planting both kinds of flowering forms, such as the early *L. p.* "Belgica" and late *L. p.* "Serotina," you can extend the period of interest throughout the summer.
HEIGHT: 22 ft (7 m)

LONICERA PERICLYMENUM

GROWING HINTS

Climbing honeysuckles grow well in any ordinary well-drained soil, but prefer sun or partial shade. They need to be trained on a suitable support and look best when surplus growth is allowed to tumble down and clothe the support. Not all species are as fragrant as common honeysuckle, so check with a supplier before buying, if this is particularly important to you.

■ *Lonicera japonica*
(Japanese honeysuckle)
A vigorous climber, produces fragrant white flowers from spring through late summer, followed by bluish black berries. Some cultivars are grown for their foliage.
  L. j. "Aureoreticulata" has yellow-veined leaves.
  L. j. var *repens* has purple-flushed foliage.
HEIGHT: 30 ft (10 m)

■ *Lonicera caprifolium*
(Italian honeysuckle)
A strongly scented deciduous climber, the Italian honeysuckle has pink-flushed cream-white to yellow flowers, which are followed by bright orange-red berries in fall.
HEIGHT: 20 ft (6 m)

VIRGINIA CREEPER

B oston ivy and Virginia creepers (genus *Parthenocissus*) are
vigorous, climbing, deciduous vines that have the merit of being
self-clinging, so you don't even have to worry about supporting them.
Grown for their stunning foliage, all of them are excellent for covering
bare brickwork and will mask even a very large wall if you allow
them the freedom to roam.

VARIETIES

■ *Parthenocissus tricuspidata*
(Boston ivy)
Ideal for clothing a large bare wall,
the Boston ivy takes up hardly any
room at the foot of the wall, yet
will clothe it with green foliage
throughout the summer, before
setting it alight with fiery red
to purple leaves in fall.
HEIGHT: 70 ft (20 m)

■ *Parthenocissus quinquefolia*
(Virginia creeper)
The dull green leaves of this vigorous
climber come into their own in fall
when they turn brilliant red.
HEIGHT: 50 ft (15 m)

■ *Parthenocissus henryana*
(Chinese Virginia creeper)
The silvery white veining on the deep
green or bronze, velvety leaves of this
attractive climber is best displayed in

PARTHENOCISSUS QUINQUEFOLIA

GROWING HINTS

Virginia creepers are undemanding
plants that survive well in most soils.
They prefer sun or partial shade; the
veined leaves of Chinese Virginia
creeper are best shielded from direct
sun. Once the leaves have fallen, crop
the plant back close to the wall so
that next year's growth will form
an even curtain of foliage.

a lightly shaded position. However,
its summer interest is surpassed
by the attention-seeking cloak of
crimson foliage that appears in fall.
HEIGHT: 30 ft (10 m)

■ *Parthenocissus thomsonii*
A woody climber valued for its
toothed leaves that are maroon when
young. The foliage turns to purple-
green in summer, maturing to scarlet.
HEIGHT: 30 ft (10 m)

PASSION FLOWER

No matter how long you grow passion flowers (genus *Passiflora*), their intricate detail never fails to impress. When trained across the top of a pergola or an arch, the exotic-looking flowers are shown at their best, offset against lush, dark green foliage. Most species are tropical and need to be overwintered in a greenhouse, but the following selection will survive winter outdoors in a temperate climate.

VARIETIES

■ *Passiflora caerulea*
(Common passion flower)
This hardy, fast-growing climber provides good summer interest, although in cold areas it may drop many of its leaves in winter. Its large, highly individual blue flowers are produced over many months, usually from early summer to early fall. It is called passion flower because the three stigmas are said to represent the three nails, the five anthers the five wounds, the corona the crown of thorns, and the ten tepals (petal-like structures) the apostles. In a warm summer, edible egg-shaped orange fruits are produced.

P. c. "Constance Elliott," which is thought to be hardier than the species, has a scented, ivory-white flower with delicate pale blue or white filaments.
P. c. "Grandiflora" has flowers up to 6 in (15 cm) across.
HEIGHT: 30 ft (10 m)

■ *Passiflora incarnata* (Maypops)
This perennial climber has large, dark green leaves. Its fragrant, white to mauve flowers crowned with dainty purple filaments are produced in summer, followed by yellow fruits.
HEIGHT: 6 ft (2 m)

PASSIFLORA CAERULEA

GROWING HINTS

Most passion flowers will grow in full sun or partial shade. Train them against a trellis or along training wires so that the flowers can be shown to best effect. Mature plants are heavy and will need strong support. Regular pruning boosts the production of flowers and extends their life span.

FIRETHORN

R espected for their stems of sharp, piercing thorns, firethorns (genus *Pyracantha*) offer year-round interest with their dark, evergreen foliage, clusters of dainty white summer flowers, and profusion of berries that often last into winter. They may be grown as specimens, but are equally striking when trained as espaliers or fans against walls or trellis screens.

VARIETIES

Firethorns will cover a large area of wall eventually but can be easily contained within a limited area by annual pruning. Although the spiny branches are largely self-supporting, it is best to secure them to horizontal or fanned-out training wires fixed to a wall or between upright posts. The eye-catching berries become showy by late summer and are usually retained for many months.

■ *Pyracantha* "Mohave"
A vigorous-growing bush grown for its clusters of long-lasting red berries.
HEIGHT: 12 ft (4 m)
SPREAD: 15 ft (5 m)

FIRETHORN

GROWING HINTS

Firethorns will grow in fertile soil with good drainage in full sun or partial shade; if grown in full shade, fewer berries are produced. In cold areas, shelter the plants from cold, drying winds. Firethorns can be grown as freestanding shrubs, but are popular for growing against walls because they respond well to training and pruning. Remember to wear gloves when handling firethorns as the stems are thorny. Tie in any shoots needed to extend the framework and cut out unwanted growth after flowering to expose the berries.

■ *Pyracantha coccinea*
This bushy shrub bears small, dark green leaves and white flowers in early summer. Bright red berries provide fall interest.
HEIGHT/SPREAD: 12 ft (4 m)

■ *Pyracantha* "Harlequin"
This spreading shrub grows best against a wall. Tinged with pink when young, the dark green leaves are variegated creamy white and make an attractive display. Small white summer flowers are followed by red berries.
HEIGHT: 5 ft (1.5 m)
SPREAD: 6 ft (2 m)

PART TWO: WATER GARDENING

The sight and sound of water will bring a feeling of tranquillity to even the busiest and noisiest of gardens. Visitors, both young and old, will always head straight for the pond, while animals, butterflies, birds, and insects are all drawn to even the simplest of water features. Anyone can have a water feature to suit their space and budget – from a mini-pond in a barrel on a balcony to a more ambitious project, complete with plants and fish, fountain, and lights. Once built and stocked, a pond or water feature needs very little looking after, so you really can sit back and enjoy it.

CREATING A WATER GARDEN

This section of the book is designed to help you create your own perfect water garden, whatever its size, shape, and style. Whether you are a total novice or an experienced water gardener, the advice given here on the materials and techniques that you will need to construct different types of ponds and water features, plus tips on the best plants and fish to choose, will help you to avoid some of the pitfalls of water gardening.

Before you rush out to buy a pond, fish, and plants, take time to think carefully about what it is you really want from a water feature and how much space and time you have. If you opt for a pond in favor of a smaller water feature, Chapter 1 looks at where a pond might best be sited in your garden; the merits of formal and informal designs; the pros and cons of a sunken pond versus a raised one; the choice of liners available; and how deep a pond needs to be. Essential guidance is given on general safety.

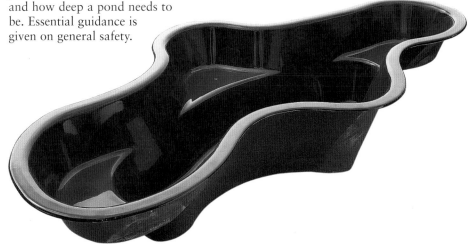

Building a pond

Work begins in Chapter 2 as the building of a pond gets under way. But even this has been made a whole lot easier with the introduction of rigid preformed shells and flexible liners. The hardest part is digging the hole! Together with the tools and materials needed, simple step-by-step instructions will enable you to construct a pond in a weekend. The whole thing can be stocked and up and running in just a few more days.

The five main groups of aquatic plants are looked at in detail, together with advice on their planting, feeding, and general care. No feature in a garden can be so relied upon to induce a feeling of relaxation as a pond reflecting sunlight, while the sound of water splashing over a cascade or from a fountain instantly cools a hot summer's day. Lighting can effect a magical transformation as dusk falls. To further enhance the enjoyment of your water feature, why not add a fountain or some lights? Pond hardware – from pumps and filters to fountains, waterfalls, and lights – are reviewed along with some suggestions for ornaments and statues.

Small water features

You don't even need a garden to have a pond. Chapter 3 looks at different ways of creating a simple mini-pond in a half-barrel and old sink. Tips and advice are also given on the plants to choose for your miniature water feature, including a selection of dwarf waterlilies. Other ideas include birdbaths, wall-mounted and free-standing fountains, a pebble pool, and a millstone bubble feature. Simple instructions are given showing how to install a pebble pool and how to create a miniature pumped feature from a simple kit.

LIFE IN THE POND

There is a simple but enormously satisfying pleasure in keeping fish. And there's an even greater thrill when a frog or toad takes up residence, or you spot your first dragonfly. Chapter 4 takes a look at how to provide the perfect habitat for both fish and other wildlife.

Keeping ornamental fish is a simple matter, provided a few basic rules are obeyed, which are given here, along with a selection of fish suitable for a garden pond and tips on how to recognize problems. If you are interested in wildlife, details are given on features to include in a wildlife pond. Information is given on what creatures you can expect to take up residence in your pond, and how to create the right habitat to attract and keep them. There is also advice on humane ways of deterring unwelcome visitors such as herons and cats.

POND CARE AND MAINTENANCE

Having built your pond or water feature and got it up and running, planted, and stocked with fish, you'll need to take care of it. Chapter 5 deals with the general care and maintenance of a garden pond, starting with the tools and equipment you will need and moving on to some of the more fundamental tasks that you will have to undertake when necessary, such as draining and cleaning the pond.

Throughout the year, season by season, there are routine jobs you can do to maintain a balance in the pond, such as removing blanketweed in spring and summer and skimming off debris in the fall. Depending on the severity of the winter in the area in which you live, there are also a number of tasks you will need to undertake to prepare the pond for the cold weather – these may range from completely closing down and destocking the pond to preventing the pond from icing over.

The troubleshooter's guide to what can go wrong with plants, fish, and water may look a little daunting at first, but few troubles ail a garden pond, so treat this guide as simply a reference to what may go wrong, not what will go wrong.

PLANT DIRECTORY

No one can fail to be impressed by the serenity and beauty of a waterlily and its dazzling waxy flowers in summer, while stately irises with their dramatic foliage rise majestically above the surface from submerged roots. Plants in and around a pond will add a new dimension to your garden, as they will grow there and nowhere else. Chapter 6 provides a directory of suitable plants for a garden pond.

Many plants perform a vital role, such as the fully submerged oxygenators that help keep a pond clean and healthy, or floating aquatics that shade the surface of the water. Marginals, on the other hand, are purely for our pleasure, whether it is their flowers, foliage, or both that are their main attraction. These should be planted in groups of the same variety, rather than singly, for maximum impact.

One square yard (square meter) of space is ample for a few oxygenators, a marginal plant or two, a waterlily or other floater, and a couple of medium-sized fish. The greater the surface area the more plants you can have – but don't be tempted to overplant, you still want to see some water and its inhabitants. And don't forget the area around the pond can be turned into a bog garden – there is a list of suggestions for plant varieties that are happy in the permanently moist conditions that are found there.

1
CREATING A
WATER GARDEN

The sight and sound of moving water and the living beauty of plants and fish will add a new dimension to your garden, and to your overall enjoyment of it.

A garden pond, whether formal, informal, or completely natural, and whatever its size, will also encourage wildlife, and so in a small way you will be providing a little sanctuary for nature in your own garden.

This chapter of the book looks at the basics of creating a pond: where it should go, how big you should make it, and the choices to be made between a formal or informal design, and whether it should be sunken or raised. Then there is a decision to be made about materials for its construction. Finally, there's the all-important question of creating, and maintaining, a healthy balance in the pond.

INTRODUCING WATER

No garden, whatever its size or style, can ever be complete without some kind of water feature to add life and movement. Even if you do not have enough space for a pond, many garden centers stock a wide range of simple, easy-to-construct water features to suit even the smallest garden. Alternatively, a pond will breathe new life into a neglected corner of a larger, more established garden.

CONSIDER THE OPTIONS

Before deciding on a water feature for your garden, first take a trip to your local water garden center or browse through a mail-order catalog – you'll find plenty of choices when it comes to flexible liners and ready-made ponds in all shapes and sizes. You'll also find the materials to construct waterfalls and cascades, as well as self-contained water features, and an impressive selection of pumps, fountains, and lights.

The wide range of materials and equipment available is designed to bring pond-making within the scope of any handy gardener. Before you part with any money, however, make sure you have the answers to the few questions in the box below.

And don't forget those optional extras – fountains, waterfalls, and lights. Provision will need to be made for electricity to be run to these features if they are to be installed.

A SOLUTION FOR LIMITED SPACE

POINTS TO CONSIDER

- How much space is available?

- Where is the best place for a pond or water feature in your garden?

- What type of pond do you want?

- Plants and fish – do you want both?

- Is wildlife important to you?

PONDS WITH A PURPOSE

■ **Patio focus** A sunken or partially raised pond on a patio forms a focal point, attracting people to linger, their senses soothed by the limpid water, and the seemingly effortless movement of fish.

■ **Lawn feature** A formal pond with waterlilies and a fountain makes an eye-catching feature set within a landscaped lawn.

■ **Wildlife haven** A natural pond, rich in native plants provides a home for frogs, toads, and newts, as well as attracting dragonflies and other insects, which in turn attract birds.

LIMITED SPACE?

If space is really tight, a mini-pond can be created in a half-barrel, deep sink, or small rigid liner, and this will provide a home for a range of aquatic plants (see Chapter 3). In cool climates, where winter temperatures drop below freezing, small features may freeze solid and will need to be dismantled seasonally at the onset of cold weather.

Self-contained water features such as pebble ponds take up little space and recycle the water – a bonus in arid areas and times of drought.

GRAND DESIGNS
A formal pond combined with modern architectural structures adds depth and reflection to a traditional garden setting.

CAREFUL PLANNING

A carefully planned garden pond that is well built, stocked, and cared for provides a constant source of enjoyment. Take care at the planning stage to address the following points, all of which are covered in detail within the pages of this book:

■ **Position** Make sure you choose the right location for the pond.

■ **Size** Take care that you build the pond to the optimum size and proportions.

■ **Planting** Choosing the right type of plants is vital to the well-being of the pond and its contents – not all will necessarily be decorative.

POSITION AND SIZE

More important than the style of a pond, whether it be formal or informal, sunken or raised, are its position in the garden and its size in relation to the range of fish and water plants you may want to introduce. Unlike most other features in a garden, once a pond has been installed, it will be very difficult to move!

CLOSE TO THE HOUSE

For maximum enjoyment, unless you have a very large garden, the best position for a pond, or water feature, is as near to the house as possible, so that it can be seen from the windows. Also, from a practical point of view, if you plan to have a fountain, waterfall, or lights, it will be easy to run electricity to the pond.

The pond should also be near a path. Not only will this make the construction of it easier, but a path leading from the house to the water feature will encourage you to visit it more often. Once planted up and stocked with fish, you will want to have easy access to it, so position your pond where it can be viewed at all times of the day...and year!

MOVABLE STONE
TROUGH FOUNTAIN

Decorative cobbles
conceal pump
equipment

THE RIGHT SPOT FOR A POND

- Visible from windows in the house.

- Easily accessible via a path leading from the house.

- In the sun for part of the day.

- Away from overhanging trees, particularly those that lose their leaves, blossoms, or fruit.

- Out of the shade of nearby buildings and walls.

- Sheltered from prevailing winds.

- As near as practical to a source of electricity for operating a fountain, waterfall, or lights.

AN OPEN SITUATION

An open situation is essential for pond life, as neither aquatic plants nor fish will thrive in deep shade, while the scourge of all pond keepers, green algae, will flourish, making the water uninhabitable.

Fish cannot tolerate the pollution caused by leaves and other vegetation that fall into the water, so keep the pond away from deciduous trees or those that shed berries or blossoms.

IDEAL SETTING
A summerhouse looks down over an informal pond. The trees are set back and the lush planting tiered to allow light to reach the water's surface.

SHELTERED FROM WIND

Make sure the spot you choose provides some shelter from prevailing winds – in spring, to prevent young foliage being scorched, and later in the season to guard against taller marginals being blown over. Waterlilies in particular are affected by wind ruffling the water's surface.

One way to provide shelter is to build up a rock garden beside the pond, using soil from the excavated hole, or plant a hedge of conifers, which do not shed their leaves.

If the pond is to be sunk into the ground, the site needs to be level. However, if the only suitable site is sloping, it would be better to build a raised pond. Avoid siting your pond in an area that is badly drained and prone to waterlogging. Although moisture-loving plants will thrive, a pond liable to flooding will be difficult to manage and maintain.

LET THE SUN SHINE IN

It is important to site the pond where the sun will shine on it for at least part of the day. Apart from the pleasure sitting in the sun gives us, there are practical advantages. Waterlilies, for instance, need sun: they appreciate at least 10–12 hours a day in the height of summer. Fish, too, will benefit from the warmth, although they are sensitive to rapid changes in temperature. This is why they need some shade, such as that provided beneath waterlily leaves and other floating aquatics. These plants will flourish in such a sunny spot and, in turn, will provide plenty of surface shade for the fish.

OUT IN THE OPEN
An informal pond in an open position supports a wide range of aquatic and marginal plants and fish and provides an attractive feature in an area of lawn.

MOVING WATER
The refreshing sound of a gently splashing
fountain brings life and movement to an
otherwise static formal feature.

STAYING CLEAR OF TREES

Few things are more lethal to the
inhabitants of a garden pond than
decaying leaves. As they slowly
decompose, they give off gases that
can be harmful to fish and are of
no benefit to plants. The pond can
deal with its own decaying matter,
but a sudden influx of any "foreign"
leaves will upset the natural balance,
leading to an excess of methane gas –
the main reason for an increase
in fatalities among fish during the
winter months.

THE SOURCE OF POWER

The proximity to an electrical
connection is important. If you plan
to have a fountain or waterfall, you
will need a pump and electricity to
operate them. Likewise, if you want
to illuminate your pond or water
feature after dark, there needs to
be a power source close by.

If possible, the power outlet should
be installed inside the house or in
a conservatory to avoid having to go
out at night or in inclement weather
should the need arise. If not, it
should be in a garage or nearby shed.

Although pond pumps, fountains,
and lights are usually low voltage,
wherever electricity is being used in
the garden, always use a residual
current circuit breaker (RCCB), or
power-breaker unit, which will trip
and cut off the current immediately
if anything goes wrong (see p. 109).

> ### Warning
>
> • Avoid planting laburnum and laurel
> close to the pond as both have toxic
> seeds as well as leaves.
>
> • Keep cherry and plum trees away
> from the water as they are host to
> the waterlily aphid (see p. 180).
>
> • While it might be tempting to have
> a weeping tree by the side of your
> pond, think again! Tree roots, such as
> those of the willow, may undermine
> and damage the fabric of the pond.

WHY SIZE MATTERS

The success of a pond relies on
a balance of fish, insect, and plant
life so, within reason, always aim to
make your pond as large – in terms
of water surface area – as you can. If
space permits, the minimum size
recommended to gain the right
conditions for clear water and the
necessary balance is a surface area of
40 sq ft (3.7 sq m), equal to a pond
measuring 8 ft x 5 ft (2.4 m x 1.5 m).
A large pond is easier to manage
than a small one, just make sure that
it blends with the rest of the garden.

RIGHT DEPTH FOR PLANTS

A garden pond need not be very
deep: many aquatic plants will be
happy in no more than 18 in (45 cm)
of water. Marginal plants, which have
their roots in the water but their
leaves and flowers out in the open
air, will need a shelf on which to
stand their pots. This shelf must be
about 9 in (22 cm) below the surface
of the water and 9–12 in (22–30 cm)
wide, and can run all, or just part of
the way around the pond. This will
accommodate a 6-in (15-cm)-deep
plant container, leaving 3 in (7.5 cm)
of water over the top of it. Most
marginals are grown at this depth.
Where plants require shallower
water, their pot or container can be
raised to the desired level by standing
it on paving stones or bricks.

RIGHT DEPTH FOR FISH

If you plan to keep fish, goldfish
will survive quite happily in a depth
of 18–24 in (45–60 cm). Koi, on the
other hand, need the water to be at
least 3 ft (1 m) deep, as they can
grow several feet long.

The deeper the pond, the safer the
fish will be during a cold winter as
the water should not freeze all the
way to the bottom. Neither fish nor
plants like sudden and frequent
changes in temperature, which are
common occurences in small ponds
both in winter and in summer.
The greater the volume of water the
more constant the temperature will
be within it. Whatever the size of
pond you choose for your garden,
the overriding factor to keep in mind
is proportion.

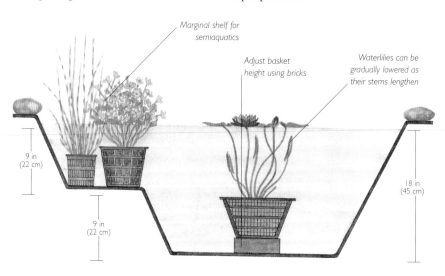

*Marginal shelf for
semiaquatics*

*Adjust basket
height using bricks*

*Waterlilies can be
gradually lowered as
their stems lengthen*

9 in
(22 cm)

9 in
(22 cm)

18 in
(45 cm)

SAFETY FIRST

When planning a water feature, always consider safety, particularly if the garden is used by young children, older people, or domestic pets. You will also need to pay careful attention to electrical installations – water and electricity can be a fatal combination.

SAFETY FOR CHILDREN

Water, even just a couple of inches, can be lethal to small children, yet it is like a magnet to them, particularly crawling babies and toddlers.

■ **Mini-features** In preference to a pond, consider a small water feature, such as a mini-pool or bubble fountain (see Chapter 3) that has no open surface of water.

■ **Out of bounds** If you want to include a pond in your garden make sure it is inaccessible to children who play there, unless there is an adult around to supervise at all times.

■ **Pond alternatives** While children are young, a raised pond can be converted into a raised bed for flowers and shrubs until they grow older. Similarly, a sunken pond can be filled in with sand to make an ideal sandbox.

ELECTRICAL SAFETY TIPS

• Check that all electrical equipment is safety approved for outdoor use.

• Switch off and disconnect electrical equipment before handling.

• Make sure that all cabling and connectors are waterproof.

• Always use a power-breaker/RCCB when using electricity outdoors.

Warning

If you sink a pond into a patio take measures to ensure that there is no possibility of anyone, young or old, tripping and falling in.

ELECTRICAL SAFETY

Electricity in the garden is a potential hazard. Low-voltage lighting and pumps for small water features are available in simple kit form and can be installed by an amateur. These work in conjunction with a transformer that reduces the voltage from the house making it safe. Place the transformer indoors as close to the wall socket as possible.

■ Make sure you always follow the manufacturer's instructions and, if in doubt, hire a qualified electrician to double-check your wiring – or even to do it for you.

■ Ask a qualified electrician to connect you to the electrical supply.

■ Once installed, all equipment must be properly maintained and serviced.

■ To prevent accidents, all cabling must be buried and protected by an armored steel casing.

■ Larger fountains and waterfalls require high-voltage electricity and should be installed by a professional.

DESIGN IDEAS

A pond or water feature will create an area of cool reflection in most gardens, whatever the size or style. Although very much a matter of personal preference, when it comes to deciding the style and shape of your pond, consider the position in which you intend to locate it. The two basic styles of a pond are formal and informal.

THE FORMAL APPROACH

Close to a building or within an area of paving, it is advisable to opt for a more formal style of a pond. A strict geometric shape – square, rectangular, oval, or circular – will link the pond with the lines of any hard landscaping close by.

In an ultramodern garden, you could consider more complex but still regular shapes, such as a triangular pond. Although formal ponds tend to be built at ground level, there is no reason why they should not be raised.

FORMAL FOCUS
A small, circular, mosaic-lined pond and stream become a focal point in this Mediterranean-style garden, helping to break up the monotony of a large paved area.

FORMAL TIPS

• Site a formal pond where it will reflect nearby objects, such as trees, a statue, or just open sky.

• Consider introducing a small fountain and underwater lighting to give added effect, especially on summer evenings.

• Avoid marginals, which may obscure the clearly defined outline of the pond. If needed, a carefully positioned container may add a degree of softness.

• An edging of paving stones or bricks makes a formal pond perfect for a patio.

A MORE INFORMAL STYLE

Away from the strictures of hard landscaping, you can adopt a more informal style, perhaps mirroring the natural curves of a lawn or border. As the outline of an informal pond is irregular and not so clearly defined, it will look more like a natural water feature, making it ideal if you want to encourage wildlife into your pond and garden.

When deciding on an informal style, bear in mind that its construction and maintenance will take slightly more effort than a formal pond. Acquiring a more "natural" look takes time and patience.

INFORMAL CASCADE
Gently trickling cascades and a decorative fountain combine with lush exotic foliage to add height and atmosphere to a partly shaded corner of a tropical-style garden.

INFORMAL TIPS

• A molded liner will give your pond a predetermined shape. A flexible liner offers more creative scope, but keep your design simple – this will make it easier to construct and the final effect will look more natural.

• Soften the outline of the pond with a selection of marginal plants or a bog garden. Marginal plantings look most effective if they appear to flow down into the water.

• Do not allow grass to grow right up to the pond's edges otherwise mowing will be awkward to carry out and clippings will have to be removed from the surface of the water before they sink and rot.

PLANNING YOUR POND

O nce you have decided on either a formal or informal pond, you need to choose whether it should be raised or sunken. Both kinds have their advantages depending on position, climate, and your own particular circumstances, but in the end it comes down to personal choice. Whatever style and shape of pond you settle on, however, before you start digging any holes, write your ideas down on paper.

RAISED OR SUNKEN?

Although there are exceptions, as a general rule a raised pond lends itself to a more formal style, while a sunken pond is more suited to an informal or wildlife setting. The list below highlights some advantages and disadvantages of each.

Most well-equipped pond and garden centers stock a wide range of pond liners (see pp. 114–15), which can be used for both types of pond.

RAISED TIMBER POND

RAISED VERSUS SUNKEN – THE PROS AND CONS

RAISED OR PARTIALLY RAISED

• Makes an excellent focal point in a formal garden or on a paved area.

• Low surrounding walls can be used as casual seating to observe pond life.

• Best suited to climates where winter temperatures remain above freezing.

• Walls can be built to varying heights, offering a solution for sloping sites.

• Needs less excavation.

• Maintenance is easier, particularly for the elderly or disabled who may find bending awkward.

• Takes longer to build than a sunken pond and tends to be more expensive.

• Surrounding wall prevents children from accidentally falling in the water.

SUNKEN

• Resemblance to a natural pond suits an informal or wildlife setting.

• Can be extended at margins to incorporate a bog garden.

• Successful even in cool climates as water below ground level is less likely to freeze solid.

• Provides a healthier environment for plants and fish, as the water temperature remains more constant.

• Less expensive to build because there is less hard landscaping to consider.

• More hazardous for young children and household pets.

• Needs excavating. The resultant spoil needs to be removed or reused elsewhere in the garden.

MAKING PLANS

■ **Sketch your ideas** On a piece of squared paper, sketch a rough plan of your garden, to scale, showing the house, boundaries, and any existing features, including trees and shrubs. This will give you an idea of just how much space you have for a pond.

■ **Make adjustments** Following your plan, mark out the outline of the pond on the ground using a length

of rope or garden hose. Leave it in place for a few days so you can view it from outdoors and indoors at different times of the day. Notice where shadows fall as the sun moves and if the pond is going to be too shady adjust the design as necessary.

■ **Think ahead** Allow space around the pond for paving or plants – perhaps even a bog garden. Don't forget to include a place to sit by the side of the pond so that once the building work is finished, you can sit and enjoy the wildlife, plants, and fish on a summer's evening.

EXAMPLE OF A GARDEN PLAN
Each square on the plan below represents 3 sq ft (1 sq m). The pond has been positioned close to the house in an open, sunny area.

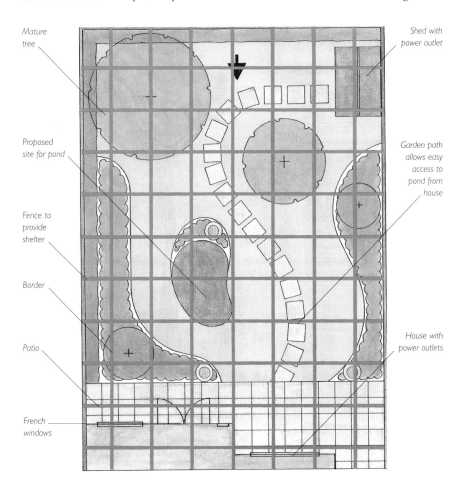

Mature tree

Shed with power outlet

Proposed site for pond

Garden path allows easy access to pond from house

Fence to provide shelter

Border

House with power outlets

Patio

French windows

MATERIALS

When it comes to building a pond, there is a wide choice of materials available, the most common being flexible sheet liners, rigid preformed liners, and concrete. The welcomed arrival of flexible liners and molded ponds has revolutionized pond construction. Easy to install, a garden pond designed to meet individual needs can be built in a weekend.

FLEXIBLE SHEET LINERS

Versatile and relatively inexpensive, flexible sheet liners can be used to line almost any size and shape of a water feature, with the exception of square and rectangular ponds. Price-wise they are relatively inexpensive and have the added advantage of being easy to take home from the garden center in the car.

Most liners can be bought either "off the roll," which will work out cheaper particularly if you are planning a big project, or in precut packs, which are ideal for a smaller pond.

There are four main types of material used for pond liners, most of which come in different weights and thicknesses. The thicker the material, the more durable it will be, but it will also be more expensive. Whatever the material, however, check that it is "fish-grade," which means it will not give off any harmful chemicals, and that it is UV-stabilized to resist ultraviolet sun damage. It should also carry a 10–20-year guarantee.

BUTYL LINER

■ **Butyl liners** Although more costly, butyl liners are virtually indestructible. Made from a kind of synthetic rubber, they are unaffected by sunlight or frost, and despite being fairly thick, are flexible even in cold weather. Their elasticity makes it possible to lay them with fewer creases and folds than PVC and polyethylene.

■ **EPDM liners** Also made from a durable synthetic rubber, EPDM liners share many of the qualities of butyl.

PVC LINER

■ **PVC** Popular, flexible, and cheaper than butyl and EPDM, PVC liners come in different thicknesses, which is reflected in their prices.

■ **Polyethylene** Although relatively inexpensive, low-density polyethylene, or LDPE, liners will not last as long as other materials. LDPE is stronger and more flexible.

COLOR CODE

Lighter colors reflect too much light, so if the liner you buy has a lighter side, put this face down in the hole. Flexible liners are usually available in a choice of black or green.

■ **Black** A black liner absorbs light and heat and creates an illusion of depth. Fish also show up better.

■ **Green** A green liner absorbs less light than black, so a green liner should help keep algae levels lower.

FLEXIBLE LINERS

ADVANTAGES

• Versatile for use in creative water garden designs as their use is not restricted to a particular size, shape, or depth. Ideal for features such as cascades and streams.

• Ideal for an informal or a natural wildlife pond and bog garden.

• Easy to transport home.

• Can be used to instantly "repair" a leaking concrete or rigid pond.

DISADVANTAGES

• Can be damaged by sharp stones or tree roots if not adequately bedded.

• Marginal shelves have to be built when using a flexible liner.

• Not suited to the angles necessary for a square or rectangular pond.

REPAIRING LEAKS

Basic repair kits can be used to patch all types of liner. Polyethylene liners are not worth repairing.

• Empty the pond and identify the damaged area.

• Thoroughly clean the surrounding area with a scrub brush and water.

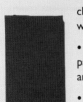

• Allow to dry then clean with a cloth wetted with alcohol.

• Place the repair patch over the leak and press firmly.

• Wait at least 12 hours before refilling the pond.

REPAIR PATCH

BEDDING DOWN

A flexible liner is usually bedded on a 1–2-in (2.5–5-cm) layer of damp sand (see Chapter 2 for construction methods). However, as a precaution against punctures, particularly if your soil is stony, it is well worth investing in a polyester matting underlay, which usually comes in rolls.

UNDERLAY

RIGID PREFORMED LINERS

Preformed, molded pond shells are available in a wide range of shapes and sizes, so it is worth shopping around until you find one that matches your requirements. For a formal raised pond on a patio, choose simple, regular shapes, such as circles and rectangles. Irregular outlines are more popular for sunken ponds, and some of these would be almost impossible to create using a flexible liner. Bear in mind that simple shapes are the easiest to excavate and backfill.

Various materials are used in the manufacture of molded liners, including fiberglass and different grades of plastic. A good-quality fiberglass liner should last a lifetime.

■ Check that planting shelves are at least 9 in (22 cm) wide – to take a decent-sized container. If the shelf is too narrow, plants will topple over in the wind or fish will knock them off.

■ Choose a dark color and before you buy, check that the minimum depth is at least 18 in (45 cm), and that it carries a 10-year guarantee.

■ If intending to stock with fish, check that the unit is big and deep enough (see p. 108).

PREFORMED LINERS

ADVANTAGES

• Ideally suited for a formal pond, either sunken or raised, especially within a paved area.

• Easy to install and maintain.

• Marginal shelves are ready formed.

DISADVANTAGES

• Too big to transport home by car.

• Tend to look bigger in a garden center than in your garden.

RESIN-FIBERGLASS

Virtually indestructible, resistant to water, frost, and ultraviolet light, fiberglass liners come preformed in a variety of shapes and can be simply bedded on sand in an excavated hole. They can be expensive, but don't compromise when it comes to size: go for the biggest you can afford and accommodate. A fiberglass pond should come with a 20-year guarantee.

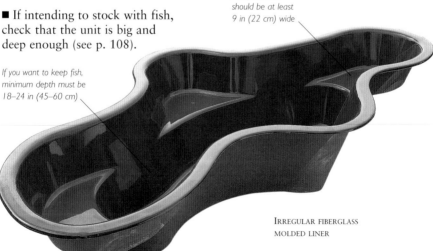

Marginal shelf should be at least 9 in (22 cm) wide

If you want to keep fish, minimum depth must be 18–24 in (45–60 cm)

IRREGULAR FIBERGLASS MOLDED LINER

NATURAL STONE-
EFFECT ROCK POOL

Fiber-glass is also used for small water features with a naturalistic rock or stone finish that encourages the growth of lichens and algae.

REINFORCED PLASTIC

Molded plastic liners look much the same as fiberglass but are thinner and more brittle. Although cheaper, they have a shorter life expectancy. Choose one with a long guarantee – usually between 10–20 years. Length of guarantee is a good indicator of durability and resistance to light degradation. Sunlight will weaken ordinary plastic liners and the corners will crack with age, so it's important when installing it in your garden to ensure that all of the liner is covered and none is left exposed.

CONCRETE PONDS

Until the appearance of flexible and molded liners, all garden ponds were built using concrete. Concrete ponds do, however, require a certain amount of expertise and their construction is probably best left to a professional.

ADVANTAGES

• Used correctly, concrete makes the strongest and most permanent pond.

• A concrete pond can be any shape or size you wish.

DISADVANTAGES

• Building a concrete pond is difficult and time-consuming, which can make it an expensive project. It is probably best left to professionals.

• Ground movement and freezing temperatures can cause cracks and therefore leaks.

• Raw concrete is harmful to fish. All inside surfaces need to be painted with a sealant before filling with water.

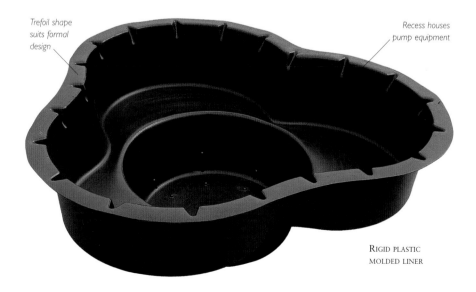

Trefoil shape
suits formal
design

Recess houses
pump equipment

RIGID PLASTIC
MOLDED LINER

KEEPING A BALANCE

A successful pond is one in which each of the components – water, plant life, fish, soil, and organic matter – interact as part of a mini-ecosystem. To prevent overcrowding and the water turning green and murky, it is essential to maintain this delicate balance.

GOOD PONDKEEPING

Here's how to create conditions that are suitable for plants and fish but which will keep algae at bay:

■ **Debris** Remove fallen leaves and other debris immediately – if allowed to decay it will pollute the water.

■ **Soil mix** Do not use peat, garden compost, or manure when planting.

■ **Plant oxygenators** Oxygenating plants (see p. 132) keep the water clean by inhibiting algae growth. They also provide oxygen for fish.

■ **Feeding** Do not give fish any more food than they can consume in five minutes. Skim off uneaten food.

■ **Size** If your pond has a surface area of less than 40 sq ft (3.7 sq m) and a depth of less than 18 in (45 cm), you may need to use a filter (see p. 141) or an algicide in the water to stop green algae and protect fish.

SURFACE COVER
The floating leaves of waterlilies and other deep-water aquatics should cover about half the surface to provide some shade for pond life.

2
BUILDING
A POND

All you really need to build your own pond are a little advanced planning, a flick through a mail-order catalog, and a visit to a water garden specialist combined with a few basic tools and materials plus some hard labor.

This chapter takes you through the various methods for constructing your own pond, using either a flexible or rigid liner. Useful tips are given for both sunken and raised ponds. There are ideas for edgings and general information on the range of water plants available and how to plant them. The chapter ends with some creative ideas for bringing movement, light, and ornamentation to your water feature.

TOOLS AND MATERIALS

A simple pond, no more than a couple of feet deep (up to 60 cm), sunk into the ground, is as easy to build as planting a tree – the hardest part is digging the hole! Whether you use a rigid or a flexible liner, this is a project that could easily be tackled over a weekend. A raised pond will need a little more time and effort spent on it.

BASIC TOOLS

Any task will be made much easier if you have the right tools for it – and in certain situations it is crucial to use the correct equipment. Consider borrowing or renting tools that you might never or rarely need again. If buying, it is well worth investing in good-quality tools if you can. They are usually longer-lasting and more comfortable to use.

■ **Leveling** Mark out the dimensions with a flexible tape measure and use a carpenter's level to ensure the pond is straight. A straightedge, such as a plank, is a useful guide for digging.

■ **Digging the hole** Use a fork and a sharp-edged spade for breaking the soil and a broad shovel for scooping out loose earth. A pickaxe is handy if there are large stones or tree roots to deal with. Remove the excavated soil from the site in a wheelbarrow.

■ **Brick and paving edging** Use a bricklayer's trowel for handling wet building mixes around the edge.

GARDEN SPADE
AND FORK

MATERIALS

The basic materials for making a pond, such as sand, mortar, and cement, should all be available from a good builders' supply store. Water garden specialists will stock a wide range of liners and underlay (see pp. 114–17).

If you are constructing a raised pool with a brick wall surround and decorative stone edging, make a trip to a local builders' supply store. Go armed with the length, height, and width of the walls for your pond, and ask them to help you work out what you'll need in terms of bricks and mortar. If the pond is going on an existing patio, try to choose materials in the same range. It is a good idea to take along a sample of the patio paving with you to be sure of a good match. If you don't have this, a photograph is the next best thing.

Don't forget coping stones for capping the walls. These will keep out damp, dirt, and debris and hide away any electrical cables for lights and fountains. Many well-stocked landscape gardening centers offer a good range of suitable stones. If you are planning to use the pond edge as a comfortable place to sit, make sure you select stones that are wide and flat enough.

WATER VOLUME

Use the following simple formulas to calculate the volume of water you will require to fill your pond. The measurements are given in imperial with metric in parentheses.

RECTANGULAR PONDS
Volume in gallons (liters) = average length in ft (m) x average width in ft (m) x average depth in ft (m) x 6.2 (1,000).

CIRCULAR PONDS
Volume in gallons (liters) = 3.14 x ½ diameter in ft (m) x ½ diameter in ft (m) x depth in ft (m) x 6.2 (1,000).

WHY YOU NEED A PUMP...

An electric pump (see p. 140) is essential for moving water in features such as fountains and cascades. The movement it creates also helps maintain oxygen levels, which is particularly important in hot, sultry weather. Pumps are also used for circulating water through filtration systems. All pumps require electricity to be brought to the pond.

AND MAYBE A FILTER

A pond filter (see p. 141) helps keep the pond water clean and healthy. Mechanical filters strain out solid particles, while biological filters use materials with large, complex surface areas on which bacteria collect and flourish to break down and purify waste products in the water. An ultraviolet purifier is an effective means of keeping algae at bay.

OTHER ACCESSORIES

When it comes to stocking your finished pond with plants, you will eventually also need a range of suitable planting baskets and containers (see pp. 134–35) as well as the plants themselves.

If you want to shed a little light on your water feature, most water garden specialists stock a good range to choose from, including lights that can be submerged in the water (see pp. 142–43).

Finally, complete the effect with a pondside ornament (see p. 144).

LINER QUANTITY

The following simple calculations will enable you to work out the approximate size of flexible liner you will require for a sunken pond, regardless of the shape of the pond and size of the marginal shelves.

Length of liner = the overall length of pond + twice the maximum depth.

Width of liner = the overall width of pond + twice the maximum depth.

USING A FLEXIBLE LINER

Flexible sheet liner is the most versatile material available to water gardeners as it offers none of the restrictions of size and shape that accompany rigid preformed liners. Use it to line containers of almost any size and shape to create your own innovative and original water features, or to renew the life of an old leaking pond by simply adding a new lining on top of the old. It really comes into its own for constructing informal sunken ponds – and as you become more adventurous, try experimenting with free-form streams and cascades.

SOLID GROUND

Flexible liner can be used to line almost any water feature, however complex. Its flexibility means it can even be laid over hard ground, as long as the site is properly prepared beforehand. Most important, always remove any sharp stones and roots and lay the liner on a 1-in (2.5-cm) layer of damp sand covered with synthetic underlay.

AVOIDING WASTAGE

To avoid wastage, it is advisable to excavate more complex water features and make any necessary amendments to the design before buying the liner. In this way, if you decide to make a part of the design bigger, you will not be stuck with the quantity and dimensions of liner you bought to construct your feature to the original plan.

FLEXIBLE-LINED
WATERCOURSE

EXTENDING PLANTING AROUND THE POND

Although many rigid preformed liners now incorporate varying depths of water to suit different plants, they cannot compete with the versatility of a flexible liner. When constructing your pond, try varying the depth around the edges to create pockets of moisture.

By extending the area of liner around the edges of the pond at the construction stage, rather than trimming it back, you can use your imagination to create bog gardens, stony beaches, and islands. Once they have been planted up, not only will these features disguise the edges of your pond, making it almost indistinguishable from a natural pond, they will also give access to a variety of wildlife.

If the flexible liner is buried beneath the soil at the water's edge, even if it is above the water level, plants in the surrounding soil will draw moisture from the pond. In small areas, this is acceptable; however, unless a large bog garden is made independent of the pond, the plants will quickly deplete the level of water in the pond. To prevent water from seeping out of the pond, allow the liner to come up out of the ground and mortar rocks or pavers on top of it.

PRACTICAL TIPS FOR USING A FLEXIBLE LINER

• The sides of a sunken pond need to slope at about 20° to prevent soil collapse during digging and to allow the liner to stretch without too many creases. It will also allow a sheet of ice to float upward without damaging the liner. You can judge the angle of slope by measuring 3 in (7.5 cm) inward for every 9 in (22 cm) of depth. If the soil is very sandy, increase the angle of slope for extra stability.

• Be careful to remove any sharp stones and tree roots from the area where you are planning to use your flexible liner, or these will cause a puncture. Repair kits (see p. 115) are available if the liner is damaged, but patching will weaken the liner. Prolong the lifespan of flexible liner by using a special underliner to cushion and protect it.

• If soil is very stony, cover it with a layer of damp, fine sand to a depth of 1–2 in (2.5–5 cm). Gently tread the base down, then rake it.

• Plan projects using flexible liner for a warm, sunny day. If you leave the liner in position in the sun for a couple of hours it will become more pliable and enable you to avoid excessive creasing.

• Do not attempt to trim the edges of the liner until you have filled your pond with water.

• Allow a generous margin of liner around the edges of a pond or water feature so you can cover it up with soil or decorative edging.

• Weight down the edges of the liner with bricks or edging stones to hold it in position while you fill the pond with water and smooth out creases.

BLUE SLATE
EDGING STONES

MAKING A SUNKEN POND

You can use a flexible liner to create a natural-looking pond in next to no time. Before you begin, calculate how much liner you will need to line the pond (see p. 121). Avoid having to join two pieces of liner to cover the area, as the water is bound to gradually seep out.

USING A FLEXIBLE LINER

1 Using your plan as a guide, mark out the shape of the pond on the ground, using a garden hose or rope. If necessary, use canes to hold the hose in position. Unfold the liner and lay it in the sun, as the heat increases its flexibility.

Mark out the shape of the pond with a length of hose or rope

Final depth should be at least 18 in (45 cm)

Angle sides to about 20°, to prevent them from caving in

2 Dig out the hole to a depth of 9 in (22 cm) and mark out marginal shelves to a minimum width of 9 in (22 cm). Excavate to the final depth. Use a carpenter's level to check that the top edge of the hole remains level. Remove any sharp stones or roots.

Allow plenty of overlap at edge

3 Line the hole with a 1–2 in (2.5–5 cm) layer of damp sand and use it to smooth any rough areas. Cover this with a layer of underlay (see p. 115). Loosely drape the liner across the hole. Make sure it is centered, with an even overlap all the way around. Let it sag gently into the hole, then weight the edges with stones.

Weight edges with edging stones

Underlay

4 Start filling the pond slowly from a hose. As the pond fills, remove some of the weights to allow the liner to settle snugly into the hole and smooth out any creases – but don't worry unduly about these, as they will not show once the pond is established. Turn off the hose when the water reaches to within 2 in (5 cm) of the rim. Trim any surplus liner using scissors, leaving about 6 in (15 cm) all the way around to allow for settle. Peg or weight this down temporarily.

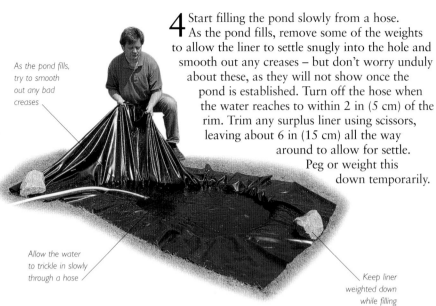

As the pond fills, try to smooth out any bad creases

Allow the water to trickle in slowly through a hose

Keep liner weighted down while filling with water

5 Conceal the plastic edge with pavers or stones set in mortar (three parts sand to one part cement), leaving a slight overhang of 1–2 in (2.5–5 cm). Make sure all the plastic is covered. Take great care not to let any mortar fall into the water. If this happens, the pond will have to be emptied and refilled. Wait a few days before adding plants to your new pond. Fish can be introduced after about six weeks.

Marginal plants can be added after a few days

In a lawn, to make mowing easier, set the edging ¾ in (2 cm) below the level of the turf

Overhanging edging casts a shadow over the water providing shelter for fish

Pond ornament

USING A RIGID LINER

Building a pond using a rigid preformed or molded liner is relatively hassle-free. Problems will only really occur if the liner is installed on the slant. Water full to the brim on one side of the pond, the liner well exposed on the other will be a permanent reminder if you don't get the levels correct right from the start. So make sure you are armed with a carpenter's level and a straight-edged board and check regularly across the width and length of the hole as you go along.

RAISED AND SEMIRAISED PONDS

Rigid, preformed pool units are generally designed to be sunk into the ground. Provided the sides are given strong support, however, they can also be used to construct attractive raised or semiraised pools.

One of the principal disadvantages of a pond installed at ground level is that it will freeze during the winter. This problem can, however, be reduced if the unit is partially buried so that its deep zones are insulated by the surrounding earth. The rigid mold can be concealed with an outer wall of bricks or log-roll edging topped with rocks or coping stones. Alternatively, for a more natural look, fill a gap of about 6 in (15 cm) between wall and liner with topsoil and stock with spreading plants.

SPECIAL FEATURES

Flexible sheet liners are not the only solution to constructing a trickling watercourse or cascade in your water garden. Most water garden specialists now stock a wide range of rigid preformed molds that are quick and easy to install. These include rock pools, tiered waterfalls, and streams. Individual pieces can be overlapped to create cascades of any length to link pools of different levels.

■ **Natural look** Unlike pond liners, which are designed to be submerged, many of the molded watercourses and cascades are produced in natural-looking finishes of rock or stone, which have been specially designed to encourage the growth of algae and lichens. Creatively displayed in a natural setting of rocks and boulders these soon blend in with the rest of the feature.

MOLDED
WATERFALL
DISPLAY

Molded stone pieces form watercourse

Flexible liner serves as foundation skin

If using a rigid pond liner for a raised pond, make sure it is adequately supported from below

RAISED POND
A rigid liner can be used to make an attractive raised pond for a patio. Place containers of plants on the edge to conceal any bare areas of liner.

Supporting wall of woven brick

USING A RIGID LINER TO MAKE A SUNKEN POND

• Prop up the liner in position and mark out its shape on the ground using garden hose or rope. Allow an extra 12 in (30 cm) all the way around.

• On a long stick, mark the depth of the pond plus an extra 2 in (5 cm) to allow for bedding sand; also mark the height of any marginal shelves. Use the stick as a guide when digging.

• At every stage of construction, make sure that the liner is level by using a carpenter's level and plank to check along the width and length.

• Cover base with 2 in (2.5 cm) sand.

• Prior to backfilling, ensure that the rim is about 1 in (2.5 cm) below the surrounding ground.

• Once liner is level, wedge it firmly in place with battens.

• Using a hose, start to fill the pond with water. When the level reaches 4–6 in (10–15 cm), remove the battens and start backfilling with sieved soil. Pack spaces beneath shelves. Continue backfilling as the pond level rises until liner and hole are full.

• Run any wiring to the pond before laying the edging so it will be hidden.

RAISED PONDS

An elevated pond will have a greater impact in a smaller garden or patio, where it will provide a strong focal point, particularly if combined with a small fountain. Bear in mind, however, that in areas with cold winters a fully raised pond will freeze solid. This problem can be overcome by sinking part of the pond below ground level. Raised ponds can be constructed using either a flexible sheet liner or a rigid preformed mold.

HOW HIGH?

The walls of a raised pond should ideally be the equivalent of about seven courses of brick or stonework high – about 24–28 in (60–70 cm). If this is too tall for your garden design, you can get away with just three or four courses – 18 in (45 cm). This would be a minimum if you want to keep fish, although one obvious solution is to dig out more depth below ground level.

■ **Patio suggestion** On a patio, you could dig down 6–12 in (15–30 cm) and then build the walls 18 in (45 cm) high and top them with wide coping stones. This will give enough depth for fish and waterlilies and a comfortable height for sitting on the wall to feed the fish, take care of the plants, or just to admire the view.

BUILDING THE WALL

Whatever materials you choose for the walls of your pond, they need to be strong enough to hold the weight of the water and to insulate it from summer heat and winter cold.

■ **Construction** A single wall of stone or brick (or wood) will be sufficient to hold a liner, but for better insulation it's preferable to build a double "cavity wall." The inner wall can be made with cheaper concrete blocks or common bricks, reserving the more expensive blocks or bricks for the outer wall. The width of the coping will dictate how far the walls need to be spaced apart. Take into account that the coping should overhang the external wall by ½ in (13 mm) and by a good 1½ in (4 cm) over the water's edge.

MAKING CURVED EDGES

When paving around the top of a circular pond, to avoid the labor and expense of hand-cut "keyed" slabs, buy preformed pavers that are produced specially for this purpose. Most landscape garden centers will stock a good range. Some pavers, such as the ones shown here, can be used as insets in conjunction with normal pavers and will help you turn corners gradually.

CORNER INSET

■ **Foundation** The walls need a good foundation or they will be likely to become unstable. Bed the bottom course on 4–6 in (10–15 cm) of mortar.

WELL LINED

It is important to plan the shape of your raised pond to suit its position in your garden, the materials you intend to use in its construction, and to your competence as a builder. Remember that a circular raised pond is easier to construct than a rectangular one. A raised pond can be lined with a standard flexible sheet liner, or it can be designed around a rigid preformed liner.

SOMEWHERE TO SIT
A flagstone shelf around this regular-shaped pond provides an additional area for ornaments or container plants as well as garden seating.

■ **Preformed rigid liner** A wide range of preformed liners (see pp. 116–17) is available.

■ **Flexible sheet liner** Be warned! A flexible liner in a circular pond will crease horribly, while in a straight-edged construction it will need careful folding at the corners. Buy a good-quality butyl liner: not only will it have to support a lot of weight, a thin liner has few insulating properties. If the pond has a surface area over 40 sq ft (3.7 sq m), you may want to pack insulating material in the cavity between the walls.

■ **Cement** If the walls are made from bricks or blocks bedded on strong foundations on a concrete surround, you may consider rendering the inside with cement. This will then need at least two coats of proprietary pond sealant.

AROUND THE EDGE

The edging you choose for your pond is largely a matter of personal taste but it should be compatible with the overall style of your garden and must also hide the liner. Hard edgings often suit a more formal style pond and may include bricks, cobbles, pavers, or even timber. If using these around a sunken pond, in the interests of safety, choose a material that will not become slippery when wet. The natural effect of an informal sunken pond can be greatly increased by growing a range of plants to overhang the edge and provide shade for wildlife.

EDGING IDEAS

The appeal of a pond can be greatly enhanced by its surrounding features. Here are a few ideas.

■ **Lawn** If setting a pond into an area of lawn make sure the edging sits slightly lower than the grass to make mowing easier.

■ **Stepped edge** Try edging a sunken pond in a patio with paving slabs or flagstones to create a gently stepped edge. For maximum effect, choose edging that either matches or contrasts with the patio paving.

■ **Hedging** Disguise the rim of a raised pond with a closely clipped hedge, such as dwarf lavender.

■ **Steppingstones** These are a popular addition to informal ponds.

WOODEN BRIDGE

■ **Bridges** A bridge can be used to link one side of a pond with another. You may want to make your own from wooden planks, steel, or iron, or take a look at the range of ready-made bridges at a good aquatic center.

■ **Marginal plants** Tall marginal plants, like irises and rushes, will hide the raw edges of a flexible liner.

PREFORMED PAVER

TIMBER RING

PAVING SLAB

■ **Boggy extension** An alternative edging to an informal sunken pond is to create an adjoining bog garden. If possible, this should be built at the same time as the pond, using one large sheet of liner for both features, extended about 3 ft (1 m) out from the edge.

■ **Wildlife access** Allow one or two edging stones to dip into the water.

■ **Paving ideas** Leave gaps between paving around an informal pond, and fill these with cushion-forming plants, such as saxifrage and thyme, or create a surface with small pebbles or cobblestones bedded into cement.

NATURAL EFFECT
Rocks and gravel complement the rich greens of this display of moisture-loving plants to lend a truly natural feel to this pond.

AQUATIC PLANTS

Water plants not only look attractive, they are vital for the overall health of the pond. Without submerged weeds to help to oxygenate the water and floating plants to provide surface shelter from the sun, the water will quickly become foul. When deciding on which plants to choose for your area's climate, select from the range stocked by a local water garden specialist. The five groups of water plants are: waterlilies, oxygenators, deep-water aquatics, marginals, and floaters.

WATERLILIES

Although we are most attracted by the blooms of the waterlily, it is the leaves that provide vital shade for fish and prevent algal growth.

■ Place newly planted baskets on brick stacks at a depth of 3–6 in (7.5–15 cm). As the plant produces new leaves and roots, remove the bricks to lower the plant to its recommended depth, which will vary depending on variety and vigor.

■ Waterlilies thrive best in still water. If you run a fountain, make sure the spray falls well away from them.

■ **Planting ratio** One lily to every 25 sq ft (2.3 sq m) of water area. This varies according to size and vigor.

OXYGENATOR PLANT

OXYGENATORS

The health of a pond depends heavily on oxygenating plants. They supply vital oxygen to water and fish, starve out green algae, and break down waste matter produced by fish.

■ Fish use oxygenators as a source of food and as a spawning area.

■ Most aquatic suppliers sell oxygenators as bunches of unrooted cuttings. To plant, either tie a stone to the bottom of each bunch and let it sink into position, or plant in a container of aquatic soil. Plant in the sunniest part of the pond three weeks before introducing any fish.

■ From time to time, trim back excessive growth using a sharp knife, to keep plants bushy and compact.

■ **Planting ratio** One bunch to every 3 sq ft (1 sq m) of water surface.

DEEP-WATER AQUATICS

Generally planted on the bottom of the pond, some deep-water aquatics produce floating leaves and flowers, while others thrust their leaves and flowers above the surface. They help provide shade.

■ **Planting ratio** One plant to every 15 sq ft (1.4 sq m) of water surface.

MARGINALS

Although they provide some shade, marginals are purely decorative plants for the shallow edges of an informal or wildlife pond.

■ Plant in baskets or directly into soil on the pond shelf at the recommended planting depth, measured from the top of the soil to the water level. The planting depth varies from water level to about 6 in (15 cm) below.

■ To acclimatize a new plant, stand the container on bricks and gradually remove these until it is established at the recommended depth.

■ **Planting ratio** One plant to every 5 sq ft (0.5 sq m) of water surface.

FLOATING PLANTS

This group of plants will provide shade in the early days of a pond, before waterlilies are established. They will, however, perish if the temperature drops below freezing.

■ As floating plants take the nutrients they need directly from the water, they can exist without soil. To plant, simply place them on the water's surface.

■ **Planting ratio** One plant to every 10 sq ft (1 sq m) of water surface.

MARGINAL DISPLAY
With its dark, glossy leaves and large, fragrant, white flowers, the arum lily *(Zantedeschia)* is an ideal choice for a more formal setting.

PLANTING UP

Most aquatics are sun-loving plants. While a few plants will grow in the water without soil, the majority must have a suitable soil mix. A medium to heavy loam is best, and specially formulated bags of aquatic soil are available. Never use peat, manure, or fertilizer, as this could pollute the water and encourage the growth of algae.

GENERAL TIPS FOR PLANTING AQUATICS

Aquatics can be planted in special deep-water beds, directly into soil on the bottom of the pond, on marginal shelves, or in specially designed plastic baskets and pots.

■ **Soil depth** The soil on the bottom of the pond must be at least 6 in (15 cm) deep. Cover it with a 1-in (2–3-cm) layer of sand, shingle, or gravel to protect it from fish.

■ **Planting depths** These vary from more than 3 ft (1 m) for some of the strongest-growing waterlilies to just 3 in (7.5 cm) for many marginals.

■ **When to plant** The best time for outdoor plantings is between mid-spring and midsummer. After planting, wait six weeks before introducing fish, water snails, and other wildlife, to allow the water to clear and the plants to settle down.

■ **Plant food** Special aquatic and waterlily foods are available from water garden specialists. These are high in phosphates but low in nitrogen – which would trigger a proliferation of algae and green water. Use according to the manufacturer's instructions.

PLANTING A WATERLILY

1 Line a basket and almost fill with a damp aquatic soil mix. Position the rhizome within 1½ in (4 cm) of the rim. Add soil to ½ in (13 mm) of the rim.

2 Firm the soil, taking care not to damage new shoots. Trim excess liner and cover soil mix with gravel to keep soil in place and protect the roots.

PLANTING BASKETS

Plastic aquatic planting baskets come in a wide range of shapes and sizes to accommodate all kinds of aquatics and make planting up a pond much simpler. The plants will also be easier to look after, as being grown in containers will control their spread. Planting baskets also make life easier when it comes to lifting the plants out when you need to divide and propagate them.

The meshed sides of the containers need to be lined. Special liners are available which keep soil in but allow roots to penetrate. Hessian, which will eventually rot away, can also be used.

Fill containers to within ½ in (13 mm) of the top with soil mix, and finish off with a layer of washed gravel or shingle.

PLANTING
BASKETS

STOCKING A NEW POND

When planting your pond, there is a set order you must follow to achieve a healthy balance. Follow the advice and planting ratios given on pp. 132–33.

• To avoid introducing rogue pests, such as snails or duckweed, or diseases into your pond, check all new plants for signs of any ailments (see pp. 179–180). Always remove new plants from their containers and wash them in cold, running water. Repot each plant in fresh soil mix before standing it in your pond.

• Start by planting oxygenators. Push two or three bunches into soil-filled aquatic baskets and place them at intervals of 2 ft (60 cm) along the bottom of the pond.

• As the water warms up, add a waterlily or two – make sure you choose a variety of the right size and vigor for your pond (see pp. 184–87).

• At the same time, drop in some floating plants to provide shade until the waterlilies establish themselves. In time, it may be necessary to remove some of these floaters as the waterlily pads take over. Plant up marginals, directly into soil or in aquatic baskets, and introduce deep-water aquatics.

• Now be patient. The plants need time to establish, and the water needs time to clear. You will need to wait at least six weeks before introducing fish (see pp. 160–65) – just add a few at a time and allow them to settle.

PROPAGATION

Most water plants can be increased by dividing the rhizome into smaller pieces and planting. Division is best carried out in late spring, every four or five years to prevent overcrowding.

SPLITTING A WATERLILY

Too much leafy growth in the center of a waterlily and smaller and fewer flowers are sure signs that the plant needs splitting. Most waterlilies need splitting every three or four years, although some of the smaller hybrids can go six or seven years without attention.

The best time to split a waterlily is late spring or early summer.

■ Lift the plant from the water and carefully wash off any soil mix from the rhizome. Remove all opened leaves.

■ The waterlily rhizome consists of a main rhizome with a number of sideshoots. Each sideshoot will produce a single healthy plant.

■ Using a sharp, clean knife, remove the best sideshoots with a portion of the rhizome. Trim off any long, coarse roots and plant them (see p. 134) individually into pond containers filled with a heavy loam.

■ Reposition the new waterlily plants in the pond on bricks at a depth of 2–3 in (5–7.5 cm) of water. As the plant becomes established, you will be able to remove the bricks until the plant is sitting at its final, recommended planting depth.

■ Throw away the old central portion of the plant.

TAKING CUTTINGS

Use a sharp knife to take a cutting directly above a leaf node

1 In spring, use a sharp knife to take a 2–4-in (5–10-cm) cutting just above a pair of leaves. Remove lower leaves and sideshoots.

2 Fill a pot with potting soil mix and insert the cutting. Water well and cover the pot with a plastic bag. Repot once the roots are established.

DIVIDING MARGINALS

Most moisture-loving marginals require little attention and can be simply divided into smaller plants when they've grown too big. Treat marginals as you would any perennial plant.

1 Carefully lift the plant to be divided from the pond and remove it from its container. Wash off any soil. Smaller plants can be gently teased apart by hand, larger specimens may need to be separated using the tines of two garden forks back to back.

2 Pot the offsets up separately. Put some crocks in the bottom of an ordinary 6-in (15-cm) plastic pot and cover these with some aquatic or loam-based soil mix. Place one new plant into each pot and add more soil mix. Firm the soil mix and finish off with a layer of shingle or washed gravel.

3 Don't return the new plants to the pond immediately, as they may float free before new anchoring roots have formed. Place all the pots in a shallow tray and fill this with water. Leave the tray to overwinter in a frost-free environment, such as a greenhouse or cold frame, until the plants are ready to be repotted early the following year. Water them regularly to ensure the soil does not dry out.

4 In late spring or early summer, when strong new shoots are starting to appear and the roots are completely filling the pots, transfer the plants into suitably sized containers filled with loam and return them to the pond.

Gently separate the roots apart with your hands

Once separated, each individual plant can be planted up separately

MOVING WATER

There is nothing quite so relaxing on a hot summer's day as the refreshing sound of a softly babbling stream, the gentle splashing of an ornamental fountain, or the constant rush of water cascading over a rocky slope. As well as soothing our senses, moving water is also of great benefit to fish and plant life as it increases the oxygen content of the water. Even the smallest garden can accommodate a moving water feature. Using one of the many self-assembly kits that are now available from garden centers, installation couldn't be simpler.

FOUNTAIN TIPS

A carefully positioned fountain will greatly influence the style of your water garden. Fountains come in a wide range of sizes and shapes, so before buying one, take a moment to consider the following three points:

ORNAMENTAL
TIERED FOUNTAIN

■ A fountain can empty a pond if the water falls beyond the edge, so make sure the model you choose is not wider than the pond.

■ Choose a fountain with a height adjuster so you can regulate the height of the spray. On windy days you may need to turn the fountain off completely to prevent losing too much water.

■ If you choose a spray fountain, the fountainhead should be raised just above the surface of the water. You may need to use fountain stem extensions in a deep pond.

WATERFALL OR CASCADE?

For maximum effect, a waterfall needs height, whereas a cascade can work well with a drop of just 6 in (15 cm).

■ Preformed fiberglass stone-effect liners (see p. 126) are available for making waterfalls and streams, but can restrict the length, width, and color of your design. The overall shape of the feature will still need softening with plants and real stones.

CASCADES OF WATER
In a small garden, a cascade of three or more shallow drops looks more natural than one high waterfall.

■ Heavy-duty flexible sheet liner will enable you to to design and construct a more natural-looking waterfall or stream. Separate sheets will be needed for each tier; always overlap higher sheets over the top of lower ones. Make the feature look more natural by placing stones and plants at the sides and bottom.

PUMPS AND FILTERS

Fountains, waterfalls, cascades, and filters all require an electric pump to move water through them. Pumps are available in all shapes and sizes, to suit every kind of water feature. Small submersible pumps operate at low voltage from a transformer and are safe and easy to install. Large features need surface pumps powered by the main electrical supply and should be installed by a qualified electrician.

PUMPS

Before buying a pump, work out what you want it to do and discuss your requirements with an expert. The two categories of pump are:

■ **Feature pumps** These are designed to move water through features such as fountains and waterfalls and may be submersible or above the surface. Most submersible feature pumps also have an integral filter.

■ **Filter pumps** These are designed to deliver water through a filter. They are capable of filtering out small solids in the water.

INSTALLING A PUMP

• Position the pump on a level surface, such as bricks or a special mounting platform, just clear of the bottom of the pond. This prevents debris from being sucked into the pump and clogging the works.

• Connect the pump to the electricity supply via a weatherproof cable connector to the extension lead. Conceal this beneath paving.

• Disconnect both the pump and the filter and remove them from the water during winter.

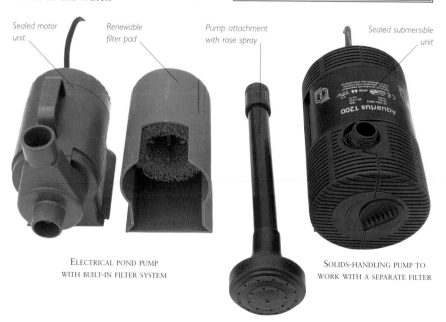

Sealed motor unit

Renewable filter pad

Pump attachment with rose spray

Sealed submersible unit

ELECTRICAL POND PUMP
WITH BUILT-IN FILTER SYSTEM

SOLIDS-HANDLING PUMP TO
WORK WITH A SEPARATE FILTER

Filters

In a well-stocked, established garden pond, the plants should keep the water clean and create a healthy environment for fish. In a new pond, however, this may take time, during which the water will go green and murky, due to the growth of algae. If this is the case, you may want to consider installing a filter system or ultraviolet purifier, which helps fight against the growth of green algae. Pond filters, most of which are sited outside the pond, generally combine the following methods of filtration:

■ **Mechanical filters** Solid particles are strained out from the water as it flows through the filter.

■ **Biological filters** The water flows through several layers of mineral materials, which have a large surface area on which bacteria flourish. These bacteria break down and purify waste products and gases on which green algae thrive.

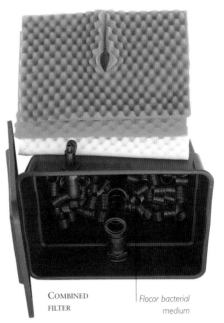

COMBINED FILTER

Flocor bacterial medium

Water garden specialists offer a wide selection of filters. To be sure you select the right filter for your pond, ask the advice of an expert. If you have a very small pond, a simple algicide may be a cheaper solution.

SPRAY EFFECTS USING A SUBMERSIBLE PUMP

The spray pattern of a fountain is dictated by the size and placing of holes in the nozzle and by the height and width of the water, which are dictated by the flow adjuster controls.

Use a small submersible pump for spray heights of up to 4 ft (1.2 m); a larger submersible pump up to 7 ft (2.2 m), and a high-head exterior pump for heights exceeding 7 ft (2.2. m).

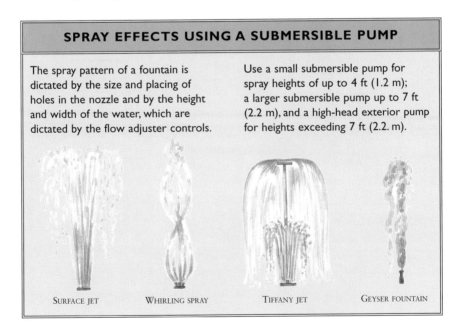

SURFACE JET   WHIRLING SPRAY   TIFFANY JET   GEYSER FOUNTAIN

LIGHTING

Any water feature can be enhanced by the creative use of garden lighting. There is a wide range of spotlights and wide-beam lights available, some of which can be floated or submerged to illuminate the water. These can create a really dramatic spectacle at night, when the water magnifies their effect.

SURFACE LIGHTING EFFECTS

The secret of good lighting is to highlight certain areas or features, leaving other parts in darkness. Floodlights produce a diffuse pool of light covering a wide area, while the beam of a spotlight will light up a specific plant or feature.

For around the pond, you can find both surface-mounted lights and spiked models that can be set in a border or lawn. Globe and searchlight styles will give general illumination; mushroom and tiered lights are used for downlighting.

LOW-VOLTAGE SPOTLIGHT

Protective rubber rim

Fixings for angle attachment

Transformer for reducing voltage of electrical supply

Ground spike for surface lighting

Swivel bracket

QUICK FIX

• Low-voltage lights operate by means of a reduced-voltage supply via a transformer, so installation is safe and straightforward.

• If possible, run the cable under edging stones around the pond where there is no risk of someone accidentally cutting through it while gardening.

• If you have to bury cable, it must be covered with a protective steel sleeve.

• Solar-powered lights do not require any cables – just a battery to be charged via a transformer.

SUBMERSIBLE
GLOBE LIGHT

MINI-HIGHLIGHTER

SUBMERGED LIGHTING

Underwater lights cast a magical spell over a water feature after dark. Floating, submerged, or clustered around a fountain, they produce an impressive effect, particularly when various colored filters are utilized.

■ **Purchasing tips** Check before you buy whether the lights are for surface or underwater use. The flex of submerged lights will need to be weighted down using a smooth stone. Do not place the lights deeper than 1 in (2.5 cm) below the surface, otherwise the effect will be lost.

■ **Maintenance** Regularly hose off any debris that collects on the lights. From time to time, you will also need to remove the lights from the water, wash them in warm soapy water, then rinse them and put them back.

■ **Caution** Remember to disconnect the power before handling lights or when taking them out of the water.

LIGHT SHOW
A submersible light positioned below a gushing fountain creates a magical illusion after dark. Different moods and effects can be achieved by the creative use of colored bulbs and lenses.

ORNAMENTS

Although plants and fish are ornamentation enough for most ponds, during the colder months, when the plants have died down and the fish are inactive, it is pleasant to have something decorative to look at, particularly in the case of a formal pond in a prominent position or themed garden design.

ORNAMENT IDEAS

A wide range of ornaments and figures are available to add extra interest to your pond.

■ **Small features** Most garden centers stock a wide range of stone figures most of which are discreet enough to blend harmoniously by the side of even the smallest informal pond.

■ **Focal points** Some ornaments, such as classical statuettes, make ideal focal features positioned either on the edge or in the center of a pond. When planning the planting of the pond, leave clear areas of water around the figure to optimize the effect of the reflection. You could also try laying an old stone urn on its side amid plants or on gravel to add a touch of fantasy.

LEAPING FISH

SHIPWRECKED TREASURE

WELL CONTAINED

■ **Containers** Terra-cotta, glazed, wooden, and even plastic pots and planters will help break up an expanse of hard landscaping around a pond, particularly on a patio, where an attractive display of color can soften the overall formality – just make sure the pots are raised off the ground so water can drain away.

Don't forget that containers can also be planted up to provide a colorful display throughout the year – even during winter and early spring. Miniature conifers, winter-flowering heathers and pansies, early-flowering spring bulbs, and trailing ivy will brighten the darkest day. The scope is endless, and a visit to a local garden center will give you plenty of inspiration – both for pots and plants.

3
SMALL WATER FEATURES

If you decide you would like a water feature but would rather it didn't overpower your garden, this chapter gives some ideas for smaller water features. Any watertight container can be pressed into service: an old sink or simply a wooden half-barrel will be deep enough for a miniature waterlily and one or two other aquatics. And you don't need a pond to enjoy a fountain: there are self-contained units that just need filling with water and the power switched on. Cobble ponds and millstone features are a safer way to introduce water to a garden where there are children about, while a simple birdbath will attract a host of feathered visitors to the garden. Find out more about creating a water garden in miniature in this chapter.

POTS OF WATER

It is amazing how soon a container of water standing out on the patio will attract wildlife, from birds dropping in for a quick drink and a bath, to a frog or toad seeking a more permanent residence. No container is too small to grow water plants in, even an old kitchen sink can be used to display a waterlily. And by choosing plants carefully, a wooden half-barrel or a large glazed pot can provide a home for a variety of aquatics.

AQUATICS ON HIGH

Where space is limited, such as on a balcony, a simple water feature can be created in a tub. Mail-order kits containing a tub, plants, baskets, and fertilizer are widely available. Plants for such a feature include a dwarf waterlily (e.g. *Nymphaea* "Pygmaea Helvola"), blue flag *(Iris versicolor)*, milfoil *(Myriophyllum)*, and water hyacinth *(Eichhornia crassipes)*.

BUBBLING OVER
Almost any container can be adapted to make a stylish water feature. A small fountain can be added to create a gentle bubbling sound.

CLEAN AND WATERTIGHT

■ Scrub out your container with clean water and a stiff brush. Do not use detergent or a cleaning agent.

■ Seal any drainage holes to make sure the container is watertight.

■ Do not use wooden containers that have held wood preservative, oil, or tar, as any residue will pollute the water and form scum on the surface.

■ Water in a barrel or pot is not a suitable outdoor environment for keeping fish.

Wooden half-barrels can be bought from most garden centers or architectural salvage specialists. New ones will usually have been made watertight already, but to be sure there are no residues in the wood that could harm plants, it is a good idea to paint the inside with a proprietary sealant. Old barrels will usually require lining with a length of flexible liner (see p. 122).

FULL TO THE BRIM
Two wooden half-barrels arranged at different levels create a compact water feature that brings sound and movement to a small garden.

BARRELS AND SINKS

A miniature pond in a half-barrel or sink will create a focus on a balcony, terrace, or small patio, or add interest to a corner of your garden. They can be freestanding, perhaps surrounded by plants, or sunk into the ground – which gives some protection against frost.

A SIMPLE BARREL GARDEN

Before planting up your barrel, check for leaks. Fill it with water, mark the level, and let it stand for a few days. If the level drops, you will need to re-waterproof it before it can be used. It is also a good idea to plant up the barrel in its intended position as it will be too heavy to move once it is full. Support the barrel on bricks to allow air to circulate underneath.

Gravel sprinkled on surface of basket

Curved planting basket fits snugly into contours of barrel

Fill slowly with hose

1 Partly fill the barrel with bricks to create a range of planting levels. Check that the depth of the bricks corresponds with the correct planting depths of the plants you have selected.

2 Plant up planting baskets (see p. 134) with your selected plants and position in the barrel. Choose curved baskets that will fit snugly around the edges. Sprinkle baskets with gravel to keep soil mix in place. Add decorative rocks and gently fill with water.

CHOOSING YOUR BARREL

• Choose a barrel about 2 ft (60 cm) in diameter, with a minimum depth of 12 in (30 cm), equivalent to a capacity of about 10 gallons (45.5 liters).

• If you are not going to use the barrel immediately, keep about 2–3 in (5–8 cm) of water in the bottom to stop it from drying out – which could cause cracks to develop in the wood.

• Block drainage holes by hammering in lengths of wooden dowling. There is no need to seal them, as they will expand when wet and fit tight.

• Check that the inside surfaces have been properly sealed and that there are no leaks.

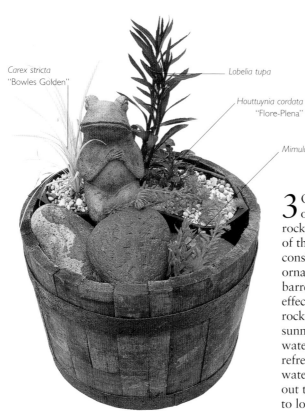

Carex stricta
"Bowles Golden"

Lobelia tupa

Houttuynia cordata
"Flore-Plena"

Mimulus lewisii

3 Once your barrel is full of water, position the rocks to conceal the edges of the planting baskets and consider adding a small ornament. The planted barrel will look particularly effective perhaps set amid rocks and flowers in a sunny corner. Check the water level regularly and refresh it if you notice that water has evaporated. Thin out the plants if they start to look overcrowded.

SINK GARDENS

If you're lucky enough to come across one, you can transform an old galvanized sink into an easy summer water feature for a cool corner of your garden. Simply clean out the sink thoroughly (see p. 146) and make sure it is entirely watertight. Then fill with water and stock with suitable water plants, such as dwarf waterlilies.

MAKING A TUFA SINK

Transform an old glazed porcelain sink into an original summer water garden by coating its exterior in tufa to create a natural-looking exterior.

• Clean the sink well (see p. 146).

• Make up the hypertufa: 2 parts peat, 1 part sand, and 1 part cement, made into a stiff mix with water.

• Score the sink's exterior with a glass cutter and coat with a bonding agent.

• While this is still sticky, spread on a ½-in (13-mm) layer of hypertufa. Plug the drainhole and cover with sealant.

• Leave the hypertufa to harden – this will take about two weeks.

• Fill the sink with water, and stock with a selection of aquatic plants (see pp. 150–1).

AQUATICS FOR POTS

Water plants grown in small containers will need more attention than those in a pond, as they can quickly outgrow their space and need regular thinning and cutting back. However, by selecting plants of differing heights, textures, and colors, you can create a stunning ensemble that will quickly become an established feature.

PLANTING AND CARE

■ Although a water garden in a container is best planted up in the spring, planting can continue until midsummer.

■ Plants in a wooden half-barrel are best grown in aquatic pots and baskets, rather than in a layer of soil spread on the floor of the barrel. Not only will this extend the barrel's life, but it will also make caring for the plants easier.

■ Submerged plants are best planted in 1-pint (0.5-liter) pots while dwarf waterlilies will need at least 3-pint (1.5-liter) pots. Marginal plants can go in small round or square pots. All these pots should be lined first. It may be necessary to stand the pots of marginals on bricks so that they are at their correct planting depth.

■ Use an aquatic planting soil mix or heavy topsoil with a clay content. Firm plants in, then cover the surface with a light dressing of gravel.

■ Aquatic plants in a ceramic or terra-cotta pot can be grown in a 3-in (7.5-cm) layer of soil spread over the bottom. Again, top the soil with a layer of gravel after planting.

■ If using soil from the garden, it must not have been given a recent application of fertilizer. Sieve it first to remove any large stones.

PLANT CATEGORIES

Water plants that suit being grown in containers such as half-barrels or large patio tubs can be divided into three categories:

• **Submerged plants** These are the oxygenating plants and most of their foliage will remain below the water level.

• **Lilies and lilylike plants** These have their root systems on the bottom but their flowers and foliage will be in full view on the surface.

• **Marginal plants** These like their roots in the water but their flowers and foliage are held above the surface.

■ Take care not to disturb the pot's contents when filling it with water.

■ The water level needs to be topped up regularly, as a surprising amount will be lost through evaporation.

■ Remove faded flowers and yellowing leaves as they appear.

■ If winter months are particularly cold, and your water feature is in danger of freezing solid, if possible, move the barrel under cover – in a greenhouse or sunroom. If not, it would be best to drain the water out, and provide a temporary winter home for any plants.

SUBMERGED

Plant these in plastic containers and place them on the bottom of the barrel.

Callitriche hermaphroditica, syn. C. autumnalis
Water starwort

Crassula helmsii, syn. Tillaea recurva

Eleocharis acicularis
Spike rush, hair grass

Lagarosiphon major, syn. Elodea crispa

MARGINALS

Plant marginals in containers and stand them on bricks, if necessary, to allow 2–3 in (5–8 cm) of water above the crown of the plant.

Acorus gramineus "Variegatus"
Japanese rush

Calla palustris
Bog arum

Caltha palustris "Flore Pleno"
Double yellow kingcup

Eriophorum angustifolium
Cotton grass

Houttuynia cordata "Plena"

Iris versicolor Blue flag

Juncus effusus "Spiralis"
Corkscrew rush

Myosotis palustris
Water forget-me-not

Sagittaria sagittifolia
Arrowhead

Typha minima
Miniature bulrush, reedmace

DWARF WATERLILIES (NYMPHAEA)

Select miniature varieties of waterlily that require a planting depth of 12 in (30 cm), spread no more than 2 ft (60 cm), and have flowers 2–4 in (5–10 cm) across. Plant only one waterlily to each barrel or tub.

N. "Andreana" (yellow to red)

N. candida (white)

N. "Caroliniana Nivea" (white)

N. "Firecrest" (pink)

N. "Froebelii" (red)

N. "Graziella" (red)

N. "Laydekeri Lilacea" (pink)

N. "Laydekeri Purpurata" (red)

N. "Pygmaea Alba" (white)

N. "Pygmaea Helvola" (yellow)

N. "Pygmaea Rubra" (pink)

N. "CAROLINIANA NIVEA"

LILYLIKE

Plant these in plastic containers and place them on the bottom of the barrel. In time, the foliage and flowers will rise to the surface.

Aponogeton distachyos
Water hawthorn, Cape pondweed

Hydrocharis morsus-ranae
Frogbit

Nuphar minima
Yellow pond lily

Nymphoides peltata, syns. Villarsia bennettii, Limnanthemum nymphoides
Fringed water lily, water fringe, yellow floating heart

SPOUTS AND BUBBLES

The sound and sight of water, splashing and sparkling in the
sunlight as it spurts from a miniature fountain or bubble feature
can alter the mood of your garden, creating an atmosphere of calm.
All you need to create such a feature are a pump, access to a power
supply, a modest reservoir of water, and an outlet
through which the water will flow.

SPOUTING WATER

A basic low-voltage electric pump
can be used to recirculate water from
a modest reservoir through a wide
range of decorative waterspouts and
fountains to create a variety of
magical features that will introduce
sound and movement into your
garden. Make a visit to your local
water garden specialist to look at
the wide range of features offered.

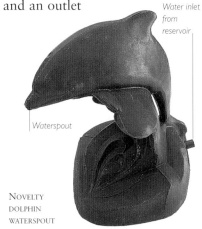

*Water inlet
from
reservoir*

Waterspout

NOVELTY
DOLPHIN
WATERSPOUT

WATER
TROUGH

Many come in kit form and can
be assembled using basic tools and
a minimum of expertise. Most will
be up and running within a few
hours of purchase and can be sited
anywhere in the garden – even in
the shadiest corner.

■ **Novelty** Most garden centers
stock a wide range of small items,
such as the dolphin waterspout
above, through which water can be
pumped to create a novelty feature.

■ **Fountain and trough** An
integral upright outlet coupled
with a stone trough makes
a useful alternative to a wall
fountain in a garden where
there are no strong walls to
support the outlet. This feature
would look perfect surrounded
by lush foliage plants against
a trellis or even across a corner
to conceal a leggy hedge.

WALL FOUNTAINS

To create a striking wall fountain, all you need is a wall strong enough to bear the weight of the fountain and an electrical outlet to power the pump. Wall fountain outlet plaques are available in real and artificial stone, cast iron, tile, concrete, terra cotta, copper, and even convincingly textured plastic and fiberglass.

A popular choice for a small garden is a classical-style mask, where water spilling from the mouth collects in a reservoir below. This can be a stone bowl, or even an old sink disguised by plants. The pump may be submerged in the pool or in a concealed chamber nearby.

Make sure the flow of water from the mouth is strong enough to spout into the center of the reservoir pool without splashing over the sides, otherwise you will find that you constantly need to top it up.

GURGLING GARGOYLES
Create an atmospheric, grotto-like feel on a shady wall by surrounding the mask with ivy – both green and variegated – ferns, and mosses.

BUBBLE FEATURES

Gurgling millstone fountains and pebble pools are an excellent way of introducing a water feature into a garden where there are children about or where a conventional pond is not practical. Both are easy to install, need little maintenance, and suit a patio, gravel bed, or border.

These features can be sited in a shady spot but will need access to an earthed electricity supply to power the pump. Turn to pages 109 and 140 for tips on installing pumps and electrical equipment. If in any doubt, always consult a qualified electrician.

No external water supply is needed for these features, as the same water is recirculated from an integral reservoir. In winter, they should be disconnected, drained, and the pump removed and stored indoors.

BUBBLING MILLSTONE
A millstone with water rippling gently over its surface makes an attractive and restful feature in a setting of differently sized pebbles and rocks.

MINIATURE LOTUS
FLOWER BUBBLE FEATURE

MILLSTONE FOUNTAINS

Original millstones are becoming increasingly difficult to find, in addition to which they are very heavy to move; however, it is now possible to buy fiberglass replicas, often as part of a self-assembly kit.

The pump is placed in a reservoir directly beneath the millstone from which a delivery pipe leads up through the hole at the center.

If a millstone is too big for your garden, smaller features are available, such as the lotus flower shown above, which work on the same principle.

PEBBLE
SPOUT

MAKING A PEBBLE POOL

A pebble pool not only looks natural, it is a safe and trouble-free way of bringing moving water into a garden and can be installed at ground level or in a raised bed. Kits ranging in diameter from 2 ft (60 cm) to 6 ft (1.8 m) are readily available. A kit usually comprises a water reservoir, a lid to keep leaves and debris out, a lining, pump, fountain, and cabling.

■ Dig out a hole to take the water reservoir – about 10–12 in (25–30 cm) deep should suffice.

■ Run electricity to the feature to power the pump.

■ Fill the reservoir with water and install the pump and fountainhead.

■ Put the lid over the water reservoir.

■ Arrange the pebbles, and switch on the fountain.

■ The pump will circulate the water over the pebbles and back into the reservoir again.

ROCKS AND BOULDERS

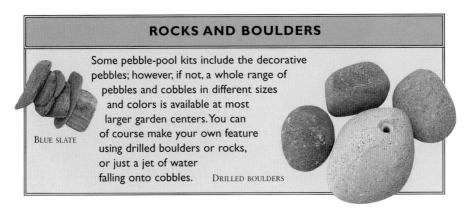

Some pebble-pool kits include the decorative pebbles; however, if not, a whole range of pebbles and cobbles in different sizes and colors is available at most larger garden centers. You can of course make your own feature using drilled boulders or rocks, or just a jet of water falling onto cobbles.

BLUE SLATE

DRILLED BOULDERS

MINI-TIRE FEATURE

With a bit of imagination, you can make a water feature out of almost anything. This novelty feature is made with a premolded plastic reservoir and lid, a low-voltage submersible pump, a ceramic fountain feature, an old car tire, river rocks, and plants in containers.

MAKING UP THE KIT

1 Plan where you want to position your water feature in the garden. Once it is planted up and filled with water it will be too heavy and awkward to move. You will need to choose a site close to a supply of electricity to power the pump. Make sure the dimensions of the plastic reservoir in the kit fit inside the tire.

ALTERNATIVE IDEAS

Instead of placing the reservoir inside a tire, you could try burying it in the ground and surrounding it with plants. Instead of rocks, experiment with differently colored gravel. Alternatively, you could partially sink the reservoir and heap earth around it, which could then be planted up.

Tough plastic reservoir

Channels to redirect water into reservoir

Lid, with hole for delivery pipe from pump

Pump cable groove

2 Line the ground at the base of the tire with a layer of fine sand. Lower the plastic reservoir so its upper rim fits snugly over the top of the tire.

Pump

3 Position the pump on the base of the reservoir. If the pump does not have its own built-in feet, place it on top of a few stones to ensure that water can flow underneath. Feed the electrical cable from the pump through the molded feed channel and fill the reservoir with water. Place the cover on the reservoir so the delivery pipe from the pump protrudes through the central hole.

4 Place the ceramic ammonite shell feature over the pump spout and decorate the cover of the reservoir with a layer of pebbles and rocks.

5 Complete the effect of your water feature by surrounding it with decorative plants. These can be planted directly into the soil or, as here, in containers to continue the shell theme. Switch on the pump and enjoy!

Bubbling waterspout

Daylily

Bistort

BIRDBATHS

Perhaps the smallest and simplest water feature, a birdbath positioned within sight of the house can bring you hours of pleasure watching the visitors splashing in the water. Choose from a wide range of styles and materials to blend in with your garden.

SIZE AND STYLES

Birdbaths are available in a variety of designs and styles. They can be mounted on a pedestal, supported on a post, hung from a chain, or sunk into the ground.

■ **Homemade bath** Sink a trash-can lid, flowerpot base, or large dish into the soil. It should have sloping sides that allow small birds to bathe at the edges and must have a central depth of about 3½ in (9 cm) to accommodate larger birds.

■ **Position** Birds will not use a birdbath unless they feel safe, so site the bath close to cover where they can take refuge to dry and preen.

■ **Check the water** In hot weather, keep the water level topped up. In winter, if the water surface freezes,

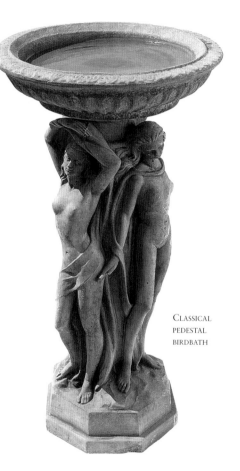

CLASSICAL
PEDESTAL
BIRDBATH

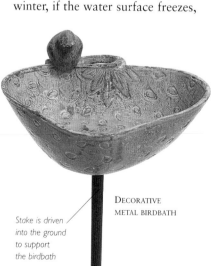

DECORATIVE
METAL BIRDBATH

*Stake is driven
into the ground
to support
the birdbath*

melt the ice. In prolonged periods of frost, a rubber ball floating on the surface will provide access to the water. Never use antifreeze or salt, which are harmful to wildlife.

■ **Cleaning** Periodically clean out the birdbath with clean water and a scrub brush. Do not use chemicals or detergent.

4
LIFE IN
THE POND

One of the charms of a water garden is that it will quickly start to teem with plant and animal life – whether it is the ornamental fish that you introduce, the frogs, toads, and newts that take up residence, or the insects and birds that soon become frequent visitors.

In this chapter, we look at choosing, buying, and caring for ornamental fish and ways of encouraging frogs and other amphibians to a wildlife pond.

However, unwelcome guests, such as herons and birds of prey, may also take an interest in your pond, and the chapter looks at humane methods of dissuading them.

ORNAMENTAL FISH

Fish bring life and interest to any pond, and there is nothing quite so restful as watching them as they glide effortlessly between strands of pondweed and lily stems. Today a wide range of exotic ornamental species is available in a variety of sizes and colors; however, the basic requirements of all healthy fish remain the same – clean, well-aerated water and adequate space, shade, and food.

BASIC REQUIREMENTS

Most ornamental, cold-water fish are resilient and need little attention: just clean water, plenty of oxygen, some shade, and room to swim and grow. Koi carp require at least a 3-ft (1-m) depth of water, while smaller fish, such as goldfish and shubunkin can survive in just 18 in (45 cm). Before buying fish, think about how visible they will be in your pond. White, yellow, orange, and red goldfish and the more active golden orfe are a safe choice as their colors contrast with the dark water and they tend to stay close to the surface.

INTRODUCING THE FISH

The best time to introduce fish to a pond is late spring to summer, when the water temperature reaches at least 50°F (10°C). Wait at least six weeks after planting before stocking a new pond with fish. This will give the plants time to root and allow the pond to find its correct balance. The level of stocking varies according to planting levels, filtration, volume of water, surface area, water movement, aeration, and the level to which you intend to maintain the pond. See the box opposite for a general guide to stocking levels.

Oxygen inside bag

Tank water

BUYING YOUR FISH

Fish can be bought from water garden suppliers, garden centers, and even mail order. Choose fish that appear healthy and active – one diseased fish can affect others already in your pond. Look for an erect dorsal fin (on the fish's back), bright eyes, and smooth scales. Never buy a fish that has white spots the size of a pinhead along its body or one that shows any sign of damage. Select medium-sized fish, about 3–5 in (7–12 cm) in length.

BRINGING THEM HOME

To transport fish home, place them in polyethylene bags, half filled with water and then inflated with air or oxygen and sealed. In the car, place the bags in cardboard boxes and protect the fish from light.

STOCKING LEVELS

If fish are to survive, it is important not to overstock your pond. Use the following ratio to work out the **maximum** number of fish you can introduce into your pond.

• A water surface area of 1 ft x 1 ft (30 cm x 30 cm) will support a fish 2 in (5 cm) long, from nose to tail. This means that a pond of 100 sq ft (9 sq m) would accommodate 200 in (500 cm) of fish. This could work out as 100 2-in (5-cm) fish, 50 4-in (10-cm) fish, or 25 8-in (20-cm) fish, or a mixture of lengths as long as the total length does not exceed the maximum of 200 in (500 cm).

• Koi carp are the exception, as one large fish needs an area of at least 4 ft x 3 ft (120 cm x 90 cm).

ACCLIMATIZING YOUR FISH

FLOATING BAG ON POND SURFACE

GENTLY RELEASING FISH INTO POND

Fish do not like sudden changes in temperature so once you get them home, you will need to spend some time acclimatizing them to their new home.

• Float the sealed bag with the fish inside on the surface of the pond for about half an hour. This allows the water in the bag to reach the same temperature as the water in the pond. If the pond is in full sun, shade the bag with a newspaper.

• Gently open the bag to allow some pond water in. Leave it for about 10 minutes, then carefully slip – do not tip – the fish into the pond. It will probably head straight for the bottom and hide itself away among the foliage until it has become familiar with its new surroundings.

FEEDING REQUIREMENTS

In a pond, fish are able to feed on the minute organisms and algae in their surroundings. You will, however, need to give supplementary food in spring and summer when they are most active. Feeding time also provides an opportunity to examine the fish for any signs of damage or disease.

■ **When to feed** Feed the fish once or twice a day, preferably at the same time and in the same place. If you have a fountain, you may find that switching it off brings the fish up to the surface. After five minutes, use a net to remove any uneaten food or this will decay and cause the water to become murky and polluted.

■ **Proprietary foods** There are many proprietary brands of fish food available, either as floating pellets or as fish sticks. Floating foods are preferable to flaked foods, which, if uneaten, will sink to the bottom to decay and pollute the water.

■ **Live foods** To vary the diet, live foods, such as daphnia and shrimp are available. If you are not squeamish, you could also feed them on chopped worms from the compost heap.

■ **Holidays** If you go away for a couple of weeks, the fish should be able to survive quite happily without any supplementary feeding.

HANDLING FISH

Fish are easily damaged by poor handling, so it is important to learn how to use a net for catching and releasing them.

• Single out the fish you want to catch.

• Very gently place the net in the water about 12–15 in (30–38 cm) away from the fish.

• Hold the net still for a minute or two before approaching the fish.

• Sweep the net to the underside of the fish, then lift gently.

• To release a fish from the net, lower the net gently into the water and allow the fish to swim out of the net at its own pace.

CATCHING FISH

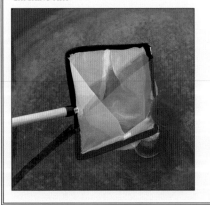

RELEASING FISH

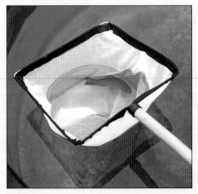

WINTER HIBERNATION

In cold weather, fish will stay in the deepest part of the pond, almost in a state of hibernation. However, a mild spell will bring them up to the surface. When the water temperature reaches 50°F (10°C), start to feed them every couple of days with a wheatgerm-rich food. Supplement their diet of floating food with a few chopped-up worms and daphnia.

In more extreme climates, where there is a risk that the pond may freeze solid, you will need to house your fish in a temporary pond in a cool part of the house or in a shed until temperatures rise in spring.

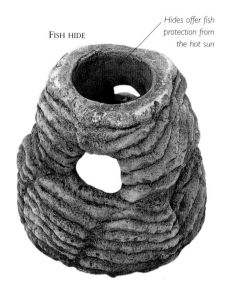

FISH HIDE

Hides offer fish protection from the hot sun

KEEPING FISH HAPPY AND HEALTHY

• Don't overstock the pond (see p. 161).

• Give the fish plenty of natural shade – waterlily leaves and other floating plants will provide this.

• Make sure the fish get plenty of oxygen by maintaining water movement. This is particularly important during a heat wave, and in periods of thundery weather. It may be necessary to keep the fountain or waterfall going all night.

• Take care when using insecticides or weed-killers near the pond to prevent spray drifting over the water.

• Water used to fill the pond should not have been stored in a metal container.

• Where a lawn surrounds a sunken pond, make sure that lawn treatments are not applied close to the pond's edge where they can be washed into the pond by rain.

• Soil used for planting underwater baskets and containers should be free from chemicals and fertilizers.

• To give your fish an extra boost in spring, food and vitamin supplements are available that will gradually release valuable minerals into the water.

FOOD TABLET

VITAMIN BOOSTER

VARIETIES OF FISH

From common goldfish and shubunkin to golden orfe and beautiful, but expensive, koi carp, you can choose from a wide variety of ornamental fish in a rainbow of colors for your garden pond. Here are just a few of the varieties you are likely to come across.

GOLDFISH VARIETIES

■ **Common goldfish** These popular yellow, orange, and red fish are inexpensive to buy and, given the right conditions, they can grow to 15 in (38 cm) and may live for 20 years. They breed easily.

■ **Shubunkin** The scales of a shubunkin produce a mottled, multicolored effect – blue, red, white, yellow, even violet and black. Shubunkins grow up to 15 in (38 cm) long and breed easily.

■ **Comet** With longer fins and tails, comets move faster and more elegantly than common goldfish. The red and white variety is known as the Sarasa Comet. They breed easily.

■ **Fantail** The metallic-orange fantail reaches 3½ in (9 cm) and breeds easily.

SHUBUNKIN
The shubunkin's scales are almost transparent, allowing pigment cells below to show through, producing a mottled multicolored effect.

OTHER FISH

■ **Tench** Both green and golden tench are sometimes sold as pond scavengers to remove waste material from the bottom of a pond – which is where they spend their lives. Put one in your pond and you may never see it again. Goldfish do the job just as well and are more visible.

■ **Koi carp** Colorful, active and long-lived, koi can become so tame they will feed from your hand. They are not, however, suitable for the average-sized garden pond as they can grow to more than 3 ft (1 m) in length – and, unlike other fish, they will carry on growing, even in the most cramped conditions. They have a tendency to stir up mud from the bottom and eat soft-leaved aquatics.

■ **Golden orfe** These golden or salmon-orange colored fish move around rapidly, just below the surface of the water, scavenging for insects. They should be easily seen, but these are timid fish when small and will hide among the plants if there are just one or two of them.

SPECIALTY KOI CARP
Highly bred and exotic, koi carp are judged by their scale types, colors, and patterns – single-color, two-color, and multicolor.

Introduce six or so, and they will patrol as a shoal.

Golden orfes grow up to 18–20 in (45–50 cm) long and so they need a pond measuring 35 sq ft (3.25 sq m) or more. They also have a high oxygen requirement, so there needs to be some movement of water, such as that provided by a fountain or waterfall.

■ **Golden rudd** Similar in appearance to a golden orfe, but not so visible in the water, the golden rudd is suitable for a smaller pond as it grows no more than 6–9 in (15–23 cm). It also needs less oxygen, but it does like higher water temperatures.

■ **Rosy minnow** The rosy minnow and the three-spined stickleback are both well suited for a true wildlife pond, moving around in shoals, and growing no bigger than 3 in (7 cm). Their dull coloring tends to make them difficult to see.

A WILDLIFE POND

Insects, birds, amphibians, and mammals will always be attracted to a pond, especially if it has been carefully planned to imitate nature. As natural wetland habitats shrink, garden ponds, however small, provide vital sanctuaries and breeding grounds for a wide range of increasingly threatened wildlife. Native plants are more attractive to indigenous wildlife, so try to include as many of these in your plantings as possible.

A POND FOR WILDLIFE

To construct a successful wildlife pond, follow the same steps as for an ornamental pond (see pp. 124–25), with one or two modifications.

■ Keep the shape of the pond very informal and at least 2 ft (60 cm) deep. Create variations in depth to provide different habitats. Deeper water protects wildlife in winter.

IMITATING NATURE
The careful selection of a range of native water plants will create a natural environment to attract birds, insects, and amphibians.

■ Create a gentle slope, perhaps in the form of a pebbly beach, on one side of the pond to give wildlife access to the water.

■ Include an area for growing bog and marginal plants to provide cover.

■ Line the pond with a heavy-duty butyl liner on a bed of sand. Place a further 2-in (5-cm) layer of sand on top of the liner and cover with a 2–3-in (5–7.5-cm) layer of soil (medium to heavy loam or specially formulated aquatic soil).

Sticky stems trap insects

VENUS FLYTRAP
(DIONAEA MUSCIPULA)

PLANTS TO GROW

Try to grow a selection of native plants, which will attract a greater variety of insects and butterflies. For inspiration, look at the kind of plants growing around ponds and streams in the countryside where you live. Do not pick or collect wild plants.

■ **Surface cover** If space allows, grow the common white waterlily *(Nymphaea alba)*. In smaller ponds floating heart *(Nymphoides peltata)* or water hawthorn *(Aponogeton distachyos)* give good surface cover.

■ **Marginals** Plant tall marginals, such as bog bean *(Menyanthes)*, bulrushes *(Typha)*, cotton grass *(Eriophorum)*, the water gladioli *(Butomus)*, and the yellow flag *(Iris pseudacorus)*. In warmer climates where there is no danger of frost, a few Venus flytraps *(Dionaea muscipula)* will add interest and attract and even catch insects.

■ **Oxygenators** Choose, among others, *Callitriche stagnalis*.

NO GOLDFISH

Goldfish are not advised for a wildlife pond, doing more harm than good, as they love to eat tadpoles. Although frogs will continue to use the pond to spawn each year, any goldfish will eat all the tadpoles long before they turn into froglets.

If you want to include fish in your wildlife pond, larger sticklebacks can be introduced, although these will also occasionally prey on tadpoles.

TAMING NATURE

Maintaining a balance between nature and garden requires some vigilance.

• Control the spread of plants such as reeds and flag irises or they will start to monopolize marginal plantings.

• In summer, skim blanketweed and other algal growth from the surface. After removing it from the water, leave it on the pondside for a while to allow any amphibians to escape.

ATTRACTING WILDLIFE

Within a very short space of time, a new pond, irrespective of whether or not it has been specifically designed with wildlife in mind, will be teeming with various inhabitants. Most of these will be beneficial, just the occasional pest will need to be rooted out.

AMPHIBIANS

Frogs, toads, and newts will soon discover and enter a new pond to breed and, once established, will return each year. Feeding on garden pests, such as slugs, these small amphibians are of great benefit in the garden and should be encouraged.

To enable amphibians to climb in and out of the pond, create ramps by placing short wooden planks or flat stones between the edge of the water and dry land.

EASY ACCESS
A few rocks sloping from the edge into the water provide wildlife with access to the pond – frogs to spawn and breed, and birds to bathe.

■ **Frogs** Female common frogs lay their spawn in jelly-like clumps in early spring, soon after they emerge from their winter hibernation. About a week later, the tadpoles hatch and start feeding on algae. Although to begin with, there will be hundreds of tadpoles – each female lays between 2,000 and 4,000 eggs – if there are fish in the same pond, few survive. Birds and newts, as well as damselfly and dragonfly nymphs, will also reduce their numbers. As tadpoles can also be cannibalistic, only the strongest will survive to develop legs and leave the pond as froglets some 12 weeks after hatching.

Although frogs must return to a pond to breed, they spend most of their life in long grass, flower beds, and other damp places on land. In summer you will often see them around the pond, sunning themselves on a lily pad or clinging to the sides cooling off, half in and half out of the water. In winter they hibernate under logs and stones.

■ **Toads** Female common toads prefer bigger ponds and lay their eggs in ribbons, some 10–12 ft (3–4 m) long, entwined around water plants. Toads are generally larger than frogs, have a drier, more warty skin, and hop or walk rather than leap. They often live well away from water and may stay in one locality for a long time. Toads feed at night on slugs and worms or small insects caught on their sticky, extendible tongue.

RESIDENT TOAD
Toads spend most of their life in the garden – keeping down unwelcome slugs – but every spring they must return to a pond to breed.

■ **Newts** These small lizard-like amphibians spend part of their life in water. The two most common species are the common or smooth newt and the great crested or warty newt. Like frogs and toads they lay spawn in spring, which hatch into tadpoles. After breeding, the adults leave the water and live under damp stones.

SNAILS AND MUSSELS

The only safe snail to introduce to a garden pond is the ramshorn snail, which feeds off scraps of decaying matter. The eggs that they produce provide a tasty treat for fish, but although they will also feed on algae, they are not really necessary in a garden pond. Never give the great pond snail a home, or they will tear your waterlily leaves to shreds and decimate other water plants. These snails will also eat frog spawn.

Swan mussels are sometimes sold to filter out microscopic algae, but they are of little value in a pond that does not have a muddy bottom.

INSECT LIFE

On warm spring and summer days you will often see dragonflies and the more delicate damselflies flitting and hovering over the water's surface in search of insect prey or a mate. Both are fierce predators, feeding on smaller insects that they have captured in flight or snatched from pondside vegetation.

Dragonflies and damselflies are the adult forms of larvae, or nymphs, that have spent the previous year under water, foraging for food, such as newly hatched tadpoles. When they are mature, the nymphs pull themselves out of the water by climbing up the nearby stems of marginal plants.

It doesn't take pondskaters, with their long, thin legs much time to find a new stretch of water on which to settle. They may be joined on the surface by water crickets, water measurers, and whirligig beetles. If you keep fish, two underwater insects to remove from your pond are water boatmen and great diving beetles, both of which are large enough to nip at small fish, often resulting in bacterial infection setting in. The larvae of great diving beetles will also attack very young fish and tadpoles, as will pondskaters and water boatmen. All aquatic insects are good fliers, so keep a regular watch for any new arrivals.

LESS WELCOME VISITORS

Birds will visit a garden pond to drink and bathe, and also to feed on tiny flies and mosquitoes that gather there. One bird you don't want to see, if you have fish, is a heron. You may not even see one as they tend to arrive at dawn or dusk, and will even visit urban ponds in search of a tasty meal.
These birds do not go directly to a pond, but land nearby, and wade in; so the more open your pond, the more vulnerable it may be, particularly the shallow areas.

PLASTIC
HERON DECOY

If herons are a problem, a plastic heron decoy is said to keep the real thing away, or the pond could be netted. A less unsightly method is to wrap two strands of wire or fishing line around 6-in (15-m) stakes positioned about 1 ft (30 cm) around the edge of the pond. Cats, particularly kittens, may take an interest in your pond, but they don't really like water, and in any case healthy fish would normally be too quick for their probing paws.

Mink and even otters have been known to take fish from a garden pond, and if these, or herons and cats are a real nuisance you could invest in an infrared sensor unit to warn them off. These emit a high-pitched alarm when a warm-blooded animal or bird strays into the area.

5
POND CARE AND MAINTENANCE

Many people worry unduly that the aftercare needed for a healthy pond involves endless time-consuming maintenance tasks, and so they are deterred from installing a water feature in their garden. This is a shame, as looking after a pond is more often than not an easy and rewarding occupation. Throughout the year it is important to remove all dead and dying organic matter, such as leaves, from the pond. Other tasks are more seasonal. This chapter looks in greater detail at basic pond management, from the tools and equipment you will need to how to completely drain the pond when it needs cleaning. A checklist of routine jobs explains what needs doing and when.

The chapter finishes off with a troubleshooter's guide to problems that can arise in a pond, and suggests how you can remedy them.

ROUTINE CARE

L ooking after a pond could not be easier. Aquatic plants do not need watering, and fish only need feeding when they are active. In order to prevent problems occurring, however, there are a few routine jobs that must be done, such as removing dead and dying plants, fallen leaves, blanketweed, and dead fish. The water level should also be checked to ensure that this does not fluctuate. Make sure that electrical equipment, such as pumps and filters, are regularly serviced.

BASIC EQUIPMENT

■ **Pond skimmer** A rake, fork, or specially designed pond skimmer can be used to remove blanketweed.

■ **Pond scissors** Long-handled, cable-operated pond scissors are used to trim out-of-reach aquatic plants.

■ **Pond pincers** Cable-operated pond pincers are used to remove debris from the surface.

■ **Garden hose** A good-quality hose is essential for keeping the water level topped up.

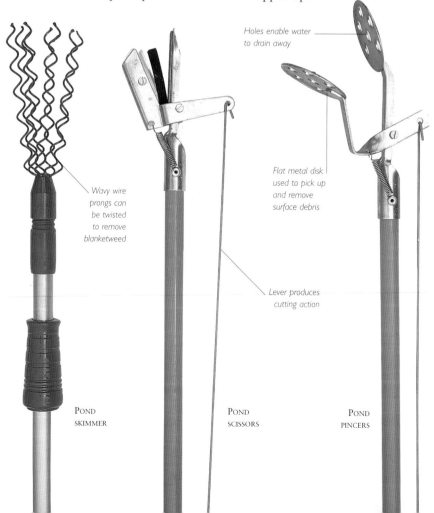

Holes enable water to drain away

Flat metal disk used to pick up and remove surface debris

Wavy wire prongs can be twisted to remove blanketweed

Lever produces cutting action

POND
SKIMMER

POND
SCISSORS

POND
PINCERS

■ **Scrub brush** A hard-bristled scrub brush is essential for cleaning off algae. Remember never to use detergent for cleaning.

■ **Fishing nets** Long-handled fishing nets in different sizes are useful for lifting out fish.

SPRING CLEANING

It is neither necessary nor desirable to change the water in your pond too frequently. If properly stocked with plants and fish, the balance of the pond should remain healthy and it is usually sufficient to remove about a quarter of the water and replace it with fresh once a year.

However, every two to three years (less frequently for a large pond) you will need to empty the pond in order to thin out overcrowded waterlilies and marginals and remove debris that has built up on the bottom. The best time to tackle this is early to mid-spring.

Before cleaning the pond, take care to avoid harming any wildlife that may have taken up residence. If your pond is home to frogs or toads, you will have to postpone any cleanup until mid-fall as there will be spawn and young in the spring.

DRAINING THE POND

Every few years, you will need to drain your pond to remove silt, debris, overcrowded plants – or fix a leak. Wear rubber boots or waders with cleated soles that will not damage the pond liner.

■ **Start emptying** Use a length of hose to begin siphoning away the water. Alternatively, if you have a pump, simply disconnect the delivery pipe and connect a hose in its place.

■ **Catch fish** Fill a large plastic holding tub or children's paddling pool with pond water and use it to place the fish in while you clean out the pond. As the water slowly drains away, catch the fish (see p. 162) with a net and place them in the holding tub. Cover the tub with netting so they cannot jump out and leave it in the shade. Keep any amphibians in a bucket filled with pond water.

■ **Remove plants** As the water drains away, remove all containerized plants. Marginals and deep-water aquatics will need to be hosed down frequently to keep them wet. Floaters and oxygenators can be kept in plastic containers filled with water.

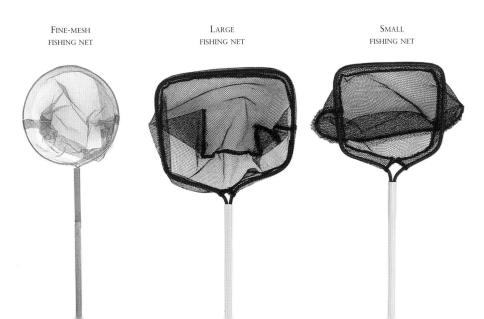

FINE-MESH
FISHING NET

LARGE
FISHING NET

SMALL
FISHING NET

CLEANING THE POND

Once the pond is drained, allow it to dry for a couple of days.

■ **Remove sludge** Use a bucket to remove sludge; spread it on a border.

■ **Wash liner** A pressure hose will remove most algal growth. Use a soft broom to sweep up debris.

■ **Refill pond** Use a hose to start refilling the pond.

■ **Replace plants** Divide plants as necessary and clean out containers. Position ornamental plants first, then add submerged plants.

■ **Replace fish** Acclimatize the fish (see p. 161) before putting them back.

BRUSHING DOWN
Use a soft broom and dustpan to sweep up any debris, taking great care not to damage the fabric of the liner. Do not use any detergent.

SEASONAL CARE

Throughout the year, as the temperature changes from season to season, so will the conditions in your pond. By being aware of the problems you could potentially face and carrying out routine seasonal tasks, you will be able to maintain a healthy balance in your pond.

SPRING

As the water temperature rises, plants begin to shoot, fish become more active, and spawn soon appears.

■ **Check pump** Bring the pump out of winter storage, check the wiring, and reinstall in the pond.

■ **Fish** Resume feeding the fish (see pp. 162–63) once temperatures rise. Check for disease (see p. 181).

REMOVING BLANKETWEED
It is essential to remove blanketweed from the pond as soon as you notice it, or it will quickly start to choke all other plant and animal life.

■ **Remove algae** Use a pond skimmer or rake to remove all algae.

■ **Tidy plants** Lift and divide overcrowded aquatics in late spring; inspect containers for stray roots, which can be cut off.

■ **Feed plants** Feed established plants in late spring. Push pellets of aquatic plant fertilizer into the soil in each individual plant container.

■ **Add new plants** Add oxygenators to inhibit algal growth and floating plants to provide surface shade.

SUMMER

At this time of year, your pond will be looking its best. The irises will come into flower, followed by water-lilies and marginals, such as lobelia.

■ **Feed fish** Now the fish are at their most active and should be fed daily.

■ **Spray plants** Occasionally spray the leaves of marginals and water-lilies with water from a hose or a can to dislodge insects, such as blackfly.

■ **Add new fish** Higher water temperatures make this the best time to introduce new fish into the pond.

■ **Top up water level** Using a hose, regularly replace water lost through evaporation.

■ **Oxygenate water** In warm, humid weather, keep the fountain running – all night if necessary – or spray the surface of the water with a hose. This increases the oxygen level – vital for fish and plant life – and lowers its carbon dioxide content.

■ **Deadhead flowers** Remove dead flowers before they set seed and trim back overvigorous marginals.

■ **Skim pond** Remove pondweed and blanketweed by winding it around a stick or fork.

■ **Clean pumps and filters** Pumps and filters will need regular cleaning to prevent their being blocked by weed and other debris.

SPRAYING LEAVES REMOVES COLONIES OF INSECTS

Fall

As plants begin to fade, it is important to deal immediately with dead and dying matter and not let it fall and rot in the water.

■ **Catch leaves** Place a fine mesh net, such as strawberry netting, over the pond surface to catch falling leaves. It is easier to keep leaves out than to remove them after they have fallen in.

■ **Remove debris** Use a pond skimmer, rake, or fishing net to remove dead leaves and other debris.

■ **Deadhead flowers** Remove faded flowers and dead leaves from waterlilies and other floating plants.

■ **Cut back plants** Once leaves and stems have turned brown, cut marginals down to about 3–4 in (7–10 cm) above the water line. This will remove any foliage pests.

■ **Prepare plants for winter** Before temperatures drop below freezing, remove any non-hardy aquatics and some of the floating plants to overwinter indoors. They should be kept in shallow bowls of water at a temperature of 50–55°F (10–13°C). The remaining floating plants – which will survive in the water during winter – can be left to sink to the bottom of the pond.

■ **Prepare fish for winter** Give fish a food high in protein to build up their strength for the winter. Put a few lengths of plastic guttering in the bottom of the pond, to give them somewhere to shelter once the cover offered by floating plants is no longer available.

■ **Remove the pump** Clean the pump and store it in a dry place over winter. Replace it with a pond heater.

CUTTING BACK MARGINALS

Cut back to 3–4 in (7–10 cm) above water level

WINTER

Besides preventing the pond surface from freezing over, there is little work to be done in the pond during the winter. The fish will be semi-dormant, remaining close to the bottom, and should not be fed.

■ **Deice the pond** In very cold climates, a pond heater is the best way of keeping an area of water ice-free. This should be installed in the fall before temperatures drop below freezing and can be connected to the electricity supply that powered the pump.

In warmer climates, place a floating object, such as a rubber ball, on the surface to prevent the pond from freezing over. This allows the gases produced by decaying matter to escape. These gases are toxic and may kill the fish. Never crack the ice with a hammer, as the shock waves can concuss or even kill fish.

If there is no power supply to the pond, a pan of boiling water placed on the ice will melt a hole. You will need to do this perhaps several times a day if the weather is really cold. Never pour the boiling water into the pond as the shock may harm the fish.

■ **Year-round algal control** Fully biodegradable straw pads are now available to float in your pond. Not only do they keep down algae, they will prevent the pond from freezing over. Each pad will usually last for about six months.

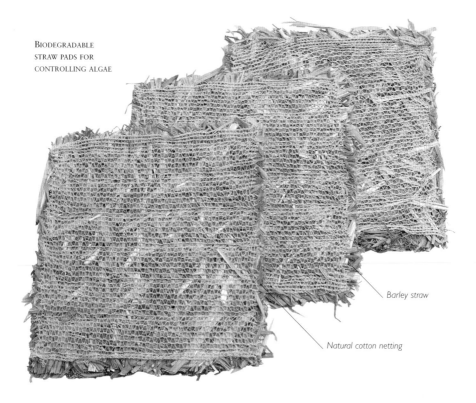

BIODEGRADABLE
STRAW PADS FOR
CONTROLLING ALGAE

Barley straw

Natural cotton netting

POND TROUBLESHOOTER

If you build and stock your pond correctly, carry out routine maintenance, avoid the unnecessary use of chemicals, and keep a close watch on your plants and fish, owning a pond should not give you too many problems. Very few pests and diseases attack aquatic plants, and if fish are well cared for, they should not succumb to ailments. There will, however, be occasions when a plant gets eaten, a fish looks off color, or the water becomes polluted.

PLANT PROBLEMS

Aquatic plants suffer from few serious pest and disease problems – which is just as well because the risk of polluting the pond water means that chemicals and sprays cannot be used as in other parts of the garden. The only spray that can be used is that from a hose to wash off insects, such as aphids, from a waterlily leaf.

One of the simplest and most efficient methods of controlling pests and diseases is to remove the affected leaf, or plant, as soon as you notice a problem.

Natural predators, such as frogs, newts, and ladybugs, as well as fish, will also play their part in helping to keep pest populations under control.

PLANT PESTS AND DISEASES		
Caddis fly larvae Mothlike adult caddis flies visit ponds on summer evenings to lay their eggs on floating leaves. When the eggs hatch, the larvae attack and feed on the roots, leaves, and buds of all aquatic plants, particularly young waterlilies. They spin cylindrical silken shelters, which they disguise with pieces of plant, sticks, and grit. The best way of reducing their numbers is to introduce fish into the pond, which will soon make a meal of them. Remove any larval cases by hand.	**Iris sawfly** This blue-gray grub, about ¾ in (2 cm) long, feeds on irises. Signs of damage are ragged or saw-toothed edges on the leaves, which should be removed, along with any grubs, and destroyed. **Leaf-mining midge** This midge lays its eggs on a wide range of soft-leaved aquatics, including waterlilies. The almost invisible larvae tunnel into the leaf, rapidly devouring the tissue between the veins, leaving a partially, or in some cases totally skeletonized leaf. Pick off affected foliage.	**China mark moth** These brown and white moths lay eggs on waterlily leaves in mid- to late summer. If left, the emerging caterpillars will cause extensive damage. They begin by biting oval-shaped pieces out of the leaf and spinning two pieces together to form a shelter, which they attach to the underside of the leaf. As the caterpillars grow, they cut larger pieces of leaf to form a protective oblong case that floats on the water – with the caterpillar safely inside. Remove these cases using a small net and destroy them.

PLANT PESTS AND DISEASES

Water snails

You can often introduce water snails into your pond on the leaves of newly purchased aquatics. Although they can be beneficial, eating both algae and fish waste as well as dead and dying plant matter, they can become a pest, particularly in spring when they may turn their attention to more succulent fresh plant growth. They should be removed with a fish net.

Garden snails

The lush growth of marginals around the edge of a pond will attract garden snails, which should be picked off by hand. It would also be a good idea to place a couple of slug traps in the vicinity. Some hollowed-out potato skins or a half-filled jar of beer sunk into the ground work well. Never use slug pellets.

Waterlily aphid

In hot, dry weather, waterlily leaves, stems, and flowers may become infested by aphids, weakening the plant and distorting both flowers and foliage. Dislodge the aphids by spraying with a jet of water from a garden hose. Alternatively, submerge the leaves and weight them down with a piece of sacking to drown the aphids.

In the fall, these aphids leave the pond to lay eggs on trees and shrubs of the *Prunus* genus. To reduce the chances of infestation, avoid siting the pond near a cherry or plum tree.

Waterlily beetle

The small brown adult beetle, the size of a ladybug, lays its eggs in clusters on the upper surface of waterlily leaves in midsummer. The yellowish brown grubs that emerge have a voracious appetite, mining the leaves, which shrivel and rot. Remove badly affected leaves, and hose down the rest. Cut down dead stalks of marginals in the fall, as this is where the lily beetle likes to hibernate.

Waterlily crown rot

Crown rot attacks the stem of the waterlily, causing the leaves to turn yellow and break away. As there is no cure, the only course of action is to remove and destroy the infected plant. If other plants have been infected, the pond will have to be emptied, thoroughly cleaned, and restocked. To guard against this disease, before planting waterlilies, inspect the rhizomes carefully. Reject any that have a black and soft area.

Waterlily leaf spot

Leaf spot is triggered by a prolonged spell of warm, damp weather. Two forms attack waterlily pads: the leaves either dry out and disintegrate, or a dark spot forms, which spreads and destroys the whole leaf. To stop the infection from spreading, remove diseased leaves immediately.

CHECK WATERLILIES REGULARLY FOR PESTS AND DISEASES

FISH

Fish are at their most vulnerable to disease and parasite attack in early spring and after the spawning season. After a long winter, or if you suspect a problem, you may want to take a closer look at your fish. To do this, each one will need to be caught and transferred into a tank of water at the same temperature as that of the pond (see p. 161). Don't chase the fish around the pond, as this will exhaust them. Before handling fish (see p. 162), make sure your hands are wet so you don't strip off their protective mucous coat. Keep any affected fish in an isolation tank until fully recovered. Treatments such as bactericides and fungicides are available; always read the manufacturer's instructions first.

COMMON FISH AILMENTS

Fin rot
This is a fairly common bacterial disease that destroys the bony rays of the tail fin, particularly of long-finned goldfish and shubunkins. If allowed to progress, fin rot will eventually reach other parts of the body, resulting in the death of the fish. The treatment is to cut away the infected area with a pair of scissors and place the fish in a solution of approved bactericide. The tail fin will regrow once the infection is cleared.

Fungus
A cottonlike growth on the fins, gills, eyes, and mouth of a fish is a sign of a fungus, which attacks a debilitated fish whose protective mucous membrane has been damaged by stress, spawning, or temperature change. Fungus can be successfully treated by using a suitable fungicide.

White spot
If a fish is seen swimming frenziedly, and looks as if it has been sprinkled with salt, it has been infected by a small parasite. Treat affected fish as soon as you notice the problem with a proprietary remedy. Do not confuse this disease with the white spots that will quite normally appear on the gills of male fish during the mating season.

Fish lice
Each fish louse is a jelly-like disk, about ¼ in (6 mm) across, which attaches itself to the body of a fish to feed off its blood. It will cause a fish to rub itself against the side of the pond and swim rapidly around. Treatment involves either removing the lice with tweezers or applying an appropriate remedy. You will need to repeat the treatment as even after you have eliminated the adult lice, there may still be eggs in the water.

Ulcer disease
Shredded fins and ulcers on the body indicates the onset of ulcer disease, which affects all types of fish. Treatment does, however, require antibiotics, which should be administered under the guidance of a vet.

KEEP AN EYE ON FISH FOR ANY SIGNS OF DISEASE

WATER

Keeping the water in the pond clean and well oxygenated is essential for the health of fish and plants. Carry out routine tasks such as skimming leaves and debris from the surface and removing blanketweed as soon as it appears. Never use garden fertilizers in or around the pond.

KEEPING WATER CLEAN

ALGAE

In small quantities algae is beneficial to the pond and provides food for fish. However, excess growth will turn the water green, indicating that the pond balance is not quite right. To create a better balance try the following:

• Introduce more oxygenating plants, and provide surface shade using waterlilies and other floating plants.

• Until the oxygenators are established and the water stays clear, skim off algae once a week.

• You can use an algicide, but always read the instructions carefully first.

• A nonchemical solution to algae is a bag of barley straw weighted down on the bottom of the pond or a floating, biodegradable pad (see p. 178).

• If fighting algae is a constant battle, install a filter for a more permanent solution.

INVASIVE PLANTS

• **Blanketweed** The scourge of pondkeepers everywhere, the long, silky green threads of blanketweed (a form of algae) choke other plants and hide fish from view. Remove the weed by winding it around a stick and put it on the compost heap. Treat the water with an algicide.

• **Duckweed** Never introduce duckweed into your pond. Before long the surface will be covered by its tiny green leaves, and as it is hardy it is almost impossible to completely eradicate. Remove as much as you can using a net before it gets out of control and check the pots of aquatics when you buy them to see that they don't contain any of this unwanted plant.

• **Fairy moss** Once introduced, fairy moss, also called water fern (*Azolla filiculoides*, syn. *A. caroliniana*), can quickly get out of hand, particularly in a small pond.

POLLUTION

Water pollution is harmful to fish and to plants and can manifest itself in several ways:

• An oily film on the surface could be due to the decomposition of waterlily leaves and other deep-water aquatic foliage. This film can be mopped up by placing a sheet of newspaper on the surface.

• Black water is the result of rotting leaves in the water. In severe cases, the pond may need to be drained and cleaned. Note that brown, or muddy water, although unsightly, is harmless to fish and plants. In fact, it is probably the fish who are to blame, stirring up soil in plant containers or on the bottom as they scavenge for food.

• Never use any kind of manure, fertilizer, or chemical weed-killer in or around the pond as this will eventually find its way into the water. The only solution is draining and cleaning.

6
PLANT DIRECTORY

Plants are essential for an attractive and successful water garden, bringing life and color to even the smallest feature.

While oxygenators and many floating plants serve a practical purpose, helping to maintain a healthy balance in the pond, many marginals are valued simply for their beautiful colors, forms, and texture, softening the hard edges of an ornamental pond and helping it to blend in with the rest of the garden.

This chapter looks at some of the most popular plants from the five categories: waterlilies, floating plants, deep-water aquatics, marginals, and oxygenators, together with some ideas for plants that can be used around the pond and in a bog garden.

WATERLILIES

There are as many as 16,000 varieties of waterlily *(Nymphaea)*, which must rank as the most popular of all pond plants. There are varieties to suit all sizes and depths of a pond, but all need sun, shelter, and still water to thrive. Take care to thin out overcrowded plants.

SMALL VARIETIES

The following varieties are all suitable for small ponds. They require a planting depth of 6–18 in (15–45 cm) and will spread 1–2 ft (30–60 cm).

N. "Andreana"
The brick-red flowers, held above the water, are shaded with yellow, with rich orange stamens. The leaves are glossy green blotched with red.

N. "Aurora"
Semi-double flowers in a wide range of shades deepening from cream to yellow, orange, and blood-red, with orange stamens. Olive-green leaves mottled with purple.

N. candida
A small variety with pure white flowers that thrives even in relatively cold water. Mid-green leaves.

N. "Ellisiana"
Star-shaped, fragrant, bright red flowers, with orange-red stamens. The oval leaves are dark green mottled with purple when young, maturing to mid-green.

N. "Firecrest"
Semi-double, star-shaped, pink flowers have orange stamens. The deep purple young leaves mature to mid-green.

N. "Froebelii"
Deep red flowers with orange-red stamens. Bronzed young leaves mature to pale green.

N. "Gloriosa"
The brilliant red, cup-shaped flowers, have rose and green variegated sepals. The green leaves have bronzy flecks.

N. "Graziella"
A free-flowering pinkish orange waterlily, suitable for the smallest of ponds.

N. "James Brydon"
Double, rose-red flowers with orange stamens. The young leaves are purple, maturing to dark green. Tolerates some shade.

N. "Odorata Sulphurea"
The sulfur-yellow flowers with orange stamens are carried above the water. Performs best in a warm summer.

N. "Pygmaea Helvola"
Small, semi-double flowers are a clear buttercup yellow. Oval, mottled purple leaves with purple undersides.

N. "Rose Arey"
A free-flowering variety with star-shaped, semi-double, anise-scented flowers, deep rose-pink when young, becoming paler with age. The young leaves are purple, maturing to green.

N. "Sioux"
The pointed petals start off a pale yellow, deepening to an orange-pink before finally turning a copper red. The dark olive green leaves are mottled with purple.

N. tetragona
Small, day-blooming, slightly scented white flowers with dark green, purple-blotched leaves.

N. "Virginalis"
Star-shaped, fragrant white flowers with yellow stamens. Rounded, pale green leaves, purplish when young.

VIGOROUS VARIETIES

The following varieties are only suitable for a large pond or lake. They require a planting depth of 1–4 ft (30–120 cm) and will spread 5–8 ft 1.5–2.4 m).

N. alba
Common white waterlily
Slightly fragrant white flowers with yellow stamens. Large, rounded, dark green leaves. Very vigorous.

N. "Amabilis"
Star-shaped pink flowers with white tips and dark yellow stamens. The dark green leaves are reddish purple when young.

N. "Brakeleyi Rosea"
The fragrant, shell-pink flowers with golden stamens are held just above the surface of the water. Large green lily pads give plenty of surface cover.

N. capensis
Cape blue waterlily
This tropical waterlily will not survive below 41°F (5°C) but can be grown as an annual in cool climates. Semi-double, star-shaped, fragrant, light blue flowers with dark yellow stamens. The young leaves have wavy edges and purple-spotted undersides.

N. "Charles de Meurville"
Star-shaped, pinkish red, white-streaked flowers that darken with age and have golden stamens. Flowers appear early. Oval, dark green leaves.

N. "Colonel A. J. Welch"
A vigorous variety with large, canary-yellow flowers that stand out of the water and stay open in the evening. The leaves have a marbled effect.

N. "Colossea"
A strong-growing variety requiring a planting depth of 5 ft (1.5 m). The large blush-pink to white blooms are fragrant and borne over a long period.

N. "Darwin"
Large, dark pink flowers striped with white and scented. The stamens are golden.

N. "Escarboucle"
Prolific, fragrant, semi-double, rich red blooms with golden stamens. The young leaves are brown tinged, maturing to green.

N. "Fabiola"
syn. **N. "Mrs Richmond"**
The inner petals of this pink waterlily turn red with age, while the leaves are a paler green than most. Very prolific.

N. "Gladstoneana"
Semi-double, pure white fragrant flowers with golden stamens, reaching up to 12 in (30 cm) across. The leaves have a wavy edge to them. Very free-flowering.

N. "Norma Gedye"
Deep rose-pink flowers and plain, dark green leaves.

N. "COLONEL A. J. WELCH"

MEDIUM VARIETIES

The following varieties are all suitable for medium to large ponds. They require a planting depth of 9–24 in (15–60 cm) and will spread 4–5 ft (1.2–1.5 m).

N. "Attraction"
Mature plants have large, star-shaped, red flowers flecked with white, while the flowers on younger plants are smaller, cup-shaped and pale pink. The stamens are pale yellow. When young, the leaves are purple, maturing to green.

N. "Carolineana Nivea"
The large, semi-double, ivory-white flowers are strongly fragrant with yellow stamens. The pale green leaves are rounded.

N. "Conqueror"
An eye-catching, free-flowering brilliant red waterlily. The large flowers, which are sometimes flecked with white, stay open in the evening. The young leaves are tinged with purple.

N. "Gonnère"
The multi-petaled white flower looks like a snowball before it opens to reveal a bright yellow center. Its more restrained spread makes it suitable for a medium-sized pond.

N. "Hermine"
The pure white flowers with their pointed petals are held well above the water. The pads are a bright green.

N. "Laydekeri Fulgens"
Free-flowering blooms through summer. Semi-double burgundy-red flowers have orange-red stamens. The young leaves are blotched with purple.

N. "Lucida"
Bright scarlet flowers with bright yellow stamens and large leaves with purple marbling make this an attractive waterlily for a medium to large pond.

N. "Mme Wilfon Gonnère"
Cup-shaped double blooms, soft pink flushed with white with a deep rose center and yellow stamens. Mid-green leaves are bronze when young.

N. "Marliacea Albida"
Fragrant, cup-shaped white flowers with yellow stamens. The young, bronzed leaves mature to dark green.

N. "Marliacea Chromatella"
Cup-shaped, semi-double golden yellow flowers set off against mottled bronze and maroon leaves.

N. "MARLIACEA CHROMATELLA"

MEDIUM VARIETIES

A reliable performer.

N. "Marliacea Rosea"
With its pink, fragrant flowers and golden stamens, this is an easy waterlily to grow and very popular. The large, fragrant blooms darken with age. Flowers produced in the first few years may be white. The dark green leaves are purplish when young.
• *N.* "Marliacea Carnea" is similar in appearance but the flowers are just a slightly paler pink.

N. "Masaniello"
Peony-like, pink flowers with darker petals at the center, standing above the surface of the water.

N. "Nigel"
This waterlily produces a mass of bright pink flowers with golden stamens, set off against large green leaves.

N. odorata
Cup- or star-shaped, fragrant white flowers with yellow stamens and glossy mid-green leaves.
• *N. o.* var. *rosea* is similar but has pink flowers.

N. "Pearl of the Pool"
Large, star-shaped, bright pink flowers have orange stamens and are fragrant. The leaves are bronzed when young, maturing to mid-green.

N. "Perry's Pink"
The deep pink, large double flowers with red centers are fragrant. Needs a lot of sunshine to do well.

N. "Pink Sensation"
Fragrant, rich pink, star-shaped flowers are held above the water and stay open late into the afternoon. Leaves are purplish when young, maturing to deep green.

N. "René Gérard"
This waterlily has distinctive upright and star-shaped, rose-pink flowers. The young leaves are bronzed, maturing to mid-green. Very free-flowering once established.

N. "PINK SENSATION"

N. "Robinsoniana"
Star-shaped, orange-red flowers with orange stamens. The leaves are light purple, with deep purple blotches and dark red undersides. Very free-flowering once established.

N. "Sunrise"
Semi-double flowers with long yellow petals and yellow stamens. The oval leaves are mottled with purple when young, maturing to mid-green. Needs warm summers.

N. "William Falconer"
A stunning deep red waterlily with dark yellow stamens. The flowers are star-shaped. The young leaves are purple but mature to dark green.

FLOATING PLANTS

It is important to introduce one or two floating aquatics to your pond as they cut down the amount of sunlight on the surface of the water and so help control blanketweed and green algae that can pollute the water. Most floating plants have attractive flowers and/or leaves, although the most attractive are usually the least hardy, and will need to be overwintered indoors.

SURFACE INTEREST

Floating plants often multiply rapidly and their growth must be constantly controlled. Some, such as water hyacinth *(Eichhornia crassipes),* while not invasive in temperate areas are so vigorous in tropical climates that their introduction may be prohibited. In areas with cold winters most floaters are killed as soon as temperatures drop below freezing. Where they are hardy, plants sink to the bottom in winter and float back to the surface in spring.

■ **Warning** Although it may provide food and shelter for fish, *Lemna*, or duckweed, should never be knowingly introduced into a garden pond. You may have seen it in stagnant ponds – a bright green blanket covering the surface. Once you have duckweed, it will be virtually impossible to eradicate.

Take care, also, when introducing other plants to your pond that there is no duckweed lurking in the water or on the plant itself.

ORIENTAL WATER
GARDEN

Lotus blossom
fountain

Floating fern

FLOATING AQUATICS

Azolla filiculoides, syn. Azolla caroliniana
Fairy moss, water fern
This plant's dense mat of pale green, fernlike foliage will quickly spread to cover the whole surface, so only put it in a pond where it can easily be removed. In late summer and fall, the fronds turn reddish. It will not stand freezing temperatures, so overwinter some in a jar of pond water and soil, and put it back into the pond in mid-spring.

Eichornia crassipes
Water hyacinth
This attractive aquatic has glossy leaves and feathery roots. However, the orchidlike lilac blue flower spikes will only appear in a warm, sunny summer: in cooler, duller conditions it may not flower. Plant out in early summer, but take inside before the first frost as it is a tender plant.

Hydrocharis morsus ranae
Frogbit
With its shiny, kidney-shaped, bright olive-green leaves and small white flowers in summer, frogbit resembles a miniature waterlily. It dies down to small buds to overwinter on the bottom of the pond. A must for a natural pond as it is a favorite haunt for aquatic wildlife. Divide in summer, by detaching young plantlets.

Pistia stratiotes
Water lettuce
This plant's common name comes from its velvety, pale green, lettucelike leaves, which are whitish green on the underside. The flowers are tiny and greenish. Thin and separate new plantlets in summer. It will not tolerate winter cold, but can be grown as an annual in cool climates.

Stratiotes aloides
Water soldier
This unusual plant spends most of its life submerged, only coming to the surface at flowering time, when white, three-petaled flowers are produced. The leaves are pointed and serrated, and look like the top of a pineapple. Once flowering is over, it sinks to the bottom and overwinters there as dormant buds. It needs deep water and can become invasive when conditions are favorable.

Trapa natans
Water chestnut
This attractive plant with floating rosettes of diamond-shaped, green serrated leaves gets its common name from the black spiny "nuts" that follow the flowers in summer. These fall to the bottom of the pond where they overwinter and produce new plants in spring. However, it will only produce its small white flower, and its fruit, in a really warm summer and will not tolerate frost.

WATER CHESTNUTS

DEEP-WATER AQUATICS

With their roots on the bottom and leaves floating on the surface, deep-water aquatics provide shade to prevent the growth of algae. Plant in containers on bricks a few inches (centimeters) under the water and gradually lower as the plants become established.

DEEP-WATER AQUATICS

Aponogeton distachyos
Water hawthorn
This is an easy plant to grow and probably one of the most reliable deep-water aquatics. The straplike leaves are often evergreen and are sometimes splashed with purple. The flowers appear throughout spring and early summer. These are borne on spikes that rise above the surface, and each has waxy white petals and black anthers and a heavy scent of "vanilla" or "hawthorn." Unlike a waterlily, water hawthorn will flourish in partial shade and moving water, but in winter you will need to check that the tubers are deep enough in the pond to sit below any ice that may form. The plant dies back in summer, but will bloom again through the fall and even on into winter.
PLANTING DEPTH 6–18 in (15–45 cm) – the deeper the better.
SPREAD 4 ft (1.2 m)
PROPAGATION Divide in late spring or sow fresh seed under glass. Plants will often self-seed.

NYMPHOIDES PELTATA

Nuphar
Pond lily
Although the pond lilies resemble true waterlilies, the flowers are smaller and carried above the water on thick stems in midsummer to mid-fall. They tolerate light shade and moving water.
• N. minima (N. pumila) has yellow flowers about 1 in (2.5 cm) across and almost translucent submerged foliage.
• N. lutea is similar to N. minima but needs a planting depth of 1–3 ft (30–60 cm).
• N. japonica (Japanese pond lily) has yellow, red-tinted flowers.
PLANTING DEPTH 6–18 in (15–45 cm)
SPREAD 4 ft (60 cm)
PROPAGATION Divide in late spring or summer.

Nymphoides peltata
Water fringe, floating heart
The leaves of this deciduous perennial look rather like those of a miniature waterlily and measure about 3 in (7.5 cm) across, but the dainty yellow flowers are more like those of a buttercup. These have fringed edges and are borne in small clusters about 2–3 in (5–8 cm) above the surface from midsummer to early fall. This is a useful plant for giving rapid surface cover early in the season before the true waterlilies become established, but it tends to be invasive.
PLANTING DEPTH 4–18 in (10–45 cm)
SPREAD 24 in (60 cm)
PROPAGATION Divide in late spring or summer.

DEEP-WATER AQUATICS

Orontium aquaticum
Golden club

This is a generally trouble-free, noninvasive plant, but it does need plenty of soil, so plant it in a deep, 6-in (15-cm) waterlily basket. Although it will grow in shallow water, if you want the leaves to float rather than stand erect, give it a final planting depth of at least 12 in (30 cm) of water. The leaves are blue-green with a silvery sheen, but it is the unusual flower spikes (spadix), carried in mid- to late spring and standing 1 ft (30 cm) or so above the water like gold and white pencils, that make this plant so appealing.
PLANTING DEPTH 3–12 in (7.5–30 cm)
SPREAD 24 in (60 cm)
PROPAGATION Seed sown in summer.

Polygonum amphibium
Willow grass, amphibious bistort

This perennial plant has long-stalked, floating leaves borne on stems that root at the nodes. In midsummer, pink flowers are held above the water. Will also grow in boggy margins.
PLANTING DEPTH To 18 in (45 cm)
SPREAD Indefinite
PROPAGATION By division.

Zantedeschia aethiopica
White arum

Although not fully hardy, this plant will survive the winter in most temperate areas and is well worth the risk, particularly if you have a larger pond. Look for the variety Z. a. "Crowborough," which is slightly more hardy than the species. The arumlike white spathes (flowers) rise 2 ft (60 cm) or more above glossy, arrow-shaped leaves throughout the summer. In the center of each spathe is a yellow, pokerlike spadix. A few weeks later, yellow berries will appear.
PLANTING DEPTH 6–12 in (15–30 cm)
SPREAD 14–18 in (35–45 cm)
PROPAGATION Divide mature clumps in spring.

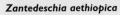

ORONTIUM AQUATICUM

MARGINALS

An attractive display of marginals at the edges of your pond will enhance its appearance and provide cover for wildlife. Although the top growth is visible above the water surface, the roots of the plants must be under water. Many will grow in bog gardens.

MARGINALS

Acorus calamus
Sweet flag

A strong-growing irislike grass with erect, swordlike leaves, which are sweetly scented when crushed.
• A. c. "Variegatus" has striking cream and yellow leaves with slightly wrinkled edges.
HEIGHT 30 in (75 cm)
SPREAD 24 in (60 cm)
PLANTING DEPTH 3–5 in (7.5–15 cm)
PROPAGATION Divide overcrowded clumps in spring or summer.

Alisma plantago-aquatica
Water plantain

This attractive plant has rosettes of bright green, oval leaves held on long stalks above the water, and a profusion of small, pale pink flowers, which are produced throughout the summer. Needs frequent deadheading to stop self-sown seedlings becoming a nuisance.
HEIGHT 30 in (75 cm)
SPREAD 18 in (45 cm)
PLANTING DEPTH To 6 in (15 cm)
PROPAGATION Sow seeds or divide in summer.

Butomus umbellatus
Flowering rush, water gladiolus

An attractive aquatic, bearing a mass of rose-pink flowers in summer. These are often fragrant. The tall, narrow leaves, triangular in section, are bronze-green at first, but lose the bronze tinge as they age. Suitable for all ponds.
HEIGHT 3 ft (90 cm)
SPREAD 18 in (45 cm)
PLANTING DEPTH 3–5 in (7.5–12.5 cm), but will also grow in boggy ground.
PROPAGATION Bulbils, which are produced on the rootstock, can be planted up. Mature clumps need dividing every three years, otherwise flowering will decline.

Caltha palustris
Marsh marigold or Kingcup

First to bloom in the water garden, the bright golden, buttercup-like flowers are held clear of the glossy dark green leaves. Marsh marigolds look best grown in small groups at the side of the pond or in a bog garden.
• C. p. var. alba is a white variety.
• C. p. "Flore Pleno" has double golden flowers. The latter two grow to 10 in (25 cm) and need a depth of 1 in (2.5 cm).
HEIGHT 24 in (60 cm)
SPREAD 18 in (45 cm)
PLANTING DEPTH To 3 in (7.5 cm)
PROPAGATION Divide overcrowded clumps in spring, or sow from seed.

CALTHA PALUSTRIS

MARGINALS

Cotula coronopifolia

Cotula coronopifolia
Golden buttons
The common name comes from the small, yellow, buttonlike flowers that cover it in summer. Although short lived and treated as an annual, it does self-seed freely. Suitable for a small pond.
HEIGHT 6 in (15 cm)
SPREAD 12 in (30 cm)
PLANTING DEPTH To 5 in (12.5 cm)
PROPAGATION Save seeds and sow in spring or transplant self-sown seedlings.

Houttuynia cordata

Houttuynia cordata "Chamaeleon," syn. H. c. "Tricolor"
Brilliantly colored red, yellow, and green heart-shaped leaves make Houttuynia a popular choice for the pond edge. The white, insignificant flowers are produced in spring. This hardy perennial thrives in wet conditions or shallow water but can become invasive and so should be planted in a container to contain its spread.
• The species *Houttuynia cordata* has red stems, blue-green foliage, and bears single white flowers each pierced by a cone-shaped center.
• *H. c.* "Flore Pleno" is a double white form.
HEIGHT 6–12 in (15–30 cm)
PLANTING DEPTH To 4 in (10 cm)
PROPAGATION Divide clumps in spring.

Iris species
Various species of iris are suitable for planting in and around the edges of the pond producing an array of lush green foliage and brightly colored flowers in all shades and mixes of white, blue, purple, and red.
• *I. laevigata* is the only species that needs to be grown in the water all the time. It produces its usually blue or white flowers in midsummer and sometimes again in early fall.
• *I. ensata* (Japanese iris) is a large-flowered iris that thrives both in and around the pond.
• *I. pseudacorus* (yellow flag) is attractive, but tends to be much too vigorous for all except the largest garden ponds.
• *I. setosa* bears its light blue or violet flowers in early summer.
• The eye-catching blooms of *I. versicolor* (blue flag) are variously variegated red-purple, green-yellow, and white, but this one does tend to seed rather too freely, and can become a nuisance.
HEIGHT From 18 in–3 ft (45–90 cm)
PLANTING DEPTH To 12 in (30 cm)
PROPAGATION Divide clumps as soon as the flowers fade.

MARGINALS

LOBELIA

Lobelia cardinalis

With purple-red leaves
and bright scarlet flowers,
this plant is equally at
home in a bog garden. It
is often attacked by slugs
and needs frost
protection.
HEIGHT 3 ft (90 cm)
SPREAD 9 in (23 cm)
PLANTING DEPTH 2–3 in
(5–7.5 cm)
PROPAGATION By division
in spring or cuttings in
summer.

Mentha aquatica
Water mint
A useful plant for softening
pond edges. The foliage is
aromatic when crushed
and the whorls of tiny
lavender flowers attract
bees in summer. Water
mint is vigorous, so plant in
a basket and trim back
stems to control its spread.
HEIGHT 9–12 in (23–30 cm)
PLANTING DEPTH To 3 in
(7.5 cm)
PROPAGATION Divide
mature plants in spring.

Menyanthes trifoliata
Bog bean
With its sprawling habit,
this is a good choice for
disguising pond edges. If
you are growing it in a
small pond, it is a good
idea to confine its spread
by planting it in a basket.
Its dark green leaves
resemble broad beans.
HEIGHT 9 in (23 cm)
SPREAD 12 in (30 cm)
PLANTING DEPTH 2-4 in
(5-10 cm)
PROPAGATION Divide
mature plants in spring.

Mimulus species
Monkey flowers
These yellow, orange, blue
or blotched snapdragon-
like flowers will brighten
up the pond margins in
summer. Equally happy in
wet conditions or shallow
water, they will readily
self-seed to produce
new plants.
HEIGHT From 12–18 in
(30–45 cm)
SPREAD 12 in (30 cm)
PLANTING DEPTH To 5 in
(12.5 cm)
PROPAGATION Raise from
seed or cuttings taken in
summer. Plants can also
be divided.

Myosotis scorpioides,
syn. M. palustris
Water forget-me-not
This is a water-loving
version of the popular
forget-me-not often seen
in flower in gardens in
spring. Free-flowering
over several weeks from
early to midsummer, it
will often creep over the
edge of the pond to root
in the surrounding wet
soil. The small bright blue
flowers each have a
central eye of pink,
yellow, or white flowers
and are produced in loose
clusters. The mid-green
leaves are narrow and
form sprawling mounds.
HEIGHT 6–9 in (15–23 cm)
There is also a shorter
growing form.
SPREAD 12 in (30 cm)
PLANTING DEPTH To 3 in
(7.5 cm)
PROPAGATION Raise from
seed or division.

MIMULUS
"LOTHIAN FIRE"

MARGINALS

PONTEDERIA CORDATA

Pontederia cordata
Pickerel weed
As one of only a handful of blue-flowered marginals, pickerel weed is a popular choice for the edge of a larger pond. A robust, deciduous perennial, it forms dense clumps of stems bearing handsome, narrow heart-shaped leaves, which are smooth and dark green in color. Dense spikes of blue flowers appear from within a leaf at the tip of the stem in late summer.
HEIGHT 30 in (75 cm)
SPREAD 18 in (45 cm)
PLANTING DEPTH 3–6 in (7.5–15 cm)
PROPAGATION Divide in late spring or sow fresh seed.

Ranunculus lingua "Grandiflorus"
Greater spearwort
Prized for its yellow buttercup flowers, some 2 in (5 cm) in diameter, which are freely produced throughout the summer, this marginal is a vigorous plant only suitable for larger ponds.
• *R. flammula* (lesser spearwort) has smaller flowers and does not grow so tall.
HEIGHT 2–3 ft (60–90 cm)
SPREAD 18 in (45 cm)
PLANTING DEPTH 3–6 in (7.5–15 cm)
PROPAGATION Divide mature plants in spring.

Sagittaria latifolia
American arrowhead, duck potato, wapato
The soft green leaves of this plant resemble arrowheads. Whorls of white flowers appear in summer.
HEIGHT 5 ft (1.5 m)
SPREAD 2 ft (60 cm)
PLANTING DEPTH 6 in (15 cm)
PROPAGATION Divide mature plants in spring.

RANUNCULUS FLAMMULA

Sisyrinchium californicum
Rather like a miniature iris in appearance but with starry bright yellow flowers. An ideal marginal for a smaller pond.
HEIGHT 12–24 in (30–60 cm)
SPREAD 12 in (30 cm)
PLANTING DEPTH To 1 in (2.5 cm)
PROPAGATION Divide in spring.

Typha minima
Dwarf cattail
An elegant plant that forms tufts of slender foliage at the pond's edge. The rust-brown flowers appear in late summer and mature into decorative seed heads.
HEIGHT 2 ft (60 cm)
SPREAD 12 in (30 cm)
PLANTING DEPTH 6 in (15 cm)
PROPAGATION Divide in spring.

Veronica beccabunga
European brooklime
Grown for its pretty dark blue flowers, which have a white eye. Although not evergreen, it retains its trailing foliage for much of the year and can be used to hide the edges of the pond. Cut back as stems become straggly.
HEIGHT 6–9 in (15–23 cm)
PLANTING DEPTH To 4 in (10 cm)
PROPAGATION Take cuttings in summer.

OXYGENATORS

Although they are not the most attractive or spectacular of all the aquatics, do not underestimate the importance of submerged, or partially submerged, oxygenating plants. Their foliage plays a vital role in keeping the water clear and supplies oxygen and shelter for fish.

OXYGENATORS

Cabomba caroliniana
Fish grass, Washington grass
This is a valuable oxygenator, used by fish for both food and for spawning. The plants form dense spreading hummocks of fan-shaped, coarsely divided bright green leaves. White flowers are borne in summer. It may be cut back by a hard frost.
PROPAGATION Take cuttings in summer or divide when dormant.

Callitriche hermaphroditica, syn. *C. autumnalis*
Autumn starwort
Ideal for a shallow pond, this plant produces star-shaped rosettes of leaves on the surface in summer, hence its common name. Under the water, it has masses of light green, cress-like leaves and is one of the few submerged plants that remains active throughout the year. It does, however, need to be kept in check.
PROPAGATION Take cuttings in spring or summer.

Ceratophyllum demersum
Hornwort
This oxygenator comes highly recommended, as it will grow in both sun or shade and is easily kept under control as it does not root. Weighted cuttings can be simply dropped into the water. The submerged whorls of dark green, feathery foliage are most attractive. In late fall the stems sink to the bottom and the plant overwinters as dormant buds, producing new stems in spring. This plant provides a popular habitat for aquatic insects.
PROPAGATION Take cuttings in spring or summer.

ELEOCHARIS ACICULARIS

Eleocharis acicularis
Needle spike-rush, hair grass
Dense mats of hairlike foliage create an attractive underwater effect. A good oxygenator and hiding place for small aquatic life and also evergreen.
PROPAGATION Divide in spring or summer.

Fontinalis antipyretica
Water moss, willow moss
An evergreen, slow-growing plant that thrives in sun or shade and prefers moving to still water. The bunches of branching stems are covered with short, moss-like, dark green leaves.
PROPAGATION Divide in spring or summer.

OXYGENATORS

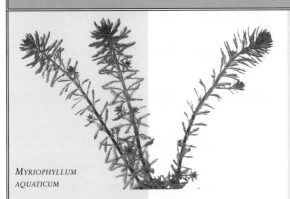

*MYRIOPHYLLUM
AQUATICUM*

Hottonia palustris
Water violet
One of the few flowering
oxygenators. The bright
green foliage below the
surface is finely divided
into fernlike leaves, while
flower spikes appear in
early summer. These rise
6–9 in (15–23 cm) above
the water level bearing
violetlike flowers, varying
in color from white to
lilac. The foliage dies
down in fall and the
plant overwinters as
dormant buds. It is not
an easy plant to get
established, needing
still and deep water.
PROPAGATION Take cuttings
in summer.

Myriophyllum aquaticum
Water milfoil,
Parrot's feather
Long trailing stems carry
very fine, feathery, olive-
green leaves. A very
effective oxygenating
plant, it is perfect for a
small pond and an ideal
habitat for fish spawn.

• *M. spicatum* has bronze-
green foliage and also
produces red-petaled
flowers an inch or so
above the water level.
Both these oxygenators
need to be kept in check.
PROPAGATION Take cuttings
in spring or summer.

Potamogeton crispus
Curled pondweed
Although large-leaved,
this oxygenator is fairly
restrained and does not
usually become invasive,
although it will spread
rapidly in mud. The
long wiry stems bear
straplike bronze or green
leaves, which are wavy-
edged and look rather
like seaweed. Insignificant,
small crimson and white
flowers appear just above
the water line in early
summer. It prefers moving
water to a still pond and
will tolerate cloudy or
shady water.
PROPAGATION Take stem
cuttings in spring or
summer.

Ranunculus aquatilis
Water buttercup, crowsfoot
This plant has two leaf
types: green and finely
divided below the water
and clover-shaped on the
surface. In early summer,
branched stems carry
masses of snow-white
buttercups with a yellow
center either on or a little
above the surface. After
flowering, the plant dies
back. This is a perfect
oxygenator for ponds of
all sizes as it does not get
out of hand, but it can be
difficult to establish.
PROPAGATION Take cuttings
in spring or summer.

Utricularia vulgaris
Greater bladderwort
This free-floating
perennial has feathery,
bronze-green, bladderlike
leaves that trap aquatic
insects. The flowers, which
are bright yellow with
red-brown streaks and
pouched, are held above
the water in summer.
PROPAGATION Separate
young plantlets in spring
or summer.

Vallisneria spiralis
Eelgrass, tape grass
A submerged perennial,
with spiraling, strap-
shaped, mid-green leaves
up to 32 in (80 cm) long.
The greenish flowers are
produced year round.
PROPAGATION By division
in spring or summer.

AROUND THE POND

Many garden plants will thrive in the permanently moist soil around the edges of a pond. Although they are often, somewhat misleadingly, sold as "bog plants," you don't need a bog garden to grow them. Just keep them well watered, particularly in summer.

PLANTS FOR THE PONDSIDE

Aruncus dioicus "Kneiffii"
Goat's beard
Similar in appearance to an astilbe, only smaller, this variety produces a froth of tiny, star-shaped creamy white flowers from mid- to late summer. The rich green leaves are feathery. Grows well in sun or partial shade.
The species (*A. dioicus*) is taller and makes an ideal specimen by a large pond.
HEIGHT 3 ft (90 cm)
SPREAD 20 in (51 cm)
PROPAGATION Divide in spring or fall.

Asplenium scolopendrium
Hart's-tongue fern
An easy-to-grow fern, which produces attractive evergreen, strap-shaped fronds. Once established, it produces spores that develop into young plants. It prefers dappled shade.
• A. s. Crispum Group and A. s. Marginatum Group look similar but are slightly smaller.
HEIGHT 18–30 in (45–76 cm)
SPREAD 18 in (45 cm)
PROPAGATION Sow spores in summer.

Astilbe species
Always a favorite around the pond, the astilbes have large feathery plumes of white, pink, and red held above deeply cut foliage, which is often coppery in color when it first emerges in spring.
HEIGHT 12–36 in (30–90 cm)
SPREAD 36 in (90 cm)
PROPAGATION Divide, in spring, every two or three years.

GALVANIZED
BATHTUB

PLANTS FOR THE PONDSIDE

Cardamine pratensis
Lady's smock, cuckoo flower
This plant's pretty purple, pink, or lilac summer flowers are a rich source of nectar for butterflies. The dark green leaves are composed of up to eight rounded or kidney-shaped leaflets.
HEIGHT 18 in (45 cm)
SPREAD 12 in (30 cm)
PROPAGATION Self-seeds.

Cyperus involucratus
Umbrella grass
This moisture-loving perennial will grow in the shallow margins of a pond or in the waterlogged soil of a bog garden. It thrives in warmer climates. The distinctive leaves are carried on tips of long, arching, slender green stems. In summer, small clusters of greenish brown flowers appear just above the leaves.
HEIGHT 2 ft (60 cm)
PROPAGATION Divide in spring.

Dierama pendulum
Angel's fishing rods
The bell-shaped, pinkish purple flowers are produced at the ends of grasslike leaves in summer.
HEIGHT 3–5 ft (90–150 cm)
SPREAD 6–8 in (15–20 cm)
PROPAGATION Divide in spring.

Filipendula ulmaria
Meadowsweet
A native bog plant with feathery spires of fragrant creamy white flowers in midsummer.
• The fernlike leaves of the variety F. "Aurea" start golden yellow in spring, turning to pale green as the season progresses.
HEIGHT 1–3 ft (30–90 cm)
SPREAD 12 in (30 cm)
PROPAGATION Divide large clumps in spring or fall.

Gunnera manicata
Giant rhubarb
This impressively sized plant is only suitable for larger water gardens. In summer it produces a bizarre, conelike flower spike, 3-plus ft (90-plus cm) high. In winter the crown will need protecting from frost, so cover it with straw or bracken.

HEIGHT 5–8 ft (1.5–2.4 m)
SPREAD 7 ft (2.1 m)
PROPAGATION Divide crowns in early spring.

Hemerocallis species
Daylily
Although each individual lilylike flower only lasts a day, most daylilies produce their trumpet-shaped flowers in succession over a period of up to six weeks in the summer. Modern hybrids, with their long, straplike leaves, come in a range of vibrant colors from bright yellow and orange to pink and maroon. The flowers have a delicate appearance and may have colored streaks or bands on the petals. They thrive best in a sunny location.
HEIGHT 2–3 ft (60–90 cm)
SPREAD 2–3 ft (60–90 cm)
PROPAGATION Divide clumps in spring or fall.

PLANTS FOR THE PONDSIDE

Hosta species
Plantain lilies

A group of handsome, shade and moisture-loving foliage plants. Many hostas produce arching spikes of white or lavender-blue flowers above distinctly colored leaves. Their main drawback is that slugs and snails find them irresistible, but a mulch of sharp gravel should help keep these pests at bay.
HEIGHT More than 18 in (45 cm)
SPREAD 1–3 ft (30–90 cm)
PROPAGATION Divide in spring.

Iris siberica

With their dense clumps of slender leaves topped with a mass of dainty flowers in early summer, the Siberian hybrids are a must for pondsides. The flowers are blue, white, and yellow, some attractively veined red.
HEIGHT More than 18 in (45 cm)
PROPAGATION Divide after flowering.

Lysimachia nummularia "Aurea"

This golden-yellow-leaved variety of creeping Jenny, will quickly spread to carpet a large area. Bright yellow flowers appear in summer.
HEIGHT 1–2 in (2.5–5 cm)
PROPAGATION Divide in spring or fall.

Lythrum salicaria
Purple loosestrife

Narrow spires of closely packed purple-red flowers add interest around the pond. Shorter hybrids are available in various shades of red
HEIGHT 2–4 ft (60–120 cm)
SPREAD 18 in (45 cm)
PROPAGATION Divide clumps in fall.

Matteuccia struthiopteris
Ostrich-feather, shuttlecock fern

A beautiful and hardy fern for the pondside, with its green and feathery fronds arranged like a shuttlecock.
HEIGHT 2 ft (60 cm)
SPREAD 18 in (45 cm)
PROPAGATION Divide crown in spring.

Osmunda regalis
Royal fern

This impressive fern grows particularly well by the water, but, owing to its size, it does need growing space and will suit a large pondside. The bright green fronds, which are pinkish when young, turn bronze in fall. In summer, pale brown flower spikes appear at the tops of the taller fronds. Cover the crown with straw or dead leaves over winter.
HEIGHT More than 4–6 ft (1.2–1.8 m)
SPREAD 3 ft (90 cm)
PROPAGATION Divide crown in spring.

LYSIMACHIA CILIATA

PLANTS FOR THE PONDSIDE

***Darmera peltata*, syn.
*Peltiphyllum peltatum***
Umbrella plant,
Indian rhubarb
Clusters of striking
white or pale pink
flowers on white-haired
stems appear in spring
before the umbrella-like
leaves unfurl.
HEIGHT 3 ft (90 cm)
SPREAD 2 ft (60 cm)
PROPAGATION Divide
crown in spring.

***Rheum palmatum*
"Rubrum"**
Ornamental rhubarb
Grown as a specimen
plant by the pond, this
variety of rhubarb is
hardy and will tolerate
sun or light shade. Its
handsome leaves, flushed
dark red, can spread 6 ft
(1.8 m) or more, so only
grow if there is plenty of
room at your pondside.
HEIGHT 8–10 ft (2.4–3 m)
PROPAGATION Divide
crown in spring.

Rodgersia pinnata
Sprays of numerous small
starry flowers, ranging
from yellowish white
through to pink and red,
are produced in summer.
The dark green leaves are
crinkled, heavily veined, and
glossy. Handsome foliage in
summer.
HEIGHT 2–3 ft (60–90 cm)
SPREAD 2 ft (60 cm)
PROPAGATION Divide clumps
in spring or fall.

Schizostylis coccinea
Kaffir lily
This attractive plant is
a useful addition around
the pond as the spikes of
crimson, red, and pink
flowers are produced in
abundance in late
summer into fall. The
leaves are upright,
narrow and swordlike,
with distinct midribs.
HEIGHT 2–3 ft (60–90 cm)
SPREAD 12 in (30 cm)
PROPAGATION Divide
in spring.

***Tradescantia* x
andersoniana
"Bilberry Ice"**
Spiderwort
Like other varieties in the
Andersoniana Group,
"Bilberry Ice" is clump-
forming perennial with
long, narrow, fleshy, green
leaves, which are
occasionally purple-tinted.
"Bilberry Ice" has white
and blue-streaked flowers
in summer.
HEIGHT More than 2 ft
(60 cm)
SPREAD 18 in (45 cm)
PROPAGATION Increase by
division in the fall.

Trollius europaeus
Globeflower
The globular, buttercup-
like flowers appear in late
spring to early summer.
The leaves are divided
into toothed leaflets.
HEIGHT Over 2 ft (60 cm)
SPREAD 18 in (45 cm)
PROPAGATION Divide in the
fall, every three years.

TRADESCANTIA
"BILBERRY ICE"

PART THREE: CONTAINER GARDENING

Growing plants in containers is perhaps one of the most rapidly expanding areas of gardening. Containers can provide focus points in a large garden, brighten up a patio, or enable homeowners with no garden at all to enjoy the pleasures of growing plants. Some of the most eye-catching and colorful displays are provided by window boxes, hanging baskets, and wall pots, bringing to life the exteriors of buildings.

CHOOSING CONTAINERS

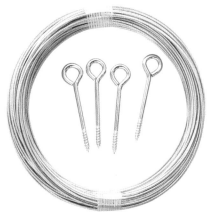

The growing idea of treating the garden or patio as an extension of the house – effectively, an "outdoor room" – has encouraged more careful planning to achieve stylish effects, using attractive containers as the "furniture." Manufacturers have been swift to respond to the interest in container gardening, and a vast range of high-quality products is available in all shapes, sizes, and styles.

PLANTING AND GROWING

No matter how beautiful the container, it needs plants to bring it to life. Choosing the right plants, and, just as importantly, knowing how to care for them and achieve the best from them, is vital if you are to enjoy your container gardening to the fullest.

This book will give you the guidance you need to make your containers a success, with tried-and-tested ideas for planting up and caring for plants in a whole range of containers. But never be afraid to experiment for yourself. One of the beauties of container gardening is that it is easy and relatively inexpensive to completely redesign your containers next season if you are not satisfied with the results of this season's efforts!

1
CHOOSING CONTAINERS

A wonderful and overwhelming selection of containers awaits anyone about to embark on container gardening. The range varies from plain and simple plastic pots, which even the smallest budget can afford, to stunningly beautiful and highly individual pieces of sculpture. In between are countless pots, tubs, troughs, and baskets in many different sizes, colors, shapes, and styles – surely something to suit everyone.

Plant containers are chosen not just for their looks – important though their appearance is. They must also be suitable for the plants that will grow in them, allowing room for roots to develop, good drainage, and the proper degree of insulation from severe weather. A careful balance between elegance and practicality is the keystone of successful container gardening.

CONTAINER GROWING

In the natural world, most plants grow in soil in the open ground. But as long as a plant can get a ready supply of water and nutrients, it is not really fussy where it puts down its roots. Any object that can hold sufficient soil to allow the roots to expand and support the plant's topgrowth is a potential plant container.

WHY USE POTS?

There are many reasons why we need, and like, to grow plants in containers. In courtyard gardens where there may be no natural soil for plants to grow or in homes that have no garden at all, the beauty of plants can still be enjoyed in wall pots, window boxes, and hanging baskets, which can equally turn a balcony or roof area into a living garden. There are many advantages to container growing in any garden:

■ **Flexibility** Plants in containers can be moved around to give different effects or used in groupings.

■ **Focal point** The container itself can be an object of beauty or can be chosen to show off a special plant.

■ **Close inspection** Container plants can be displayed in a raised position, where their fine detail and their scent can be more readily appreciated.

SPECIAL SOILS

Pre-packaged commercial soil mix is easier to handle and is often of better quality than garden soil, giving more consistent results from plants. If you live in an area with lime-rich soil but long to raise lime-hating plants in your garden, grow them in containers of special ericaceous soil mix.

■ **Young and old** Small children and older, less flexible gardeners enjoy the easy access of container gardens.

■ **Made to measure** The limited root space in a container restricts the overall size of many plants, allowing potentially large plants to be enjoyed in a small garden, whereas they would soon outgrow their space if raised in the open ground.

■ **Keeping trim** The more controlled growth often makes pruning and shaping plants easier, too.

■ **Prompt rewards** Containers are often quick and easy to plant: there is no backbreaking soil preparation required. Gardeners in a hurry can plant up containers to give instant results, using bedding plants that are about to bloom. An afternoon's easy work can produce a garden filled with color, which looks as though it has been established for weeks.

Containers can be planted up with trees, shrubs, and perennials that will thrive for many years, but most are used to display plants that last for just one season. This makes it easy to change the entire look of the garden every year or even every season.

IN SUN AND SHADE
The versatility of containers means that they can be sited to suit the need of most plants, either sun lovers or shade dwellers.

CONTAINER MATERIALS

Pots, tubs, and baskets are available in a variety of materials. Which one you choose will depend mainly on the style of your existing garden and house, your own preferences, and your budget. As far as plants are concerned, the type of material the container is made from is usually less important than its size and shape.

TRADITIONAL POTS

Color and texture are the key differences between the materials most commonly used in containers.

TERRA-COTTA
CONTAINER

■ **Terra-cotta** The wide range in price of terra-cotta containers, in their familiar warm, brick-red shade, depends on their size and design. Clay is porous, which can provide good growing conditions for plants, but it also means that clay containers are likely to break up in freezing weather unless they are guaranteed frostproof. They are also fragile and will shatter if dropped. Glazed earthenware containers, which are often finished in bright colors or a pattern, are rarely guaranteed frostproof.

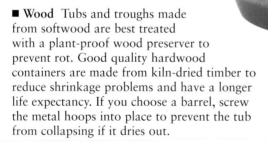

DECORATED
CERAMIC POT

■ **Wood** Tubs and troughs made from softwood are best treated with a plant-proof wood preserver to prevent rot. Good quality hardwood containers are made from kiln-dried timber to reduce shrinkage problems and have a longer life expectancy. If you choose a barrel, screw the metal hoops into place to prevent the tub from collapsing if it dries out.

■ **Stone** Natural stone comes in a range of colors and finishes and it weathers quickly to give an attractive "aged" effect. Stone containers are heavy and not suitable for moving around in the garden frequently or for balancing on ledges or balconies. They are surprisingly easy to damage unless treated carefully.

GLAZED
URN

ANTIQUE-FINISH
WALL MANGER

LOOK-ALIKES

Where weight, budget, and weather-resistance are important factors in your choice of container, imitation materials offer an attractive solution.

■ **Concrete** Commonly used to imitate natural stone, concrete is not quite as realistic as reconstituted stone. It is used to make a range of relatively inexpensive, heavyweight containers. Straightforward, simple shapes are the most effective style of pot, and are preferable to many of the whimsical designs offered.

■ **Reconstituted stone** Made from crushed stone chips mixed with concrete, this material is not as attractive as real stone, but it is considerably less expensive. Like genuine stone, it is heavy and unwieldy, and containers are likely to break if dropped or mistreated.

■ **Metal** Containers made of metal may be galvanized or treated to mimic antique lead. They are best used as outer covers for lightweight pots, with the inside lined or treated to prevent rusting. Wall mangers are an attractive alternative to wall pots.

■ **Plastic** Containers made of plastic are inexpensive and easy to handle. A matt finish and stylish detail can give them a very convincing appearance, especially terra-cotta look-alikes. Being lightweight, plastic containers are prone to toppling over and break easily with age.

■ **Fiberglass** Used to mimic stone, metal, or wood, fiberglass is lightweight and tends to be tougher than plastic. Fiberglass containers are easily blown over in strong winds and should be weighted down.

Stylish matt finish

Broad base reduces risk of overbalancing

PLASTIC
CONTAINER

CONTAINER STYLES

Because plants will grow in almost anything that will hold soil, the possible styles and types of container are almost endless. Whether you are looking to decorate a large expanse of wall, a patio area, or a window sill, there is a pot to suit your site.

POTS AND BASKETS

Probably the most familiar type of container, pots range from the simple, standard-shaped flowerpot to large patio tubs, planters, and troughs. The standard pot shape is round, with the sides tapering slightly toward the base, making it easier to slide a plant out of its container when repotting.

Large wicker baskets make ideal patio tubs, while a hanging basket adds interest and height in any garden. The traditional basket is an open-dish shape made from

PUNCH BOWL
ON PLINTH

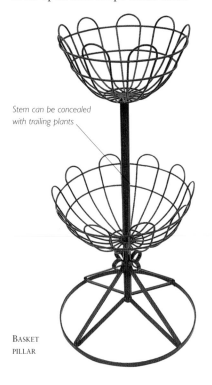

Stem can be concealed with trailing plants

BASKET
PILLAR

a network of plastic-covered wire, and hung on chains. Plants are positioned in the top as well as through the sides of the basket to give an all-round effect that covers the basket (see p. 298). Variations include square, slatted-wood baskets, rigid metal baskets with lengthwise slits, and freestanding tiers of baskets held by a central pillar. Remember that all wire baskets need a liner to retain the soil. Solid-sided baskets are often fitted with a saucer, making them easier to plant up and less prone to drying out.

FOR WALLS AND LEDGES

There are several types of container designed to suit homes without any growing space, or where hardstanding is limited.

■ **Wall pots** A display of wall pots helps to give a three-dimensional effect to a garden and makes good use of all available space. Wall pots are generally small, and may be rectangular, half round, or almost completely round, with one side flattened to allow them to be fixed against a wall. Decorative versions add interest to plain walls and containers made in the form of heads, hands, or animal masks can provide an element of fun.

■ **Window boxes** Long, rectangular containers, usually of wood or plastic, are intended for display on window ledges. They can either be held by brackets, or the boxes may

WICKER HORN OF PLENTY

fit inside a decorative outer case, which is firmly fixed in position (see pp. 282–83). Shallow wooden and stone troughs are ideal for shallow-rooted alpine plants and can be used as window boxes or displayed in freestanding trough holders.

NOVELTY CONTAINERS

All manner of unusual items can be turned into containers, limited only by your ingenuity and, frequently, your sense of humor. It is usually old and worn-out objects that find a new lease on life as plant containers: wheelbarrows, chimney pots, sinks, tires, logs, – even old boots and lavatory pans have been planted up. Provided that there is adequate drainage and sufficient soil you should succeed. Experiment with objects of little or no value, so that they can, if necessary, be thrown away at the end of the season.

CERAMIC FROG PLANTER

MAKING A CHOICE

No matter how handsome the container, its appearance will be ruined by plants that are failing to thrive, or that are ill suited to its shape. To avoid disappointment, it is best to prepare a checklist of practical considerations so that you find the right pot for the right site. If you really can't resist an elegant but impractical piece, treat it as an ornament and leave it unplanted.

THINKING AHEAD

It is all too easy to select a container just because it is beautiful, without giving too much thought to its suitability for growing plants.

■ **Weight** The portability of a container is an important consideration, especially if you intend to change its position in the garden at regular intervals.

■ **Size** Any container must hold sufficient volume of soil or soil mix to support the plant for at least one season – longer if it is a perennial planting. It must also balance the topgrowth of the plant, so that it is not likely to become top heavy and fall over.

■ **Shape** It is not just the volume of soil that a container holds that is important; it is the ratio of its surface area to its depth. A wide, shallow sink may hold exactly the same amount of soil mix as a tall, slender pot, but the soil mix in the sink will dry out more rapidly and be of little value to a plant that has a deep, penetrating taproot. Shallow containers suit only shallow-rooted plants such as alpines and short-term bedding plants – even then they are likely to need frequent watering. Deep containers are essential for trees, shrubs, and perennials that have a long life expectancy.

DRAINAGE

It is vital that surplus water can drain away from the soil mix in containers; if the roots become waterlogged, the plant will die. In the open ground, water has plenty of opportunity to seep away, but in the restricted space of a container it can easily become trapped, and the effects of overwatering soon become evident.

Plastic containers often have several small drainage holes around the edge of the base; in stone and clay containers there may be one large, central hole. If the container has no drainage holes, it may be possible to add them yourself; otherwise place a deep layer of broken rubble at the base as a reservoir for excess water.

AWKWARD SHAPES

Choose fancy containers carefully as they may be impractical when it comes to planting or repotting. The necks of some tall pots, such as ali-baba jars, are narrower than the waists. This gives an elegant appearance, but makes it impossible to remove plants for repotting once their roots have grown into the widest area. Sometimes this problem can be overcome by setting a separate pot to contain the plant in the top of the jar, where it will be concealed, but can be lifted out easily.

PICK 'N' MIX POTS
A collection of containers in a variety of shapes
and styles and made from different materials
makes an attractive grouping on a patio.

Woven and wire containers drain
very freely and demand more
attention to watering than others.
Hanging baskets and wall pots hold
a large number of plants in a small
area, and so need frequent watering
and supplementary feeding during
the season to keep them at their best.

Warning

Check that your container is made
from plant-friendly material. Some
treated wooden or metal tubs may
contain chemicals that are toxic to
plants: if you are in any doubt, line
the containers with plastic sheeting
or seal them with bitumen-based
paint to prevent minerals or chemicals
from seeping into the soil mix.

POINTS TO CONSIDER

As well as being pleasing to look at and effective plant holders, containers need to suit your requirements, the size and situation of your garden, and the style or effect that you want to achieve. The most important consideration of all is that they should not demand any more of your time than you are able to spare.

TIME AND EFFORT

One advantage of a container garden is its flexibility; it allows you to reposition the containers and change their plants around to achieve a new look. You will often want to bring forward a plant when it is at its best, and return it to a less prominent position when its moment of glory is over. If you are growing short-term plants such as seasonal bedding, the

SHALLOW
DISH OF HERBS

containers will also need to be cleared out and replanted regularly. These tasks will be made much easier if you choose containers that are easy to lift, so opt for models that are moderately light in weight and not too large to handle.

If you intend to use plants that will stay in place for years, then stone troughs and heavy, awkward items present less of a problem. For gardeners with little time on their hands, a few large containers will require less attention than lots of small ones, and laborsaving ideas such as self-watering containers are worth considering.

STAYING PUT

Once a large pot has been planted up, it becomes quite an obstacle to move. Make sure that you are happy with its position before filling with soil mix and planting up.

PAIRING UP

The size and shape of the container should complement the plant growing in it (and vice versa). An elegant, statuesque container is usually most satisfying when balanced by a tall, graceful plant; while an intricate design on an ornate pot will be wasted if it is obscured by the foliage and flowers of trailing plants.

Some gardeners may be prepared to choose the container first and select the plants to suit it, but if you have a strong idea of the type of plants you want to grow, choose the containers with those plants in mind. To do justice to an arrangement of mixed plants, choose a wide-necked container or trough. If you want to grow tall plants that will need support, make sure that the container is deep enough to hold the base of the support firmly.

CLIMATE AND LOCATION

Variations in climate and prevailing weather conditions can have a considerable impact on certain types of containers; indeed, some are better suited to particular regions and areas. For example, heavy, stable items are more practical on a windswept site; wooden planters will need more frequent weatherproofing when used in exposed and coastal areas.

In areas that experience severe winters, choose frostproof containers with thick walls that will provide some protection for plant roots. Look for containers that offer good insulation for the roots when growing plants in a baking hot, sunny position, as it will help to keep the roots cool and moist. Small and shallow containers should be avoided in such a situation, as they dry out very rapidly.

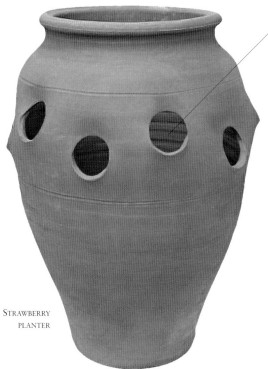

Fruits are trained through planting pockets

STRAWBERRY PLANTER

STRAWBERRY PLANTERS

If you would like to try growing something for your kitchen, you might like to consider using a terra-cotta strawberry planter. These containers are fitted with side planting pockets through which herbs or strawberries can be trained. Provided that the plants are fed and watered regularly, you can count on a healthy crop each summer.

WHICH POT WHERE?

The beauty of containers is that they are equally at home in the country or the city, on the grounds of a large classical mansion or on the terrace of an ultramodern apartment building. To achieve the best possible effect in a chosen location, bear these points in mind.

POSITIONING CONTAINERS

Plants play an important role in linking a house with its garden; they help to soften hard landscaping and add color, fragrance, and interest. When grown in containers they can be kept tidy and under control more easily than in the open garden and fulfil the role of outdoor "furniture."

■ **Patio** With its practical hard surface and proximity to the house, the patio tends to become an outdoor room. Freestanding pots, tubs, and troughs of all shapes and sizes all suit patios, according to the space available, while wall pots and hanging baskets can be used to decorate an adjoining wall or fence.

■ **Paths and steps** A few well-placed containers clustered at various points or sited at regular intervals along a plain garden path can improve its appearance greatly and mark out its route from a distance.

AN OLD BATHTUB ADDS
INTEREST TO A FORGOTTEN
CORNER OF A GARDEN

Wide flights of steps also form an ideal display area – raising plants often helps to increase their impact.

Most freestanding containers can be used on paths and steps, but they and their contents should be small and neat enough not to interfere with people's progress past them. Wall pots and window boxes can be particularly effective fixed to the tops of balustrades and handrails, but again must not present a hazard.

■ **Walls** In gardens where there is no growing space at all, walls are particularly important to increase the area available for plants. Wall pots and mangers, hanging baskets, and window boxes are the containers to be used here. They must all be fixed securely to the wall and positioned in such a way as to make routine maintenance tasks such as watering and deadheading easy.

■ **Balconies and roof gardens**
A balcony or roof garden is an ideal surface for plants, but it is important to assess the load-bearing capability of the area. Site lightweight freestanding pots at the strongest points (usually around the edges). Adorn bordering walls or railings with troughs and window boxes.

ROOFTOP TERRAIN
Exposed to strong daytime sun, this rooftop garden provides the desert-like conditions enjoyed by cactuses and succulents.

GARDEN STYLES

There are no hard-and-fast rules about the correct use of containers in garden design – it is all a matter of personal preference. Whether your containers blend harmoniously with the garden style or provide a complete contrast, full of impact – both are equally effective.

SETTING THE TONE

Many gardens do not have a particular style of their own, and in small gardens especially, it is often the containers that will set the style. A distinct style can be achieved by selecting containers made from one type of material. A mixture of different materials tends to give an unsettled look but can be effective where an informal look is required. Generally, the most restful and pleasing effects are obtained by suiting containers to the style of your garden; bold contrasts require more courage and artistic flair to succeed. The material and style of the house is another factor to consider. An informal garden is more appropriate than a starkly modern design for a country cottage, and the regular lines of a formal garden suit a classical style house. Many gardens will fall into one of these categories.

■ **Formal** A formal style is made up of regular, symmetrical shapes and straight lines. The types of plants used may include clipped shrubs and topiary shapes, regular beds bordered by low hedging, and color-themed plantings. The overall impression is of neatness and regularity.

In a formal garden, containers should be made from one material, or just two or three different but blending materials. Matching pairs are essential when used to flank a doorway or to line a path.

■ **Informal** An informal style makes use of flowing lines and irregular forms rather than hard edges and symmetrical shapes. Plants are allowed to billow and mingle and are not kept rigidly clipped and shaped. Garden paths are more likely to meander than march straight through the center of the plot.

A TASTE OF MOROCCO
Hot, spicy colors, cool blue water, and ali baba-style containers conjure up the exotic, sultry charms of a Moroccan courtyard.

SPRING GREENS
The look of a traditional kitchen garden
is translated into the modern style by
the bold lines of this aluminum trough.

A mixture of styles and types of
container suits an informal setting,
with mixed groups of odd numbers
rather than rows of matching pots.

■ **Practical** Containers can be used
with great success for growing
a wide range of fruit and vegetables
(see pp. 236–37); even hanging
baskets and window boxes can
provide salad crops and herbs, and
the delights of early strawberries.
Straightforward plastic containers
or rustic-style earthenware usually
look more appropriate than classical,
highly ornamental containers.

■ **Classical** Stone balustrades,
Greco Roman-style urns and vases
on stone plinths and pedestals, all
in a strictly formal setting, help to
create a timeless classical style. Look

for containers with classical
decoration, such as lion masks,
acanthus, and foliage swags.
A fountain, bust, or sundial in
matching materials will further
enhance the classical theme.

■ **Modern** A modern style is
particularly suited to the town
gardens of contemporary buildings.
The clean, uncompromising lines of
bold, unornamented containers can
be very striking. Steel, fiberglass,
and plastic are common materials,
in either neutral or strong colors.

■ **Oriental** Glazed earthenware pots,
which are usually colorwashed and
decorated with a Chinese- or
Japanese-style design, are very
attractive and often inexpensive.
In a simple setting such as a gravel
garden, enhanced by a sympathetic
planting of bamboo or Japanese
maple, they can provide a calm,
relaxing atmosphere. A small water
feature will add authenticity.

CREATING AN EFFECT

Once you have chosen your containers, you need to assess the best possible position for them in the garden to achieve maximum impact. In the right spot, containers can help to create illusions, altering the size and proportions of your garden area.

ANOTHER DIMENSION

A range of containers enables more than just one level to be used for growing plants. Window boxes, wall pots, and hanging baskets can be placed on adjacent surfaces for a three-dimensional effect. When a planting theme based on similar shades or textures is applied to all containers, it helps to link the surfaces together in a satisfying way. Extra interest will be added by using groups of containers to emphasize or create changes of level.

The hard angles of a patio and other paved areas can be softened by containers of flowing or trailing plants. The transition from a paved area to grass or flower borders can be smoothed by containers of plants placed where the two meet.

LARGE GARDENS

In a large garden, a container can prove useful as a focal point; for example, a grand, dramatically styled urn placed on a pedestal for extra height, and planted with a mixture of upright and trailing plants, will simply demand attention.

Containers may also be used as "pointers" to draw the eye to a feature, perhaps a flight of steps, or to a different aspect of the garden. They can also be used to make a garden's dimensions look different. Long, narrow plots appear wider if grouped containers are placed at intervals along both sides of the garden. By using pots that gradually decrease in size the farther away they are from the viewpoint, a small area can be made to look larger.

VISUAL TRICKS

• Unless the size of the container is deliberately being used to create optical illusions, it should be kept in scale with the area in which the container is sited. Very small containers will be lost in a large garden, and a grand, imposing container on a tiny patio can look ridiculously out of proportion.

• Avoid pairing a brilliant display of plants with a very striking, decorative container – they will vie with each other for attention and reduce impact.

• Sympathetic planting is essential. If the container is the main point of interest, the planting should be discreet but complementary. If the focus centers on a bold display of plants, a simple, neutral-colored container is usually the most effective. Delicate-looking foliage, such as ferns, is best offset against a plain terra-cotta pot.

LIVING SCREENS

Many gardens or balconies contain or overlook an object or area that is not particularly attractive. A group of container plants can be the perfect way to disguise an eyesore, forming a living screen that can be replaced, if necessary, as it dies down or passes its best. Containers can liven up a dull area of the garden temporarily – plants in full flower can be sunk in to the soil in their containers to boost up a border when it is needed. Later, when the border starts to come into its own, the container plants can be removed and used elsewhere.

TO THE POINT
Geometric, electric blue containers, raised on metal tripods, accentuate the striking spiky foliage of blue grass (Festuca glauca).

GROUPING CONTAINERS

Dotting odd containers here and there around the garden is never the best way to use them – they will have far more impact if several are grouped together. Grouping also makes regular tasks, such as watering, easier and will improve growing conditions for the plants.

Grouped pots do not have to be made from the same material, but the best effect is obtained if they are all of a similar shade and texture; red sandstone, brick, and terra-cotta blend harmoniously. Containers grouped in odd numbers – three, five, or seven – have a more satisfying appearance than groups of even numbers (unless they are lined up in pairs in a formal setting).

A triangular layout makes an effective arrangement. The apex of the triangle may be in the center of the group or to one side; if no pot is tall enough to form an apex, stand one of them on a concealed brick to give extra height. A wall pot or hanging basket could also be used to form the apex.

Keep fluidity in the display by linking the plantings – either through a common color or by making their outlines "flow" from one container to the next.

PAINT EFFECT

• If your budget will not stretch to buying large numbers of the same container, or if you already have a wide selection of containers made from different materials, you can help to unify them to form groups by painting them.

• Unglazed terra-cotta and earthenware pots are easy to color with matt-finish paints; metal and plastic containers usually need coating with primer before applying the paint.

• Sand down glossy plastic to provide a key for the paint. Some of the best effects can be obtained by using two-toned colors to give a "distressed" effect; vary the emphasis of the colors within the group to avoid too regular an appearance.

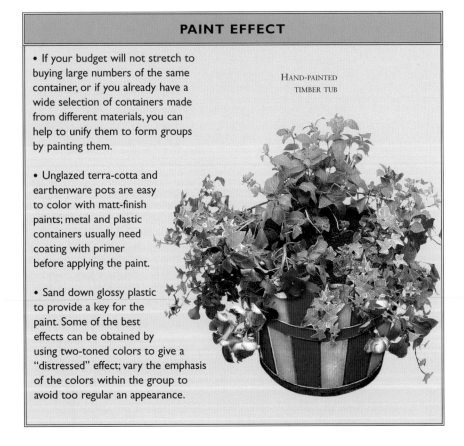

HAND-PAINTED
TIMBER TUB

2
PLANTS FOR CONTAINERS

Some container plants give their all to provide a glorious show of color for a single season; others will survive to give pleasure for many years. The choice of suitable plants is extensive: architectural plants provide strong shapes and outlines; flowers and foliage supply a wide variety of color and form; softly flowing trailing plants make an effective contrast to stiffly upright specimens.

A pleasing balance of shape and form, texture, and color can be obtained from a mix of annuals, perennials, bulbs, shrubs, and trees. While the range of plants that will grow successfully in containers is surprisingly wide, it pays to know which ones adapt most happily to container growing.

PLANT ESSENTIALS

Virtually any plant can be grown in a container for at least part of its life – but that does not mean that all plants are suitable or worthwhile for growing in a container garden. A look at the basic requirements of plants helps in our understanding of the part that containers play.

WHAT PLANTS NEED

All garden plants require water and dissolved minerals; air, containing oxygen and carbon dioxide; and light, which is converted into energy for development and growth.

In most instances, the water and mineral solutions that a plant needs for growth are supplied by soil, from where they are taken up by the plant's roots. The surface area of the roots is increased by the presence of millions of tiny root hairs that absorb moisture in the soil. As the root system spreads it provides a firm base for the plant, allowing the aerial parts to develop above the ground.

TAKING ROOT

Different types of plants have different types of root systems, varying from a single, large, deep-growing taproot to a shallow mat of many slender, branching roots.

Only a tiny amount of soil may be needed to keep a plant growing: weeds spring up through tarmac and paving, and alpine plants survive on pinches of soil in mountain crevices. However, once the supply of water and nutrients in the soil is exhausted, the plant dies. In general, the larger and more vigorous the plant, the more water and nutrients it needs to grow – and, in theory, the larger the volume of soil that is needed to supply them.

Leaves absorb oxygen and sunlight for growth and development.

Dissolved nutrients are carried up to the foliage by the plant's stem or trunk.

Plants take up water through their roots. The larger the plant, the bigger its root system, so the bigger the volume of soil it will require.

HALF-STANDARD *CUPRESSUS ARIZONICUS*

Pinching out dead flowers will help prolong flowering.

Adding a liquid fertilizer to the water once a week helps promote lush green foliage.

A SUMMER DISPLAY OF SURFINIA

Self-watering pot has a built-in reservoir of water to help prevent the soil from drying out.

Plastic containers help retain moisture in soil.

Position plant in a sheltered but airy, well-lit, preferably partly shaded, spot.

GROWING IN CONTAINERS

A plant container of any sort limits the volume of soil available to the roots. However, in a garden, we can make sure that a supply of water and nutrients always remains available to the plants, even after the soil's own supply has run out. Regular watering and the application of fertilizers can keep plants developing healthily for many months and even years.

Once a plant's roots become physically constricted by the lack of space in the container, the development of the topgrowth will be affected, too; while still healthy, growth will be slowed despite feeding and watering, and the plant will usually remain smaller than if grown in the open ground. This can often be a benefit, because it allows potentially large plants to be grown successfully in small gardens.

In other cases, however, a plant in a container may never be able to develop sufficiently to reach the stage at which it would become attractive, making it unsuitable for container growing. Very large, fast-growing trees and shrubs, and plants with deep taproots, are not usually the best choices for growing in containers, because the root will never manage to reach the depth it requires and growth will be stunted.

Some plants can be grown very happily for a single season in a container and are then fit only for throwing away; they are replaced by new plants in the following year. Others can be grown for several years in the same container, with just occasional repotting to keep them healthy and looking good (see p. 255).

Plants are often broadly grouped by their natural cycle of growth. The main categories are annuals and biennials; perennials; bulbs; and trees and shrubs. The next few pages highlight suitable container-friendly examples from each category.

ANNUALS AND BIENNIALS

When you are looking for an instant display of color and foliage to brighten up your garden throughout the summer season, look no further than the wide variety offered by annuals and biennials – the number-one choice for container gardens.

A SEASON OF FLOWERS

Most annuals and bedding plants are grown for their colorful flowers, although some are valued for their foliage. Their form may be bushy, spreading, or upright; trailing varieties spill over the sides of pots, baskets, and troughs, while climbers make good, fast-growing screens.

Many annuals, biennials, and bedding plants used to be sold only in mixed colors, but single shades are becoming more common, making effective color scheming possible.

An annual plant is one that grows from seed, flowers, and dies within a single-growing season; a biennial grows from seed in one season, overwinters, then flowers and dies the following season. Annuals and biennials can be further subdivided.

POPULAR ANNUALS AND BIENNIALS

HARDY ANNUALS	HALF-HARDY ANNUALS	BIENNIALS
Calendula officinalis Pot marigold	*Ageratum houstonianum* Floss flower	*Campanula medium* Canterbury bell
Centaurea cyanus Cornflower	*Antirrhinum majus* Snapdragon	*Dianthus barbatus* Sweet William
Clarkia amoena Satin flower	*Begonia semperflorens* Bedding begonia	*Matthiola incana* Brompton stock
Helichrysum bracteatum Everlasting flower	*Callistephus chinensis* China aster	*Althaea rosea* Hollyhock
Lathyrus odoratus Sweet pea	*Impatiens walleriana* Impatiens	*Bellis perennis* Double daisy
Nigella damascena Love-in-a-mist	*Papaver nudicaule* Iceland poppy	*Digitalis purpurea* Foxglove
Papaver rhoeas Shirley poppy	*Pelargonium* Bedding geranium	*Erysimum cheiri* Wallflower
Tropaeolum majus Nasturtium	*Phlox drummondii* Annual phlox	*Myosotis sylvatica* Forget-me-not
Viola x wittrockiana Pansy	*Portulaca grandiflora* Sun plant	*Viola x wittrockiana* **Floral Dance series** Winter-flowering pansy
	Salvia splendens Salvia	

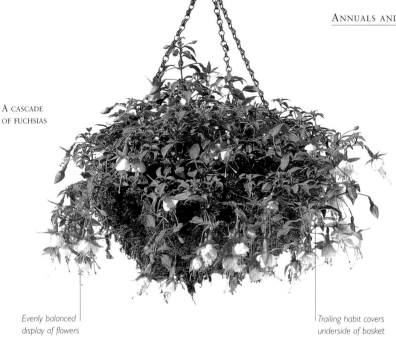

A CASCADE
OF FUCHSIAS

Evenly balanced
display of flowers

Trailing habit covers
underside of basket

■ **Hardy annuals** Fully hardy means that plants can withstand frost, so they can be sown at any time in the spring, or sometimes in the preceding fall for early flowering plants.

■ **Half-hardy annuals** Half-hardy indicates that plants will be killed by frost, so they must not be taken outdoors until all risk of frost is over in spring; their flowering season is cut short by the first frosts in fall.

■ **Perennials treated as annuals** (or biennials) Plants that fall under this category botanically are not true annuals or biennials – they do not die after flowering – but they are discarded at the end of their first flowering season in the garden because their appearance deteriorates in their second and subsequent years. Here, they may be referred to as annuals or biennials for simplicity.

■ **Bedding plants** Bedding is a general term used for many types of annual and tender perennial that are usually bought as young plants and transplanted into the garden or containers for one season only.

Bedding plants are discarded after flowering, although some tender perennials are worth overwintering in a greenhouse or conservatory to provide cuttings for the following spring.

POPULAR CLIMBERS AND TRAILERS

CLIMBERS	TRAILERS
Convolvulus tricolor Convolvulus	***Anagallis monelli*** Blue pimpernel
Eccremocarpus scaber Chilean glory flower	***Convolvulus sabatius***
Ipomoea tricolor Morning glory	***Fuchsia*** Some varieties
Lathyrus odoratus Sweet pea	***Lobelia erinus*** Lobelia
Thunbergia alata Black-eyed Susan	***Lotus berthelotii***
Tropaeolum majus Nasturtium	***Pelargonium peltatum*** Ivy-leaf geranium
	Sutera grandiflora Purple glory plant
	Verbena x hybrida

PERENNIALS

The most familiar use for perennials is in perennial borders, but many species make excellent container plants. They are nowhere near as popular for container growing as bedding plants, and this is a shame, as they have great potential.

COLOR AND FOLIAGE

A perennial is a plant that persists from year to year; normally its topgrowth dies down in winter and new shoots appear from the crown at or below ground level in spring. A few perennials, such as euphorbia and bergenia, are evergreen, but tender perennials, which cannot withstand temperatures that fall to below freezing, are often treated as annuals and simply discarded after their first flowering season; others can be kept from year to year as long as they are brought under cover in the winter. Commercial plant breeders have introduced a wide range of short, compact varieties of perennials, many of which are ideal for growing in containers.

Perennial plants tend to increase their spread over several seasons, which can present a problem where more than one plant occupies a container – a strong-growing plant will eventually swamp a weaker one. Growing perennials as single specimens in containers overcomes this problem; dramatic species such as spiky *Phormium tenax* or the golden foliage of hakonechloa make splendid candidates.

The flowering season for perennials runs from early or mid-summer to early fall; the foliage may persist for longer. The one drawback of growing perennials in containers is that they remain dormant over winter. This means that the containers cannot be planted up with winter and spring bedding. The best solution is to use a selection of perennials, combined with evergreen shrubs, to provide an extended season of interest.

SPIKES OF COLOR
Lupins grown in individual containers provide spikes of instant summer color, ranging from creamy yellow to delicious raspberry pink.

PERENNIALS FOR GROWING IN CONTAINERS

FLOWERING

Cosmos atrosanguineus
Chocolate cosmos

Dianthus species
Pinks

Diascia cordata and hybrids

Erysimum "Bowles Mauve"

Geranium "Johnson's Blue"
Cranesbill

Lysimachia "Outback Sunset"
Loosestrife

Paeonia lactiflora
Peony

Penstemon hybrids

Phygelius aequalis
Cape figwort

Primula vulgaris
Primrose

DIANTHUS SPECIES

FOLIAGE

Ajuga reptans "Multicolor"
Bugle

Alchemilla mollis
Lady's mantle

Arum italicum
Lords and ladies

Bergenia hybrids
Elephants' ears

Euphorbia amygaloides "Purpurea"
Purple wood spurge

Festuca glauca
Blue grass

Hakonechloa macra "Aureola"

Helichrysum petiolare

Helleborus argutifolius

Heuchera micrantha var. diversifolia "Palace Purple"
Coral flower

Hosta species and cultivars
Plantain lily

Ophiopogon planiscapus "Nigrescens"
Black grass

Stachys byzantina
Lambs' ears

Phormium tenax
New Zealand flax

TENDER

(Protect from frost)

Argyranthemum frutescens
Marguerite

Brugmansia sanguinea
Angels' trumpets

Canna hybrids
India shot plant

Dahlia cultivars

Gazania cultivars

Osteospermum cultivars

Tibouchina urvilleana
Brazilian spider flower

FALL FLOWERS

Aster novi-belgii
Michaelmas daisy

Chrysanthemum cultivars

Dahlia cultivars

Helenium autumnale
Sneezewort

Liriope muscari
Lilyturf

Sedum spectabile
Ice plant

WINTER INTEREST

Bergenia cordifolia
Elephants' ears

Euphorbia characias
Wood spurge

Festuca glauca
Blue grass

Lamium maculatum "Beacon Silver"
Deadnetttle

Phormium tenax
New Zealand flax

Heuchera "Pewter Moon"
Coral flower

FLOWERING BULBS

Bulbs are easy to plant, flower reliably in their first season, and make compact growth, so in many ways they are ideal for growing in containers. They can be mass planted to make a truly spectacular display for relatively little effort.

WHAT IS A BULB?

A bulbous plant is one in which part of the plant is swollen with a supply of stored food. This store enables the plant to survive dormancy and resume growth when conditions are right. Bulbous plants include bulbs, corms, tubers, and rhizomes, though it is sometimes difficult to tell them apart simply from their appearance.

■ **Bulb** A bulb consists of fleshy scales (modified leaves) attached to a basal plate and is often covered by dry, papery skin, or tunic. Narcissus, tulip, and hyacinth are all bulbs.

■ **Corms** From the outisde, corms look similar to bulbs but they are swollen stem bases, not scales.

Unlike a bulb, a corm disappears as its food supply is used up, and is replaced each year. Popular corms include crocus and freesia.

■ **Tubers** Like corms, tubers are also swollen stems, but unlike corms they do not have a basal plate – roots may grow all over the surface, and growth buds are carried at several points on the surface, too. Examples include cyclamen and begonia.

■ **Rhizomes** Rhizomes often grow horizontally at or just under the soil surface; border iris is probably the best-known type.

AFTERCARE

The main season of interest for bulbs is spring, although the earliest of these appear in winter, and there is a good selection of useful summer-flowering bulbs, too. Once bulbs have finished flowering they can be planted in open ground if space is available; leave the foliage until it dies down naturally to provide a food supply for next year's growth. Alternatively, bulbs can be discarded in the same way as bedding plants.

A mixed container planted with shrubs, bedding, or annuals, to take over once the bulbs have flowered can be successful, but remember to feed the bulbs with liquid fertilizer to ensure a repeat performance the following year.

SPRING-FLOWERING BULB

Nose of bulb

Protective paperlike skin

Basal plate

BULBS FOR ALL SEASONS

BULBS FOR WINTER

Chionodoxa luciliae
Glory of the snow

Crocus ancyrensis
Golden bunch crocus

Crocus tommasinianus

Cyclamen coum

Cyclamen persicum

Eranthis hyemalis
Winter aconite

Galanthus nivalis
Common snowdrop

**Galanthus nivalis
"Flore Pleno"**
Double common snowdrop

Iris danfordiae

Narcissus cyclamineus
Miniature daffodils

TULIPS IN A MIXED PLANTING

BULBS FOR SPRING

Anemone blanda

Convallaria majalis
Lily of the valley

Crocus chrysanthus

Erythronium dens-canis
Dog's tooth violet

Fritillaria imperialis
Crown imperial

**Ornithogalum
umbellatum**
Star of Bethlehem

Hyacinthus orientalis
Hyacinth

Muscari azureum
Grape hyacinth

Narcissus cultivars
Daffodil

Tulipa cultivars
Tulip

BULBS FOR SUMMER

Allium species
Ornamental onion

Alstroemeria cultivars
Peruvian lily

Begonia x tuberhybrida

Canna hybrida
Indian shot

Dahlia cultivars

Gladiolus callianthus

Iris cultivars

**Lilium species and
cultivars**

Ranunculus asiaticus
Persian buttercup

**Rhodohypoxis baurii
"Douglas"**

Tigridia pavonia
Peacock flower

BULBS FOR THE FALL

Amaryllis belladonna
Belladonna lily

Colchicum autummnale
Autumn crocus

Crocus speciosus

Crocus laevigatus

Cyclamen hederifolium

Dahlia cultivars

Leucojum autumnale
Autumn snowflake

Merendera montana

Nerine bowdenii

Schizostylis coccinea
Kaffir lily

Sternbergia lutea
Autumn daffodil

Zephyranthes candida
Rainflower

TREES AND SHRUBS

Whether grown as specimens or as a backdrop to colorful borders, trees and shrubs help to form the framework of a garden. This applies just as strongly to container gardens, where they can act as "reference points" around which to plan the rest of the planting.

SIZE MATTERS

The distinction between a tree and a shrub is not as clear-cut as it might first appear, as a degree of overlap exists between the categories. In general, trees have a single clear stem forming a trunk, while shrubs usually have several small stems arising from the base; trees are normally also taller than shrubs.

The majority of trees and shrubs will grow very large, which restricts their suitability for containers. Although their likely height and spread, and the extent of their root growth may rule them out as container plants, several species will make attractive short-term exhibits until they outgrow their container.

Shrubs and trees can be treated as single specimens or may share a tub with bulbs or bedding plants around their base to add extra color and extend their season. Some shrubs, such as hebe and erica, have small, neat forms that enable them to grow happily in medium-sized containers, for at least one season. Most trees and shrubs, though, are likely to stay put for several years, so choose a sturdy, weatherproof container.

STRUCTURE AND FOLIAGE

Permanent container plantings need to work hard to justify their place, so make sure they offer more than one feature of interest. Evergreens, which carry their leaves all year round, form a valuable background of foliage, especially in winter when there may be little else of interest in the garden. Deciduous trees and shrubs change with the seasons, bearing fresh new leaves in spring, offering cool shade in summer, and shedding their often fiery colored leaves in the fall, to reveal a striking network of branches during winter.

COOK'S DELIGHT
A small bay tree grown in a terra-cotta urn makes a handsome specimen, adding height and interest to a grouping of small foliage plants.

TREES AND SHRUBS AS SPECIMEN PLANTS

SMALL TREES

Acacia dealbata
Mimosa

***Acer palmatum* "Dissectum"**
Japanese maple

Eucalyptus gunnii
Gum tree

***Juniperus scopulorum* "Skyrocket"**

Laurus nobilis
Sweet bay

Magnolia stellata

***Malus* x *zumi* "Golden Hornet"**
Crab apple

***Prunus* "Kiku-shidare-zakura"**
Flowering cherry

***Pyrus salicifolia* "Pendula"**
Weeping pear

***Salix caprea* "Kilmarnock"**
Kilmarnock willow

Trachycarpus fortunei
Fan palm

SHRUBS

Camellia japonica
Camellia

Choisya ternata
Mexican orange blossom

Cotoneaster microphyllus

***Euonymus fortunei*
"Emerald 'n' Gold"**

Hydrangea macrophylla
Common hydrangea

Pieris japonica

Pyracantha watereri
Firethorn

***Skimmia japonica* "Rubella"**

Viburnum tinus
Laurustinus

Vinca major
Periwinkle

***Weigela* "Victoria"**

***Yucca gloriosa* "Variegata"**

LOW-GROWING
COTONEASTER MICROPHYLLUS

CONTAINER FOODS

It is surprising how many edible crops can be grown successfully in containers, which can be placed within easy reach of the kitchen. They won't yield a constant supply of summer produce, but they will contribute several interesting varieties to enjoy with your meal.

POTTED CROPS

To be a suitable candidate for container growing, the variety needs to be reasonably compact, without very deep or spreading roots, and it must be able to produce a worthwhile crop from a small number of plants. In order to earn its place in a garden, the variety should also be attractive to look at; those offering bright flowers, striking foliage, or fall color as well as edible produce double their value.

FRUIT TIPS

Apple
• Varieties on dwarfing rootstocks such as M27 grow well in deep tubs.
• For single specimens, choose a family tree grafted with three different varieties.
• Ballerina and Minarette trees are columnar varieties specially raised for container growing.

Blueberry
• Orange and copper leaf color in the fall.
• Grow in large pots of lime-free soil mix.
• Choose "Herbert" for the best flavor.

Cherry
• Dwarfing rootstock Inmil allows cherries to be grown in deep tubs.
• Self-fertile varieties include "Stella," "Sunburst," and "Cherokee."

Peach
• Dwarf varieties "Bonanza," "Garden Annie," "Garden Lady," and "Nectarella" (nectarine) are ideal for growing in deep tubs.
• Needs shelter from mid-winter to spring in cold climates.

Plum
• Suitable for growing in a deep tub.
• Grow trees on the dwarfing rootstock "Pixy," which requires rich soil.
• Self-fertile varieties include "Czar" (cooking plum), "Denniston's Superb" (greengage), "Opal," and "Victoria."

Strawberry
• Many different varieties, including small-fruited but tasty alpine types. Strawberries may crop

STRAWBERRY PLANTER

between early summer and fall, depending on variety.
• Suitable for growing bags, pots, window boxes, terra-cotta planters, and hanging baskets.
• The small fruits of alpine strawberries, such as "Baron Solemacher," are less prone to attack by birds.

VEGETABLE TIPS

Beans
- "Purple Teepee" and "Golddukat" have attractive colored pods.
- Suits window boxes, growing bags, and pots.
- Runner bean "Hestia" is a dwarf variety for tubs, with red and white flowers.

Beetroot
- Suitable for growing in bags or tubs.
- Roots are best pulled at golf-ball size.
- "Pronto" and "Monaco" are good for pots and growing bags. "Action" is ideal for baby beet.

Carrot
- Choose short-rooted varieties such as "Amini" and "Mignon," or globe-rooted "Parmex," valued for its sweet taste.
- Suitable for raising in pots, growing bags, and window boxes.
- Take care not to overwater.

Eggplant
- Good for a warm, sheltered position.
- Bears up to six glossy, purple-black fruits during late summer.
- Try "Bonica" or "Mini Bambino" in a tub or growing bag.

Lettuce
- Try baby iceberg "Blush," cut-and-come-again, frilly-leaved "Frisby," or purple, crimped "Lollo Rossa."
- Suitable for raising in pots, growing bags, or window boxes.

Sweet pepper
- Pick fruits when green, or leave them until they are red, when they are fully ripe and sweet.
- "Redskin" and "Apache" are good container varieties for raising in pots or growing bags.

Tomato
- Small-fruited types, with cherry-sized fruits, are the most decorative.
- Try "Totem" or "Tornado" in pots or growing bags.
- Trailing variety "Tumbler" suits hanging baskets.

Zucchini
- Produces large, rich yellow flowers.
- Different shapes and colors of fruit available.
- Bush varieties such as deep green "Supremo" or golden "Sunburst" suit growing bags or tubs.

CONTAINER-GROWN KALE AND CHIVES

POPULAR PLANTS

Of the many container-friendly plants, some species and varieties are especially popular, valued for their particularly brilliant color, a graceful or compact habit of growth, ease of cultivation, resistance to pests and diseases, or a long and prolific flowering season. The following selection of popular plants includes new varieties as well as established favorites but all are reliable choices for containers.

POPULAR CONTAINER PLANTS

Ageratum houstonianum
Floss flower
A summer-flowering bedding plant with fluffy heads of purple-blue flowers forming a dome over the mid to dark green, oval, toothed leaves. Varieties include "Blue Champion," "Blue Horizon," "Neptune," and "Blue Mink." Sow under cover in spring; plant out after frosts. Suitable for window boxes and tubs.
HEIGHT: 9 in (23 cm)

Antirrhinum majus
Snapdragon
Half-hardy annual bearing elegant, tapering spikes of lipped flowers in a range of colors and bicolors. Varieties include Crown and Coronette series; double-flowered "Madame Butterfly;" and low-growing Magic Carpet and Candelabra groups – ideal for hanging baskets as well as tubs. Sow under cover in spring; plant out after frosts.
HEIGHT: 6–16 in (15–40 cm)

Begonia cultivars
Begonia
Two types of this half-hardy annual/tuber are popular for containers. The fibrous-rooted Semperflorens begonias have small, yellow-eyed flowers in red, pink, and white shades; the rounded foliage is often bronzy green. Devil, Super Olympia, and Victory series are reliable. Tuberhybrida begonias have large, showy blooms. The long-flowering Nonstop series is the most popular. Good for all containers; trailing types are especially useful in hanging baskets. Buy plants or tubers and plant them out after frosts. Keep soil just moist and provide good ventilation during winter.
HEIGHT: 6–12 in (15–30 cm)

Fuchsia cultivars
Fuchsia
A tender perennial/shrub bearing delicate, usually drooping flowers of distinctive shape, with colored petals and often contrasting colorful sepals. Hardy varieties make good tub plants; try the upright dwarf varieties of "Tom Thumb" (very free-flowering) or "Mrs Popple." Fuchsias are commonly grown as frost-tender bedding plants. The trailing varieties are well suited to window boxes, hanging baskets, and troughs. Plant outside after frosts.
HEIGHT: 24–48 in (60–120 cm)

POTTED FUCHSIA

POPULAR CONTAINER PLANTS

Hedera helix
Ivy

A hardy climbing shrub with lobed leaves on sturdy climbing or trailing stems; there are many attractively variegated types such as "Glacier," "Harlequin," "Gold Child," and "White Knight." Ivies are well suited to all types of container, especially when they are allowed to trail over the edge, or trained up stakes to give height. Green-edged varieties tolerate shade, but variegated ones prefer sun. Excellent winter interest, but attractive all year round. Set out young plants at anytime. Contact with the sap may irritate skin or provoke an allergy.
HEIGHT/SPREAD: indeterminate

TRAILING IVY

Helichrysum petiolare
Helichrysum

The long, trailing or arching stems of this tender shrub are clothed with felted, oval leaves of dusty silver. Its daisylike flowers are usually white or yellow. Popular varieties for hanging baskets include "Limelight" (lemon-yellow foliage) and "Roundabout" (small-leaved with cream variegation). Set out young plants after frost. Overwinter under cover to provide cuttings for the following spring.
HEIGHT/SPREAD: to 3 ft (to 90 cm)

Impatiens walleriana
Impatiens

This half-hardy annual has bronze-green foliage and produces flat-faced, spurred flowers in a wide range of colors. Impatiens are very free flowering and provide summer-long interest. They are tolerant of shade and suit all types of container. Reliable series include Accent, Tempo (some bicolors and picotees), and Super Elfin; Confection and Carousel series feature semidouble and double flowers.
Sow in spring; plant out after frosts. Protect from cold winds.
HEIGHT: 6–10 in (15–25 cm)

Lobelia
Lobelia

Lobelia erinus is a half-hardy annual with small, lance-shaped or oval leaves and lipped flowers, usually in shades of blue. Plants are upright and bushy or trailing, according to variety. Riviera series (early flowering) and "Crystal Palace" (dark green leaves) are bushy varieties; Regatta and Fountain (profuse flowers) series are good trailing plants. Easy to raise from seed in spring or buy as a bedding plant.
HEIGHT: 4–6 in (10–15 cm)
Lobelia tupa is a robust perennial with red-purple stems and fiery orange-red flowers. It makes a striking display in barrel gardens and large tubs.
HEIGHT: to 3 ft (to 1 m).

LOBELIA TUPA

POPULAR CONTAINER PLANTS

Nemesia strumosa
Nemesia

"Sundrops Mixed" and other modern selections of this half-hardy annual offer a wide range of bright shades and a prolonged flowering season. Nemesia is compact and rounded, free-flowering and early to come into bloom after planting out. It is suitable for growing in all types of containers. Transplant carefully to avoid root disturbance and keep well watered in dry spells.
HEIGHT: 6–8 in (15–20 cm)

Nicotiana hybrids
Tobacco plant

A half-hardy annual with trumpet-shaped flowers in shades of red, pink, salmon, and white. Old varieties have a strong fragrance but close their flowers in the middle of the day; modern varieties stay open all day but many have lost their scent. The Domino series has compact plants with flowers in a good color range; "Lime Green" has unusual green flowers. For fragrance, try the taller "Heaven Scent." Plant out in spring in full sun or partial shade. Contact with the foliage may cause skin irritation.
HEIGHT: 10–24 in (25–60 cm)

Osteospermum cultivars
South African daisy

A tender perennial bearing large, daisylike flowers in an extensive range of colors. Varieties in the Starlight series are compact and early flowering; "Pink Whirls" and "Whirligig" have spoonshaped petals, which are rolled in the center; "Silver Sparkler" has variegated foliage and white flowers. Good for raising in tubs. Choose a sunny position because the flowers tend to close in shade. Deadhead regularly to prolong the flowering period.
HEIGHT: 14 in (35 cm)

Pelargonium cultivars
Geranium

These tender perennials are probably the most familiar of all bedding plants and suit all types of containers. Pelargoniums are drought-resistant and prefer full sun. Bedding varieties have rounded, scalloped and globe-shaped heads of brightly colored flowers on long stalks. The foliage may be attractively variegated (try "Frank Headley" or "Robert Fish"), or their flowers may have slender petals, which give a starry effect (Stellar series). Ivy-leaved pelargoniums have fleshy leaves and trailing stems set with dainty, open-faced flowers: free-flowering, Continental-style "Balcon" and "Ville de Paris" varieties are popular. Plant out in spring after frosts have past. Deadhead regularly to prolong flowering.
HEIGHT: 6–12 in (15–30 cm)

NICOTIANA "LIME GREEN"

POPULAR CONTAINER PLANTS

Petunia cultivars
Petunia

A tender perennial bearing large, trumpet-shaped, velvety flowers, with a scent of honey. Upright varieties are suitable for troughs and window boxes, while the semi-trailing types are popular in hanging baskets. Grandiflora cultivars have large blooms and are best kept in a sheltered site, to avoid damage in heavy rain; one exception is "Lavender Storm," which is wet-weather resistant. Multiflora types, such as the Resisto series, have small flowers that are produced in large quantities; these flowers are more resistant to rain damage. Recent introductions include Milliflora petunias, with a mass of small flowers; "Million Bells" has unusual bell-shaped blooms with contrasting-colored throats referred to as "halos;" the Surfinia series (Grandiflora) is vigorous and very free-flowering, with a strong trailing habit. Choose a sunny site for planting, with shelter from strong winds. Deadhead regularly to prolong the season, from late spring to late fall.
HEIGHT/SPREAD: to 18 in (to 45 cm)

Rudbeckia "Toto"
Coneflower

Rudbeckias are most familiar as tall border plants, but this half-hardy annual is very compact and ideal for growing in tubs. Its daisylike flowers are rich gold, with a prominent brown central "cone." "Toto" is free-flowering over a long season, and lasts throughout the summer until the first frosts. Flowers have good weather resistance.
HEIGHT: 10 in (25 cm)

Sanvitalia procumbens
Creeping zinnia

This half-hardy annual produces bright yellow to orange flowers with distinctive black centers. The dainty yellow daisies of "Little Sun" show up well against a background of bronzy foliage on trailing stems. Creeping zinnias are ideal for hanging baskets and are also useful for growing in patio containers and troughs. The flowering season lasts into the fall until stopped by first frosts. Plant in full sun.
HEIGHT: to 10 in (to 25 cm)

PETUNIA "MILLION BELLS"

Scaevola aemula
Fairy fan flower

A tender perennial with a vigorous trailing habit, which produces strong stems clothed with dark, bronzy green leaves. The flowers are very freely carried and are usually colored deep purple with a white eye. All five petals are carried on one side to give a distinctive fan shape. Popular varieties include "New Wonder," "Blue Shamrock," the compact "Saphira," and white-flowered "White Charm." A good choice for all containers, especially hanging baskets.
HEIGHT/SPREAD: 1 ft (30 cm)

POPULAR CONTAINER PLANTS

Sutera cordata
Bacopa

A very vigorous, branching or trailing tender perennial with neat, rounded leaves and small flowers produced in great profusion. The original variety "Snowflake" has been superceded by the trailing "Blizzard," with relatively large white flowers. "Knysa Hills" is an upright growing variety with pale purple flowers; "Sea Mist" and "Pink Domino" are trailers with pale lilac blooms. "African Sunset" has red flowers, each with a yellow eye. Choose a sunny position. Protect from frosts.
HEIGHT/SPREAD: 16 in (40 cm)

TRAILING NASTURTIUMS

Tropaeolum
Nasturtium

These hardy annuals are easy to grow and ideal for novice gardeners. Nasturtiums may be trailing or more bushy and are suitable for all types of containers. The edible, rounded leaves are light green (marbled white in the Alaska series) and the spurred flowers are red, yellow, salmon, or orange. Double-flowered varieties include *Tropaeolum majus* "Darjeeling Gold" and *T. m.* "Hermine Grashoff." Plants are easily raised from seed sown in spring. Aphids may need to be controlled.
HEIGHT/SPREAD: 12 in (30 cm) or more

Verbena x *hybrida* cultivars
Verbena

Verbenas are tender perennials with pointed, bright green, tacky-textured leaves topped with heads of brightly colored flowers, often with a white eye and sometimes bicolored. Stems are lax and semi-trailing or trailing, making the plants useful for all types of containers. Bush varieties include "Blue Lagoon" with deep blue flowers and "Peaches and Cream" in shades of coral, yellow, and pink. Trailing varieties include the fragrant "Pink Parfait," with pale pink and red flowers; "Aphrodite" bearing deep purple flowers striped with white; and "Tapien Pink" and "Tapien Violet," both extremely free-flowering selections. Bush types can be raised from seed and planted out after frosts. Trailing types are best obtained as bedding plants. Avoid overcrowding in the container to prevent damage by mildew.
HEIGHT/SPREAD: 12 in (30 cm)

3
PLANTING AND GROWING

A plant in a container is almost entirely dependent on the gardener for its well-being – far more so than a plant growing out in the open ground in a flowerbed or border. No matter what type of container is being used, there are certain watchpoints that must be observed if container plants are to thrive and give of their best. Ample drainage, regular watering, and supplementary feeding are the foundations of good plant care. Subsequent training, pruning, and repotting as and when required will ensure that long-term plants become well established and thrive in their container garden.

As well as the routine, day-to-day care of plants, you need to know what steps to take if problems develop and be able to identify the cause, rectify the problem, and prevent any further damage or repeat occurrences as soon as possible. And when a plant has performed really well, it is rewarding to be able to propagate it for future years, or to supply plants for friends and neighbors.

WATER AND DRAINAGE

Certain growing techniques apply to all container plants, whether they are in patio tubs, window boxes, or in hanging baskets. Knowing when to add water and when to stop to ensure the right balance for healthy looking plants is the way to overcome a problem that is common to all container gardens.

DRAINAGE HOLES

Plants in containers often swing between having too little water for their needs and far too much. Both states can be fatal. In order to prevent waterlogging, containers must provide free drainage; there should be sufficient holes in the base of the container to allow excess water to drain away. The holes are often all round the edge of the base, but clay and ceramic pots usually have a single, large, central hole.

If there are not enough drainage holes present, they can be added. In wooden, fiberglass, and plastic pots, an electric or hand drill fitted with a fairly large bit will quickly puncture holes of a useful size. A heated metal skewer held with an oven glove or thick cloth is just as effective for making holes in the base of most plastic containers.

Rather than risk damaging fragile pots without drainage holes, use the container as an outer cover for a plain pot with drainage holes, which should stand on a deep layer of grit or stones in the base. Lift out the inner pot occasionally to empty any excess water that has collected in the base of the nondraining container.

KEEPING THE FLOW

The presence of holes is not sufficient drainage on its own, because the flow of water through them can easily be impeded. Large drainage holes should be covered with a piece of narrow-gauge wire mesh to prevent the soil mix from washing through them. In all containers, a layer of coarse

TERRA-COTTA POT ON FEET

Pot feet ensure good drainage

SELECTION OF CERAMIC POT FEET

material at the base of the pot will allow excess water to percolate through. Concave pieces of broken clay pots (crocks) are excellent for the base layer, expecially over large drainage holes. For large containers, bulky rubble or stones should follow the broken pots; in smaller containers, use coarse gravel, grit, or similar material.

If the container is standing flush on a flat surface, water may not be able to get away from the drainage holes sufficiently well. Raise the container off the ground slightly, setting it on blocks of wood or bricks. A more attractive option is to use "pot feet" made from clay or terra-cotta, which will do the same job.

GRIT

Retaining water

Keeping container gardens supplied with sufficient water can present just as much of a problem as making sure that they do not suffer from having too much water. Use a container that is large enough for the plant to produce a reasonable amount of growth before its roots fill all the available space, and avoid very shallow containers for deep-rooting plants. Using a soil mix that retains moisture well will cut down the amount of watering required; water-retaining granules added into the soil mix are very efficient, as each granule is able to store up to 400 times its own weight of water (see p. 252).

WATER-RETAINING GRANULES

CONTAINER SOILS

Although it is possible to use garden soil to fill containers, proprietary soil mixes will nearly always give better results. They are sterile, and unlike garden soil, they do not contain weeds, weed seeds, pests, or diseases; they also usually have a better physical structure to allow good drainage.

SOIL MIX TYPES

Proprietary brands of soil mix are either soil based or soilless.

■ **Soil-based mixes** Made from loam (rotted down meadow turf), soil-based mixes, such as multipurpose types, look and feel like fine garden soil. They retain water well, contain a long-lasting supply of plant nutrients, and are very stable when used in containers. On the downside, they are heavy and awkward to handle in bulk and messy to work with. In containers, they are most appropriate for long-term plants such as trees and shrubs.

MULTIPURPOSE SOIL-BASED MIX

■ **Soilless mixes** Based on peat or peat substitutes, such as coconut fiber, shredded bark, and sewage sludge, soilless mixes are clean, lightweight, and pleasant to handle. They contain low levels of nutrients, so plants need supplementary feeding quite soon after planting; they drain freely but also dry out quickly. Soilless mixes are suitable for nearly all types of container-grown plants, but particularly for short-term subjects such as annuals and bedding. On the downside, their light weight makes them less suitable for very tall plants that tend to become top heavy and topple over.

PEAT-FREE SOILLESS MIX

SPECIAL-PURPOSE SOILS

Ericaceous soil mix is suitable for lime-hating plants such as camellias; hanging basket soil mix is formulated to retain water well, with a long-lasting nutrient supply. Soil mixes with added insecticides protect plants against soil-borne pests, and free-draining, low-nutrient mixes provide an ideal medium for raising plants from seeds and cuttings.

SEED AND CUTTING SOIL MIX

PLANTING UP

Whenyou plant up your containers, you are providing the plants with their only home for the rest of the season – so it is important that you get the planting technique right. Once you have understood the basic needs of plants and know how to provide them, planting up becomes a simple and straightforward procedure.

WHAT YOU NEED

Gather together everything you will need before you start planting. Your basic equipment should include:

■ **Trowel** Wide-bladed trowels make good-sized planting holes for bulbs and small bedding plants. Narrow-bladed versions are more practical when planting in confined spaces.

■ **Hand fork** A hand fork is useful for loosening the soil when removing weeds and when repotting a plant.

■ **Dibble** Available in a range of sizes, dibbles are used to make planting holes. Small ones are ideal for cuttings and seedlings; large ones for planting bulbs.

■ **Container** Make sure that the style of container suits the growing needs of your plants and rinse it clean before planting up.

■ **Drainage material** To prevent waterlogging, use pieces of broken clay pots or coarse gravel (see p. 245).

■ **Water-retaining granules** Refer to the manufacturer's guidelines to assess the correct amount for your container (see p. 252).

■ **Soil mix** Choose a soil mix that is appropriate to your plant's growing needs (see p. 246).

■ **Plants** Use healthy plants that are large enough to be handled comfortably (see pp. 248–49).

■ **Watering can** Make sure that your can is a manageable size, especially if you need to lift it to reach hanging baskets and wall mangers. A long spout will allow you to reach plants.

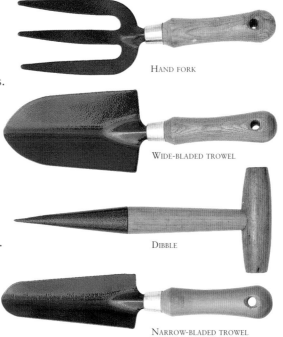

HAND FORK

WIDE-BLADED TROWEL

DIBBLE

NARROW-BLADED TROWEL

BUYING PLANTS

There is no shortage of outlets selling suitable plants to grow in containers, especially in spring, when it seems almost every shop has a display of bedding plants. For some of the more unusual plants, however, a little more advance planning is required. There are three main ways to buy plants.

WHERE TO BUY

■ **Garden centers** Specialist nurseries are perhaps the most popular places for gardeners to buy container plants. They usually offer a good choice of plant types and varieties, and you are able to make your own selection. Staff are likely to be knowledgeable and the plants should be well looked after – although this is variable.

■ **Nonspecialist retailers** Market stalls, private sellers, and hardware and chain stores often sell more popular types of plants, although their quality may be rather poor as staff usually have no special training in plant care. However, prices are likely to be very competitive, and you can see what you are buying.

■ **Mail order** Probably the largest range of varieties, including new and unusual types, is available from specialist mail-order outlets. Many seed companies, as well as specialist nurseries, supply young plants in the spring. Orders have to be made several weeks in advance of the plants being needed, and shipping costs will add to the overall price. The quality of the plants cannot be seen until they arrive, but most reputable firms will replace damaged or substandard stock.

TYPES OF PLANTS

Plants are sold at different stages of growth, from tiny seedlings that will need transplanting into pots and hardening off before going outdoors to pot-ready plants that are ready to be planted out immediately. The type of plant that you choose will depend on your time and budget.

Healthy buds indicate good plant growth

SUN OR CAPE DAISY
(*OSTEOSPERMUM*)

■ **Seedlings** The least expensive way of buying seedlings is an open tray, although the seedlings in them are not as easy to transplant. Open trays of seedling plants need to be transferred to compartments within larger trays or individual pots of soil mix and grown for several weeks. You will need a suitable light, frost-free place in which to grow the seedlings, as well as spare pots or trays, soil mix, and the time for transplanting.

Tray plants

Damage-free foliage indicates good health

■ **Plug plants** Available in a wide range of sizes, plug plants are grown individually in small cells of soil mix in a molded tray. Plug plants are larger and sturdier than seedlings and each have their own, firm rootball. They usually need to be potted up for growing before they can be planted out, but otherwise they are easier and less time-consuming to look after than seedlings.

■ **Tray plants** Older seedlings are often sold divided into compartmented trays to give them extra room to grow into sturdy young plants. They are not quite as easy to transplant as plug plants because they are likely to suffer more root disturbance, but they are generally less expensive. You will usually need to have facilities to harden off the plants before setting them outside.

Pot-ready plant

■ **Pot-ready plants** Although more expensive, large plug plants or plants that have been grown on in individual pots will be ready for planting at the time of purchase. Some may need to be hardened off before planting outside.

PROPAGATION

If you have the space and equipment, you might like to try raising your own stock of plants to fill your containers. A frost-free greenhouse is the ideal environment for propagating, but a warm conservatory or a bright window sill will also serve the purpose.

GROWING FROM SEED

■ **Tray preparation** Fill a seed tray with seed and cuttings soil mix, level it and firm the surface with a wooden presser. Water the soil mix using a can fitted with a fine rose.

■ **Sowing** Sprinkle the seed thinly over the surface of the soil, and cover it lightly with a thin, even layer of soil mix or silver sand. Cover with a propagator hood or another seed tray turned upside down.

■ **Cultivation** Leave the seed tray in an evenly warm place, and mist well whenever the surface looks as though it is drying out. As soon as the first few seedlings are showing through, make sure that the tray is kept in bright but diffused light. When the seedlings are large enough to handle, separate them out into another tray or individual pots to give them more growing room. Always handle them by their first pair of leaves, never by their stems.

CLOCHES

Cloches provide young plants and seedlings that need to be hardened off with additional protection against the cold. They also shield tender young leaves from attack by birds and slugs.
  Readymade cloches are available in a range of sizes, suitable for covering individual plants or seed trays. The more expensive models are made from glass, which is the traditional material, but transparent plastic is just as effective and less prone to breakage. Homemade versions can be fashioned from wire hoops and horticultural film or, simpler still, from a transparent plastic bottle cut in half and placed over an individual plant.

SOWING SEED

Allow even spacing between seeds

TAKING CUTTINGS

If you find that a cultivar does not come true from seed, or if it is not possible to increase a plant by division, then taking cuttings is your best solution. Cuttings can be taken at anytime during the growing season and should produce root systems within two to three weeks of cultivation.

1 Select a strong-growing, healthy, preferably non-flowering shoot and cut it off just above a node (where the leaves join the stem). Trim the cutting so that it has about four pairs of leaves, cutting just below a node and removing the bottom pair of leaves cleanly.

Use a clean, sharp blade

Insert cuttings evenly around the edge

2 Insert the cutting into a pot of moist seed and cutting soil mix topped with a layer of silver sand, and firm it in well. Cover with a propagator hood to maintain a humid atmosphere and water regularly to keep the soil moist. Leave the pot in light shade until roots have formed and the cutting starts to grow away at the tip.

ROUTINE CARE

Whether your containers are planted up with short-term summer displays or long-term shrubs and specimen trees, they will need regular attention and maintenance, especially during the growing season, to ensure a prolonged period of interest and pleasure.

WATERING

Perhaps the most time-consuming task associated with container gardening is watering, with demand reaching its peak during the flowering season, especially if you have densely planted containers. Most containers will need watering daily in summer, and some may need to be refreshed two or three times a day. The need for water is greatest in hot, dry weather, but even when it rains, the dense leaf cover over the surface of the soil will probably mean that little rain water penetrates the soil mix to any depth.

A well-balanced watering can with a long spout is useful for reaching hanging baskets and wall pots, but if you have lots of containers to look after, a hose is much quicker. Fit it with a long lance that can be turned on and off at the end farthest from the tap. If you are unable to spend much time on watering your plants regularly, you can set up an automatic drip or trickle watering system, which is controlled by a fully adjustable computer fitted to the tap.

Water-retaining granules, which look like grains of sugar when dry (see p. 245), can absorb many times their own weight in water. If they are distributed through the soil mix, they retain water that would otherwise drain away, making it available to the plants. Mix a small quantity of granules with the soil mix when planting up and it will cut down the subsequent need for watering considerably.

Long spout allows access to high wall pots and hanging baskets

LONG-SPOUTED
WATERING CAN

FEEDING

In densely planted containers, plants compete for nutrients from the soil. Soil-based mixes are able to keep plants supplied with food for a while, but soilless mixes may need supplementary feeding soon after planting. One or two specialist soil mixes are also available (see p. 246).

Fertilizers contain the major plant nutrients of nitrogen, potassium, and phosphorus, as well as other minor nutrients. For flourishing foliage, choose a nitrogen-rich fertilizer; for good flowering, opt for one that is high in potassium. Fertilizers are available as granules, powders, or liquids. One of the most useful forms is slow-release granules or feedsticks: added to the soil mix at the start of the season, these release their nutrients gradually, sometimes lasting all season long. Powders and liquids are usually diluted and applied with a watering can; they are quick acting, and often weak solutions can be applied at every watering. The fastest results are produced by foliar feeds, which are taken up by the plants' leaves; they help to reduce nutrient deficiencies and act as a general "pick-me-up" for plants under stress. They can be very useful for supplying nutrients to lime-hating plants that are not in their ideal soil conditions.

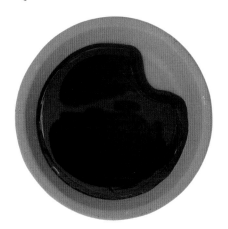

LIQUID FERTILIZER

POWDER FERTILIZER

FERTILIZER FEEDSTICKS

Warning

When applying any fertilizer, always follow the application instructions on the package, and remember that too much food can be just as damaging to a plant as can too little food.

PLANT SUPPORTS

The necessity for plant supports
depends upon the size and type of plant
being grown and the position of the
container – whether it is in a windy
or sheltered place.

Climbing plants, unless they are
grown as trailers, need a framework
on which to grow. This can be
provided by a section of wooden
or plastic trellis, either fixed in the
container or attached to a nearby
wall. If the plant is tall and leafy, the
depth of soil in the pot may not be
sufficient to support it, and the trellis is
then best fixed to a firm base outside the
container. A wigwam constructed from bamboo
canes placed around the edge of the container
and tied together at their tips is also effective.

The stems of bushy and shrubby plants may
need individual supports to maintain their shape.
Dark green split canes are less obvious when set
among the branches and tied to individual stems.

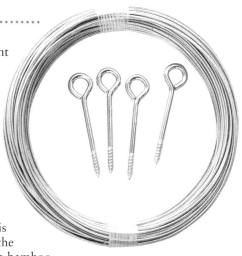

HORTICULTURAL WIRE
AND VINE EYES

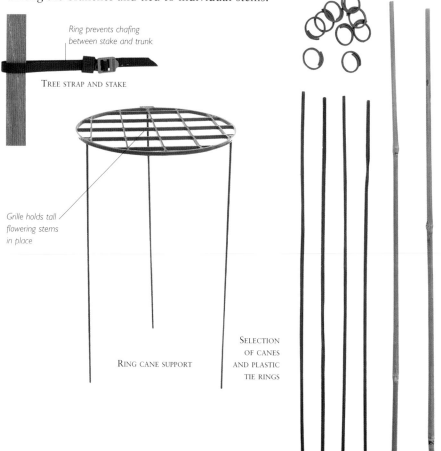

*Ring prevents chafing
between stake and trunk*

TREE STRAP AND STAKE

*Grille holds tall
flowering stems
in place*

RING CANE SUPPORT

SELECTION
OF CANES
AND PLASTIC
TIE RINGS

KEEPING IN TRIM

Container-grown trees and shrubs and perennial climbers are most likely to need pruning; this may be to keep them to an attractive shape, to encourage flowering or to restrict them to a practical size. Use sharp pruning shears and make cuts just above a bud. Always remove damaged, dead, or diseased wood completely, whenever it is seen; otherwise, the timing and type of pruning depends on the individual plant.

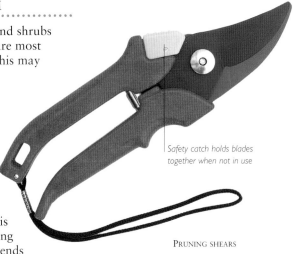

Safety catch holds blades together when not in use

PRUNING SHEARS

Deadheading is a form of pruning that can be carried out to advantage on nearly all container plants. As well as making the plant look tidier by removing faded flowers, if it is done early enough it will prevent energy being wasted in seed production and stimulate further flowering throughout the season. Faded flowers can be pinched off with the fingers or removed with shears, cutting the stem down to a leaf joint or removing it completely.

Warning

Hands need to be protected by gardening gloves when carrying out routine tasks in the garden. Choose heavy duty gauntlets when pruning thorny stems and brambles; use lightweight cotton gloves when weeding and deadheading.

REPOTTING

Perennial plants, including trees and shrubs, will need occasional repotting to ensure healthy growth.

■ **Repotting in a new pot** Once a young plant has filled its pot with roots, it should be repotted into a larger pot. Water it well an hour or two before removing it from the pot. Stand the plant on a layer of fresh soil mix in a new pot that is one or two sizes larger. Backfill around the rootball with more soil mix, pushing the soil down well, until it just covers the old surface. Water well.

■ **Repotting with new soil** Once a plant has reached as large a size pot as it requires, it can be repotted in the same pot. Remove it as before and crumble away some of the old soil mix from the outside of the rootball. Tease out any constricted roots; some of these can be pruned back carefully if you want to restrict the plant's size. Mix some fresh soil mix with slow-release fertilizer granules and place a layer of this in the original pot. Return the plant to the pot, filling in down the sides with more soil mix. Water well.

PROBLEM-SOLVING

Like all living things, plants are prone to their share of problems. Pests and diseases are always the chief suspects, but there may be a whole range of other causes such as inappropriate feeding and watering, poor soil, or weather damage. An accurate identification of the trouble is an essential first step toward putting things right.

CULTURAL PROBLEMS

When things go wrong with plants, pests and diseases tend to get the blame, but it may well be a cultural fault that is causing the problem.

■ **Nutrient deficiencies** These show up as yellowing foliage, or leaves with marked yellow patches or yellow veins; a fertilizer containing trace elements will usually cure these.

■ **Wilting foliage and stems** This may be caused by lack of water at the roots, or even waterlogged soil.

■ **Stunted growth** This may be due to sudden cold or windy conditions, or lack of nutrients in the soil mix.

■ **Leaf scorch** Strong sun can cause leaves to blotch and shrivel.

COMMON PESTS AND DISEASES

Good observational skills are the key to coping with pest and disease attacks; if an infestation is spotted at an early stage, it is much easier to deal with than when it has become well established. Look particularly at the growing points of plants and check the undersides of leaves, as symptoms may first show themselves here.

• **Slugs** Have voracious appetites for tender foliage and can reduce susceptible plants such as hostas to skeletons almost overnight. Remove slugs by handpicking them after dark; or use beer traps, proprietary organic controls, or slug pellets containing metaldehyde or methiocarb.

• **Caterpillars** Chew holes and ragged pieces out of leaves and shoots. Remove caterpillars by handpicking or by spraying with derris or bifenthrin.

• **Aphids** Colonize growing tips, shoots, and buds of plants in vast numbers. They can distort and stunt growth and may spread viral diseases. In the early stages of an attack, aphids can be washed away from affected shoots with soapy water. Chemical controls include pirimicarb, bifenthrin, derris, and horticultural soap.

• **Powdery mildew** Powdery white patches on plant foliage; most common in hot, dry weather and often caused by overcrowding plants in one area. Treat outbreaks with a fungicide such as carbendazim.

• **Rusts** Pale spots on the leaf surface with brown or orange powdery spores on the underside. Leaves fall early and growth is stunted. Remove and burn affected leaves; spray with a fungicide such as propiconazole.

VACATION CARE

To keep your container plants well watered while you are away from home, group them together and set up an automated sprinkler or drip system; this need not be too costly and can be very effective. Always test the system in advance and ask a friend or neighbor to check that it is working while you are away. Just before you leave, prune back bedding plants and tender perennials; this will encourage new growth and produce a flush of flowers for your return.

TAKING SHELTER
A neighbor will find it easier to water and care for your plants if you group your containers together in a sheltered, lightly shaded spot.

OUT-OF-SEASON INTEREST

Containers come into their own in summer when they are filled with an abundance of colorful flowers, but there is no need to store them away when the first frost arrives. Plants in containers can brighten up gardens and window sills right through fall and winter and into spring, when they are often even more welcome than in summer.

MAINTAINING INTEREST

■ **Fall** Perennials such as Kaffir lilies *(Schizostylis coccinea)* and michaelmas daisies help to continue the summer's flowers into fall, and are followed by fall-flowering bulbs like nerines, colchicums, and cyclamen. Brilliant fall foliage colors are provided by Japanese maples and witch hazels, while glossy orange-red berries from firethorn and cotoneaster develop their rich red tints.

■ **Winter** Delicate flowers are provided by laurustinus *(Viburnum tinus)*, witch hazel, winter iris, and the sweet-scented shrubby honeysuckles. The bold colors of winter-flowering pansies and the more subtle shades of heathers, such as *Erica carnea* varieties, are ideal for growing in window boxes, wall pots, and other small containers. Bright, glowing foliage from golden-variegated ivies, euonymus, and *Eleagnus* compensates for the lack of sun on a dull winter day.

■ **Spring** Snowdrops and the earliest crocuses and miniature narcissi help to ease the transition between winter and spring. As the days lengthen, myriad other bulbs come into flower,

accompanied by primulas and polyanthus, double daisies, and a renewed flush of winter pansies. Several varieties of heather *(Calluna)* bear beautifully colored foliage tips in spring, and hellebores carry their nodding heads of green, purple, or white cupshaped flowers.

BERRY BRIGHT
The blazing-orange berries of firethorn provide a splash of color in the fall garden once the last of the summer flowers have died down.

4
POTS, TUBS, AND TROUGHS

Freestanding pots, patio tubs, and troughs are perhaps the most popular types of container. Planted with spring-flowering bulbs, summer blooms, or winter foliage, they can be moved around the garden to give an attractive display throughout the year. Whether they are filled with flowers and displayed in a grouping or planted up with a single specimen, perhaps trained as a standard and used as a focal point, containers are infinitely versatile.

POSITIONING POTS

Freestanding containers are valued for their versatility. Ornamental pots can be used to make bold statements in a garden; large tubs can be moved to form a temporary screen, while oversized troughs and urns are ideal for accommodating large specimen plants, or for cramming full with long-lasting displays of colorful annuals.

MOVING CONTAINERS

One of the advantages of freestanding containers, such as pots, tubs, and troughs, is that they can be moved around the garden. This means that they can be brought into a prominent position when the plants they contain are at their best, and then moved to somewhere less obvious when their main display is over.

Some containers are very heavy, and moving them around the garden is not a job to be undertaken lightly.

TIMBER TUB

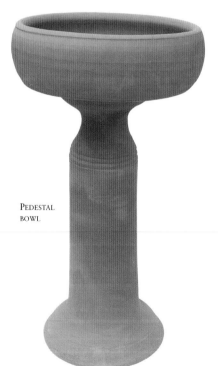

PEDESTAL BOWL

Try to place any heavy, awkward containers in their final positions before planting, as the weight of damp soil once they are filled may make it almost impossible to move them. If you move your containers regularly, it might be worth your while investing in a small, purpose-made trolley on casters; these are generally available from large garden equipment suppliers.

Lightweight containers are quite easy to move about, although even with these, you should not underestimate the weight of soil once they are planted up.

In order to drain freely, pots should be slightly raised from the ground; three or four small blocks of wood or purpose-made pot feet do the job well. Make sure the pot is stable on these blocks, as delicate pots can easily be damaged or broken if they are knocked over.

CHANGING THE LEVEL

Pots and tubs do not all have to be displayed at ground level; raising them helps to give height to a garden and allows a well-planted container to be more easily admired, perhaps forming a focal point. It also allows trailing plants to fall gracefully, extending below the base of the container. Garden walls, raised beds, flights of steps, and purpose-made plinths and pedestals offer suitable places for raised pots.

It is important to ensure that a raised pot is fixed securely; if it falls, there is not only the risk of damage to the pot, but of human injury.

■ **Walls** A flat, level coping stone on the top of a wall enables a pot to be positioned centrally and reasonably safely; on walls extending above

BATH TIME BLUES
A decorated metal trough provides ample room for this *Hydrangea macrophylla* bearing large blue mopheads of flowers.

Warning

Containers set on pedestals or tall pillars can be particularly dangerous, especially if there are children in the garden who may pull the container on top of them. To reduce the risk of accidents, cement the container firmly to the top of the pedestal, or use an all-in-one arrangement whereby the container is constructed as an integral part of the pedestal.

head height, extra measures are advisable. Hold troughs in place with an L-shaped metal bracket, set railings along the edge of the wall to act as restraints, or simply cement the container into place.

■ **Steps** Pots should be placed well to the sides of flights of steps so that they do not impede access. Trim back trailing or spreading plants regularly to ensure that their foliage does not present a hazard to passersby.

GENERAL CARE

The shape of a container plays an important part in the amount of care it needs once planted. If the surface area of the soil is large in proportion to its volume, the soil will dry out more quickly. Shallow bowls and troughs have a large surface area, and therefore need much more frequent watering than a deep pot.

MATERIALS

The material a container is made from will also have an effect on plant growth. Porous materials like terra-cotta lose water by evaporation; they can also draw moisture out of the soil when first filled and planted up. Glazed or plastic containers are nonporous and need less watering, but they are more likely to become waterlogged. Where items have been adapted to become plant containers rather than being purpose made, they may need special treatment before planting. A coating of bitumen-based paint will seal the inside of a wooden or metal container, helping to prevent rot and rust as well as protecting the plants from the presence of damaging chemicals. A plastic liner can be used instead of bitumen-based paint, but it is important to ensure that the base of the polyethylene is well punctured to allow water to drain away.

PREPARED HALF-BARREL

ROUTINE CHECKS

■ **Roots** When growing trees, shrubs, and perennials in containers, check the base of the pot regularly. Roots emerging through the drainage holes indicate that the plant is ready for repotting (see p. 55). If the pot is left standing on open ground, the roots will penetrate down into the soil; when the pot is eventually lifted, these roots will be damaged or destroyed and the plant's growth could be severely checked.

MAKING A SINK GARDEN

Stone troughs can be expensive and difficult to obtain. A good substitute can be made from a glazed kitchen sink covered in hypertufa, which is a mixture of peat and cement.

• Clean the sink and coat the outside in a bonding agent; leave it to dry.

• Mix equal parts of peat or peat substitute with coarse sand and cement; add water to give a suitable consistency for coating the sink.

• With gloved hands, apply a ¾-in (2-cm) layer of hypertufa to the sink.

• Leave the sink to dry for several days, then roughen the dry surface with a wire brush to achieve a stone-textured finish. Add moss and lichen to complete the effect.

■ **Moisture** Water your containers regularly; if too much moisture is lost, the soil will dry out and shrink away from the sides of the pot. Any subsequent watering will pass down the gully between soil and pot, rather than soaking through the soil. Stand the container on a gravel-filled saucer to prevent drying out (but do not leave the base of the pot standing in

SHELTERED IN SHADE
This cool, shady corner provides welcome shelter from bright midday sun, which can scorch foliage and deprive roots of much-needed moisture.

water at anytime) or add a layer of gravel over the surface of the soil. This mulch helps to retain moisture and usually sets the plants off well.

PLANTING A POT

Your first attempt at planting up a container can often be a little daunting. Gather together a couple of inspirational pictures to use as reference and make sure that you have everything that you need at hand before you start; then simply follow the steps below.

A POTTED POSY

1 Rinse out the container with water then place some broken pieces of clay pot (crocks) directly over the drainage hole. Add a layer of coarse gravel, grit, or small stones to the base of the pot to ensure that the soil can drain freely. If the container has small holes round the edge of the base rather than a single, large, central drainage hole, the layer of stones or gravel will be sufficient on its own.

Sprinkle water-retaining granules evenly through soil mix

2 Fill the pot three-quarters full with soil-based or soilless mix; the latter tends to be the most popular because it is lightweight and clean (see p. 246). When using soilless mix, it is a good idea to add some slow-release fertilizer and water-retaining granules at this point; follow the manufacturer's instructions to assess the correct quantity. Sprinkle the supplements over the soil and mix them in by hand.

3 Top up the pot with soil mix to just below the brim. Keeping the plants in their pots, set them out on the surface of the soil until you are satisfied with the overall appearance. Start with a tall, upright plant in the center, then place lower-growing, bushy plants around it, and add some trailers at the edge of the pot. Keep an even balance of plants around the pot, if the arrangement is going to be viewed from all sides.

4 Remove the central plant from its pot by turning it upside down, holding the stem between your fingers, and tapping the rim sharply; the rootball should slide out cleanly.

5 Make a hole in the soil and insert the plant so that the top of the rootball is just covered with fresh soil. Firm it lightly into position. Treat the rest of the plants in the same way.

Balanced all-round display of flowers

6 Once the planting is complete, water the finished pot overhead with a fine rose on the can. As well as settling the plants into place, this will freshen them up, washing off any traces of soil mix from the leaves and flowers. Check the moisture content of the soil after a couple of hours if water-retaining granules have been used – it may need a further watering once the granules have absorbed moisture.

A POT FOR WINTER

Containers for winter interest tend to rely mainly on foliage plants, but there are some flowers available that will help to brighten up dull winter days. The Universal series of winter-flowering pansies produce their best blooms during late fall, but in a fairly sheltered position they will continue to flower through the winter until they have a further large flush of blooms in early spring. Winter-flowering heathers are another good choice; varieties of *Erica carnea* are available in a wide range of shades and are undeterred by the weather.

FROST AND SNOW

A simple arrangement of green and white is particularly suitable for winter days, adding brightness but with a suggestion of frost and snow. *Euonymus fortunei* "Harlequin" is a new variety of compact growth, its foliage heavily mottled and splashed with brilliant white; the white-margined *E. f.* "Silver Queen" could be used as a substitute. *Erica carnea* "Springwood White" is a favorite and reliable winter-flowering heather variety. It makes a vigorous plant with bright green foliage and a mass of white flowers, each bloom tipped with rusty brown. The rambling stems of *Vinca minor* carry neat, oval, glossy, dark green leaves. In late winter or early spring, the form *V. m.* f. *alba* bears white periwinkle flowers that tone perfectly with the white and green theme.

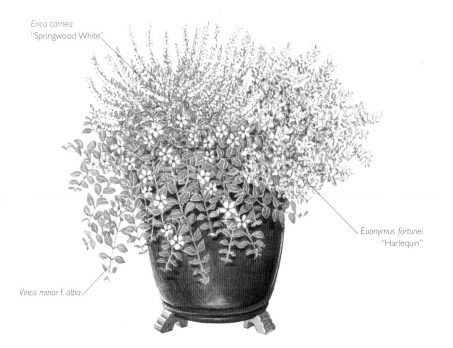

Erica carnea
"Springwood White"

Euonymus fortunei
"Harlequin"

Vinca minor f. alba

SPRING SUNSHINE

Many winter-flowering plants redouble their efforts as spring arrives, but there is also a good range of spring bedding plants and spring-flowering bulbs to provide instant color. Most bedding plants should be able to withstand light frost but they will need to be hardened off before being set outdoors permanently.

TOUCH OF SUNLIGHT

The bright golden color scheme of this container display brings a touch of sunlight to the garden just as it emerges from winter. The most prominent plant is the *Ranunculus asiaticus* Turban Group, with heavily ruffled flowers of soft yellow-orange laced with deeper color on the edges of the petals. The deeply cut, fresh green foliage is also attractive. Yellow and white primroses produce prolonged flushes of bloom; the white-flowered form has a deep yellow eye that picks up the color of the ranunculus. *Tulipa* "Glück" is one of the Kauffmaniana group, with streaked and mottled foliage; the elegantly shaped flowers have creamy yellow petals with a central stripe of rusty orange-red. Curling around the pot are tendrils of *Hedera helix* "Yellow Ripple," a variety of ivy with attractively shaped, variegated deep yellow and light green leaves.

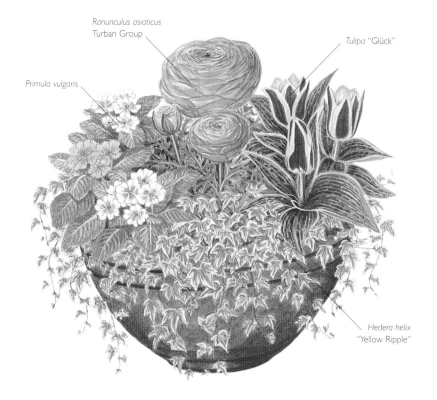

Ranunculus asiaticus Turban Group

Tulipa "Glück"

Primula vulgaris

Hedera helix "Yellow Ripple"

SUMMERTIME PLEASURES

In summer, there is almost an embarrassment of choices for the container gardener. This is the peak season for pots, tubs, and troughs; wherever you look there are containers spilling over with a mass of color from a vast range of flowering plants.

COOL AND LIGHT

Many containers are planted up without a great deal of thought or planning. The ensuing "riot of color" may be just what is wanted, but a more careful selection of shade can often give far more effective results. The "hot" colors – red, orange, and bright yellow – are lively, vibrant, and instantly attract the eye. In contrast, "cool" colors – blue, white, and green – are more restful and appear more distant and less obtrusive. Container gardens may be planned on a theme of either hot or cool shades, depending upon the effect you want to create, but in each case a small touch of contrast helps to intensify their effect.

In the wooden trough illustrated, the main tones used are cool and light. The trailing stems of golden creeping Jenny (*Lysimachia nummularia* "Aurea") are studded with round leaves of a sharp citrus-green shade; the flowers of the tobacco plant (*Nicotiana* "Lime Green") produce a soft haze of palest green above the deep green foliage. Dotted in among them, the relatively few brilliant red blooms of *Nicotiana* "Domino Red" are given maximum impact by their sharp contrast with the cool tones surrounding them.

In the same way, a planting of bright reds, oranges, and intense, deep yellows can be thrown into more effective relief by the addition of some cooler shades – a silver-foliaged plant such as *Helichrysum petiolare* is an excellent choice.

Lysimachia nummularia "Aurea"

Nicotiana "Domino Red"

Nicotiana "Lime Green"

PINKS AND PASTELS

Different shades of pink and pastels feature in the illustrated tub, which teams a weeping standard rose (here, *Rosa* "Nozomi") with garden pinks *(Dianthus)* around the base of the plant. "Nozomi" makes a very attractive informal standard, with its spreading, slightly weeping branches festooned in summer with delicate shell-pink, single flowers. The small, ferny, dark green leaves have a bluish cast, which is echoed by the silver-gray foliage of *Dianthus* "Houndspool Ruby," while the rich pink double flowers complement the paler pink of the roses.

Using a wider range of adjacent colors gives more scope for incorporating different plants and varieties. Pink, salmon, magenta, lilac, purple, and blue all harmonize well but allow a wide range of individual shades to form part of the scheme, giving an impression of a varied, multicolored container that still retains a satisfying and well-integrated color scheme.

A single-color planting scheme can make a very striking container arrangement, but needs the skill of an experienced gardener to successfully incorporate the green of the plants' foliage into the scheme. White- or golden-variegated foliage is

Rosa "Nozomi"

Dianthus "Houndspool Ruby"

WEEPING STANDARDS

Most ramblers, lax climbers, and trailing ground-cover roses can be trained as weeping standards, including: *Rosa* "Dorothy Perkins" (rose-pink); *R.* "Excelsa" (crimson); *R.* "Grouse" (blush pink); and *R.* "Sander's White Rambler."

---

particularly useful in helping to link foliage into a single-color scheme; equally, you may find a color wheel useful when planning a planting scheme. Reading clockwise, the wheel colors are blue, green, yellow, orange, red, and purple. Adjacent colors on the wheel tone with each other, while opposite colors contrast. Red and green are directly opposite each other on the wheel, giving a strong contrast between red flowers and green leaves, but purple, blue, or orange flower shades can be more difficult to work with. White makes an effective combination with green foliage, as does yellow which is adjacent to green on the color wheel.

HEIGHT AND TEXTURE

The overwhelming choice of colors offered by container plants, especially annuals and biennials, makes it easy to overlook other features in a container garden. For example, differently shaped flowers, from trumpets to bells, can increase variety and interest in a display. Many schemes, especially those comprising mainly low-growing bedding plants, could benefit from some additional height. Areas of dull foliage in a planting can be interspersed with more textural plants, such as spiny, soft-haired, or delicately divided leaves.

RAISING STANDARDS

The most usual way of adding height is by including one or two tall specimens in a mixed planting, or by devoting some containers entirely to tall plants that can be positioned among containers of low-growing subjects. The clear-stemmed tree shape of a trained standard also makes an ideal choice for adding height to containers because it allows additional low-level planting around its base. Standards can be formed from a wide range of plants, some of the most popular of which are flowering crab apples and cherries, roses (see p. 269), marguerites, bay *(Laurus nobilis)*, and fuchsias. Another way of adding height is to grow climbing plants up a support. A narrow piece of trellis, a wigwam of canes, or specially made decorative wire or wooden globes or pyramids can all make effective features. Climbing or scrambling plants such as ivy, nasturtiums, clematis, honeysuckle, and black-eyed Susan *(Thunbergia)* are all suitable for training on supports.

HOLLY STANDARD
A holly tree grown as a standard produces an eye-catching sphere of glossy, spiny foliage, adding height to the colorful underplanting of fuchsias and trailing plants.

ADDING TEXTURE

The word "texture" is usually used to describe the feel of a substance, but while some plants are, indeed, very tactile, texture when applied to plants usually describes a visual effect. Most containers are planned around flower or foliage color and plant form, but the texture of flowers or foliage is another aspect to take into consideration. The sympathetic use of different textures can make the difference between a run-of-the-mill planting and one that has a really outstanding effect. Plant foliage may be sturdy, firm, and bold, or feathery, light, and hazy; it may be sharply pointed and swordlike or softly rounded. As a general rule, feathery plants provide a good background and margin for a container planting, with bolder shapes displayed against them. It is the finely cut or fluffy plants, such as ferns and grasses, that usually supply the contrast of texture in a mixed planting.

Texture can be introduced by means of a planting prop. A wire shape such as a pyramid or ball can be filled with soil mix held in place by sphagnum moss around the outside, and low-growing plants such as pansies, lobelia, or double daisies planted through the moss – rather like an upside-down hanging basket.

TEXTURED FOLIAGE

Alchemilla mollis
Lady's mantle
Softly scalloped, downy leaves that hold sparkling drops of dew, with open, fluffy heads of tiny lime-green flowers.

Artemisia
Wormwood
Bright steel-blue or silver foliage, often finely cut or filigreed, and sometimes aromatic. *A. schmidtiana* "Nana" or A. "Powis Castle" are good choices.

Cordyline australis
New Zealand cabbage palm
A strong palmlike outline with spiky, swordshaped foliage with bold stripes and margins. Suitable for patio tubs and conservatories.

Festuca glauca
Blue fescue, Blue grass
A fully hardy, fine-leaved evergreen bearing tufted blue-green to blue-gray grass that forms a hazy mound (see p. 23).

Gypsophila paniculata
Baby's breath
Delicate branching flower stems bearing clusters of tiny trumpetshaped flowers that form a misty white cloud.

Nigella damascena
Love-in-a-mist
Blue-petaled flowers, surrounded by a collar of green, slender leaves, arise from finely cut, bright green foliage. *N. d.* "Dwarf Moody Blue" and N. d. "Blue Midget" are dwarf varieties.

Phormium tenax
New Zealand flax
A striking rosette of bold, swordlike, sturdy leaves, in yellow-green to dark green, often striped. *P. t.* "Bronze Baby" is a dwarf hybrid with attractive bronze leaves.

Sempervivum andrachnoideum
Cobweb houseleek
Rosettes of succulent, fleshy leaves are laced together at their tips with a cobweb of fine hairs.

Stachys byzantina
Lambs' ears
Silver-green leaves covered in silky-soft hairs that give them a velvety look and feel. Spikes of pink-purple flowers appear in summer.

SPECIMEN PLANTS

Acontainer planted up with a single, impressive specimen can make an excellent focal point for a garden and can be more effective than a colorful and varied mixed planting. Specimen plants should be striking in terms of their flowers and foliage but, more often, it is their overall shape that earns them the title of "architectural" plants.

MAKING A STATEMENT

Many specimen plants have a bold, imposing, even eccentric outline that needs to be offset against a plain background for maximum effect. Examples include the spiky, swordlike forms of cordylines and phormiums, the strangely twisted and contorted corkscrew hazel (*Corylus avellana)*, or the bold mounds of giant feather grass.

Other plants can be trained and clipped to achieve impressive shapes. Bay laurel and box are favorite candidates for training into standards, balls, pyramids, spirals, cones, and a range of other stately forms.

FLOWERS AND FOLIAGE

Many shrubs, including flowering species, make excellent specimen plants when they are grown as standards: fuchsias, marguerites, roses, and hollies are popular, but willow, laurustinus, and photinia make more unusual focal points.

The delicate foliage and fall color of Japanese maples make these small trees popular to use as specimens for containers. Specimens grown for their flowers have a short but spectacular season of interest. In early spring, the perfect, waxy flowers of camellias shine richly among the dark green, glossy foliage; a few weeks later, the loosely formed

FERN PALM AS A SPECIMEN

white flowers of star magnolia (*Magnolia stellata)* deck the bare, spreading branches. Angels' trumpets (*Brugmansia* x *candida* "Knightii") make a rounded shrub with impressive leaves, and beautiful, trumpetshaped flowers that release their perfume on summer evenings.

ARCHITECTURAL PLANTS

Acer palmatum
Japanese maple
A low, spreading, mound-forming shrub with delicate foliage that colors well in the fall. "Dissectum" has finely cut leaves.

Agave americana
Century plant
A bold rosette of strong, fleshy, pointed leaves, armed with sharp spikes along their margins. "Marginata" has leaves edged with gold bands.

Astelia chathamica
Silver spear
Upright rosettes of silver-gray, sharply pointed foliage, reaching up to 5 ft (1.5 m) in length.

Brugmansia x candida "Knightii"
Angels' trumpets
Tender plant with large, drooping, double flowers, creamy white and heavily scented. All parts are highly toxic if eaten.

Canna
Indian shot plant
Large, oval leaves, often bronze and sometimes finely striped in an array of red, orange, and cream shades. Showy, exotic-looking blooms are carried on tall stems; "Assaut" has scarlet flowers; "King Midas" has golden yellow flowers.

Dicksonia antarctica
Woolly tree fern
Very showy, unusual, treelike fern with a stout, fibrous trunk topped with wide-spreading, mid-green fronds. New fronds unfurl from tightly curled "croziers" in the center of the plant.

Fatsia japonica
Japanese aralia
Large, bold, palmshaped leaves of a deep, glossy green. Drumstick heads of small white flowers appear in the fall, turning to black fruits.

Laurus nobilis
Bay laurel
Pointed, dark green, aromatic leaves with small, fluffy yellow flowers in early spring. "Aurea" has golden yellow foliage. Can be clipped to shape and trained as a standard. Contact with foliage may irritate skin.

Stipa gigantea
Giant feather grass
Arching mounds of slender, mid-green foliage and airy, feathery plumes of flowers carried on tall stems in late summer.

Trachycarpus fortunei
Chusan palm
Rounded, deeply divided, palmlike fronds are carried at the ends of long stems on top of a rough, fibrous trunk. Slow growing.

Yucca filamentosa
Adam's needle
Evergreen rosettes of long, swordshaped leaves with fibrous threads unraveling along their margins. Established plants bear panicles of creamy white, cupshaped flowers in summer. "Variegata" has white-margined leaves, tinged pink in winter.

GIANT FEATHER GRASS

UNUSUAL FEATURES

Containers can be used to create an unusual and individual garden feature. An old bathtub or wheelbarrow makes an ideal showcase for a collection of special plants, while a teapot that has lost its handle or a favorite old pair of garden boots make whimsical outer pots.

MAKING A SCENE

■ **Full to the brim** A tall, elegant water jug filled with trailing plants such as deep blue anagallis and white-flowered sutera gives the effect of foaming water flowing out. Tilt the jug slightly to give the impression of contents spilling out.

■ **Alpine fresh** An old trough filled with alpine plants can nestle among scree and rocky outcrops to echo a mountainside scene.

■ **Secret dell** A hollowed-out log makes an excellent setting for ferns, violets, and other woodland plants.

■ **Along the coast** Rope-coiled pots or a disused lobster pot planted with sea holly, dorotheanthus, rosemary, and tamarisk can be set on pebbles, shells, and driftwood to conjure up a harborside setting.

■ **Forgotten corner** A tall, slender traditional-style chimney pot can be planted and wreathed with ivy to give a deliberate tumble-down effect.

STACKED TOGETHER
A selection of slender chimney pots filled with summer flowers adds old-world charm to the tumble-down look of a cottage garden.

5
WINDOW BOXES

*Lushly planted window boxes really help to strengthen
the link between a house and its garden, by echoing
the style and colors of a planting theme. In courtyard
gardens and on apartment balconies they provide
virtually all of the growing space available. They not
only improve and enhance the appearance of the building
from the outside, but when planted with a well-thought-
out scheme, they can be appreciated just as much from
within the home as without.*

*There are many practical points to bear in mind
when fixing and planting window boxes, to make sure
that they are safe, easy to care for, and have long-lasting
appeal. Herbs and foliage plants can be used as well
as flowers, and scented plants are particularly welcome
beneath an open window, where their scent can drift
into the house.*

WINDOW DRESSING

Designed to suit platforms and ledges, window boxes are low, rectangular troughs, which can be fixed to external walls, just below the level of a window. They make use of otherwise sterile wall space, and are particularly important for houses without gardens where, along with hanging baskets, they provide a vital growing area.

POINTS TO CONSIDER

■ **Light-saving** Exactly where a window box should be positioned depends to some extent on the style of the window. It may seem obvious to stand the window box on an outer sill, but this is not always practical. Unless the windows are tall, the box and the plants it contains are going to block out quite a lot of light from the room. If casement-type windows that open outward have been fitted, a box will prevent them from being opened. For this reason, sash or inward-opening windows are better suited to having window boxes placed in front of them.

■ **Secure fixing** It is essential that window boxes are fixed securely. This protects your plants and passersby from damage and injury should the box become dislodged in bad weather or accidentally knocked off. In general, it is best to attach boxes below the sill (see pp. 84–85).

■ **Room with a view** Window boxes make the outside of the building more attractive, but they can also be appreciated from the inside, too – a fact that is sometimes forgotten when planning their planting. Rather than creating a one-sided display that is best enjoyed by your neighbors, arrange the plants in an evenly balanced display so that you can appreciate them from indoors, too.

■ **Alternative uses** Window boxes do not always have to be positioned outside windows. They can be used as freestanding troughs on walls or steps; they also look effective when secured to railings, particularly on balconies, or used to decorate the roof of a garden shed. A dull, blank wall can be easily livened up by painting on some representations of simple window frames and fixing window boxes below them to form an effective *trompe l'oeil*.

LIGHTWEIGHT PLASTIC WINDOW BOX

Drip tray stops water from spilling over

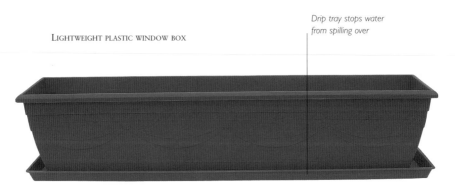

ROOM WITH A VIEW
Scarlet-red pelargoniums make
an eye-catching contribution
to this floral window display.

SIZE AND SHAPE

Most window boxes are rectangular, but their
size varies considerably. If the box is to be fixed
below the window sill, you will not be restricted
to finding one that fits the space exactly; for the
most pleasing effect, try to keep the length of
the box in proportion to the width and the height
of the window. The best appearance is usually
obtained from a window box that is slightly
wider than the window, and you may find that you
need to use two boxes to fill the space available.
Remember that a deep box retains moisture better,
but if a deep box is placed on a window sill it
will block too much light from the room.

Warning

Bear in mind that
deep window boxes
are very heavy once
they have been filled
with soil and plants.
Take care when lifting
and moving them, and
check that they are
fixed securely in place.

FLOWERING LEDGES

When choosing a window box it is particularly important to select one that will blend happily with the style of your house, as the window box will become a fixture of the house itself. However eye-catching the plants, an inappropriate box will jar and spoil the display.

THE RIGHT TYPE

Most window boxes are made from wood, plastic, fiberglass, or terra-cotta. Given that window boxes are invariably suspended off the ground, it is best to keep the weight of the box to a minimum so as to reduce stress on the fixings. A lightweight box will also be easier to handle if you need to move the box to a more convenient place when tending to your plants. Alternatively, choose a plain, lightweight trough as the inner container, which can then be housed in a more decorative outer box.

Window boxes usually follow the same formal pattern in which house windows are arranged; where more than two or more boxes are used, make sure that they are all the same style to create a coherent effect. Wooden boxes can be painted to blend with the house, or to give them a distinctive individual style.

HUES OF BLUE
A cool-colored planting scheme of low-growing and trailing blue-flowered plants provides a refreshing window-box display.

TOP TIPS

• A spare inner container can be prepared with fresh plants as an instant replacement for a fading display.

• Painted walls and white-curtained windows make good backdrops for bold, colorful plantings.

• Apply a plant-safe, weatherproof preservative to wooden troughs before planting up (see p. 215).

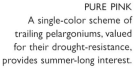

PURE PINK
A single-color scheme of trailing pelargoniums, valued for their drought-resistance, provides summer-long interest.

WATERING AND DRAINAGE

Like all containers, window boxes hold a relatively small amount of soil, which gives rise to the usual problems of regulating the water supply. Because window boxes are sheltered from rainfall by their position against the house, they will need frequent watering. This can be a problem if access to them is difficult. If a window box is fixed below the level of an upper-story window sill, it should be possible to water the plants by reaching through the window. If the window opens outward, however, the plants may eventually grow too tall for the window to be opened without damaging them. If it is not possible to water plants through the adjacent window, you may need to use an attachment to your watering system to help you reach. Various hose fittings and devices are available to make watering from below easier (see p. 99).

Water must also be able to drain away from a box – but preferably not down the wall of the house, where it can leave unattractive stains and possibly cause damp to penetrate the wall. Like any other container, a window box should have drainage holes in its base, preferably situated toward the front of the box, keeping the drainage water clear of the wall. A drip tray fitted below a window box is useful to prevent water from overspilling, but do not allow the box to remain standing in water.

PLANTING UP

B efore starting to plant a window box or trough, you need to decide
whether it will be practical to transport and fix the container in
position after planting, or whether it will be best to part plant or
postpone planting until it has been placed in its final position. Once
the box has been filled with soil, planted up, and watered, it is too late
to discover that it is heavy and awkward to maneuver through the
window frame or to carry up a ladder. If planting up the box *in situ*
is likely to be difficult, then look for a lightweight container that will
fit comfortably inside your window box. This "inner box" can then
be planted up and placed into the fixed "outer" window box.

STEP-BY-STEP PLANTING

1 When planting directly into the window box,
check that there are sufficient drainage holes
in the base. Make additional holes, if necessary,
and cover these with crocks and a layer of coarse
gravel to ensure they do not become blocked.
An internal reservoir tray may be fitted in the
base of the window box to ensure a constant
supply of water for the plants.

*Internal reservoir ensures
constant water supply*

*Water-retaining
granules absorb
and release moisture*

2 Half-fill the box with a lightweight, potting
soilless mix; supplement the mix with water-
retaining granules and slow-release fertilizer,
applied at the manufacturer's recommended rate.

Trailing plants will curtain trough front

Young evergreen adds height to display

3 Position the plants (still in their pots) in the window box to achieve the best arrangement of their upright, flowering, or trailing features. If your box is to be visible from both sides, adjust the planting to ensure a well-balanced, all-round display.

4 Once the plants are arranged to your satisfaction, ease each plant gently out of its pot and insert firmly in the soil. Seasonal plants can be set within separate pots to make them easier to remove once they have passed their best and are ready to be replaced.

5 Position any individually potted plants within the window box, and fill in around and over the top of them with soil mix so that they are completely concealed. Water the arrangement well, then fix the window box securely into position.

6 As individual plants start to fade, the inner containers in which they are growing can be removed without disturbing the long-term plants. Replace them with an appropriate seasonal plant that is ready to flower, water well and enjoy the display.

FIXING A WINDOW BOX

Even on the ground floor, a window box that falls from its position
means a ruined display, wasting your time and money. Secure
fixing is therefore very important, and as far as safety is concerned,
its importance increases the higher up the window box is displayed.

USING THE WINDOW SILL

A planted-up window box is
surprisingly heavy. Its long, narrow
shape – and often narrow base – can
also make it unstable, especially as
the plants grow in size. If a window
box is positioned on an upper-story
window sill it must be sitting on a
level surface and properly secured
with hooks and screws to prevent it
from falling or being knocked off.
To avoid a potentially lethal accident,
run through the following checklist:

■ **Window opening** Check which
way a window opens before siting
a window box in front of it. If the

window opens outward, it be will
obstructed by the box and you will
not be able to use it for ventilation.

■ **Sound window sill** The sill must
be broad and sturdy enough to hold
the weight of a freshly watered box
at the peak of its growth.

■ **Sloping sills** Most window sills
slope downward in order to drain
water away from the window frame,
so wedges need to be placed under
the front edge of the window box
to level it. This will also improve
drainage from the base of the box.

KIT FOR FIXING A WINDOW BOX
BENEATH A CASEMENT WINDOW

Fixings

*Adjustment to fit
brackets to
width of box*

Wall bracket

*Window-box
support*

FIXING TIPS

If you are positioning your window box below the sill, it must be securely attached to the wall with L-shaped or angle brackets. First, screw the brackets to each side of the box, and then to the wall.

■ **Fixings** When fixing brackets to walls, drill holes with a masonry bit and use a special wall plug fixing which will ensure that the bracket is held securely in the brickwork. Alternatively, use wooden dowels inserted into holes drilled in the brickwork, fixing the screws for the brackets into the ends of the dowels.

■ **Making a ledge** To make a ledge for the window box to sit on, screw two or more (depending on the length of the box) sturdy metal brackets directly into the wall at a suitable distance below the window sill; a piece of timber can be fixed across the brackets to make a solid shelf, if desired.

BRIGHTER BRICKWORK

• When hanging troughs to relieve the monotony of a plain brick wall, position them at different heights to divert the eye away from the parallel rows of bricks.

• Avoid positioning window boxes one directly beneath the other as the lower box will be set in shade and receive less rainfall.

• Create a tiered focal point in your garden by placing a ground-level grouping of containers below an arrangement of window boxes on a wall. Repeat a key color, container style, or range of plants throughout the display for maximum impact.

• Create a showcase on which to display your boxes. Fix a series of shelves on the wall and encase them with a frame. Alternate two different styles or colors of boxes along the shelves for a striking effect.

■ **Adding chains** For extra security, run chains from the front edge of the box to the window frame, hooking them into metal eyes at each end.

■ **Using wall mangers** Wrought-iron mangers may be fixed to the walls below windows. These look attractive even when empty, and can be used to hold a lightweight window box.

■ **Metal bar** A slim metal bar can be fixed as a restraint across the width of the window frame, about 4–6 in (10–15 cm) above the sill. This acts as a reassuring check that the box cannot fall, and allows small pots to be stood on the sill, too.

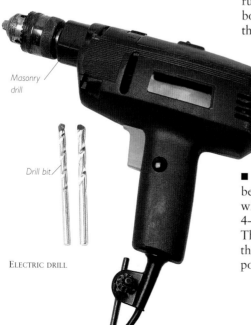

Masonry drill

Drill bit

ELECTRIC DRILL

WINTER WINDOW BOX

Generally, window boxes tend to be regarded as summer fixtures – emptied as soon as the first frost arrives, and stored away until the following spring. They can, however, provide plenty of interest during other seasons, even in the depths of winter.

STRIKING WHITES

Although *Helleborus niger* is commonly known as the Christmas rose, the wide, saucerlike blooms do not usually appear until early January in the open garden. In a sheltered window box, Christmas roses will bloom earlier; their sheltered position and the warmth radiated through the house walls, means that the plants are less subject to weather damage.

Borne on sturdy purple-marked stems, the ivory-white flowers boast a central boss of gold stamens. They will remain perfect in their elevated position, and can be appreciated more easily than when they are nodding at ground level.

For a dramatic contrast in your planting, add *Helleborus* x *hybridus* "Ballard's Black," which bears deep, dark purple flowers or *H.* x *h.* "Peggy Ballard," with its large flowers colored dark red on the outside and heavily veined dusky-pink inside.

Common snowdrops *(Galanthus nivalis)* make the perfect partners in a winter window box; the single varieties, such as *G. n.* "Scharlockii" and *G. n.* "Sandersii," have more elegance and grace than the stocky, frilly edged doubles. Their dainty, nodding white flowers often bear green markings or, in the case of "Scharlockii," pale yellow markings and a yellow base.

Curling tendrils of a white-variegated ivy such as *Hedera helix* "Glacier" complete the snowy theme. They can be trailed down the sides of the window box to soften the hard edges of the container.

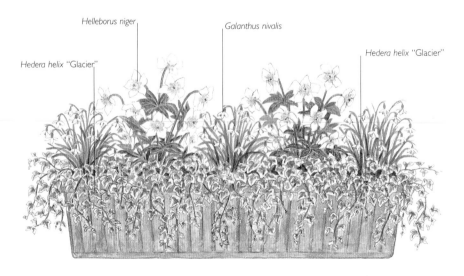

Helleborus niger

Galanthus nivalis

Hedera helix "Glacier"

Hedera helix "Glacier"

Spring Pleasures

Flowering spring bulbs are always among the most welcome plants in the garden and need little in the way of elaborate styling to give a cheerful display. A bold and simple contrast of colors, interspersed with bright green foliage, makes a most effective window box.

Fresh blooms

The hardy grape hyacinth *(Muscari armeniacum)* is a prolific plant; its bellshaped flowers, which are clustered on short stems like bunches of grapes, are an intense, bright blue, an unusual shade among spring bulbs. *M. a.* "Early Giant" has large, deep cobalt-blue blooms that have a pleasant perfume.

The buttercup-yellow flowers of the dwarf daffodil *Narcissus* "Tête-à-Tête" contrast well with grape hyacinths. Its slightly nodding flowers are perfect golden trumpet daffodils in miniature.

For the best flowering display, raise the bulbs in pots until the flowerbuds have formed, then transfer them to the window box to flower; this gives more control over the final result than planting directly into the box.

SPRING BULBS

Below is a small selection of the many small, spring-flowering bulbs suitable for growing in containers.

• *Anemone blanda* "Ingramii"

• *Crocus chrysanthus* "Eye-catcher;" *C. c.* "Snow Bunting;" *C. minimus*

• *Hyacinthus orientalis* "Ostara;" *H. o.* "Delft Blue;" *H. o.* "City of Haarlem"

• *Iris danfordiae; Iris winogradowii*

• Dwarf tulips *(Tulipa)*: Choose from the Kaufmanniana and Greigii groups

• Dwarf daffodils *(Narcissus)*: Choose from the Triandrus, Cyclamineus, and Jonquilla groups

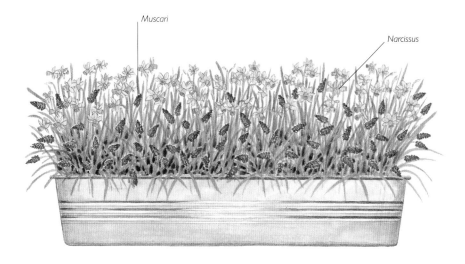

Muscari

Narcissus

SUMMER SPECIALS

The vast array of colors offered by summer flowers often tempts us to throw caution aside and go for a "riot of color" approach when planting. This does not always work successfully within the confined space of a window box, making individual colors look "spotty" and disjointed. A restrained color scheme is usually more satisfying.

SUNNY SPLENDOR

Yellow is always a popular color, with its sunny, cheerful effect. There are many shades of yellow, from gentlest pastel primrose to glowing golden orange; all can be offset attractively by fresh green foliage.

Creeping zinnia *(Sanvitalia procumbens)* and its cultivars make a popular container plant, valued for their long flowering period from early summer to early fall. Large numbers of bright yellow daisylike flowers with distinctive black eyes spangle the foliage in summer. *S. p.* "Gold Braid" is a compact variety; the dwarf creeping zinnia *S. p.* "Golden Carpet" produces small, lemon flowers that are set off against very dark green foliage.

The large many-petaled flowers of *Gazania* Daybreak Series closely resemble small sunflowers. The flower centers are accentuated by a brown ring, and petal colors range from creamy yellow through gold and orange to deep mahogany, some with contrasting stripes. All of the shades blend well together and are enhanced by the deep green, linear leaves with silver, felted undersides.

Another plant with soft-haired foliage is helichrysum *(Helichrysum petiolare)* whose woolly, semi-trailing stems are set with neat, oval leaves covered in fine hairs. *H. p.* "Limelight" has lime-green foliage; *H. p.* "Variegatum" has gray leaves, with cream variegation.

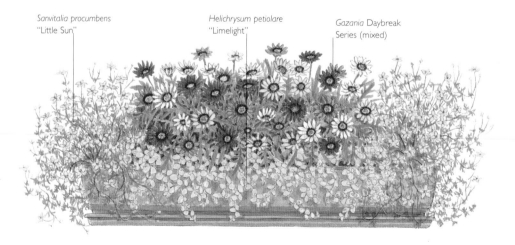

Sanvitalia procumbens
"Little Sun"

Helichrysum petiolare
"Limelight"

Gazania Daybreak
Series (mixed)

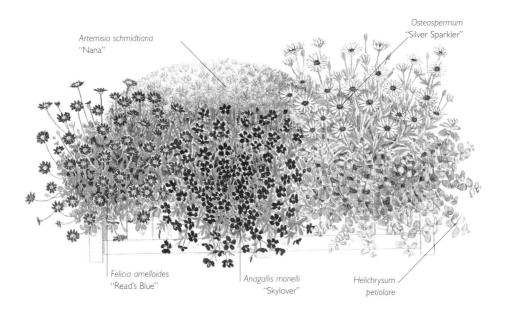

Artemisia schmidtiana "Nana"

Osteospermum "Silver Sparkler"

Felicia amelloides "Read's Blue"

Anagallis monelli "Skylover"

Helichrysum petiolare

COLOR CHOICES

YELLOW	BLUE
Chrysanthemum multicaule "Moonlight"	**Ageratum "Blue Mist"**
Dorotheanthus bellidiformis "Lunette"	**Brachyscome "Blue Mist"** Swan river daisy
Lotus maculatus	**Convolvulus sabatius** Bindweed
Lamium maculatum "Cannon's Gold" Dead nettle	**Lobelia erinus "Crystal Palace;" L. e. "Sapphire"**
Nemesia strumosa Triumph Series	**Nemesia strumosa "Blue Gem"**
Thymophylla tenuiloba Golden fleece	**Plumbago auriculata** Cape leadwort
Viola Crystal Bowl Series (yellow) Pansy	**Scaevola aemula** Fairy fan-flower
	Surfinia "Violet Blue"

COOL BLUES

At the opposite end of the color spectrum, blue shades offer a cool and sophisticated effect and look particularly good against a white background. *Artemisia schmidtiana* "Nana," a perennial wormwood, has very finely cut, silver-blue foliage that makes a series of overlapping rosettes to form a distinctive rounded mound. The vigorous blue daisy, *Felicia amelloides* "Read's Blue" has strong blue petals offset by yellow centers. The informal outline and saucer-shaped flowers of blue pimpernel, here *Anagallis monelli* "Skylover," tumble over the front of the box.

The inclusion of white flowers in a scheme usually helps to highlight blue shades more effectively. This planting is lightened by the cream-variegated foliage of *Osteospermum* "Silver Sparkler," with sparkling white flowers pierced by powder-blue centers. The cool tone is continued with the silver, furry stems of *Helichrysum petiolare.*

WINDOWBOX HERBS

Culinary herbs have so many qualities – they look attractive, smell wonderful, and turn almost any food you prepare into something special. A window box is, in many ways, an ideal place in which to grow herbs, keeping them close at hand so they are ready to use.

COOK'S DELIGHT

Most compact herbs suit window boxes, although large, shrubby kinds raised as rooted cuttings or small plants will tolerate the confines of a box for up to three years.

■ **Preparation** Clean and prepare the window box, ensuring adequate drainage and using a good quality potting soil mix (see pp. 280–81). Most gardening experts advise against giving herbs too much fertilizer, as strong, lush growth is less aromatic than the hard growth produced by poor soil. Apply a moderate amount of slow-release fertilizer to encourage plenty of new

growth to replace shoot tips as they are harvested. Most herbs are perennial, but if you cut window box herbs regularly, you may find it more useful to treat them as annuals.

■ **Siting** Ideally, herbs should be placed where they will receive at least some direct sun daily. Place the box by a window that can be opened, so that you can pick the herbs and enjoy their aroma.

HERBS GALORE
With its good looks and tasty foliage, a tiered trough crammed full of kitchen herbs will delight cooks and gardeners alike.

HERBS FOR CONTAINERS

***Ocimum* spp.**
Basil
• Greek or bush basil
(*O. campechianum* var.
minimum) is ideal for
growing in small
containers. Its clove-
scented leaves are good
with tomato dishes. *O.
basilicum* "Spicy Globe"
makes a compact plant.
• Can be harvested until
late fall.
• Raise from seed.

Anthriscus cerefolium
Chervil
• Soft, lacy, fernlike leaves
have a mild
aniseed flavor.
• Useful in salads and
with eggs.
• Raise from seed.

Allium schoenopraseum
Chives
• Grassy upright leaves
are onionflavored.
• Harvest by cutting the
leaves right to the base
with sharp scissors.
• Buy young plants.

MINT

Origanum
Marjoram
• Sweet marjoram
(*Origanum majorana*) has
a warm, sweet fragrance.
• Good with chicken
dishes and tomatoes.
• Buy young plants.

Mentha
Mint
• Mint is a rampant
grower so confine it to
an individual pot sunk
in the soil.
• Pineapple mint (*M.
suaveolens* "Variegata") has
creamy variegated leaves;
ginger mint (*M.* x *gracilis*)
is beautifully veined gold.
• Buy young plants.

Petroselinum
Parsley
• Curled, frilly leaved
parsley(such as *P. crispum*
"Afro") has mossy, deep
green foliage that suits
decorative use.
• Flat-leaved varieties,
such as French or Italian
parsley (*P. crispum* var.
neapolitanum), have the
best flavor.
• Grow as an annual
from seed. Presoak the
seed in hot water to
speed up germination.

Rosmarinus
Rosemary
• Pretty blue flowers and
silvery, needlelike leaves
with a distinctive aroma.
• Use the low-growing,
creeping rosemary
(*R.* Prostratus Group)
for window boxes.
• Good for flavoring
oils and vinegars.
• Buy young plants.

SAGE

Salvia
Sage
• Gray-green, wrinkled
leaves have a warm and
pungent scent.
• *Salvia* "Icterina" has
creamy yellow foliage.
• Buy young plants.
• The leaves of scarlet
or red sage (*S. coccinea*)
can be dried for use in
potpourri.

Artemisia dracunculus
Tarragon
• Slender, spearshaped
leaves have a minty
aniseed flavor.
• Buy young plants; seed-
raised tarragon is said to
have an inferior flavor.

***Thymus* spp.**
Thyme
• Thyme's tiny, oval leaves
are intensely fragrant.
• Ideal for growing in
window boxes.
• Lemon thyme
(*T.* x *citriodorus*) is
a culinary favorite.
• Buy young plants.

THE VALUE OF FOLIAGE

By far the majority of window boxes are filled with flowering plants, but a foliage-only box can make a refreshing change. The subtle blend of cool green shades creates a lush effect for hot, parched summer days and contrasts with other boxes brimming with flowers.

FOLIAGE FAVORITES

■ **Senecio** *Senecio cineraria* "Silver Dust" has bright silver, lacy, deeply cut leaves while *S. c.* "Cirrus" has round, silver-white leaves with less deeply indented margins.

■ **Coleus or painted nettle** *Solenostemon scutellarioides* has serrated-edged foliage in a stunning assortment of brilliant colors. *S. c.* "Pineapple Beauty" has yellow-green leaves with purple markings *S. c.* "Royal Scot" has bright red leaves with khaki centers.

■ **Perilla** *Perilla frutescens* var. *crispa* has deep bronze-purple foliage with serrated, crisped, and wavy margins.

■ **Burning bush** The soft, light green leaves of the coniferlike *Bassia scoparia f. trichophylla* turn bright red or purple toward fall.

■ **Houseleeks** *Sempervivum* are evergreen succulents with rosettes of thick, pointed leaves. The cobweb houseleek *(S. arachnoideum)* is coated in soft white hairs; the vigorous-growing common houseleek *(S. tectorum)* has blue-green to red-purple leaves.

FLATTERING FOLIAGE
The broad, lush-green leaves of the hosta and delicately variegated ivy uplift this small group of containers in a shady corner.

COMPACT SHRUBS

Although shrubs and subshrubs may eventually outgrow a window box, some make worthwhile short-term tenants. Spotted laurel *(Aucuba japonica)* is an excellent choice for a winter box; particularly variegated varieties, such as the yellow-speckled "Gold Dust." Several hebes are also suitable, including *Hebe* x *andersonii* "Variegata," which is freely available as a small plant. Spindle tree *(Euonymus)* is another good choice, particularly variegated varieties such as *Euonymus fortunei* "Harlequin" and *E. f.* "Emerald 'n' Gold."

Dwarf conifers provide variations in color, form, and texture in a window box, from the upright, deep green column of the common juniper (*Juniperus communis* "Compressa") to the starry blue pyramid of the spruce, *Picea glauca* "Alberta Blue," and the fluffy textured, bronze-green Japanese cedar *Cryptomeria japonica* "Vilmoriniana."

CREEPERS AND TRAILERS

Many foliage plants are widely used as trailing subjects in mixed plantings. *Glechoma hederacea, Helichrysum petiolare,* and *Lamium maculatum* are among the most popular, and an exciting range of colored and variegated forms is available.

Coral gem *(Lotus berthelotii)* has, in warm summers, showy scarlet blooms, but it is valued for its cascades of silver, needlelike foliage. The variety names of creeping bugle *(Ajuga reptans)* – "Burgundy Glow," "Multicolor," "Pink Splendor," "Purple Brocade," and "Silver Shadow" – give an idea of the wide range of color forms that exist.

Attractive variegated leaf adds color interest

VARIEGATED TRAILING IVY

FINE FRAGRANCE

Scented plants are the perfect choice for planting in window boxes with the window open, their fragrance can drift into the house on the warm summer air. Scent from flowers is the most valuable, as it is freely released; fragrance from aromatic foliage can usually only be appreciated if the leaves have been bruised or handled.

CHOOSING SCENTS

Flowers generally have sweet scents, which in most cases, it is impossible to describe accurately, although "honeylike," "fruity," or "spicy" may give an idea of their fragrance. The appreciation of fragrance is a very personal sensation, and what is a strong, pleasant scent to one person can appear light or even nonexistent to someone else.

Sadly, some modern varieties of plants that were once well known for their scent may no longer have any fragrance – the perfume has been bred out of them in the quest for other attributes. This may apply particularly to plants that are suitable for window boxes, as modern, dwarf varieties often seem to have sacrificed scent for compact growth. Dwarf varieties of pinks *(Dianthus)*, sweet peas *(Lathyrus)*, and flowering tobacco *(Nicotiana)* all need to be selected carefully to ensure the ones chosen retain a reasonable perfume.

Many flowers release most of their perfume in the early evening, and this is often the best time to enjoy a scented window box. Fragrance may also be intensified by a shower of rain – an effect that can be re-created by watering a plant lightly with a fine spray fitted on a watering can.

Plants with aromatic foliage often have insignificant flowers, but this is a small price to pay for their sensual delights. Scented-leaved pelargoniums, for example, make a valuable addition to a box, offering a range of aromas from apple, lemon, and orange to nutmeg and balsam. As is the case with all aromatic foliage, be sure to plant them within reach where they can be gently squeezed in passing to release their heady scents.

LAVENDER SPRIG

SCENTED FLOWERS

Dianthus (dwarf varieties)
Pinks

Exacum affine
Persian violet

Heliotropum peruvianum
Cherry pie

Hyacinthus orientalis
Hyacinth

Laurentia axillaris
Shooting stars

Lathyrus odorata (dwarf varieties)
Sweet pea

Lavandula species
Lavender

Nemesia denticulata

Nicotiana hybrids
Flowering tobacco

Verbena hybrids

NICOTIANA "LIME GREEN"

6
HANGING BASKETS AND WALL POTS

Hanging baskets and wall pots add a completely new dimension to a garden. Their care can sometimes be difficult, but using a few simple tricks when planting and hanging will help to ensure a trouble-free, long-lasting display.

Although baskets and wall pots are usually features of summer gardens, there is no reason why they cannot be decorative through the winter months and into spring as well. They can even be used to grow food crops, providing a miniature kitchen garden.

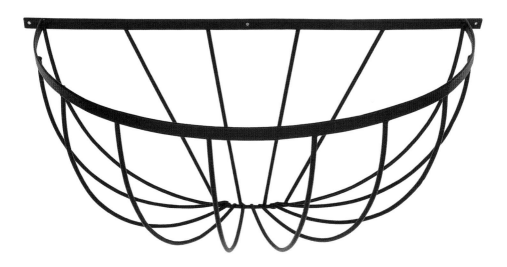

HANGING BASKETS

Unlike other types of plant containers, hanging baskets are designed to be viewed mainly from below. With a little skill and careful planning, you can create a stunning sphere of color, such that the container itself is completely hidden by flowers and foliage.

BASKET STYLES

■ **Open sided** The traditional basket is made from plastic-coated wire, and can be hemispherical, hexagonal, or bowl shaped with a flattened base. When choosing a wire basket, make sure the spaces between the wires are large enough to insert plants through, otherwise the point of such a basket is lost.

■ **Solid sided** The main advantage of hanging containers with solid sides is that they conserve water. Trailing plants can be set around the edges of the basket so that they hang down and disguise the container itself, but the effect is never quite as dramatic as a traditional wire basket with plants emerging through the side walls. Because the sides are more likely to be seen, look for containers made from materials that have an interesting texture or design; for example, coiled-rope, wicker, and stained wood versions all provide an attractive backdrop for plantings.

■ **Basket pillar** If you do not have any available hanging space in your garden, but would still like to have a basket feature, choose a freestanding basket pillar (see p. 12). Basket pillars comprise three or four tiers of wire, hemispherical baskets, fixed to a central stem. The baskets are arranged by size, with the smallest at the top of the pillar. When fully planted, they create an attractive cascade of flowers and foliage.

HEXAGONAL
WIRE BASKET

Trailing foliage can be trained around wire framework

■ **Flower tower** This comprises a shallow bowl and hanging frame joined together by a long tube of polyethylene. The tube is filled with soil mix, and the walls are pierced with planting holes. Plants soon cover the entire tower, and the bowl at the base acts as a water reservoir, making routine care easy.

Basket linings

The one major drawback of hanging baskets is that they dry out extremely quickly. To hold the soil mix in place and to keep moisture loss to a minimum, all open-sided baskets need to be lined. Remember that open, porous lining materials such as moss and grass clippings need to be partly covered with a sheet of pierced polyethylene before soil mix and plants are added to the basket, otherwise water drains through them too rapidly.

■ **Moss** Sphagnum moss still has much to commend for lining baskets. It looks attractive, holds moisture well, and allows plants to be inserted around the sides of the basket. Compressed, dried moss (harvested from renewable resources) is available as shaped liners or in small bales, swelling to shape rapidly once watered; it is easy and convenient to buy and to use.

■ **Grass** Clippings of grass collected by the lawn mower can be recycled for basket lining, though they need to be wilted by just the right amount to make them manageable – leave them in a heap for a day or two before use.

■ **Liners** Proprietary liners are made from substances such as coir fiber, wool and wood waste, pulped paper, or plastic, and usually cut or molded to fit a specific size of basket. They are all effective at holding in soil and moisture but some are difficult to pierce with holes or do not allow any side planting – which defeats the object of using a traditional-style open-weave wire basket.

MOLDED, RIGID LINER

COMPRESSED MOSS LINER

Shaped to fit circular baskets

COIR-FIBER LINER

SPHAGNUM MOSS

HANGING THE BASKETS

The ideal position for hanging baskets is at a suitable height to prevent them from getting in the way, but not so far out of reach that watering becomes impossibly difficult. The basket will need several hours of sunshine but some light shade for part of each day to cut down water loss; it should also be sheltered from winds.

FIRMLY FIXED

Most hanging baskets are supported by three chains evenly spaced around the rim and brought together at a large hook above the top of the basket. While the basket is being planted up, the chains can be removed to prevent them from getting in the way, but make sure that the plants are not positioned where they will be damaged by the chains once they are linked up again for hanging.

Although a hanging basket is quite small, it is, like most containers, surprisingly heavy when fully planted and watered; for this reason, a sturdy support system is essential. In some cases a basket can hang from a simple hook fixed to the overhead beam of a pergola or porch, for example, but usually a bracket is necessary to hold the basket away from a wall. The safest type is a triangular rather than an L-shaped bracket, with a diagonal strut to help spread the load. Some baskets are not suspended from the bracket but designed to fit on top of it instead, held in place by a upward-facing spike that fits in a socket. This

TRIANGULAR
HANGING BRACKET

Hanging point

D-ring hook
for fixing to
basket

HANGING CHAINS AND HOOK

arrangement eliminates having to use chains, which can restrict the plants' growth. A padlock can also be fitted through the spike and socket to prevent baskets from being stolen.

WATERING

FLOWERING BELLES
Whether planted up with a single- or mixed-color scheme, hanging baskets provide a most satisfying way to display summer flowers.

It is hardly any wonder that hanging baskets dry out so rapidly: they are shallow and densely planted, the soil is exposed to the air, and they are hung in open positions, where they are exposed to full sun and drying winds. The majority of baskets require watering at least daily during the summer, sometimes twice a day, and any steps that can be taken to make watering easier are worthwhile. Always allow space for watering when filling and planting up the basket (see pp. 298–99).

■ **Pulley systems** A simple pulley device will enable high baskets to be lowered to a more convenient height for watering and maintenance.

■ **Within reach** Hang the baskets where they can be watered easily.

■ **Water reservoir** If watering your basket on a daily basis is not convenient to your schedule, opt for self-watering hanging baskets. Fitted with built-in water reservoirs, these supply water to the soil via capillary-action matting.

■ **Watering can** Purposemade, pump-action watering cans are available for reaching high baskets, if a hose is not available.

■ **Flow control** When using a hose, adjust the flow to a gentle trickle; too much pressure will wash plants and soil out of the basket.

■ **Hose extension** A watering lance, with a long, rigid stem and down-turned tip can be fixed to the end of a hose to water above head height.

■ **Water-retaining granules** Added to the soil, these granules are useful in all types of container (see p. 245).

PLANTING BASKETS

It is worth taking the time and trouble to plant up a traditional hanging basket, to be rewarded with a spectacular feature for many weeks over the summer. Stand the planted basket in a sheltered place for several days before hanging so that the plants can begin to establish themselves. When you are hanging the basket, ask someone to take the weight of it from below.

TRADITIONAL STYLE

1 Support the empty basket firmly on a large pot or bucket for planting, temporarily removing the chains if they are likely to get in the way. Line the basket with your chosen material. Position a square of pierced plastic or a saucer on top of the lining at the base of the basket to prevent water draining through the liner too freely. Fill one-third of the basket with potting soil mix – a soil-based mix retains moisture better than soilless, but can make the completed basket too heavy. Add water-retaining granules and slow-release fertilizer, applied at the manufacturer's recommended rate.

Make slit central to basket hole

2 Using a sharp blade make 1-in (2.5-cm) slits through the liner at even spaces around the basket. These slits will allow you to insert small flowering plants and trailing foliage to ensure full coverage of the wire framework.

3 Insert the trailing plants through the sides of the basket. It is usually easiest to push the roots of the plants through from the outside, spreading them out on the soil; for other plants it may be easier to gently pull their topgrowth through from the inside of the basket. If plants are awkward to position, gently wash some of the soil off the roots and wrap the plant in a cone of newspaper to protect it as you insert it through the side of the basket.

Guide plant through from the outside

4 Top up with more soil mix, firming the plants in gently. Add another layer of plants through the side, if desired, until the basket is almost full. Plant the top of the basket with bushy and trailing plants, with an upright in the center to add height. Firm them in and water well.

WINTER BASKET

Of all plant containers, hanging baskets are the most difficult to keep going successfully through the winter months and virtually impossible in extreme climates. However, if you can find a sheltered sunny spot, out of the way of icy winds, perhaps close to the house, it is possible to create an attractive winter display.

VELVET TOUCH

Pansies *(Viola* x *wittrockiana)* are among the most reliable winter-flowering plants. Their main flushes of bloom are in fall and spring, but in sheltered positions they will carry on flowering through the winter. The Universal Series is perhaps the best-known variety, but several others offer a wide range of colors and petal markings too. Pansies can be planted both through the sides of baskets and around the top.

Ivy *(Hedera helix)* is hardy and tough and will help to cover the base of the basket with its trailing stems. A dark, glossy green shows off the colors of the pansies well, and a variety such as "Green Ripple" has interestingly shaped foliage.

Winter-flowering heather provides some height in the center of the basket; *Erica carnea* "Ann Sparkes" has the double bonus of rose-purple flowers and bronze-red foliage.

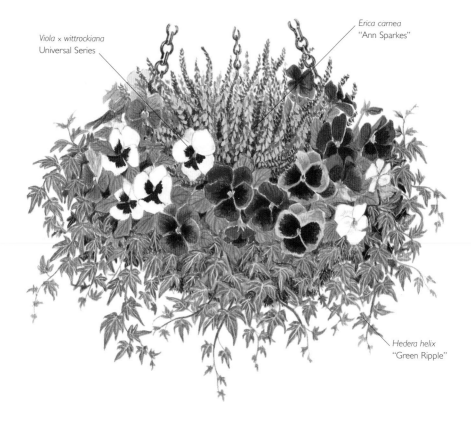

Viola x wittrockiana
Universal Series

Erica carnea
"Ann Sparkes"

Hedera helix
"Green Ripple"

WELCOMING SPRING

As the days lengthen, the choice of suitable flowering plants for a basket increases. Spring can be a treacherous time – hard frosts and chilling winds are just as likely as warm sunshine and soft breezes – so before hanging up the basket outdoors, remember to gradually harden off any plants that have been raised under glass.

RASPBERRY RIPPLE

Line the basket with moss, so that it will not matter that the basket sides can be seen as well as the plants. The most suitable trailing plant for a spring basket is, once again, ivy; this time a variegated variety such as green and white *Hedera helix* "Glacier" brings a fresh, light note to this mainly pink and white scheme. Winter-flowering pansies have a renewed flush of bloom in spring; try one of the single-color varieties like this creamy white selection. The pompom flowers of double daisies *(Bellis perennis)* appear in early spring, in a variety of rosy pinks. *Anemone blanda* has deeply cut foliage and cheerful, daisy flowers that are freely produced; *A. b.* "Radar" bears deep pink and white flowers. Both the daisies and anemones can be tucked at intervals through the sides of the basket, as well as being planted in the top.

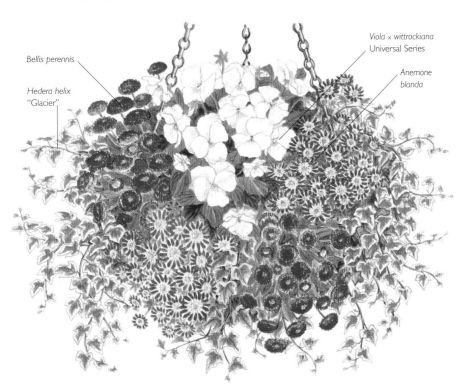

Bellis perennis

Hedera helix
"Glacier"

Viola x wittrockiana
Universal Series

Anemone
blanda

SUMMER SPLENDOR

The variety of plants suitable for summer hanging baskets is vast, and some wonderfully colorful, luxuriant displays can be created, with lush waterfalls of flowers and foliage. Before planting, consider whether you want a mass of color as a feature in its own right, or a themed color planting to be repeated in a number of baskets.

BLAZE OF COLOR

A mass of different colors works best in a basket displayed on its own, because it is difficult to reproduce a second basket, and two non-matching, boldly planted containers are likely to work against each other.

The "Surfinia" varieties of petunias (*Petunia*) make strong, vigorous growth, even in poor weather conditions and produce numerous flowers, some with darker veining or a pronounced dark eye. The showy, cream-splashed leaves of the blue daisy, *Felicia amelloides* "Santa Anita Variegated," provide foliage interest, and *Diascia* "Coral Belle" has unusual lipped, salmon-pink flowers. A host of golden daisies on tumbling, bronze-foliaged stems is provided by *Sanvitalia* "Little Sun," while the silver-leaved *Convolvulus sabatius* is set with clear blue, funnel-shaped blooms. The whole blaze of color is gently cooled down by the plain, silver foliage of the trailing *Helichrysum petiolare*.

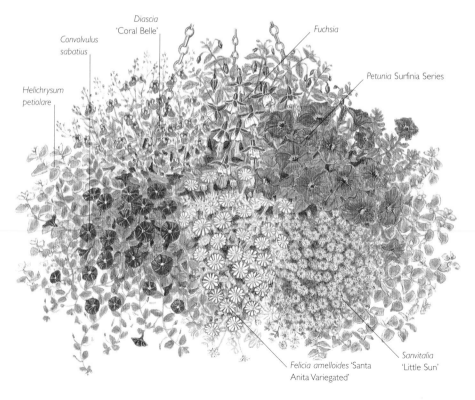

Diascia 'Coral Belle'

Convolvulus sabatius

Fuchsia

Helichrysum petiolare

Petunia Surfinia Series

Felicia amelloides 'Santa Anita Variegated'

Sanvitalia 'Little Sun'

IN THE PINK

A well-tended basket planted with a single plant variety can be every bit as eye-catching as a basket crammed with a whole range of different, multicolored plants. The type of plant chosen should be vigorous and free-flowering and you will need several plants for each basket. You will probably need to pinch and prune the stems carefully as they develop to obtain a good shape.

The specimen shown here is a trailing snapdragon, *Antirrhinum* "Chandelier Rose Pink." Its spreading, arching habit of growth makes it quite distinct from the common border snapdragons and is well suited for use in hanging baskets.

Other plants that suit a solo performance include nemesia, anagallis, trailing fuchsia, impatiens, ivy-leafed pelargonium, sutera, trailing petunia, and verbena. It is important that you make sure you buy plants of all the same variety for each basket – one of a different color would ruin the effect. Select plants in labeled pots, and reject any whose foliage color is markedly different to the others, as this often signifies a different flower color.

Fuchsias are excellent plants for hanging baskets and their drooping, bell-like flowers can be easily appreciated from below. Upright-growing varieties, such as *Fuchsia* "Tom Thumb," are suitable for forming the center of a planting arrangement, while trailing types can cascade over the edges; there are also some semitrailing varieties of lax growth, which is somewhere between the two. *Fuchsia* "Patio Princess" is a pretty bush variety with clear red sepals and double, frilled white petals.

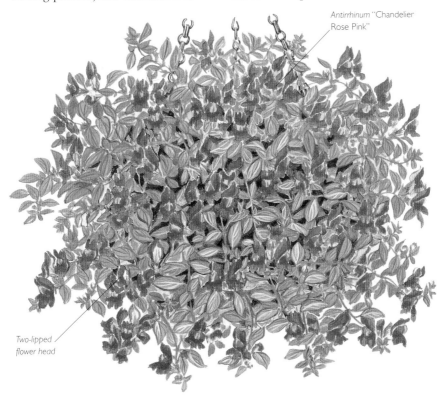

Antirrhinum "Chandelier Rose Pink"

Two-lipped flower head

HARVEST FESTIVAL

No one can pretend that you will be able to keep yourself in homegrown vegetables from a few hanging baskets – but growing edible crops in baskets is great fun and always makes a good conversation piece. Hang vegetable baskets close to the kitchen for some really fresh garden produce.

COLORFUL SALADS

Salad vegetables are always welcome, even if there is only enough of a crop to make a garnish. Loose-leaf lettuce such as "Salad Bowl" grows quite well in baskets, or try the mini-iceberg "Blush," which grows 3–4 in (6–8 cm) across; trim away the spreading outer leaves as the heart develops. With their blue-green foliage and profusion of bold red, yellow, and orange flowers, nasturtiums (Tropaeolum majus) have an ideal trailing habit for baskets. Both the foliage and flowers are edible, adding a peppery taste and color to mixed salads.

KITCHEN HERBS

Herbs are well worth growing, as only small amounts need to be harvested for use. Many herbs are compact in habit and can tolerate relatively dry, poor conditions, so are well adapted to basket growing (see also p. 289).

- Basil (Ocimum)
- Parsley (Petroselinum)
- Rocket (Eruca vesicaria)
- Chives (Allium schoenoprasum)
- Summer savory (Satureja)
- Marjoram (Origanum)
- Oregano (Origanum)
- Rock hyssop (Hyssopus)
- Thyme (Thymus)
- Mint (Mentha)

TASTY VEGETABLES

Several vegetables are worth trying in baskets, too – and make an attractive display when interspersed with herbs.

■ **Tomato** The cherry-sized, bright red fruits of "Tumbler," which has been specially bred for containers, are carried in abundance on trailing trusses and have an excellent flavor and handsome appearance. "Phyra" is another cherry variety that grows well in baskets and other containers.

■ **Root vegetables** Carrots have very pleasing ferny foliage; try the variety "Parmex," which produces small, globe-shaped roots with a sweet taste. Radishes are quick growing and tolerate crowded conditions. Choose a globe-rooted type such as "Pink Beauty" or "Scarlet Globe" for a hanging basket.

■ **Beans** Dwarf French beans make compact plants with clusters of slender pods that hang over the sides of the basket; grow and cook them with summer savory for a really special flavor.

■ **Peppers** Capsicum peppers vary in strength, from mild and sweet-tasting to very hot, but are striking to look at. "Super Cayenne" grows well in containers and bears hot, deep red fruits; "Firecracker" produces tiny, conical peppers of purple, orange, and red, and lives up to its name!

FRUIT DESSERTS

To round off a meal on the patio or just provide a sweet, summer snack, strawberries are perfect. Alpine varieties, with their tiny, intensely flavored fruits, are perhaps the best for hanging baskets; "Mignonette" can be grown from seed and bears a particularly heavy crop. Large-fruited strawberries can also be grown, with

TRIUMPHANT ARCH
Glowing red tomatoes take pride of place in a display that is determined to catch the eye of visitors as they pass through the arch.

their clusters of fruit hanging attractively over the edge of the basket. Keep them well watered and fed, and pinch out runners as soon as they are formed to direct the plants' energy into fruit production.

GROUPING BASKETS

Perhaps more than most other types of containers, hanging baskets tend to be displayed in matching pairs, or in larger groups, and are rarely used for solo performances. Whether used in a formal or more casual arrangement, grouped baskets create a stunning effect.

FORMAL SITUATIONS

Hanging baskets are often used to add height, suspended from pillars or columns that form the framework of the garden. Filled with bold, simple arrangements, their purpose is to provide another tier to the planting scheme and to define the garden borders. Possibly the most popular position for baskets, though, is as a pair, flanking either side of a front door or gateway. For this formal arrangement to work well, the baskets and supporting brackets need to be as near identical as possible to achieve strong symmetry. Individual plantings will always differ slightly even if you have made every effort to use the same linings and varieties – two sets of plants simply will not grow and develop in exactly the same way. However, by using the same color scheme and balance of trailing, bushy, upright plants, a satisfactory result can be obtained. Sometimes the effect is spoiled because one basket develops more slowly than the other; this usually arises when one side of the grouping is in constant shade, or subject to cold winds. In this case, swap the positions of the baskets regularly to produce a more evenly balanced development.

FORMAL AND INFORMAL STYLE TIPS

FORMAL

• Highlight the geometry of the design, by repeating symmetrical plantings that use neat, strong shapes.

• Hang groups of baskets at an even height to maintain strong lines.

• Keep baskets in proportion to the design by using just one size of basket.

• Site hanging baskets to draw the eye to a focal point or vista, for example under an arch or either side of a gate.

• Train foliage-only baskets to create striking green globes, spirals, and mini-standards that mimic the geometrical shapes used in formal topiary.

INFORMAL

• Make the most of trailing plants and nodding flowers to produce organic, freeform shapes that soften harsh lines. Use trailing blue-flowered plants to mimic cascading water.

• Adapt unusual items, such as an old teapot, for use as containers (see p. 274) to achieve an unsophisticated look.

• Hang baskets at different heights to add interest to an arrangement. Grade the sizes of the baskets, with the smallest at the bottom and the largest at the top (or vice versa).

• Choose gentle, pastel shades to give a soft-focus effect to the planting scheme.

INFORMAL EFFECTS

In an informal arrangement, planting schemes can differ from basket to basket, although it does help the display if there is at least one common theme running through each of the baskets – the same variety of ivy, perhaps, or a white flowering plant occupying a prominent position in each.

An effective way to display two nonmatching baskets is to hang them slightly offset, one below the other, and to use plant colors that make it look as though the plants are flowing from one basket to the next. For example, let a trailing white petunia spill over like white froth into a lower basket planted with matching white plants.

DECORATED BOUGHS
A well-established mature tree with bare lower boughs is given a new lease on life by a pair of colorful baskets hung from its branches.

WALL CONTAINERS

Like hanging baskets, wall pots and mangers offer an ideal solution for breaking up expanses of bare wall and maximizing plantings where growing space is limited. Wall containers may be of solid construction – literally, a pot flattened on one side with a fixing point for attachment – or of open ironwork.

CHECKLIST

■ **Container styles** Wall pots are made from a variety of materials, from terra cotta to metal. Remember that unusual, decorative shapes may be awkward to plant up. If there is no provision for drainage, or no room for root development, use the pot as an outer vessel and plant up a more suitable, lightweight container that will fit inside.

■ **Fixing** Make sure that the method of fixing provided is sufficient to support the planted pot safely. Where the only fixing is a single hole in the back of the pot, add small L-shaped or mirror brackets to share the load.

■ **Planting up** When using decorative pots, arrange the plants so that the container itself remains visible – just the opposite of planting up a hanging basket. Remember that the display can only be viewed from one side, and that there is no room for plants to grow or develop at the back of the

CERAMIC ANGLED WALL POT

pot. Open-work mangers should be lined in the same way as hanging baskets (see p. 295).

■ **Watering** Wall containers receive virtually no rain, so make sure that they are within easy reach to allow regular watering.

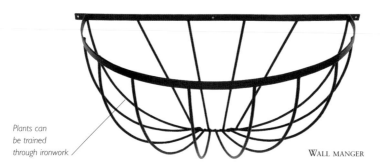

Plants can be trained through ironwork

WALL MANGER

TIPS FOR CHOOSING PLANTS

• Upright plants such as pelargoniums, bush fuchsias, heathers, primulas, and spring-flowering bulbs allow a highly decorated wall pot to remain visible once planted up.

• Avoid using very tall plants that are out of proportion to the depth of the pot.

• One or two strands of ivy or a similar trailing plant will help to soften the outline without obscuring the container; stems can be cut back to the base if they start to become untidy looking.

• Where pots are of specific and unusual designs, it can be fun to try to find a particularly appropriate plant for them. A classical style, stonework face, for example, is a popular design; plant it up with the fine-textured blue grass *Festuca glauca* to give it a shock of steely blue "hair." A lion's mask can be provided with a golden "mane" of creeping jenny (*Lysimachia nummularia* "Aurea"): pinch the shoots back regularly so that the stems frame the head rather than cover it.

CREEPING JENNY

GOLDEN CREEPING JENNY

PART FOUR:
PROBLEM-SOLVING FOR THE BUSY GARDENER

1
SOIL MAINTENANCE AND PLANTING

Soil is the medium in which all garden plants grow. Maintaining soil fertility allows plants to flourish and give their best. Strong-growing plants are disease-resistant, survive pest attack, and will rapidly form a weed-suppressing barrier. Many gardening problems can be reduced, or in some cases eliminated, if due attention is given to the soil. If you are making a new garden, you will ease the burden of maintenance by carefully assessing the soil, which will provide valuable clues as to which plants will do well for you. Once the garden is planted, regular mulching will keep the soil fertile and the plants growing strongly.

ASSESSING SOIL

It is worth spending time getting to know your garden soil. Many gardeners waste time, money, and effort trying to grow unsuitable plants in the prevailing conditions. A few minutes spent carrying out some simple tests can repay healthy dividends in the long term.

SOIL-TESTING KITS

A range of simple-to-use soil-testing kits are available at garden stores. Some measure the availability of the major plant nutrients nitrogen, phosphorus, and potassium, although home-testing kits can be unreliable; if you think an accurate analysis is necessary, send samples to a professional soil-testing laboratory. Most soils contain satisfactory nutrient levels, however, and detailed analysis is necessary only if you suspect a serious mineral deficiency.

Soil acidity/alkalinity is expressed in terms of the pH scale. This runs from 0 to 14: 7 is neutral; lower numbers indicate acid conditions and higher ones show alkaline.

Most soils fall within the range 5.5 to 7.5, with the majority being neutral to acid. Soil pH should be tested in several areas, as it is possible to discover pockets of acid soil in predominantly alkaline soil, and alkaline soil in acid areas. While the pH value of your soil can be altered by chemical means, you will save much effort by working within the restrictions imposed by your soil rather than try to change them.

Kits that measure the acidity and alkalinity of soil are cheap and accurate, and worth using. Many plants will grow in either type of soil, but a few – notably rhododendrons, camellias, and some heathers – must have an acid soil. A pH-testing kit could save you time, money, and effort that would be wasted if you tried to grow acid-loving plants in an alkaline soil. Chemical pH-testing kits are the most reliable.

■ Using a teaspoon, take a sample of soil from about 3 in (7.5 cm) below the soil surface. Place it in the test tube supplied with the kit and add the chemical reagent and water as directed. Seal the tube and shake it, then wait for the contents to settle.

■ The color of the liquid indicates the acidity/alkalinity of the sample. Yellow/orange indicates the soil is acid. Bright green indicates the soil is neutral. Darker green indicates the soil is alkaline.

ALKALINE

NEUTRAL

ACID

VERY ACID

SOIL-TESTING KIT

SOIL STRUCTURE

The structure of soil is as important a factor as pH in determining which plants will do well in your garden. For an instant assessment, carry out the following simple test. Pick up a handful of soil and squeeze it in the palm of your hand. If it sticks together in a lump, leaving the impression of your fingers, it is clay soil. If it fails to hold together but trickles through your fingers, it is light sandy soil. The ideal soil – friable loam – will bind into moist crumbs that leave your hands clean when rubbed through your fingers.

Whatever the structure, you should choose plants that will do well in the prevailing soil type rather than attempt to change the soil to suit certain kinds of plant.

■ **Friable loam** Crumbly soil that contains both sand and clay without either predominating is called friable loam. It drains well and is easy to work. It usually contains high levels of humus (decayed organic matter) that make it fertile.

■ **Clay soil** Soil that compacts easily is clay soil. It is made up of tiny particles, making it heavy, sticky,

---

TIMESAVING TIPS

• To gain a better idea of your soil type, and the plants you will be able to grow successfully, find out what is growing in your neighborhood. Notice those plants that are doing well and those that are doing badly.

• Avoid walking on beds of clay soil in winter, as it compacts the soil, making it difficult to dig. Instead, stand on steppingstones or a length of wood.

---

and moisture retentive. It sets like concrete in hot weather; it also tends to freeze solid in winter. Heavy soils generally have poor drainage, which often results in a greenish film or moss on the surface. On the plus side, clay soils are potentially very fertile, since they retain nutrients and moisture well.

■ **Light soil** Soils that are dustlike and dry out rapidly in hot weather are too light to maintain nutrients. This is a characteristic of sandy soil, which requires more maintenance than clay soil. However, light soil quickly warms up in spring and is easy to work.

STEPPINGSTONES

Whenever planning large borders, think ahead by placing small slabs or brick pavers among the plants. This will allow you access to the plants without having to stand on the soil, which compacts it. Quarry tiles and timber rings can also be used.

QUARRY TILE

TIMBER RING

IMPROVING SOIL

Soil structure can be improved quite significantly by methods that are neither difficult nor time-consuming. Making the initial effort will save you valuable time later by ensuring plants thrive with the minimum of maintenance, as well as increasing the range of plants you can grow.

ADDING ORGANIC MATTER

Improving soil before planting will improve its texture, nutrient content, drainage, and moisture retention. All soils benefit from the addition of organic matter. On heavy soils, it improves drainage by opening up the texture. It has the opposite (but equally beneficial) effect on light, sandy soils, binding them into larger crumbs that retain moisture. Soil improvers can be forked in over a large area, or added in smaller quantities when planting individual plants (see pp. 320–21). They can also be spread around existing plantings as a mulch (see pp. 324–5).

ANIMAL MANURES AND COMMERCIAL SOIL IMPROVERS

■ **Animal manures** Farmyard manure can be added to the soil and is good for adding bulk to light soils, but it does have disadvantages. It contains variable amounts of nutrients and may contain weed seeds. Cow and horse manure are most widely available; horse manure is preferred because it has a lighter, drier texture. Poultry manure is rich in nutrients, but is described as a "hot" manure because it can scorch young roots. All animal manure must be well rotted before being added to the soil; if the manure you collect is fresh, you will have to stack it until it breaks down. This can take a year, so a gardener with little time is likely to use a proprietary soil conditioner.

■ **Proprietary soil conditioners** These are based on animal manures, but already rotted and concentrated. They are weed free, pleasant to handle, and easier to transport and apply than animal manure.

CHICKEN
MANURE PELLETS

TIMESAVING TIPS

• Manure and other organic matter that is not fully rotted can be spread on vacant ground in the fall. It will then be ready to be dug in by the following spring.

• It is quicker and easier to use a mechanical cultivator – rented on a daily basis – than to dig by hand.

MAKING YOUR OWN LEAF MOLD

Rotted down leaves make a superb soil conditioner. Leaf mold has the texture of peat (the use of which is generally frowned upon, because it is not a renewable resource) and, properly made, is weed free. However, it contains relatively few nutrients.

• Gather fallen leaves in the fall and place them in a black plastic bag.

• Make a few holes in the bag. Loosely tie the top and store it in a cool, dark place such as a cellar or garage.

• The leaves take at least a year to break down and are ideally left for longer.

• No heat is generated, since various fungi are responsible for breaking down the organic matter.

FALL LEAVES

PLANT-BASED SOIL IMPROVERS

■ **Garden compost** Made up of decayed vegetable matter from the garden and kitchen, garden compost (see pp. 326–7) can be an excellent soil improver, with a high nutrient content. Although it is difficult to make it in sufficient quantities to satisfy all your gardening needs, a compost heap or bin is a useful way of disposing of garden refuse.

■ **Spent mushroom compost** This is available from mushroom farms. It is usually chalky, so should not be used around acid-loving plants or on soils that are already very alkaline.

■ **Composted bark** Available commercially, this material is light and pleasant to handle but like leaf mold contains few nutrients.

GARDEN DEBRIS

INORGANIC IMPROVERS

Grit is inorganic and is a useful additive where the soil is very heavy and poorly drained. Horticultural gravel will improve drainage without affecting nutrient levels. It should be dug in with a fork to a depth of roughly 12 in (30 cm). If you wish to use it in conjunction with acid-loving plants, check that it is not from a limestone quarry. Do not use gravel obtained from a builder's yard.

WEED CONTROL

The presence of weeds in any area of soil is a sign that the soil is fertile. Some form of weed control is necessary in nearly all gardens, particularly in new gardens. Prevention at an early stage can save the inconvenience of large-scale eradication later. Which method you choose depends on the scale of the weed problem, when you need to deal with it, and the amount of time at your disposal.

WHAT IS A WEED?

A weed is simply a plant in the wrong place. In a wildlife garden (see pp. 366–7), "weeds" form a desirable part of the planting. Some garden plants spread their seeds so freely as to become weeds.

■ **Annual weeds** Weeds of this kind complete their life cycle in a single season. Some will produce two or more generations a year. Digging the soil can bring to the surface buried weed seeds, so planting can cause weeds to appear on a patch of soil you thought was weed free.

■ **Perennial weeds** Some weeds persist from year to year. These include taprooted plants, such as dandelions, and any with spreading root systems such as the troublesome bindweed and couch grass.

■ **Woody stemmed weeds** Often present on neglected sites, these weeds include elder and brambles.

Thistle

Dock

COMMON
GARDEN WEEDS

WEEDING TIP

Bruising the leaves of weeds prior to treating them with an application of chemical weed killer helps to improve its take-up. You may find that you need to carry out repeat applications to clear a site of really pernicious weeds.

CHEMICAL WEED KILLERS

When used correctly, chemical weed killers can save hours of backbreaking work. Some are formulated for specific areas of the garden, such as lawns, vegetable gardens, or paving. Many weed killers can be applied as a spray, and are useful for clearing large areas of weeds.

■ **Soil-acting weed killers** Weed killers that "poison" the soil are described as "soil-acting." They are applied just before growth begins and effectively kill any plant in the area, persisting in the soil for some months. Taprooted weeds between paving are best killed with a chemical product.

■ **Contact weed killers** Specific plants and problem areas can be treated with weed killers that kill only the part of the plant they touch. They are effective on all annual weeds but have less impact on perennial weeds, which regenerate from the section of root that remains in the ground.

■ **Systemic weed killers** All soft plant material can be destroyed by systemic weed killers. These are absorbed by the plant, leaving the soil untainted, so replanting can begin as soon as the weeds have died.

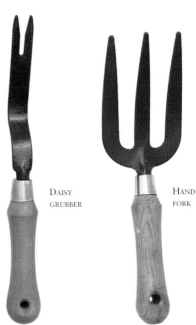

DAISY GRUBBER

HAND FORK

SUPPRESSING WEEDS

Laying black plastic sheeting directly on to the soil kills weeds by depriving them of light, air, and moisture. Weight the sheeting down at the edges with large stones. To get around the fact that it takes at least a year to eradicate weeds by this method, try planting through the plastic and treat it as a mulch (see p. 325).

HAND WEEDING

Although hand weeding is an often hated chore that can be one of the most time-consuming tasks in the garden, it is sometimes unavoidable. Pulling out seedling weeds as soon as they occur may take only a few minutes and can prevent a more serious problem developing. A few spells with a hand fork or daisy grubber, or pushing a hoe, can often be quicker than getting out a sprayer to apply a chemical weed killer. Hoes should always be kept sharpened to easily and effectively slice off the topgrowth of weeds from their roots. Hoe or hand weed on a dry, breezy day so that weeds wilt and die quickly. Annual weeds should always be removed before they flower and set seed, to avoid work later.

If you prefer nonchemical controls, a flame gun is very effective for large areas, especially on surfaces such as gravel paths or on empty flower beds in early spring.

PLANTS AND PLANTING

The quickest way of stocking a garden is to select from the wide range of ready-grown plants that are available from garden centers, nurseries, and home improvement stores. Specialist nurseries also sell by mail order. Container-grown plants are great timesavers because they can be planted at virtually anytime of the year, except when the ground is frozen.

TYPES OF PLANTS

■ **Container-grown plants** Most plants are sold in full growth in containers. When buying plants check that the roots fill the pot without being unduly restricted. Weed seedlings on the surface are no cause for concern, but moss may suggest that the plant has been overwatered. On shrubs, check that

TRAY OF BEDDING PLANTS

the topgrowth is in proportion to the root system. The shrub should be well branched and not lopsided.

■ **Rootballed plants** Some trees, such as conifers, are sold "rootballed," with the soil still

CONTAINER-GROWN
ROSE

Healthy-looking flower buds

TIMESAVING TIPS

• Take a good horticultural reference book with you to the garden store, to check before buying that a specific plant is suitable for your soil and conditions.

• Container-grown plants can be purchased in leaf and flower, allowing you to see what the plant really looks like.

• Add planting mix and fertilizer to the base of the planting hole to help the plant grow.

clinging to the roots. To keep the rootball intact, it is wrapped in hessian, netting, or in a wire basket.

■ **Bulbs** Usually sold when dormant, bulbs are effectively bare-root plants. Look for plump, firm bulbs; reject any that feel soft or that are diseased, withered, or blemished.

■ **Bare root** These are trees and shrubs that have been raised in open ground and lifted in the dormant season for sale from late fall to late winter. Bare-root plants are less convenient for busy gardeners because they need to be planted as soon as possible after purchase. If they cannot be planted straightaway, bare-root plants should be "heeled in" (dug in to a shallow depth) to a spare piece of ground to temporarily cover the roots with moist soil to prevent them from drying out.

PLANTING

Most plants are best planted in mild, damp weather during spring or fall. Container-grown plants can be planted at other times of the year, but not during freezing weather or periods of drought.

Prepare the site by removing any weeds and lightly turn over the soil with a garden fork. Dig a hole at least twice the size of the container or rootball. Ease the plant from its container, making sure that you support the main stem on large shrubs. Tease out the roots gently with a hand fork, then set the plant in the middle of the hole. Backfill with the excavated soil supplemented with garden compost and a little slow-release fertilizer. Firm the soil around the neck of the plant and water it thoroughly to ensure good initial growth.

SITING PLANTS

Most plants do best in a sunny, open site. Some prefer partial shade (either in the dappled shade of deciduous trees or in a position that is shaded when the sun is at its hottest). Relatively few plants do well in full shade. Many plants will thrive in sun or partial shade. However, these usually flower less freely in shade, but the flowers will last longer and hold their color better.

• Yellow-leaved and variegated plants need some sun to enhance the leaf coloration, but can scorch in full sun.

• Purple- and gray-leaved plants produce their best leaf color in full sun.

• Most green-leaved foliage plants can be relied on to perform well in shade.

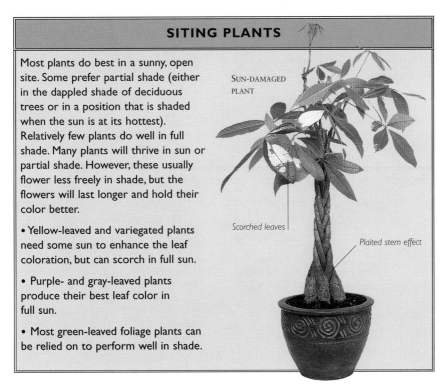

SUN-DAMAGED PLANT

Scorched leaves

Plaited stem effect

AFTERCARE FOR PLANTS

Once they are in the soil, plants benefit from a certain amount of aftercare, but this need not impose a heavy burden on the busy gardener. The suggestions here will help keep the soil in good condition and the plants growing strongly with the minimum of effort.

WATERING

Water is essential to plant growth. It is the medium by which nutrients are carried by the roots to the rest of the plant's organism. Properly maintained, the soil should provide all the moisture that established plants need.

■ For individual plants, a watering can fitted with a coarse spray rose can be used; for all but very small areas, a hose fitted with a spray nozzle, or a sprinkler, is quicker and more efficient. For maximum timesaving, automatic irrigation

systems can be installed. A water computer fitted to an outdoor tap will deliver a fixed amount of water to a number of plants through a system of small-bore tubing and sprinklers or drip nozzles.

■ Only annuals, container plants, and new plantings need additional water during dry spells. Carry out watering in the evening, when the water will evaporate more slowly from the soil surface, and irrigate to ensure that the water penetrates to the base of the plant's root system.

TIMESAVING TIPS

• Slow-release fertilizers need applying only once a year and will keep plants going all season.

• In beds and borders, mulch the soil surface between plants to reduce the need for watering.

• When planting containers and hanging baskets, incorporate some water-retaining granules in the soil mix to reduce watering.

• A hose-end diluter can be fixed to make liquid fertilizer easy to apply.

FEEDING

Plants need three main elements for healthy growth: nitrogen (N) stimulates lush, leafy growth; potassium (K) promotes good flowering and fruiting and also helps firm woody stems; phosphorus (P) is beneficial to plant roots. Other elements ("trace elements"), such as magnesium (Mg), are also required, but in much smaller amounts.

Your choice of fertilizer should be guided by what you want the plants to do. In spring, it is best to apply high-nitrogen fertilizers for good foliage and vigorous regeneration after winter dormancy. High-potassium feeds can improve the performance of plants that have a long flowering season, such as roses, pelargoniums, and annuals. High-phosphorus feeds are of benefit in the fall, when plants experience an increase in root activity.

■ **Soluble or liquid fertilizers**
Usually diluted with water, liquid and soluble fertilizers should be applied as near to the roots as possible, so the nutrients are readily available to the plant. However, a certain amount is wasted as water leaches through the soil.

■ **Powdered and granular fertilizers**
Sprinkled around the plants and forked in, powders dissolve quickly in the soil. Slow-release fertilizers are coated with a special resin that breaks down when the soil reaches a certain temperature. Some are effective for three months, others for longer periods.

■ **Foliar feeds** Liquid feeds designed to be sprayed on to the topgrowth make nutrients immediately available to plants. Foliar feeds are invaluable for giving plants an instant boost after a period of unexpected cold or if they have suffered from disease or pest attack. They are often the most practical way of feeding climbers trained against walls or fences whose roots are inaccessible because they are beneath grass or paving.

Warning

Always follow the manufacturer's instructions when applying fertilizers, especially regarding dosage. Over-generous applications can have harmful effects on plants.

ORGANIC FERTILIZER

PHOSTROGEN, A MIX OF PHOSPHORUS AND NITROGEN

MULCHING

A mulch is a material – usually organic – spread on the surface of the soil around plants. Mulches prevent evaporation of moisture from the soil surface, thus reducing the need for watering and can also suppress the germination of weed seeds.

TYPES OF MULCH

Plants should be mulched on planting and after watering to limit moisture loss from the soil surface. Mulch established plants annually, in spring or fall, after a heavy rainfall. When mulching plants that need protection from slugs and snails, such as hostas, apply slug pellets before the mulch. The mollusks are active underneath the mulch, so any pellets applied on top will not be effective.

■ **Organic mulches** All of the organic materials suitable for use as soil conditioners (see pp. 316–17) can also be used as mulches. Well-rotted compost or animal manure makes an excellent mulch, adding nutrients to the soil as it breaks down, but it is not easy to handle and can be hard work to spread among plants.

TIMESAVING TIPS

• Make sure the soil is moist before putting down a mulch.

• Apply most mulches at a depth of at least 2–3 in (5–8 cm) around plants, since shallow mulching does not work efficiently.

■ **Proprietary mulches** Prebagged mulching materials are available from garden outlets and are easy to transport and clean and easy to handle. Wood chips and cocoa shells are two popular products readily available in most outlets.

■ **Grit** Plants that need swift drainage rather than a rich soil should be mulched with grit.

WOOD CHIPS

GRIT

USING PLASTIC SHEETING

Mulching with black plastic (see p. 319) suppresses weeds and prevents the soil from drying out. The more expensive water-permeable type is perforated to allow rainwater through and is useful for light soils that would otherwise dry out quickly, even under plastic. Spread the sheeting over the area you want to clear and hold down the edges with stones. Covering the surface with wood chips will improve the appearance. Once the area is weed free, the plastic can be removed for planting. Alternatively, cut slits in it with a knife and leave it as a mulch.

1 Using a sharp knife, scissors, or pruning shears, make X-shaped slits in the plastic. Pull back the flaps to make a planting hole through the sheeting in the ground below.

2 Dig a hole slightly larger than the plant's rootball. Gently tease out the roots and insert the plant. Backfill gently with the removed soil and firm after planting.

DECORATIVE MULCHES

• Gravel can make an excellent top-dressing as well as a decorative mulch. Gravel provides quick drainage away from the "collars" of plants that are sensitive to excess moisture. Gravel has the timesaving advantage of discouraging the growth of mosses or lichens on the soil surface.

• Clump-forming dwarf shrubs, such as sea pink or thrift (Armeria maritima), are an excellent choice for growing through gravel. These fully hardy, evergreen plants require plenty of sun and well-drained soil.

THRIFT IN GRAVEL

GARDEN COMPOSTING

A compost heap is an excellent way of dealing with plant refuse, breaking it down to a rich, fertile subtance that will improve the structure of your garden soil and provide an eco-friendly way of feeding your plants. As long as a few basic rules are followed, a compost heap needs very little attention and provides a quick and easy way of disposing of otherwise awkward garden waste.

COMPOST CONTENT

Almost any material of organic origin (that is, material that has once been living) can be composted, but some are more suitable than others.

■ **From the garden** Almost any soft, green plant material including most weeds can be composted. Grass clippings are suitable as long as they are mixed with other, more open-textured refuse.

■ **From the house** Raw fruit and vegetable peelings and trimmings, tea leaves, ground coffee, and crushed eggshells are all suitable, as well as cage cleanings from family pets.

■ **From the farm** Animal manure makes an excellent activator. Small amounts of old straw and animal bedding can also be used.

■ **Materials to avoid** Weeds with running rootstocks (such as bindweed and couch grass) or thick taproots (such as dandelions) should be avoided as they are unlikely to be killed in the composting process. For the same reason, avoid weeds that are setting seed. Do not use cooked food scraps or anything containing meat or dairy products, as these will attract vermin. Avoid woody material, as it takes too long to rot down.

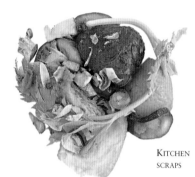

KITCHEN SCRAPS

GRASS CUTTINGS

COMPOST ACTIVATOR

COMPOST BINS

Compost bins help to provide the
right conditions for rapid breakdown
and keep the heap looking tidy.
There are several types of proprietary
bin available, made from timber
or plastic, in kit form or ready
assembled. When choosing a bin,
bear in mind how easy it is to
assemble, how much space it takes
up, whether it is the right size for
your needs, and how easy it is
to access the finished compost.

MAKING COMPOST

To turn into dark brown, crumbly,
sweet-smelling soil mix, garden
refuse needs moisture, warmth,
and the right type of naturally
occurring microorganism.

■ Build the heap in layers, as far
as possible mixing fine- and coarse-
textured material.

■ Compost activators can be
sprinkled on between layers to
encourage rapid breakdown; follow
the directions on the package. Fresh
animal manures have a similar effect.

KITCHEN REFUSE
Keep a small bin by the kitchen door for
collecting scraps to save time going out
repeatedly to the compost bin.

■ Sprinkle on a handful of garden
lime to reduce the acidity of
the heap; this allows the micro-
organisms to work more efficiently.

■ When the bin is full, cover it to
retain the heat and keep out excess
rain. Leave it for three to six months
(breakdown is faster in summer than
in winter) to mature.

DISPOSING OF REFUSE

Bulky material that would be very
slow to break down can usually be
added to a compost heap if it is
shredded; powered garden shredders
can be bought or rented for a
weekend after a major tidy up.
    Otherwise, ask your local authority
if a special collection of garden refuse
is made. Few household collectors
will deal with garden waste, in which
case it will have to be taken to the
local garbage site. Some dry waste
can be burned at home: however,
bonfires can be time consuming
and should not be left unattended.

SPREAD IT AROUND

• If you fail to make good compost
during the summer, don't despair.
Cold, wet compost can be spread
around plants in the fall, provided it
does not actually touch them. It will
break down over winter and the
nutrients will be available to the
plants the following spring.

• There are many good ready-made
compost substitutes for the busy
gardener, including peat, coconut
fibers, and shredded tree bark.

MAKING A WORMERY

In a small garden, you are unlikely to have enough room for – or generate enough waste plant material to justify – a large compost heap. Under these circumstances, the best way to recycle organic matter is to install a wormery.

WORKING WORMS

A wormery is a plastic bin that houses special composting worms, which work their way through organic matter to produce a high-quality compost rich in nutrients. As a by-product, fluid can be drained from the bin and diluted for use as a liquid feed.

Although you can make a wormery at home, commercial ready-made models are available. The worms (tiger worms) can be bought by mail order or from fishing-tackle shops. Earthworms are not suitable.

Everything that can be added to a compost heap (see pp. 326–7) can be used in a wormery, as well as cooked food and meat.

■ Site the wormery in a sheltered place out of direct sunlight. Place a plastic bowl underneath to catch any fluid.

FEEDING A WORMERY
Add further layers of kitchen scraps only when the worms have worked their way through the existing material.

■ Place a 3-in (7-cm) layer of rotted garden compost in the base to act as a starter, and introduce the worms.

■ Cover them with a shallow layer of material for composting. Add further layers of kitchen scraps only when the worms have worked their way through the existing material.

■ To empty the bin, sieve the compost so that any undigested material is left behind, as well as the worms themselves. Return these to the bin along with a little of the finished compost (to act as a starter) and begin the cycle again.

Warning

Activity in a wormery slows down during winter. Protect the worms from cold by bringing the bin under cover in winter, either into a shed or greenhouse, where temperatures are unlikely to drop below freezing.

2
LAWNS

To many gardeners, a lawn is an essential part of the garden – a green, grassy carpet providing the perfect foil for ornamental plants. Mowing and edging the lawn can be unnecessarily time-consuming, however, unless you know how to do these chores in as quick and easy a manner as possible. If you want to create a new lawn from scratch, this chapter will show you the best way to lay turf to produce an almost instant effect.

EQUIPMENT

K eeping lawns and other surfaces in good order can be made much
easier if you use the right type of equipment. There are plenty of
laborsaving gadgets available; which ones you select will depend on
the size and style of your garden and your budget.

LAWN MOWERS

Regular summer mowing is essential
to keep a lawn looking neat and tidy.
A manual mower may be adequate
for a small lawn, but for a larger
area of grass a powered mower will
save considerably on time and effort.

■ **Powered mowers** Electric mowers
are lightweight and easy to operate,
but the trailing cable can be a
dangerous nuisance. Special holsters
are available to run the cable over
your shoulder, helping to keep
it out of the way of the blades. A
circuit breaker should always be used
with outdoor electrical equipment.

■ **Battery mowers** Mowers with
batteries avoid the problem of
a trailing electrical cable, but are
heavier than electric mowers and
the batteries need regular
recharging. They have a limited
range per charge and are
only suitable for
small lawns.

■ **Gas-powered mowers** Gas-
operated mowers are good for large
areas of grass and where there is no
access to electricity. However, they
are heavy, high-maintenance, and
can be tricky to start.

HALFMOON
EDGER

LAWN RAKE

as they can be used on patios and gravel without damaging the surface. To improve your lawn quality, you can scarify the grass in the fall with a powered raker; this is far quicker and easier to use than a hand rake.

■ **Powered trimmers** Trimmers can be fitted with a nylon line for cutting soft growth, or a blade to turn them into brushcutters. Nylon line trimmers are excellent for trimming tufty grass and other plant growth against the base of walls, around established trees, and at the edges of paving. Some have heads that can be turned through 180° for use as lawn edge trimmers. Brushcutters deal quickly with areas of more woody growth that need tidying, such as ground-cover shrubs.

■ **Garden vacuums and blowers** These make quick work of gathering up fallen leaves and other debris from lawns, paths, and patios, and are especially good at clearing difficult corners.

■ **Irrigation systems** To keep lawns green in times of drought, use a sprinkler attached to a hose; for more ornamental, luxury-style lawns, a pop-up irrigation system can be installed. However, if you cannot be bothered to water the turf, leave it – it will green up quickly as soon as rain arrives, though its quality may suffer slightly.

LABORSAVING TOOLS

Some equipment is only designed for lawn care, but many tools can be used for other surfaces as well. If tools are used only occasionally it may be best to rent them – that way you do not have the trouble of storing and maintaining them.

■ **Powered edgers** These are made specially for lawn edges and are much quicker to use than long-handled shears. They must have a neat, straight, right-angled edge to work to, which should be cut beforehand with a halfmoon edger.

■ **Lawn rakers** For small lawns, a spring-tined rake is light and easy to use for gathering clippings, fallen leaves, and garden debris. Rubber-fingered rakes are particularly useful,

Warning
To avoid injury and potentially fatal electric shock, always install a circuit breaker when using electrical tools in the garden. Do not use electric mowers on wet grass.

LAYING A LAWN

Although lawns require more maintenance than other surfaces, grass is restful to the eye, complements plants and flowers well, and is soft and safe to walk on. If you decide a lawn is right for your garden, you can achieve a rapid result by laying turf.

TURF OR SEED?

For a busy gardener, laying turf is far more practical than growing a lawn from seed – the effect is instant and the new lawn requires far less initial care. However, on the downside, the quality of turf can vary greatly, and it is more expensive than seed.

Meadow turf has been stripped from farmland and may contain poor-quality grass and lots of weeds, although it can be a good buy; try to inspect a sample before ordering. It generally comes in standard-sized rectangles of 3 x 1 ft (100 x 30 cm), folded into three. Seeded turf has been grown specifically for lawns and is high quality, though more expensive. It is usually cut thinner than meadow turf and comes in long rolls, which makes laying quicker.

SOIL PREPARATION

Taking trouble over soil preparation is worthwhile in the long term, as it will save time and effort later on when the lawn is established.

Clear the ground of any existing grass, weeds, and rubble. It may be necessary to use a total weed killer such as glyphosate, or a flame gun to kill off plant growth. Roots of perennial weeds such as dandelions and docks must be removed.

Cultivate the area thoroughly; a powered cultivator does the job easily and quickly. Break the soil surface down to fine crumbs.

LAYING OUT TURF
Turfs should always be laid in a straight line. Stagger the joints to ensure an even finish and maximum bonding.

CUTTING A CURVE

If, when you have laid a basic rectangle of turf, you decide you want to soften some of the edges to allow for rectangular or semicircular borders, follow these simple steps. All you will need is some sand, string, a small plastic cup, a peg, a halfmoon edger, and a spade.

1 Drive a peg into the grass and attach a length of string to it. Tie the free end to a plastic cup with a hole in the base and fill with sand. Pull the string taut and mark out the curve with the sand.

2 Following the sand marks, cut through the turf with a halfmoon edger. Using a gardem spade, remove the semicircle of turf that you no longer want. This can be added to the compost heap.

LAYING THE TURF

Late fall is the best time to lay turf, but you can lay turf in mild spells of weather throughout the winter and into early spring. Ensure the turf is delivered within two days of when you intend to begin laying it, or it will start to deteriorate. Choose a convenient place for stacking the turfs, preferably near the prepared site.

■ Tread the prepared soil firm and rake it level, making sure there are no bumps or hollows. Sprinkle on some general fertilizer granules to ensure the turf has a good start.

■ Mark out the area to be turfed with pegs and string, or perhaps with a garden hose for irregular shapes.

Lay the first strip of turf nearest the stack, overlapping the proposed lawn edge slightly. Tamp each turf down lightly with the head of a rake, and butt turfs up closely to each other.

■ Lay the next strip of turf alongside the first, working from a plank on the newly laid turf. Butt the edges as closely as possible and stagger the joints like a brick wall. Continue until the whole area is covered.

■ Trickle sandy loam soil along the joints between turfs to help them knit together, and water the new lawn. Wait a day or two before cutting the edges to shape to allow any shrinkage to occur first.

CUTTING GRASS

How often you cut your grass depends on the type of lawn, the weather, and personal preference. Some people will tolerate a shaggy, uneven stretch of grass, while others want a more manicured appearance throughout the summer.

MOWING

Regular mowing helps to create an attractive, high-quality lawn. Coarse grasses and many weeds will not tolerate frequent mowing and will die out, leaving the finer grasses to dominate. However, regular mowing is a time-consuming task, so any ways of making the job quicker and easier will be of great benefit to the busy gardener.

STRIPED LAWN
Cylinder mowers fitted with rollers can create a classic striped effect for the lawn, with an even attractive finish.

■ **Slow-growing grasses** There are some varieties of grass that grow slowly and need less frequent mowing while still retaining a high-quality appearance. These varieties can be used if you are raising a lawn from seed, but there is less choice if you want to use turf.

■ **The right mower** Mowing can be much quicker if you use the most suitable mower for your lawn. For example, a lightweight hover mower is easier to maneuver on a lawn with lots of curves and difficult edges,

Warning

If stones or twigs catch in the blades of any powered mower and inhibit its action, make sure the machine is properly switched off (and disconnected, in the case of electric-driven tools) before attempting to remove the obstruction.

while a rotary mower is easier to use on long, rough grass than a cylinder mower (see page 330 for more details on mowing equipment).

■ **Frequent cutting** Mowing the lawn at frequent intervals means that the very short clippings can be allowed to lie on the grass and do not have to be collected up. This saves a lot of time spent emptying a grass box. Mulching mowers can deal with longer grass, chopping it up finely enough to be left on the lawn in the same way.

■ **Mowing height** For the majority of lawns, the grass does not need to be cut any lower than 1 in (2.5 cm). This keeps it green and helps it withstand wear.

■ **Lawn shape** A rectangular- or square-shaped lawn is straightforward to mow in parallel lines, but involves lots of turns at each end. A lawn that is a gently curved or round shape can be mowed in one continuous, decreasing circle, which tends to be quicker.

■ **Forget the stripes** Mowers fitted with a rear roller will produce stripes; some rotary mowers have a rear roller, but rollers are more common on cylinder mowers. Stripes look attractive, but make mowing

time-consuming because so much care has to be taken over getting the stripes neat and evenly spaced.

■ **Feeding and watering** Fertilizers may improve a lawn's appearance, but they also cause increased growth – which means more mowing – so don't feed your lawn just for the sake of it. Slow-release fertilizers applied in spring have a more gradual, sustained effect. Watering will also increase grass growth in dry summers and is often unnecessary. Tolerate the brown turf for a while: the grass will soon recover when rain arrives.

■ **Lawn edges** Instal a mowing strip to make mowing your lawn edges much easier.

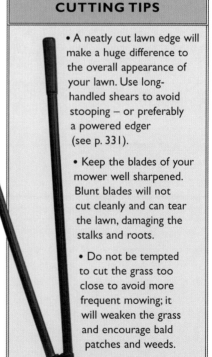

CUTTING TIPS

• A neatly cut lawn edge will make a huge difference to the overall appearance of your lawn. Use long-handled shears to avoid stooping – or preferably a powered edger (see p. 331).

• Keep the blades of your mower well sharpened. Blunt blades will not cut cleanly and can tear the lawn, damaging the stalks and roots.

• Do not be tempted to cut the grass too close to avoid more frequent mowing; it will weaken the grass and encourage bald patches and weeds.

ROUTINE LAWN CARE

There is no need to spend hours on lawn care to keep the turf looking good. Many of the time-consuming tasks detailed in some gardening books can be dispensed with altogether, and shortcuts can often be found for essential chores.

SPRING

■ **Mowing** Begin mowing as soon as the grass reaches 2 in (5 cm) tall, with the blades set to give a 1.5-in (4-cm) cut.

■ **Feeding** If your lawn needs feeding, use a fertilizer designed for spring use. Granular fertilizers can be applied more quickly and accurately with a calibrated spreader, which can be rented from the fertilizer supplier.

■ **Weeding** Broad-leaved (nongrass) weeds can be controlled with a selective weed killer. If the whole lawn is weed-ridden, apply a "weed-and-feed" treatment that saves time by combining fertilizer and herbicide

application. If there are just a few weeds, use a herbicide spot treatment; long-handled applicators save stooping.

■ **Moss treatment** A lot of moss on a lawn means conditions are too shady or wet for good grass growth; consider replacing the lawn with an alternative surface (see pp. 49–62). Otherwise, use a moss killer such as lawn sand and rake out the dead moss with a spring-tined rake on small areas, or with a powered lawn raker on large lawns. Isolated, compacted areas with mossy grass can be improved by spiking the surface with a fork.

RAKING AWAY DEAD GRASS

SPIKING A LAWN WITH A FORK

SUMMER

■ **Mowing** Cut the lawn regularly – as long as the clippings are short, they do not need to be removed but can be left lying on the lawn surface. Do not cut grass lower than ¾ in (2 cm).

■ **Watering** Resist the urge to water, even in drought conditions. If you feel it essential to maintain a green lawn, use a sprinkler, selecting a pattern that will cover the lawn in the most efficient way. Water in the evening and ensure enough water is given to soak the root area.

FALL

■ **Mowing** Cut the grass less frequently than in the summer.

■ **Leaf clearing** Fallen leaves will smother grass if allowed to lie on it for any length of time. A garden vacuum will clear them up rapidly.

■ **Feeding** High-quality turf will benefit from a feed, but it must be one formulated for use in fall. While time-consuming, topdressing with a mixture of peat, sand, and soil gives a real boost to a quality lawn.

■ **Scarifying** A powered lawn rake will remove dead grass and improve the quality of the grass.

DON'T WALK

Avoid walking across a lawn when there is frost on the grass, as black footprints will be left where the grass has been trodden on and killed.
Try to keep off the lawn during wet weather too – you will compact the soil and inhibit lawn growth.

LAWN SAND

GRANULAR LAWN FERTILIZER

WINTER

■ **Mowing** Occasional mowing may be necessary during mild spells. Try to keep the grass to a height of roughly 1.5 in (4 cm).

■ **Lawn edges** Avoid treading on lawn edges – they are prone to crumbling during the winter, which will mean time has to be spent recutting them or constructing new edges in the spring.

■ **Mower maintenance** In late winter, send mowers for servicing well before the spring rush, otherwise you may have to wait weeks for them to be returned.

AROUND THE EDGE

Most lawns show signs of wear and tear occasionally, especially if they are subjected to heavy use. Tidy edges are essential for maintaining a neat effect. Fortunately, most damaged edging can be quickly repaired, saving considerable time and effort in the future.

CUTTING A NEW EDGE

To make a new edge for a lawn (for example if you are extending a flower bed), lay a plank on the grass to mark the new edge and cut along it with a halfmoon edger. This will prevent you from damaging the edge when you step on it.

TIDYING A RAGGED EDGE

Lawn edges easily become ragged. but tidying them is a simple task.

■ Using a halfmoon edger, cut a square section of turf that incorporates the damaged edge and lift it carefully.

■ Turn the turf around so that the damaged section is now facing inward and what was the inside edge is flush with the edge of the lawn.

■ Prepare the bare area thoroughly and then resow lawn seed. You will now have a neat, straight edge.

PREPARING A MOWING EDGE

Preparing a mowing edge will make mowing quicker and easier and avoids the necessity of frequent trimming of the lawn edge. As well as using grit, you can lay a row of bricks set in concrete along the lawn edges. Flexible plastic or metal edging strips can also be used to protect lawn edge, and are very simple to install; edging tiles – such as the rope-topped style favored in the 19th century – are another option.

1 Remove all weeds along the edge of the lawn with a hand fork. Dig a trench 2–3 in (5–8 cm) along the edge of the lawn.

2 Fill with grit, making sure it remains slightly below the level of the lawn. This will avoid the mower kicking it up.

3
SHRUBS, TREES, AND CLIMBERS

Ideal for the busy gardener, shrubs, trees, and climbers provide beautiful features and year-round interest while requiring the minimum of work. Once the plants are established, they virtually look after themselves and continue to grow and develop year after year with very little intervention from the gardener.

With the right choice of plants, you can have some feature of interest and color in every month of the year, whether it is provided by plant shape, foliage, flowers, or fruit. Apart from their beauty, shrubs, trees, and climbers can also have a practical value as windbreaks, screens, barriers, and hedges.

SHRUBS

Ideal plants for the busy gardener, shrubs need far less maintenance than borders filled with perennial or annual plants. With a careful selection of flowering and variegated shrubs, you can ensure year-round color and interest in the garden.

CHOOSING PLANTS

A shrub is a plant that makes a permanent framework of branches above ground. Shrubs may be evergreen or deciduous, and may be grown for their leaves, flowers, or berries. Choose a variety for a prolonged season of interest.

PRUNING SHEARS

■ **Evergreens** These will provide the backbone of the garden throughout the year and have the added advantage of not shedding leaves in fall. Variegated foliage is valuable for its bright color, especially on dull winter days. Good examples include *Euonymus japonicus* "Ovatus Aureus," *Elaeagnus pungens* "Maculata," and *Skimmia japonica* "Rubella."

CUTTING BACK TO SHAPE
There are many shrubs that need pruning at a specific time each year to produce a good crop of flowers.

■ **Deciduous shrubs** Shrubs that lose their leaves in fall help to add variety to the garden as the seasons change. Many produce brilliant colors before the foliage falls, and some have an attractive winter outline of bare branches. Good examples include *Acer palmatum atropurpureum* and *Corylus avellana* "Contorta."

■ **Flowering shrubs** Shrubs can be found in flower through every month of the year. Some types need pruning at specific times of the year to produce the best show of flowers, so make sure you know a plant's pruning requirements before you buy it. *Mahonia aquifolium, Escallonia* "Apple Blossom," and *Hebe* "Autumn Glory" come into this category.

■ **Berrying shrubs** Berries are carried from late summer right through the winter. Shrubs with berries include *Pyracantha* "Orange Glow," *Viburnum davidii*, and *Cotoneaster conspicuus* "Decorus."

SHRUB MAINTENANCE

Once they are established, shrubs usually need very little maintenance. Most are deep rooted so they do not normally need watering; mulching moist soil in spring aids moisture retention and also keeps down weeds. Many shrubs require no regular pruning; others require cutting back to shape only if they start to outgrow their space.

Shrubs that flower in the first half of the year flower on old wood and should be pruned immediately after flowering, cutting back stems between one-third and one-half. Shrubs that flower from midsummer produce flowers on new shoots. These should be pruned at the end of the dormant season, cutting back old stems to stimulate new growth.

PRUNING REQUIREMENTS

CLIP INTO SHAPE

Buxus
(Box)
Elaeagnus
Hebe "Boughton Dome"
Heteromeles
(Christmas berry)
Ilex
(Holly)
Lavandula
(Lavender [do not cut into bare wood])
Ligustrum
(Privet)

BLUE HYDRANGEA

Lonicera nitida
Phillyrea
Prunus laurocerasus
(Cherry laurel)
Prunus lusitanica
(Portugal laurel)
Taxus
(Yew)

MINIMAL PRUNING ONLY

Callistemon
(Bottlebrush)
Calycanthus
Ceanothus thyrsiflorus
Chimonanthus

Cistus
(Rock rose)
Convolvulus
Corylopsis
Daphne
Hamamelis
(Witch hazel)
Hippophäe
Kalmia
Magnolia
Paeonia
(Peony)
Pittosporum
Prunus (deciduous)
(Cherry)
Rhododendron
Sophora
(Kowhai)
Stachyurus

CUT BACK ANNUALLY

Brugmansia
(Angels' trumpets)
Buddleja davidii
(Butterfly bush)
Caryopteris
Ceratostigma
Cestrum
Fuchsia
Hydrangea paniculata
Indigofera
Lavatera
(Tree mallow)
Perovskia
Phygelius

ROSES

Although roses must be among the best-known and most popular garden plants, they have an undeserved reputation for being difficult to grow well. Advances in rose breeding are helping to remove this prejudice; however, if you select the right varieties, roses are as easy to grow as any other shrub.

CHOOSING VARIETIES

Traditionally, roses were difficult plants, with a short flowering season, a tendency to suffer from pests and diseases, and requiring specialized pruning. However, modern varieties are much easier to look after; most are compact growing, repeat flowering, and resistant to insects. In most cases, a simple pruning regime is adequate.

■ **Disease resistance** Fungus diseases such as blackspot and mildew are common and can decimate plants in some seasons. Disease-resistant varieties are much less likely to be badly affected. If treatment is necessary, ready-to-use sprays are convenient and save time.

■ **Flowering season** Many old-fashioned roses have one glorious but brief season of flowering in midsummer. Repeat-flowering varieties, which flower throughout the summer, offer more value and keep the garden filled with color.

■ **Type** Different types of roses require different amounts of care. Shrub roses are generally trouble free, needing little pruning except to remove dead or weak shoots. Most are repeat-flowering. Ground-cover roses are good for growing in beds to reduce weeding, while patio roses are low-growing and excellent for containers and in mixed borders.

TALL AND STRIKING
Standard roses should be pruned to produce an evenly shaped, floriferous head with many good-sized flowers.

Warning

All rose prunings – whether from a damaged plant or not – should be burned rather than composted as they can harbor disease.

ROSE MAINTENANCE

Roses do not need much specialized
care. For the best flowers, hybrid teas
and floribundas should be pruned
in early spring: cut the stems straight
across, to about half their height.
Give plants an application of rose
fertilizer in spring. Treat pests or
diseases with a suitable ready-to-use
spray. Improve the plants'
appearance and encourage blooms
by removing dead flower heads.

DEADHEADING A ROSE
When the central flower begins to fade,
roses should have their whole central
truss cut back to an emerging bud.

ROSE TYPES

There are hundreds of naturally
occurring species of roses and many
natural hybrids. The type of roses you
choose to grow will depend on your
garden and the time you have available.

• **Old garden and species** Generally
freely branching roses with flower
clusters borne in midsummer. While
old garden roses require extensive
pruning, species are easier to maintain.

FREEDOM
ROSE

• **Hybrid tea** (large flowered)
Upright, repeat-flowering shrubs with
large flowers in summer and fall.

• **Floribunda** (cluster flowered)
Upright, repeat-flowering shrubs
with a better continuity of bloom
than hybrid tea varieties.

• **Patio and miniature** Similar
to floribunda, but with a neater
habit. Invaluable in confined spaces
and containers.

• **Ground cover** Low-growing,
trailing or spreading roses. Ideal for
planting at the front of a border.

• **Shrub** Widely varied group,
ranging from mound-forming cultivars
to wide-spreading shrubs.

• **Climbing** Roses with stiff, upright
growth and blooms borne on
sideshoots. Most are repeat-flowering
in summer and fall.

• **Rambling** Roses with long, strong
shoots and large flowers. Some bloom
once, but most are repeat-flowering.

TREES

Valued for adding height, permanence, and foliage interest, trees require very little care from the busy gardener once they have become established. However, it is important to choose the right type of tree to complement the size and shape of your garden; you will also need to assess carefully the right spot for it – a tree in the wrong position can cause a lot of unnecessary work.

SHAPE AND SIZE

If you are lucky enough to have a very large garden, you can plant almost any tree you like, but if like most garden owners you have a small garden, the choice is much more limited. Trees that are too large cast unwelcome shade, deprive other plants of light, nutrients, and moisture, and can cause damage to nearby buildings, especially on clay soil. Avoid the dense leaf canopy of evergreen trees and fast-growing, thirsty trees with wide-spreading roots, such as willow and poplar.

The busy gardener should check the following features to obtain trouble-free trees.

■ **Eventual height** It is difficult to specify exactly what height a tree will reach at maturity because so much depends on its growing conditions, but most good nurseries will be able to offer advice on the likely height after 5 to 10 years of growth. While tall trees can be kept small by regular pruning, this takes unnecessary time and effort, and it often spoils the shape of the tree.

■ **Features of interest** It is always a good idea to choose a plant that has more than one feature of interest, so that it really earns its place in the garden. Trees come in many varieties and can have a graceful shape, colorful leaves, attractive bark, flowers, berries, or fruits.

■ **Evergreen or deciduous** Deciduous trees can be a nuisance in fall – particularly if they are large – as leaves will need clearing from paths, lawns, and ponds. However, small leaves, such as those from a birch tree *(Betula)*, do not normally cause a great problem.

PLANTING A SMALL CONTAINER-GROWN BEECH TREE

PRUNING A MATURE WILLOW
Willows need only minimal pruning with either loppers or pruning shears to maintain a healthy framework.

ESTABLISHED TREES

Established trees are usually trouble free, but occasional intervention may be necessary to keep them growing vigorously.

■ **Check tree ties** Remove or slacken tree ties if they are chafing or constricting the trunk of the tree. Trees do not normally require a stake for more than the first two or three years of growth.

■ **Replace broken leaders** The central leader of a tree is quite easily damaged, and if the leading shoot is broken, the shape of the tree can be spoiled. Cut a damaged leader back to the next vigorous shoot that is showing a tendency to grow into the desired position. Rub out any other nearby shoots that may compete with the new leader. In some cases, you might need to attach an extension cane to the new leader to aid growth. This should be removed once the leader is growing strongly.

■ **Cut out dead or diseased wood** Any dead or damaged branches should be cut back to healthy wood with shears or a pruning saw.

PLANTING TREES

When buying a young tree, look for one that has already received formative training, and so will need minimal pruning after planting. Container-grown trees can be planted at anytime of year, but establish most quickly in the fall.

■ Prepare the ground thoroughly before planting, adding rotted garden compost or proprietary planting mix to the base of the hole.

■ Container-grown trees should be supported at both the top and the bottom, until the tree becomes established. Provide a new tree with a stake to keep it upright while it becomes established; the stake should be hammered into position before the tree is planted to avoid damage to the tree's roots.

■ Specimens that have not been staked before planting should have a slender cane attached, which will do less damage to the trunk and the overall shape of the tree than a stout stake.

> ## Warning
>
> Mature trees in existing gardens may carry a preservation order. You should contact your local authority before attempting to do any major work on them, or if you wish to remove them.

SPECIAL EFFECTS

While all busy gardeners prefer to keep pruning to a minimum, it is possible to use pruning to enhance a particular decorative aspect on certain plants. However, there is often a loss as well as a gain. For example, if you cut back a dogwood *(Cornus)* hard to stimulate new stems, it is at the expense of the flowers, since these are carried on old wood.

COPPICING

Known as coppicing, regular pruning of a tree close to the ground will encourage strong, basal shoots to grow. It can be used to restrict tree size. The technique has differing results on a variety of shrubs. Most often it results in larger, showier leaves, so it is often used on shrubs that are grown for their foliage rather than their flowers or fruits. Coppicing *Eucalyptus gunnii* encourages it to produce a crop of fresh young leaves, which most gardeners consider more attractive than the older leaves, that become elongated and lose their sheen as they mature.

On some shrubs (notably *Cornus* and *Rubus*), coppicing is a means of ensuring that there is a good supply of strikingly colored young stems. These shrubs are at their best when bare in winter and when there is little else of interest in the garden.

■ **Method** To coppice a shrub, let it grow unpruned during the first two seasons to allow it to establish. In either late winter or early spring, cut back all the growth to leave a woody framework 6–12 in (15–30 cm) above the ground. Repeat this task annually. Otherwise, cut back in alternate years, but remove only the two-year old stems. For large plants, stagger the pruning over two or three years, only removing older wood.

BERRY BRIGHT
Grown for its bright, decorative, orange-red fruit, *Pyracantha* "Orange Glow" can be displayed trained against a wall.

■ **Exposing berries** Some shrubs, such as *Pyracantha*, are grown for their bright berries, although these are often masked by the flush of new growth put on after the fruit has set. To expose the berries, cut back the new growth emerging from behind the fruit clusters to two or three leaves. This increases the decorative appeal of freestanding plants.

PLEACHED TREES
These beech trees have had their branches woven together to create a suspended hedge with an intricate branch structure.

POLLARDING

Pollarding is a similar technique to coppicing, except that the plant is allowed to develop a clear trunk. It is suitable for trees such as *Catalpa, Eucalyptus,* and some willows *(Salix).*

To produce a pollard, it is best to buy a young tree with a clear trunk and a well-branched crown. Allow the tree to grow with minimal pruning for two seasons or until well established. Before cutting, consider the shape, size, and habit of the mature tree. In late winter or early spring, cut back the trunk just above the lowest branches on the crown. Cut these branches back to within 3 in (8 cm) of the trunk. Thereafter, cut the new growth back as for coppicing, either annually or every two or three years.

HEDGES

A hedge provides an attractive barrier or border that has a softer, often more pleasing appearance than a wall or fence. Hedges can be hard work if they require frequent clipping, so choose easy-to-care-for plants that need minimal maintenance.

MAKING YOUR CHOICE

Consider the function of your hedge before deciding on the plants – it may be that a nonliving alternative such as a fence would suit your needs just as well and be less labor intensive (see p. 349).

Hedges make attractive boundaries that can bear flowers and berries as well as foliage; many hedging plants change with the seasons to provide variety in the garden. By filtering the wind, hedges – especially deciduous ones – make better windbreaks in

exposed areas than solid barriers such as walls. Hedges may be formal or informal. The choice depends on the style of garden and the space available, but generally, informal hedges are less work for a busy gardener. Formal hedges need to be closely clipped to keep them neat, and clipping can be very time consuming. Informal hedges also need occasional clipping, but this can be done with less regularity and with less precision.

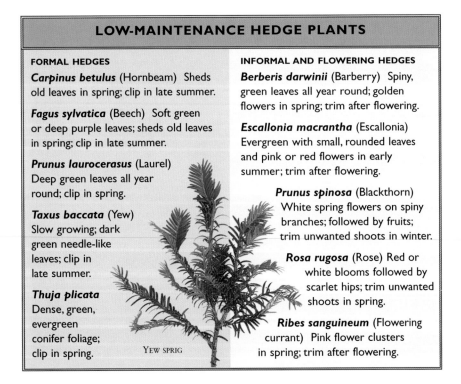

LOW-MAINTENANCE HEDGE PLANTS

FORMAL HEDGES

Carpinus betulus (Hornbeam) Sheds old leaves in spring; clip in late summer.

Fagus sylvatica (Beech) Soft green or deep purple leaves; sheds old leaves in spring; clip in late summer.

Prunus laurocerasus (Laurel) Deep green leaves all year round; clip in spring.

Taxus baccata (Yew) Slow growing; dark green needle-like leaves; clip in late summer.

Thuja plicata Dense, green, evergreen conifer foliage; clip in spring.

YEW SPRIG

INFORMAL AND FLOWERING HEDGES

Berberis darwinii (Barberry) Spiny, green leaves all year round; golden flowers in spring; trim after flowering.

Escallonia macrantha (Escallonia) Evergreen with small, rounded leaves and pink or red flowers in early summer; trim after flowering.

Prunus spinosa (Blackthorn) White spring flowers on spiny branches; followed by fruits; trim unwanted shoots in winter.

Rosa rugosa (Rose) Red or white blooms followed by scarlet hips; trim unwanted shoots in spring.

Ribes sanguineum (Flowering currant) Pink flower clusters in spring; trim after flowering.

TRELLIS EXTENSION

Treated with preservative
for a longer life

HEDGING ALTERNATIVES

A hedge may mark a boundary, form a barrier, or act as a windbreak. However, busy gardeners can also use a low-maintenance alternative such as a wall, fence, or screen. It is possible to combine the two, growing a low hedge and topping it with a trellis extension for extra height.

■ **Walling** Traditionally, building a wall requires good bricklaying skills, but special walling units make the job quick and easy for amateurs.

■ **Screening** This has a shorter life than fencing but is simple to erect. Traditional hurdles are made from hazel, but willow, reed, and bamboo screens are also available.

■ **Fencing** Make sure timber fencing posts are treated with preservative; concrete posts have a longer life and save maintenance. Posts must be firmly fixed in the ground: for this purpose, metal post spikes are easier to use than setting posts in concrete.

MAINTAINING HEDGES

Hedges require regular trimming to keep their growth under control, but the amount of clipping they need depends on the type of plant used and the effect required.

■ If possible, choose hedging plants that need only one trim a year, such as those recommended on p. 348.

■ Try using the growth regulator dikegulac: it reduces the need for cutting on some species and helps make the hedge denser and bushier.

■ A strip of paving running alongside the hedge is easier to work from than soil or grass.

■ Use a powered hedge trimmer rather than shears. Always use an electric circuit breaker in case of accidents.

■ Keep the height of the hedge low so that it is not necessary to use a ladder when trimming. This is safer as well as easier.

TIMESAVING TIPS

• Informal hedges require less attention and are easier to trim than closely clipped, formal hedges.

• Use a plastic groundsheet at the base of the hedge when cutting – this makes clearing up the clippings afterward much easier.

• Fast-growing hedging plants, such as *Leylandii,* need to be clipped several times a year. The busy gardener should consider replacing these plants as well as very tall, formal hedges with low-maintenance fencing or walling.

CLIMBING PLANTS

One of the most versatile plant groups, climbers provide enormous scope for imaginative design in the garden. Grown with support, climbers can combine with other garden features, such as fences, garages, and walls, to add further color and texture.

CHOOSING CLIMBERS

Climbing plants can provide a living screen to mask unsightly features, such as drab-looking garages, plain brick walls, and fences. They are also effective when used as weed-smothering ground cover across banks, or to add an extra vertical dimension to gardens where growing space is limited. Climbers attach themselves in a number of ways.

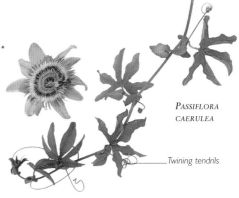

PASSIFLORA CAERULEA

Twining tendrils

■ **Tendril climbers** These kinds of climber have specialized leaf stalks (as in clematis) or modified shoots (passion flower and sweet pea) that coil tightly around the support.

■ **Scandent climbers** Shrubs with no means of attaching themselves to a support are called scandent climbers. These include trailing plants such as winter jasmine and a few clematis (see p. 354).

■ **Self-clinging climbers** Some climbers, such as ivies, Virginia creeper, and climbing hydrangea, have aerial roots or suckering pads that will adhere to most surfaces.

■ **Twining climbers** Climbers such as wisteria and honeysuckle have stems that twist around their support.

■ **Hooked thorns** Plants such as bougainvillaea have hooked thorns that grip the bark of host plants.

TRAINING CLIMBERS

• Avoid planting self-clinging climbers on a wall with a flaky surface or loose mortar. They will worsen the problem and further damage the wall.

• Spread out the stems of young climbers to encourage the plant to cover the whole width of the allotted space rather than just the center.

TIMESAVING TIPS

• Grow self-clinging climbers to save time spent training them on supports.

• A trellis fixed to a batten (see p. 352) with screws or hooks allows you to lower the plant and its support to carry out wall maintenance.

• Avoid climbers that need regular pruning to keep rampant growth under control or to produce flowers.

PLANTING CLIMBERS

When siting climbers, bear in mind that they are vigorous plants that make heavy demands on soil moisture and nutrients. Water them well until established and feed them regularly.

Protective cap

CONTAINER-GROWN IVY

Stem tied in

1 Set the plant 12 in (30 cm) away from the base of the wall. Angle the topgrowth toward the wall and aim the roots toward the garden, so they can gain plenty of moisture.

2 Soak the rootball and fill the hole. Insert a stake for the strongest shoots and tie the climber, using garden twine to make a figure-eight loop (this avoids the plant chafing).

CLIMBING SUPPORTS

The type of support you choose for your climbers can make all the difference to the display. Fixed trellis panels and netting enable you to transform a bare wall or to mask an unsightly feature, while creative use of freestanding supports, such as obelisks and wigwams, can bring color and height to a border or patio. Select your support according to the habit of the climber you want to grow.

FIXED SUPPORTS

■ **Trellis panels** Ready-made trellis panels can be used with solid fencing panels or can be fixed to walls or fences. Wooden panels are the hardest wearing and need little maintenance. Use trellis panels for thorny, scandent, and twining climbers. They can also be used for tendril climbers, provided the timbers are thin enough for the tendrils to coil around. Trellis can be brightened up and protected with a coat of colored wood preservative.

■ **Netting** Available in a wide range of gauges from heavy-duty pig wire down to lightweight plastic mesh, netting provides an ideal support for tendril climbers. Ensure that you choose one that is robust enough for your choice of climber. Netting can be fixed to walls and fences or wrapped around wigwams, obelisks, or tree trunks.

■ **Vine eyes** Used with horticultural wire, vine eyes are driven into masonry or fencing uprights, and wires are stretched between them.

Make sure timber has been treated before fixing

TRELLIS PANEL

FANTAIL TRELLIS

FREESTANDING SUPPORTS

■ **Obelisks and wigwams** Designed to be used as a feature in borders or on patios, obelisks and wigwams suit less vigorous climbers, such as some hybrid clematis or annual sweet peas.

■ **Host trees** Any established tree will support climbing roses, honeysuckles, and species clematis – too vigorous a climber may swamp or even pull down a less-than-sturdy host. When planting a climber to grow into a tree, plant at least 3 ft (90 cm) from the base of the trunk. Angle two canes toward the tree trunk and tie the climber's stems to them. Once the climber has grown into the tree canopy, remove the canes.

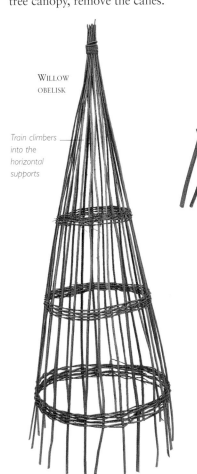

WIGWAM

Movable joints allow the height and width of the obelisk to be adjusted according to its position in the garden

WILLOW OBELISK

Train climbers into the horizontal supports

FIXING TRELLIS

• Fix wooden battens at least 2-in (5-cm) thick to the wall. Attach the trellis panel to the battens so as to leave a gap between the trellis and the wall. This will allow air to circulate behind the plant and reduce the likelihood of fungal diseases caused by stagnant air.

• Before fixing trellis to a painted wall, apply a fresh coat of paint to the surface to avoid time-consuming difficulties after the trellis is fixed.

POPULAR CLIMBERS

There are many different types of climbing plants, and planting a selection of different species could ensure there is something of interest the whole year round. Flowering types are always popular, but don't neglect the many trouble-free and reliable foliage climbers that are available from garden stores.

FLOWERING CLIMBERS

Many flowering climbers need pruning in order to ensure the best display of flowers, which can put off many busy gardeners from cultivating them. Some, however, need minimal attention in order to create an eye-catching feature.

■ **Clematis** Most clematis attach themselves by means of twining leaf stalks and need no tying in once established. Strong-growing types such as cultivars of *Clematis montana* can be used to rapidly cover outbuildings or garages but may be too rampant for a small area. The large-flowered hybrids are less vigorous but may need specialized pruning. When you are buying plants the label should indicate to which pruning group it belongs. Best choices for the busy gardener are those in pruning Group 1, which need pruning after flowering only to tidy them as necessary. They flower in spring and include varieties of *C. alpina*, *C. armandii*, *C. macropetala*, and *C. montana*. Group 2 clematis (including "Rouge Cardinal") need to be pruned back after their first flush of flowers in early summer, while Group 3 varieties should be pruned in late winter or early spring.

■ **Honeysuckle** The fragrant, tubular honeysuckle flowers are immensely popular. *Lonicera periclymenum* "Belgica" flowers in early summer, and *L. p.* "Serotina" in late summer. Older stems can be thinned as required after flowering.

■ **Hydrangea** *Hydrangea petiolaris* is self clinging, producing woody stems and lacy heads of creamy white flowers. It does well on shady walls and needs no regular pruning.

■ **Jasmine** The common white jasmine *(Jasminum officinale)* has attractive ferny leaves and very fragrant, trumpet-shaped white flowers, but it needs a sheltered spot to do well. Winter jasmine *(J. nudiflorum)* is a wall plant with leafless green stems, which are spattered with bright yellow stars in winter. It may need tying back against a wall to keep it neat.

CLEMATIS "ROUGE CARDINAL"

WISTERIA SINENSIS
Ideal for high walls and fences, there are few more spectacular sights than a mature wisteria in full flower in early summer.

■ **Wisteria** This is a spectacular plant with great racemes of pealike, pendent flowers. However, it needs pruning to channel its vigor into flower production. Ideally, wisteria should be grown in a south-facing position to gain maximum sunlight. *W. floribunda* is easier to control than *W. sinensis*. Cut the sideshoots back to 6 in (15 cm) in midsummer.

FOLIAGE CLIMBERS

Some foliage climbers, such as ivy, are evergreen and a valuable addition to any garden all year round. Choose large-leaf varieties that will give rapid cover. Other foliage climbers are deciduous and may only produce brightly variegated leaves between spring and fall. Some climbers, such as Virginia creeper, have a single, magnificent display in fall, when their leaves turn brilliant scarlet and crimson. Deciduous climbers will need their leaves clearing up in fall.

FOLIAGE CLIMBERS

Actinidia kolomikta White- and pink-banded leaves

Hedera helix **"Glacier"** (Ivy) Green- and white-variegated leaves

Humulus lupulus **"Aureus"** (Golden hop) Lime-green foliage

Parthenocissus henryana Bronze leaves with white and pink veins

Parthenocissus quinquefolia (Virginia creeper) Red fall foliage

Vitis vinifera **"Purpurea"** Red fall foliage

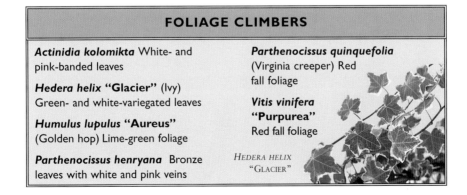

HEDERA HELIX "GLACIER"

GENERAL MAINTENANCE

Many shrubs, trees, and climbers need occasional pruning to trim back stems and shoots in order to produce well-balanced, free-flowering, healthy plants. Always prune to retain an open framework that allows the free passage of air. Pruning will be quicker and easier if you have the right tools to do the job.

TOOLS

Good-quality tools are essential and will save time in completing pruning jobs quickly and efficiently.

■ **Pruning saw** A pruning saw is designed for cutting thick, woody stems on both shrubs and trees. Most models have a folding blade.

■ **Gloves** A stout pair of gloves is necessary if you are pruning thorny plants such as roses and pyracanthas and for plants such as euphorbias that exude a milky sap that may irritate the skin.

PRUNING SAW

LONG-HANDLED LOPPERS

GARDEN SHEARS

> ### TOOL TIPS
>
> Keep all your pruning tools in good condition. Clean the blades carefully after use by rubbing them with an oily rag and have them sharpened regularly. Tools with rusty or dirty blades will not make clean cuts. They are likely to snag the outer skin or crush stems, making the plant vulnerable to disease. Clean cuts will heal more quickly.

■ **Pruning shears** Most pruning jobs can be performed by pruning shears. Do not attempt to cut stems thicker than that recommended for the shears. Not only will the blades not cut cleanly, but you risk damaging the implement.

■ **Long-handled loppers** Inaccessible shrubs and high branches can be pruned with long-handled loppers. They are also useful for reaching into the interior of dense, thicket-forming shrubs.

■ **Shears** Hedges can be trimmed with shears and can also be used for light pruning on other plants such as shrub roses. Powered hedge trimmers are best for a large hedge.

■ **Goggles** Wear goggles when pruning large plants and trees.

ROUTINE TASKS

There are a number of minor, regular tasks that will keep your trees, shrubs, and climbers in peak condition without taking up too much of your time.

■ **Watering** It is only necessary to water young or newly planted specimens in a dry spell. Use a hose or can, making sure the water soaks right down to the roots of the plant. Once a plant is properly established, it should not need additional watering. Never direct a jet of water at the base of the plant, as this will wash the soil from the roots.

REMOVING DEAD STEMS
Dead stems are recognizable from their blackened wood. The stems of shrubs should be pruned when in leaf.

DEADHEADING FLOWERS

Deadheading is a basic and essential pruning job. By removing old flowers, new blooms can be encouraged. Removing faded flowers also helps prevent the onset of fungus, such as *Botrytis cinerea* (see p. 364). Use sharp pruning shears to remove blooms as soon as they start to fade. Cut back the stem to a strong shoot lower down the stem. Soft-stemmed plants can be pinched out by hand.

REMOVING
BLOOMS

■ **Feeding** Flowering plants can benefit from an application of high-potash fertilizer in spring. On poor soils, a slow-release, granular fertilizer applied once a season helps keep shrubs growing well, but routine feeding is not normally necessary.

■ **Mulching** A mulch applied over moist soil in spring will help the soil retain moisture throughout the growing season and will also improve soil structure.

■ **Weeding** Remove weeds regularly while they are still young. Prevent excessive weed growth by using a mulch. Chemical weed killers, like dichlobenil, are specially formulated for use around shrubs.

■ **Removing dead stems** All dead and dying stems should be cut back to healthy wood to avoid the spread of disease.

STAKES AND TIES

Tall plants, especially those growing in exposed areas, often need extra support to prevent their being blown over. These should be of an appropriate type to secure the plant without restricting the stem.

EQUIPMENT

■ **Horticultural wire** Used in conjunction with vine eyes, either screwed into masonry or fencing posts.

■ **Garden twine** This is adequate for most tying jobs and stronger than raffia, which can disintegrate.

■ **Tree tie** Ties are useful for fixing a young tree to a supporting stake. The tie should be loosened as the tree grows to avoid damage.

■ **Canes and stakes** Bamboo canes are useful for supporting single-stemmed plants, but split and rot in time. PVC stakes and plastic-covered steel rods are more robust and likely to last longer.

■ **Ring ties** Designed to fit easily around the plant stem and its support, plastic-covered rings are suitable for light jobs, such as attaching a plant to a cane.

TYING IN

• When using garden twine, tie it in a figure-eight loop around the stem and the cane to prevent the plant from chafing against the stake.

• Plastic-coated horticultural wire is strong and lasts for many years. It is good for fixing labels to training wires or trellis and joining canes.

• Purpose-designed plant stickers can be used to secure the stem of a climber direct to its support.

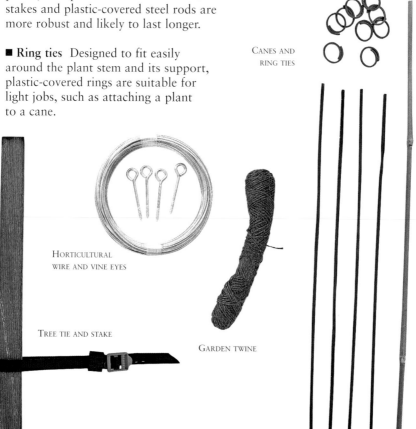

CANES AND
RING TIES

HORTICULTURAL
WIRE AND VINE EYES

TREE TIE AND STAKE

GARDEN TWINE

4
PESTS
AND DISEASES

Pests and diseases can strike in even the best-maintained garden. However, prompt action can usually prevent any problems from reaching a critical level. Although many gardeners are increasingly wary of using chemicals, these are usually highly effective, and as long as their use is localized, long-term damage can be avoided.

However, provided you can tolerate the occasional blemished or eaten flower, leaf, or fruit, a live-and-let-live approach can be effective. It will be to your advantage to maintain a healthy and diverse ecosystem that supports a variety of beneficial insect predators as well as the plants that attract them. Most pest and disease problems can be avoided by good garden hygiene and careful planting of disease-resistant varieties.

PREVENTING PROBLEMS

Good garden hygiene can greatly reduce the risk of diseases developing and spreading, while growing as wide a range of plants as possible ensures a healthy balance between pests and their natural predators (see also pp. 366–7). Save time having to deal with problems later by introducing a few simple preventive measures now.

GOOD GARDEN HYGIENE

Allways buy strong, vigorous, healthy plants. Do not buy any plants showing signs of infestation, or that have dieback or discolored stems. Check that the plant is suitable for its intended position, taking into account the soil type and site. Plant carefully, making sure the ground is well prepared and the roots spread out (see pp. 320–21).

■ **Avoid overcrowding** Take care not to overcrowd your borders, which will lead to poor air circulation and encourage fungal diseases. Planting too tight means you will have to thin your plants at a later stage; cover the gaps between them with a mulch (see pp. 324–5).

■ **Pruning** Prune shrubs to ensure good air circulation among the branches (see pp. 369–90) and routinely cut back any diseased wood to healthy growth. You should also prune out growth that has been heavily attacked by pests, since this will be vulnerable to disease. Regularly remove and dispose of diseased plants and plant matter. All debris from diseased plants should be burned. This will prevent the pest surviving and reinfecting the plant later.

■ **Feeding** Keep plants well fed to keep them growing strongly and help them recover quickly from pest infestations. Do not feed plants in late summer, however, since this can promote sappy growth that will not ripen fully before winter and will be vulnerable to disease.

EARWIG TRAPS

Earwigs are mainly beneficial insects, feeding on aphids and insect eggs. However, they do cause unsightly damage to the flowers of clematis, dahlias, and chrysanthemums.

An inverted flower pot provides a nighttime feeding place and convenient trap for earwigs

• Pack flower pots with straw and invert them on canes positioned among vulnerable plants. Earwigs will congregate in the straw overnight.

• Collect earwigs each morning and either destroy them or move them to another part of the garden.

CLEARING DEBRIS

Keeping the garden clear of plant debris is an effective way of reducing the likelihood that fungal diseases will take hold or that viruses will spread. Viruses, such as blackspots in roses, can be transferred to the soil from leaves and flowers and affect growing plants the following year. Fallen leaves also provide an ideal habitat for a range of pests, such as slugs and snails.

Compare the advantages of keeping borders tidy against the benefits of leaving decaying plant remains, which provide winter protection and help to improve the soil. Be selective; clearing spent plant material away from plants that are hardy (such as hostas) but vulnerable to slugs and snails, while leaving a protective layer around plants of borderline hardiness.

GROUND PROTECTION
Surrounding your flower beds with gravel mulches will help prevent slug and snail attacks, as well as create a neat and tidy display.

COMPANION PLANTINGS

Many gardeners believe that growing particular plants in association improves the health and vigor of both, though it is difficult to demonstrate this conclusively. Alliums are commonly held to deter aphids from roses (perhaps because of their pungent smell) and rhododendrons and foxgloves (Digitalis) seem to give an improved performance when grown together.   FOXGLOVE

ORGANIC CONTROLS

Some chemical preparations originate from natural sources. Pyrethrum, for example, is derived from a daisy. Other organic treatments include derris dust, soft soap, and sulfur dust. They are safe to use as powders or sprays, but require regular application to be effective.

TIMESAVING TIPS

• Treat all pest and disease outbreaks as soon as they are noticed to prevent more serious problems later.

• Check that plants are healthy when you buy them. Ease the plant gently from its pot to inspect the root system and look under the leaves for signs of potential problems.

• Ready-to-use formulations of chemical pesticides are much easier to use and store than concentrates that have to be diluted.

COMMON PROBLEMS

Early recognition and diagnosis of garden pests and diseases will enable you to find a quick and effective solution. The following pages list some of the most common problems, which can usually be eradicated by preventive measures or chemicals.

CHEMICAL CONTROL

Contact insecticides must be sprayed directly onto the pest concerned. The effect is usually immediate. Alternatively, systemic insecticides are absorbed by the plant and poison the pest that feeds on it. Repeated applications are usually necessary.

■ **Disposal of chemicals** Excess chemicals in solution should not be emptied down domestic drains, lavatories, sinks, or any natural source of water. They are best poured over driveways, gravel paths, or other plant-free areas of the garden. If you need to dispose of large quantities of unused chemicals, contact your local authority.

BIOLOGICAL CONTROL

It is a good idea to encourage wildlife into your garden: spiders, hedgehogs, birds, wasps, bees, and toads will eat many of your animal pests. Certain biological controls – such as a nematode parasite – are effective within a controlled area such as a greenhouse. Always introduce biological methods as soon as possible, before the infestation of pests becomes too much for the predators to control.

SAFE STORAGE
A garden shed is ideal for storing potentially hazardous materials like insecticides. These should be kept out of the reach of children and out of direct sunlight.

PLANT DAMAGE

Bulb blindness

Shoots that fail to flower are referred to as "blind." Bulb blindness is most often caused by a lack of water during the growing season or, particularly in the case of daffodils, by congestion.
Treatment: Make sure bulbs have adequate water. Dig up crowded daffodil bulbs, split them, and replant.

Leaf spots

Caused by a variety of bacteria and fungus, brown or black oval or rounded spots appear on the leaf surface. The area around the spot sometimes discolors to yellow. Roses and certain fruit bushes are most often affected, but this is a seasonal condition that will vary in its severity from year to year. Most leaf spots do not cause serious problems and develop only on plants that are already in poor condition.
Treatment: Cut back and destroy any affected growth to improve the overall health of the plant. Spray the plant with fungicides that include mancozeb, carbendazim, or Bordeaux mixture. Varieties that are resistant to leaf spot are available from garden centers and nurseries.

Toadstools

Most toadstools appear in damp fall weather. On lawns they often grow in circles ("fairy rings"), which cause the grass to discolor. However, toadstools are short lived and rarely survive the first winter frost.
Treatment: There is no effective means of preventing the emergence of toadstools, but to prevent them spreading, knock them off with a stiff brush before they release their spores. Toadstools sometimes grow on buried organic matter, such as old tree roots. These should be dug out.

BULBS MAY BE PRONE TO BLIND SHOOTS

Damping off

The roots of seedlings can darken and rot, causing the seedling to die. A fluffy, fungal growth may appear on the soil as well as on dead seedlings. This is called "damping off," and is caused by various soil- or water-borne fungi, in particular *Pythium ultimum* and *Phytophthora*, attacking the roots and the stem. *Treatment*: There is no effective control. To prevent the disease, sow seed thinly, maintain strict hygiene, improve ventilation, and avoid overwatering. Use only sterilized soil mix, main-supply water, and clean trays.

Rust

Various fungi are responsible for rust infections. This is most severe in damp, stagnant conditions. Orange, brown, and beige pustules appear on the leaves, mostly on the undersides. The upper surfaces may also have yellow blotches.
Treatment: Pick off affected leaves and improve air circulation in and around the plants. To decrease humidity, avoid wetting the foliage. Spray the plant with fungicides containing mancozeb, or bupirimite with triforine.

PLANT PROBLEMS AND DISEASES

Mildew

A powdery white or grayish fungus that appears on stems, leaves, and flower buds (which may wither and fall), mildew commonly occurs in hot, dry spells after midsummer. It is linked with stagnant and humid air around plant stems. Roses, clematis, and some other climbers are particularly at risk.
Treatment: Prune back overcrowded growth to improve air circulation. Affected growth should be cut out and burned, after which the plant should be kept well watered and mulched. Chemical treatment is possible with dinocap or triforine.

SOME TYPES OF CLEMATIS ARE PRONE TO MILDEW

Gray mold (Botrytis)

Many plants are susceptible to this fungus, especially those with soft growth. Fuzzy patches of light gray mold appear on leaves and flowers, causing surrounding tissue to become discolored and eventually die back. It commonly occurs where ventilation is poor, either in a greenhouse or where plants are overcrowded.
Treatment: Prune infected tissue and improve air circulation around the plant. Affected tissue should be disposed of immediately. On herbaceous plants, remove moldy leaves and flowers and spray the plant with a fungicide containing carbendazim. Severely affected plants should be burned.

Virus

A number of viruses can attack plants, resulting in poor growth, leaf spots, or discoloration, and distortion of the flowers. Viruses are often spread by aphids and other pests, so controlling these will lessen the risk of disease (see p. 362). Plants in the Rosaceae family, including *Malus, Pyracantha, and Prunus,* are vulnerable.
Treatment: Dig up and burn affected plants. You can reduce the risk of transferring viruses around the garden by cleaning equipment well, especially pruning tools, after use. Some viruses are soil-borne, so if you need to replace an ailing plant, choose a resistant variety. Buy guaranteed virus-free stock (especially bulbs). Some plants show better virus resistance than others.

Foot and root rot

Bedding plants are particularly susceptible to this soil- and water-borne fungus, which causes discoloration and shrinking of stems.
Treatment: Maintain a high degree of hygiene by using sterilized, proprietary soil mix, main-supply water, and clean trays and pots. Water seeds with a copper-based fungicide.

PLANT PESTS

Aphids

The term aphid covers a vast range of sap-sucking pests that are usually endemic in gardens. Not only do the pests cause damage and carry viruses, but their sticky excreta encourages sooty mold to take a hold.
Treatment: A variety of chemical controls are available, some of which will leave beneficial insects such as ladybugs unharmed. A healthy ladybug population will help control the number of aphids.

Slugs and snails

Among the most common of garden pests, slugs and snails attack the young growth of many plants, mainly at night and in damp weather.
Treatment: Slugs and snails can be controlled by hand, picking them off as you see them and disposing of them. Chemical controls such as slug pellets and liquid metaldehyde are effective. Biological control is available in the form of a parasitic nematode, but is effective on slugs only. Other eco-friendly methods include surrounding plants with crushed eggshells, grit, or cocoa shell, but are likely to be of limited effectiveness.

Earwigs

The young leaves and flowers of many plants such as chrysanthemums, dahlias, and clematis, may be decimated by earwigs.
Treatment: Earwigs can be controlled with pirimiphos-methyl of malathion. For an eco-friendly alternative, set traps around vulnerable plants (see p. 360).

Vine weevils

Container plants are commonly attacked by vine weevils. Both adults and larvae cause damage, but the latter are the more serious. Adults eat leaves and can be removed by hand. Larvae are active below soil level and attack roots, so are less immediately apparent. You are often only aware of their activity when severe damage has been done. Check for their presence when repotting plants.
Treatment: Larvae can be controlled biologically by introducing parasitic nematodes (*Steinernema* and *Heterorhabditis* species) or by chemicals such as pirimiphos-methyl.

Caterpillars

The larvae of butterflies and moths, caterpillars eat holes in leaves, soft stems, and flowers.
Treatment: They can be picked off by hand or treated with the biological control *Bacillus thuringiensis.* A variety of pesticides are available, such as pyrethrum, permethrin, and pirimiphos-methyl.

Moles

Mounds of soil ("mole hills") in borders and on lawns are caused by moles burrowing underground.
Treatment: If this problem exceeds your level of tolerance, employ a professional mole catcher. Mole smokes and ultrasound devices that emit a note inaudible to the human ear are also effective. There is no evidence that the caper spurge or mole plant *(Euphorbia lathyris)*, a common weed in some gardens, deters the pest.

SLUG-DAMAGED
OSTEOSPERMUM

ENCOURAGING WILDLIFE

A carefully planned wild garden often needs less rigorous attention than a formal garden and can provide a haven for beneficial wildlife. By maintaining a natural ecological balance, many common problems will be kept under control without the need for intervention.

FRIEND OR FOE?

Insects and other creatures found in the garden are by no means all destructive. Many are not only useful, but are actually essential for plant survival. Attracting birds to the garden may well help keep down the slug and snail population, but they will also peck at fruit bushes. Caterpillars are acknowledged pests, but are beneficial pollinating insects once they metamorphose into butterflies, besides being an ornament to the garden in their own right. Earwigs cause much unsightly damage to many flowering plants, but they are useful predators and feed on aphids and insect eggs. Hedgehogs, shrews, and frogs feed on many ground-dwelling plant pests.

BIRDS WILL FEED ON ROTTING WINDFALLS

ENCOURAGING BIRDS

Many birds are useful predators of garden pests, especially slugs, caterpillars, and aphids. While they can cause some damage to fruit and berries, this damage can be reduced by using nets and other barriers.

All trees will provide shelter for birds, and you can hang bags of nuts from their branches in winter when natural supplies of food are scarce. If there is no suitable specimen in your garden, plant a few berrying shrubs and allow other plants to set seed. Many birds will also take pieces of fruit scattered on the ground or on a bird table. Provide water in freezing weather. Birdhouses can persuade birds to nest in your garden. Your local natural history society or nature reserve can tell you which birds visit your area most frequently and will advise on a suitable birdhouse.

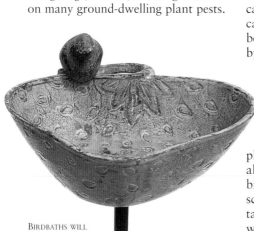

BIRDBATHS WILL ATTRACT BIRDS TO THE GARDEN

ATTRACTING INSECTS

The vast majority of insects are harmless to plants and help to create a well-balanced garden environment. Many are actually beneficial and should be encouraged.

Grow as wide a range of plants as possible to create varied food sources for insects throughout the year. *Helianthus, Nicotiana, Stachys,* and fennel are particularly useful because of their open flowers.

■ **Flowers** Most flowering plants rely on pollinating insects, such as honey bees, to enable them to produce seeds and fruit. Attracted by the scent or bright colors of the flowers, the insects settle to eat the nectar, also picking up pollen, which they can then transfer to the next flower, so fertilizing the plant.

Bees tend to prefer single flowers that have more accessible reproductive parts, so include some wild plant species in your beds and borders. Butterflies need a range of plants to feed them throughout their lives. Nettles and long grass provide an ideal food source for caterpillars, while adults prefer scented, nectar-rich flowers such as *Buddleja davidii.*

■ **Uncultivated land** Leave a section of the garden uncultivated. This will eventually be colonized by native weeds that will attract a large number of beneficial insects. Nettles are a valuable food source for caterpillars. A pile of logs will provide shelter for beetles and wood lice and may in turn attract hedgehogs, which will feed on slugs.

Warning

Many of the berries and seeds that birds will eat are poisonous to humans, so make sure that anything planted for this purpose is inaccessible to young children.

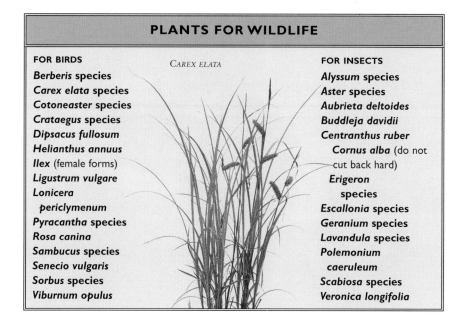

PLANTS FOR WILDLIFE

FOR BIRDS	FOR INSECTS
Berberis species	**Alyssum** species
Carex elata species	**Aster** species
Cotoneaster species	**Aubrieta deltoides**
Crataegus species	**Buddleja davidii**
Dipsacus fullosum	**Centranthus ruber**
Helianthus annuus	**Cornus alba** (do not cut back hard)
Ilex (female forms)	
Ligustrum vulgare	**Erigeron** species
Lonicera periclymenum	**Escallonia** species
Pyracantha species	**Geranium** species
Rosa canina	**Lavandula** species
Sambucus species	**Polemonium caeruleum**
Senecio vulgaris	**Scabiosa** species
Sorbus species	**Veronica longifolia**
Viburnum opulus	

CAREX ELATA

WILDLIFE POOLS

As well as making your garden more appealing, a water feature will attract beneficial creatures, including birds, toads, frogs, and various insects, into the garden. For more information, see "Water Gardening," pp. 95–201. A dedicated wildlife pool will greatly increase their chances of survival and encourage them to multiply. Ideally, you should not have any fish in your wildlife pond, as they eat frog spawn. Large stones and areas of rough vegetation near the water's edge will provide hiding places for frogs and toads. Marginal plants will shelter creatures that prefer moist conditions.

PLANTED POND
A well-built wildlife pond can include a wide variety of native plants, as well as providing food and water for a great number of animals.

PLANTS FOR POOLS

SHALLOW MARGINALS
Acorus gramineus
Carex elata "Aurea"
Iris ensata
Juncus effusus
Peltandra alba
Typha minima

DEEP MARGINALS
Acorus calamus
Butomus umbellatus
Iris pseudacorus
Myriophyllum aquaticum
Ranunculus lingua "Grandiflora"
Typha angustifolia

DEEP-WATER PLANTS
Aponogeton distachyos
Nymphaea
Nymphoides indica
Orontium aquaticum

5
PRUNING

When left to their own devices, plants such as shrubs and trees, roses and climbers, fruit trees and berry bushes, and even houseplants and greenhouse tomatoes, will all grow, as long as they have adequate water, light, heat, and food. By giving them some assistance in the form of pruning, however, you can help them to grow better and stay healthier and, in consequence, they will reward your efforts by flowering and fruiting more prolifically.

This chapter looks first at the reasons behind why pruning is necessary for the well-being of certain cultivated plants, and the best times to take up the pruning shears and tackle the job. It then covers topics such as how much of the plant to remove at any one time and how to select the correct tools for the job. It also gives more in-depth advice on pruning common plants such as shrubs, roses, and fruit trees and bushes. At the end of the chapter, there is a useful glossary of pruning terms.

WHY PRUNE?

Some inexperienced gardeners may find pruning a puzzling and complex task. Put simply, pruning is the cutting back of unwanted shoots, stems, or branches of woody plants, such as shrubs, trees, and roses. It serves both to curb any straggly overgrowth of the plant and also to stimulate the production of fresh, new growth. This creates a well-shaped specimen that is strong and healthy, with improved flowering or fruiting capabilities.

REASONS TO PRUNE

■ **Encouraging growth** Pruning is only strictly necessary when something begins to go wrong with a plant. There are several reasons for needing to cut back a shrub or tree. For example, if it starts to outgrow its allotted space in the garden; if it becomes straggly and untidy; or if flowering or fruiting starts to decline. Removing old wood encourages the production of new shoots which, in turn, will flower and fruit more prolifically. The harder you prune the more vigorous the new growth. This is the basic principle that lies behind why most pruning is carried out.

■ **Staying healthy** If a plant starts to die back, cut out any dead or diseased shoots to promote fresh, healthy growth, giving the plant a new lease on life.

■ **Increasing fruit yields** Fruiting plants need a more structured annual pruning routine if they are to produce optimum yields. In this case, pruning is a preventative measure rather than a cure. For successful crops, remove old wood regularly to ensure the constant production of new and vigorous flowering and fruiting shoots.

REVERTED SHOOTS
Variegated-foliage plants such as *Euonymus fortunei* sometimes produce shoots with all-green leaves. Remove any of these as soon as you see them, using sharp pruning shears.

UNWANTED GROWTH

■ **Retaining color** If a variegated plant "reverts," meaning that it produces shoots with all-green leaves, swiftly remove any rogue shoots to restore order. Reverted shoots should be pruned out as soon as they occur, otherwise they will take over the plant. These shoots have a higher chlorophyll content than variegated shoots and are more vigorous.

■ **Suckers** These unwanted growths often appear around the base of trees and roses; always remove them as soon as you spot them.

■ **Water or epicormic shoots** These fast-growing shoots sometimes arise from dormant buds or near pruning cuts on tree trunks. They proliferate quickly and sap energy from the tree. Remove them immediately by cutting them right back to their point of origin, otherwise they will deprive healthy new growth of valuable nutrients.

RECOGNIZING ROSE SUCKERS
Rose suckers arise from a plant's base and bear leaves that have a different appearance than those on the rest of the plant.

IMPROVING SHAPE AND CONDITION
You can quickly improve the shape and health of a mature tree or shrub, such as this flowering quince, by taking out any shoots or branches that look either dead or diseased, or that are crowding or crossing over each other. This will allow light and air into the center.

SHAPING AND TRAINING

Another reason for pruning is to improve the existing shape of a tree or shrub. To do this, you need to remove healthy but unwanted wood as well as unhealthy growth. Cut out all dead, dying, congested, and crossing shoots and branches. This will allow light and air to enter and circulate the plant, helping it to produce new, strong, healthy growth in a neat and balanced shape.

Fruit trees are often trained to make the most of limited space or to open them out. By removing crossing and crowded branches, air and light are allowed in to ripen the fruit on lower branches. Ornamental and fruit trees can be trained in decorative shapes, such as espaliers, or fanned out against walls. On fruit trees, branches are often trained horizontally for ease of harvesting.

SIX GOOD REASONS FOR PRUNING

• To improve the condition of the plant, by removing unhealthy branches.

• To stimulate growth, by letting light and air into the center of the plant.

• To encourage more prolific flowering and cropping.

• To control size or restore the stability of an overgrown plant.

• To improve or change the shape of a plant, such as in pleaching or topiary.

• To create special effects, such as colored winter stems.

■ **Special pruning** Topiary and bonsai are special pruning methods used for training shrubs and trees to a specific shape or purpose. This "creative" pruning is a little more complicated and calls for patience and a steady hand but, as with all pruning, the results can be immensely satisfying. Other decorative features that demand careful pruning include creating a laburnum arch, a rose swag, or a standard plant.

Exactly where and how much to prune depends on the health of the individual plant and what you want it to look like in future years. Both timing and technique depend on the age and type of plant. Pruning will inevitably cause the plant some stress, so always have a clear idea of exactly what you are trying to achieve before you start to cut.

SHAPED IVY
This variegated "Gold Heart" ivy has been trained on a support and shaped with pruning to create an eye-catching feature for the patio.

WHEN TO PRUNE

The timing of pruning is crucial and depends on the growth habit of the plant. Most flowering shrubs, including roses, produce flower buds either on new growth or on wood that is just one year old, and it is this that determines the best time to prune them. Deciduous trees are best pruned when they are dormant during winter, but evergreens should be left until the weather warms up.

TYPES OF PLANT

■ **Flowering shrubs** For the vast majority of flowering shrubs, and especially those that bloom in spring and early to midsummer, the ideal time to prune is immediately after the flowers have finished their display. This will give the plant plenty of time to produce strong new flowering stems for the following year.

For shrubs that flower in late summer and fall, it is better to delay pruning until the following spring, rather than cutting back the plant straight after flowering. Pruning late in the season will encourage tender, young shoots to grow, leaving them exposed and likely to succumb to frost damage over the winter months.

■ **Fruiting plants** For both edible and ornamental types of fruiting plant, pruning is usually carried out during the fall or winter months after fruiting has been completed. However, some of these plants will also need attention during the summer months.

■ **Deciduous trees** These should be pruned from late fall until late winter, when they are not producing any new growth. With the arrival of warmer weather in spring, strong new growth will be encouraged and any wounds will quickly heal.

CONTROLLING PLANT GROWTH
If a plant's stems are spilling onto a lawn making it difficult to mow or if it is crowding out other plants in a bed, you may need to cut it back, even when it is in flower.

Warning

Never prune in frosty or cold weather or during hot, dry spells, when plants are more vulnerable to disease and damage. The cooler and damper months of fall and spring are much more suitable for pruning.

■ **Evergreens** It is best to prune evergreen shrubs and trees in spring, after all danger of frost has passed. They may also benefit from a light trim after flowering to tidy up the stems that have flowered.

■ **New plants** When planting out, it is a good idea to tidy up the topgrowth and roots of pot-ready and bare-rooted plants.

Prune out any broken or torn branches and roots, making clean cuts. Untangle the roots of bare-rooted plants and spread them out in the planting hole, cutting off any that are twisted or very long.

A RIOT OF ROSES
The rewards of good pruning are clearly visible in this delightful rose garden. The plants are all strong and healthy, and flowering profusely.

CONTROLLING GROWTH

In addition to the basic pruning carried out to improve shape and stimulate new growth, shrubs, climbers, and roses also need cutting back regularly. For example, access along paths may become difficult or even hazardous if the plant in question has thorns or prickly leaves. These plants may also encroach on space needed by other plants or spill onto a lawn. In the growing season and spring, you may need to perform basic cutting back, as well as tying in, once a month in order to regain control. Some tidying up may also be needed in spring to repair any winter damage.

AFTER PRUNING

Pruning can be a bit of a shock to a plant's system. The plant also has to work harder to produce new growth. After spring and summer pruning, it is best to water the plant thoroughly and apply the appropriate fertilizer. Take time to weed around the plant too, then add a layer of mulch. For plants that were pruned in winter, do not feed or water them until spring, when they start back into growth after dormancy.

LAVENDER HEDGE
This lovely hedge is at its prime, and provides the perfect example of a plant that should be trimmed back only when flowering has finished.

A QUICK GUIDE TO PRUNING TASKS	
TIME	**SUBJECT OR TASK**
Early to midspring	Late summer- and fall-flowering shrubs. Shrubs with colorful stems. Gray-leaved shrubs. Bush, shrub, climbing, and standard roses. Clematis (except early flowering kinds) and wisteria. Cut back dogwoods (Cornus) for winter stems.
Late spring	Spring-flowering shrubs, such as forsythia and the flowering currants (Ribes), as their blooms fade. Reshape evergreen shrubs if necessary. Thin and cut back any unwanted growth. Check fan-trained fruit and remove any unwanted shoots.
Early summer	Look for signs of silver-leaf disease on stone fruits, such as plums, cherries, peaches, and apricots, and cut away any infected branches.
Midsummer	Late spring- and early summer-flowering shrubs, such as broom (Cytisus) and lilac (Syringa), as blooms fade. Stone fruit, such as cherries and plums. Espalier- and cordon-trained fruit trees. Lightly prune vigorous large-flowered (hybrid tea) roses and wisteria.

A QUICK GUIDE TO PRUNING TASKS

TIME	SUBJECT OR TASK
Late summer	Clip evergreen hedges, such as box and yew, and trim topiary to shape. Trim lavender hedges after flowering.
Early fall	Prune rambling roses.
Late fall	Lightly prune roses to reduce the possibility of damage caused by wind-rock.
Winter	Cut back and trim beech (*Fagus*), hawthorn (*Crataegus*), and privet (*Ligustrum*) hedges. Prune deciduous trees and shrubs to improve their shape and maintain balanced growth.
Midwinter	Finish pruning apple and pear trees. Cut back stems of newly planted bush fruits. Halve the lead shoots of gooseberries and red and white currant bushes. Cut back black currant bushes.

YEW

HOW TO PRUNE

Cutting techniques and methods vary according to the type of pruning being carried out. It is very important that you use the correct one for the plant and style that you have chosen, otherwise the plant may suffer. If in doubt, it is better to err on the side of caution.

DEGREES OF PRUNING

There are, in general, three degrees of pruning: hard (or severe), moderate, and light. Hard pruning encourages vigorous growth, while a light prune slows down the rate of growth.

■ **Hard pruning** This involves removing a large amount of new growth from all over a plant or cutting a few shoots back hard where more growth is desired. When hard pruned, existing growth is cut back by at least three-quarters or down to about three or four buds from the base.

■ **Moderate pruning** This style of pruning results in about half the amount of any new growth on a plant being reduced by around half of its length. Cutting is spread evenly over the entire plant.

■ **Light pruning** A light prune cuts down about one-quarter of any new growth by no more than one-quarter of its length. In some cases, just the the tip of each shoot, about 2–3in (5–7.5cm) is removed. As in the case of moderate pruning, the pruning is spread across the whole plant.

ALTERNATE BUDS
Where the buds are arranged alternately, meaning they are staggered along the stem, make a slanting cut about ¼in (5mm) above a bud.

Thin blade nearer bud

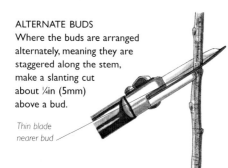

OPPOSITE BUDS
Where the buds are in opposite pairs, cut straight across the stem about ¼in (5mm) above them.

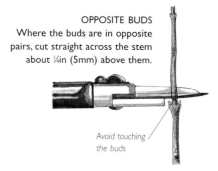

Avoid touching the buds

CREATING A WELL-BALANCED SHAPE

• When pruning any shrub, tree, or rose, try to imitate the plant's natural growth habit.

• Avoid overdrastic pruning: be sympathetic to the natural size and shape of a plant, and give it the amount of space it deserves.

• In order to encourage well-balanced and symmetrical growth, cut back any strong shoots lightly, and cut back weaker ones heavily.

• If strong shoots are cut back very hard, leaving too much weak growth, the plant will not flourish.

Principles of pruning

■ **Removing unhealthy growth** Aim to remove all dead, damaged, and diseased wood and weak, straggly, or misshapen growth. Always cut back to healthy wood. Cut away and burn dead and diseased wood before the problem spreads through the plant. Straggly growth is unsightly and saps a plant's energy.

■ **Creating an open framework** Cut back some of the main stems to the base. An overcrowded plant will suffer, so prune it back sufficiently to allow air and sunshine to reach the ripening wood and swelling buds. Remove any suckers, as well as branches that are crossing or rubbing against others.

■ **Making a clean cut** Always tidy up any jagged edges or tears to prevent disease entering the wound.

■ **Collecting up all prunings** Soft and healthy wood may be composted, but burn or otherwise dispose of any woody or diseased prunings.

■ **Feeding and mulching** After pruning, apply a generous handful of general fertilizer around the base of the plant, then apply a good mulch of leaf compost, shredded bark, or wood chips to retain soil moisture and suppress weeds.

■ **The golden rule** Too little pruning is always better than too much.

Making the right cut

All pruning cuts should be as small, clean, and neat as possible, which is why it is so important to have the right tools (see p. 386). Prune before shoots become too woody and before twigs become branches because young wood heals faster.

■ **Slanting or straight?** When cutting between buds arranged alternately on a stem, always make a slanting cut, to let water roll off the cut surface. When cutting above a pair of healthy opposite buds, make a straight cut, taking care not to damage the buds.

■ **Where to cut** If you cut too far from a bud, the wood left above it will wither and become susceptible to disease. If you cut too close to a bud, you risk damaging the bud itself. Never cut just beneath a bud, and avoid snagging or tearing the bark. Always prune just above a bud or a leaf, and new shoots will then sprout from just below the cut.

COLORFUL WINTER STEMS
Cutting this dogwood (*Cornus alba* "Sibirica") back hard in spring produces these attractively colored young stems the following winter.

PRUNING SHRUBS

Ornamental shrubs generally grow and flower without any help, and most require little or no pruning other than the removal of dead or diseased shoots. In some cases, however, it becomes necessary to use the pruning shears – to encourage better flowering or to keep the plant within bounds, controlling the height, shape, or thickness of growth. Left alone, shrubs keep growing upward and outward, with any flowers appearing higher and higher on the plant each year.

ORNAMENTAL SHRUBS

Whatever the shrub, there are several important points to bear in mind when pruning.

■ **Shape and balance** The purpose of pruning is to form a shapely shrub with strong, young branches that are well-spaced to allow light and air into the center.

■ **Cutting cleanly** You should always use sharp tools to make a clean cut, either close above a healthy bud, slanting away from it or, if removing a branch or sideshoot, flush with the main stem. Any jagged edges and crushed stems should be trimmed neatly with a sharp knife.

■ **Unwanted growth** Aim to take out all dead and diseased wood, crossing or rubbing branches, and any weak and spindly shoots. Depending on the individual plant, remove stems at ground level, either to an outward-facing bud or to sound, green wood.

■ **Treating pruning wounds** In the past, it was recommended that all cuts of more than 1in (2.5cm) across should be treated with a wood sealant or fungicide in order to prevent disease entering the plant. This course of action is no longer considered necessary; it may, in fact, do more harm than good.

FLOWERS OR FOLIAGE?
If unpruned, the smoke bush (*Cotinus coggygria*) bears lots of flowers; if pruned in spring it will produce more leaves for bright fall color.

SHRUB-PRUNING CHECKLIST

BERBERIS
Thin out old wood after flowering in spring. Clip hedges after flowering.

BUDDLEIA
Cut back *B. davidii* in early spring to within 4 or more buds of the base. Shorten shoots of others after flowering.

CALLUNA
Trim off old flower spikes in early spring.

CAMELLIA
Cut back leggy mature plants after flowers fade.

CEANOTHUS
Prune spring-flowering types grown against a wall to within 2 buds of the previous season's growth after flowering. Thin freestanding plants in spring, also removing dead wood. Cut back summer-flowering types to 2–6 buds in spring.

CHAENOMELES
After flowering, take out old wood and thin and shorten sideshoots.

CHOISYA
Cut out any old wood and prune to shape in spring if necessary.

COTINUS
Trim in early spring if you want more foliage.

COTONEASTER
Hard prune old bushes in spring.

CYTISUS
Perform an annual tidy-up after flowering, but take care not to cut beyond the previous year's wood.

ELAEAGNUS
If necessary, thin and shape in spring.

ERICA
Trim the plant with hand shears to remove dead flowers and retain shape.

ESCALLONIA
Thin and prune wall-trained plants to maintain shape as flowers fade.

FORSYTHIA
If growing against a wall or fence, remove old flowering shoots after flowers fade. Thin freestanding shrubs every 3–4 years.

FUCHSIA
Remove any dead growth from small plants in spring. Large (hardy) types do not usually need pruning.

GARRYA
Prune after flowering, if necessary, to retain shape.

JASMINE
Hard prune winter jasmine after flowering. Thin out summer jasmine after the flowers have faded.

PHILADELPHUS
After flowering, take out old flowering shoots and thin the rest. Give older plants a new lease on life

by pruning them back hard in spring.

PIERIS
Prune after flowering in late spring.

RHODODENDRON
Rejuvenate old bushes by hard pruning in spring; otherwise remove dead flower heads.

RIBES
Older bushes benefit from a hard spring prune.

SPIREA
Remove old flowering shoots of spring-flowering types after flowering. Hard prune late summer-flowering types in early spring.

WEIGELA
Remove any leggy shoots after flowering.

LAUREL
(LAURUS)

PRUNING ROSES

Roses are in a class of their own when it comes to pruning as the various types have their own different needs. If you want them to perform at their very best, giving a stunning show of color and sometimes also fragrance, it is best to give them a helping hand.

WHEN TO PRUNE

Late winter or early spring is the best time to prune repeat-flowering roses, when the plants are dormant or new growth is just beginning to show. Prune too early and new growth will risk being tipped by frost, and you will then have to prune again, cutting back to undamaged wood.

Ramblers should be pruned once flowering has finished, that is in late summer or early fall. Established roses can be pruned at the beginning of winter, too, but bear in mind

that, although this may be fine in a sheltered, warm garden, in colder, more exposed spots heavy pruning at this time may lessen a plant's chances of survival. The best advice, therefore, for all areas, is to give roses a light pruning at the end of their season.

Shorten the stems of large- and cluster-flowered, tall-shrub, and climbing types by about one-third, and finish the job when the weather improves during the spring. The light, prewinter pruning will help to protect the plant from the damaging effects of winter winds, particularly in exposed sites or coastal gardens.

MODERN SHRUB ROSE
"Octavia Hill" is an example of a Modern shrub rose. It produces a profusion of fragrant pink blooms from summer to fall.

PRUNING A NEWLY PLANTED ROSE BUSH

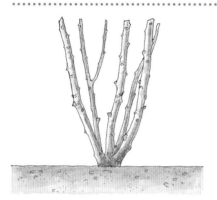 

1 Once a rose has been planted, you will need to prune it back quite hard to stimulate healthy growth from low down. These stems are long and some are crossing and even damaged.

2 Prune each shoot down to about 3–6in (7–15cm) above the base. Make a slanting cut just above an outward-facing bud, so that the new growth forms an open-centered bush.

HOW TO PRUNE ESTABLISHED ROSES

All roses need pruning to develop their shape, to control their size and vigor, to help them remain healthy, and to encourage flowering. Remove old and spindly growth regularly, cutting as low down on the plant as possible, to make room for new growth to sprout from the base. Reducing strong, healthy growths by about one-third will encourage side growth. It will also lessen the risk of damage from wind-rock, which can cause broken shoots and weakened stems.

The aim is to create an open-centered plant, giving space, light, and air to the stems so that they can develop freely. Always use a pair of sharp pruning shears and wear gloves. Cut back to a dormant, outward-facing bud to encourage an upward and outward growth habit. Make each cut at an angle, sloping down and away from the bud, leaving a clean edge. After pruning, apply a layer of rose fertilizer, watering it in if the ground is dry, followed by a mulch to prevent moisture loss.

■ **Dead and diseased growth** Cut right back to healthy wood – the cut surface will be white rather than brown.

■ **Weak growth and spindly stems** You should remove all of these so that the plant can concentrate its energy on the good shoots.

■ **Crossing and inward-growing stems** Removing these will prevent overcrowding, which would otherwise hinder healthy growth.

FALL INTEREST

Roses that produce ornamental hips in late summer or fall, such as *Rosa rugosa* "Alba" and *R.* "Frau Dagmar Hastrup," should not be pruned until late winter or early spring.

PRUNING FRUIT

Both top fruit, such as apples and pears, and most soft fruit, such as currants and raspberries, need careful and regular pruning to keep them in good condition, healthy, and productive. Pruning is best performed annually, either when the plant is dormant during the winter months or in the summer after cropping is complete.

WHY PRUNE?

Pruning encourages new shoots to grow: the harder a branch is cut back, the more vigorous the new growth will be. During the first few years, the aim of pruning is to establish a basic framework, building a strong, large plant as quickly as possible. Once established, a different pruning regime will encourage a good crop of fruit each year.

Initial pruning and training aims to: develop a particular shape, be it bush, cordon, or fan, for example; to keep branches and stems well spaced to allow in light, air, and sun to ripen the wood and fruit; to encourage fruit to form by removing unwanted growth shoots but leaving fruit buds; and to remove all weak, dead, and diseased wood.

FRUITING RED CURRANT
Correct pruning will ensure that you achieve good results. This red currant is bushy and healthy and producing an excellent crop of fruit.

THE BEST TIME TO PRUNE SOFT FRUIT	
Blackberries	In fall after fruiting
Black currants	Late fall or early winter
Blueberries	Early spring
Gooseberries	In winter while dormant
Gooseberry cordons	Summer and winter
Raspberries, summer-fruiting	In summer after fruiting
Raspberries, fall-fruiting	Late winter
Red and white currants	In winter while dormant
Red and white currant cordons	Summer and winter

PRUNING SOFT FRUIT

All woody soft fruits, except fall-fruiting raspberries, produce on stems that are at least one year old. There are two main pruning periods (see also panel on p. 384). Winter pruning improves the shape of a plant, while summer pruning restricts growth and maintains form. Always dip the pruning shears in disinfectant before pruning each plant.

PRUNING TREE FRUIT

■ **When to prune** Fruit trees are usually pruned in late winter or early spring, when they are still dormant. Prune hard at this time and again, lightly, in fall (see also panel below). Established free-standing apple, pear, and plum trees can be largely left alone, apart from removing diseased, crossing, weak, or unwanted branches. Do this in winter for apples and pears (pip fruit) or summer for plums (stone fruit).

■ **Training to shape** Fruit trees can be pruned and trained into a variety of forms, the most natural being a freestanding, compact tree known, confusingly, as a bush. Apples, pears, and plums can all be grown in this fashion. The other forms, such as cordons, espaliers, and fans, are discussed in detail later in this chapter, because they all require a slightly different pruning routine.

■ **How to prune** First take out dead, damaged, or diseased branches (when removing diseased limbs, disinfect the pruning tool before making the next cut to prevent the spread of disease). Then remove crossing or crowded branches. If established trees are too productive, weighing down branches with large quantities of undersized fruit, remove some of the fruit buds in spring. Fruit buds are normally fatter and more rounded than an ordinary growth bud.

THE BEST TIME TO PRUNE TREE FRUIT

Apples	Bush trees	Winter or early spring
	Trained trees	Summer
Apricots	All forms	Late summer after fruiting
Cherries	All forms	Midsummer after fruiting
Figs		Spring and summer
Peaches and nectarines	All forms	Midsummer, after fruiting
Pears	Bush trees	Winter or early spring
	Trained trees	Mid- or late summer
Plums	Bush trees	Midsummer
	Trained trees	Midsummer

TOOLS FOR THE JOB

Having the right tools for each garden task is of vital importance, and this is especially true when it comes to pruning. Always buy the best-quality tools you can afford and make sure they stay sharp. Pruning tools include various shears, saws, knives, and loppers.

WHAT YOU NEED

■ **Loppers** A pair of pruning loppers or long-handled pruning shears is useful for removing thick branches and old, hard wood. The longer the handles the longer the reach and the more leverage you will have, meaning you will have to exert less effort. Loppers will tackle wood up to ¾in (2cm) thick. For tall-growing shrubs and climbers, a pole pruner with extendable arms is a good investment.

■ **Sharp pruning shears** Pruning shears must always be sharp: blunt blades will tear or crush the stem, which can lead to dieback or allow infection to set in. This is particularly important when pruning roses.

There are two types of cutting blade: single (anvil) and double-bladed (bypass or scissor). The single-bladed model has one sharp, hard metal blade, which cuts through with a biting action to a softer metal anvil. The double-bladed model works with a scissorlike action, in that the two blades bypass each other.

A good pair of pruning shears can be used to prune all soft stems as well as woody ones up to ½in (1cm) in diameter. Brightly colored handles make it easier to find the tool if you put it down somewhere, and make sure it is fitted with a safety catch to keep the blades closed when not in use.

■ **Chain saw** Always wear protective clothing when using this tool, and handle it with extreme care. Consider using a chain saw if you have branches more than 4in (10cm) thick to tackle. Rather than buy one, borrow a chain saw from a local tool-rental company. Alternatively, use a professional tree surgeon, but obtain an estimate for the work beforehand.

SINGLE OR
ANVIL LOPPERS

BYPASS PRUNING SHEARS

■ **Shears** Hand or hedging shears need to be kept sharp and oiled. They are useful for trimming hedges and general tidying. Crinkle-edged blades cut through thick shoots more easily, but are difficult to sharpen.

■ **Powered hedge trimmer** An electric hedge trimmer makes light work of trimming a hedge, although hand shears are better for a short hedge or for trimming individual shrubs. The longer the cutting length, the quicker you will cut the hedge. The more teeth there are on the blade, the finer the finish, although wide-spaced teeth will cope better with thicker shoots. Make sure there is a protective hand shield on the machine, a lockoff switch to prevent accidental starting, and a ground-fault circuit interrupter (GFCI) on the electrical supply.

■ **A pruning knife** This needs a keen edge to clean up any jagged pruning cuts, but take great care not to cut your fingers. After use, wipe the blade dry and rub it with an oily cloth after use.

PRUNING SAW

■ **Pruning saw** Use a bow or other narrow-bladed pruning saw for thick wood. Unlike a carpenter's saw, a pruning saw has wide-set, splayed teeth, that are less likely to get clogged up when cutting through live, green wood.

■ **Gardening gloves** A pair of heavy-duty gardening gloves, preferably leather, is essential to protect your hands from sharp blades and prickly stems or foliage.

■ **Shredder** Use this to reduce trimmings in bulk before composting.

CARE OF PRUNING TOOLS

• Store all tools in a dry place to prevent rusting.

• After use and before putting them away, clean and dry tools thoroughly.

• Oil all the moving parts from time to time.

• Keep tools sharp. Either sharpen them yourself or take them to a specialist at least once a year.

• Never leave your tools lying around outside.

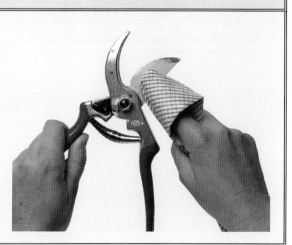

PRUNING TERMS

There is a whole new vocabulary for you to learn when it comes to pruning. Most of it is just common sense and you will soon become familiar with the terms. Use this glossary regularly to remind yourself of precise meanings as you read through the rest of the book.

PRUNING GLOSSARY

ALTERNATE BUDS
Buds that grow singly at different heights and on different sides of a stem.

ANGLED CUT
The cut used when pruning stems that have alternate buds (compare "Straight cut"). Make a slanting cut just above and sloping away from the bud.

BRANCH COLLAR
A thickened ring of tissue at the base of a branch.

BUD
A swelling on a plant stem containing an embryonic leaf or flower. A growth bud produces either leaves or a shoot, and a fruit bud produces flowers, which are followed by fruit.

CALLUS
The scar tissue that forms over a pruning cut.

COPPICING
Regular pruning back of shrubs or trees close to ground level to stimulate the growth of vigorous new stems.

CORDON
A method of training a tree (either an ornamental or, more usually, a fruiting tree) to produce a single, upright stem with no large side branches.

DEADHEADING
The removal of spent flowers from flowering shrubs to stimulate further flowering. It prevents seed production at the expense of plant growth and the formation of the following season's buds.

DIEBACK
Death of shoot tips, usually caused by damage such as frost or disease.

ESPALIER
A method of pruning and training fruit trees to grow flat against a wall, fence, or other support.

FAN
A method used for growing fruit trees, such as cherries, up against a wall or fence. Branches of a young tree are encouraged to grow up in a fan shape from as close to the base as possible, supported by wires and ties to keep them in place.

CALLUS OR SCAR TISSUE

PRUNING GLOSSARY

FEATHERED MAIDEN
A one-year-old tree that has developed lateral shoots, which are known as "feathers."

FRUIT BUD
On a fruit tree, a bud that produces flowers and fruit rather than foliage or a shoot. A fruit bud is larger and rounder than a growth bud.

FRUIT SPUR
A growth from a branch or three-year-old sideshoot.

GRAFT UNION
The point on the stem of a shrub, tree, rose, or woody climber where the topgrowth has been grafted onto the rootstock, resembling a ring of callus.

GROWTH BUD
On a fruit tree, a bud that produces foliage or a shoot rather than fruit.

LATERAL
A side growth arising from a root or shoot.

LATERAL BUD
A bud that will form a sideshoot.

LEADING STEM OR LEADER
All trees and some shrubs produce a main or central stem, or trunk, from which all the side branches develop. Growth can be controlled by cutting the leader out.

MAIDEN
A tree that is in its first year of growth.

PINCHING OUT (OR STOPPING)
The removal of the shoot tip or bud to encourage sideshoots to form and to restrict growth.

PLEACHING
The training of deciduous (sometimes flowering) trees on a post-and-wire framework, so that their branches entwine to form a green wall or hedge, or overhead canopy, such as a laburnum or wisteria arch.

POLLARDING
Severe pruning of tree branches at regular intervals in order to promote the growth of more young shoots, thereby preventing the tree from reaching its natural size and form.

PLEACHED LIME TREES

PRUNING GLOSSARY

RENEWAL PRUNING
A method of pruning by which the plant is cut back really hard, removing older growth in favor of younger shoots, to give it a new lease on life.

ROOT PRUNING
Trimming the roots of a plant before planting or replanting it. When you buy a bare-rooted plant, as opposed to a container-grown one, you may need to trim the roots to make planting easier. This is usually the case with bare-rooted roses. Trim back roots to 9in (23cm), and also remove any dead, diseased, or damaged ones. Root pruning is also carried out on established trees and shrubs. For example, a fruit tree such as a plum that produces lots of leafy growth and very little fruit may have an overdeveloped root system. When the plant is dormant, dig a trench around the tree or shrub 2–5ft (0.6–1.5m) away from the main stem. Cut through any thick roots that are uncovered.

ROOTSTOCK
A plant used to provide a root system for the topgrowth of another plant (scion) that is grafted on. This method is commonly used for roses.

SIDESHOOT
A shoot growing outward from a stem.

SPUR
A short shoot or branchlet on fruit trees, bearing flower buds then fruits.

STANDARD
A tree or trained shrub with a single straight stem devoid of branches.

STRAIGHT CUT
The cut used when pruning stems with opposite buds (compare "Angled cut").

SUBLATERAL
Sideshoot from a lateral shoot.

SUCKER
A shoot arising from below ground level, some distance from the plant, or growing from the rootstock of grafted plants.

TIP PRUNING (OR TIPPING BACK)
Pinching or cutting out shoot tips to encourage sideshoots to develop or to remove damaged growth.

VEGETATIVE GROWTH
Nonflowering, usually leafy growth.

WATER (EPICORMIC) SHOOTS
Unwanted, fast-growing, sappy shoots, usually arising from the site of damage or pruning cuts.

WEEPING
A shrub or tree with a pendulous habit, either natural or induced.

WEEPING STANDARD
This tree has been trained as a weeping standard. It has a single stem crowned with a head of pendulous branches.

6
DIRECTORY OF RELIABLE PLANTS

Plants that are most suitable for the busy gardener are those that are trouble free and will thrive in a wide range of soils and conditions, needing no special care or attention. This directory lists some of the most reliable garden plants; most of them are hardy apart from a few popular tender kinds that are suitable for growing as annuals or are easily overwintered. However, many equally worthwhile plants are omitted simply because of lack of space.

The height, and where appropriate the spread, of each plant is given as a guide, though their eventual dimensions will vary according to the conditions in which they are grown.

RELIABLE PLANTS

ACER
Maple
Deciduous shrubs and trees grown for foliage and fall color. Grow in a sheltered, sunny or part-shaded site in moist soil.

A. japonicum "Vitifolium"
Japanese maple
Small red flowers. Leaves turn orange in fall.
HEIGHT: 15 ft (5 m)
SPREAD: 10 ft (3 m)

A. negundo "Flamingo"
Young leaves edged white and pink. Prune in winter.
HEIGHT: 40 ft (12 m)
SPREAD: 30 ft (9 m)

A. palmatum "Bloodgood"
Reddish purple leaves turning scarlet.
HEIGHT: 15 ft (5 m)
SPREAD: 10 ft (3 m)

ALLIUM
Ornamental onion
Bulbs with rounded heads of summer flowers carried on erect stems. Tall varieties add style to a mixed or herbaceous border; small types are good in a rock garden. Leaves are often pungent. Some have culinary uses, such as A. sativum (garlic) and A. schoenoprasum (chives). Grow in a well-drained site in full sun.

A. giganteum
Has star-shaped, lilac-pink flowers in summer.
HEIGHT: 6 ft (2 m)

A. karataviense
Has curving, red-rimmed, dull pink leaves.
HEIGHT: 6–8 in (15–20 cm)

ANTIRRHINUM
Snapdragon
Cheerful annuals with a long succession of two-lipped flowers in shades of pink, red, purple, yellow, orange, and white. Good tolerance of wet weather. Grow in well-drained soil in full sun.

A. Coronette Series
Tall and weather-resistant in a wide range of colors; ideal for cutting.
HEIGHT: 26 in (65 cm)

A. Sonnet Series
Bronze, pink, crimson, white, and burgundy flowers are produced early. Good for cutting.
HEIGHT: 2 ft (60 cm)
SPREAD: 12 in (30 cm)

ALLIUM

RELIABLE PLANTS

BEGONIA
Half-hardy annuals and tuberous perennials with pink, cream, white, orange, or red flowers. Many suitable for summer bedding and containers. Grow in fertile, well-drained soil in partial shade. Tuberous begonias can be overwintered in frost free conditions.

B. Cocktail Series
Compact annuals with bronze leaves and single flowers through summer.
HEIGHT: 6 in (15 cm)

B. "Illumination Orange"
Tuberous trailing bergonia, with brilliant double orange flowers.
HEIGHT: 2 ft (60 cm)

BEGONIAS

BERBERIS
Barberry
Evergreen and deciduous spiny shrubs grown mainly for their foliage; some have attractive spring flowers and colorful berries. Grow in any but waterlogged soil in full sun (deciduous) or partial shade (evergreen).

B. darwinii
Evergreen shrub with bright orange flowers. Ideal for hedging.
HEIGHT: 5 ft (1.5 m)
SPREAD: 4 ft (1.2 m)

B. x ottawensis "Superba" syn. B. x o. "Purpurea"
Rounded, deciduous shrub with oval, rich purple leaves and clusters of pale yellow flowers.
HEIGHT/SPREAD: 5 ft (1.5 m)

BUDDLEJA
Fast-growing, arching, evergreen or deciduous shrubs grown for their fragrant summer flowers. Grow in well-drained soil in full sun.

B. alternifolia
Deciduous shrub with hanging clusters of mauve flowers in early summer.
HEIGHT/SPREAD: 8 ft (2.4 m)

B. davidii and vars.
Deciduous shrubs that produce dense panicles of fragrant flowers in late summer and fall.
HEIGHT/SPREAD: 5 ft (1.5 m)

B. "Lochinch"
Compact deciduous shrub with lilac-blue flowers in late summer.
HEIGHT/SPREAD: 6 ft (2 m)

RELIABLE PLANTS

CAMPANULA
Bellflower
Summer-flowering perennials with bell-shaped, white, pink, or blue-purple flowers. Grow in fertile, well-drained soil in part shade.

C. cochleariifolia
Creeping with solitary white-lavender flowers suited to rock gardens.
HEIGHT: 3 in (8 cm)
SPREAD: 20 in (50 cm)

C. lactiflora "Loddon Anna"
Upright border plant, with soft lilac-pink flowers.
HEIGHT: 36 in (1 m)
SPREAD: 2 ft (60 cm)

C. portenschlagiana
Mat-forming rock plant with purplish blue flowers.
HEIGHT: 6 in (15 cm)
SPREAD: 20 in (50 cm)

CEANOTHUS
California lilac
Sun-loving evergreen and deciduous shrubs, grown for their mainly blue flowers in summer. Many can be wall-trained. Grow in fertile, well-drained soil in a sheltered site, in sun.

C. "Autumnal Blue"
Evergreen shrub with rich, sky-blue flowers from late summer to fall.
HEIGHT/SPREAD: 5 ft (1.5 m)

C. x delileanus "Gloire de Versailles"
Deciduous shrub with late, pale blue flowers.
HEIGHT: 5 ft (1.5 m)
SPREAD: 3 ft (1 m)

C. "Southmead"
Dense evergreen with early, dark blue flowers.
HEIGHT/SPREAD: 5 ft (1.5 m)

CEANOTHUS

CHOISYA
Mexican orange blossom
Rounded, evergreen shrub with attractive, fresh green, divided leaves, which are aromatic when crushed. Starry white flowers appear in spring and again in the fall. Prefers a reasonably sheltered position and free-draining soil.

C. ternata
Dense, bushy shrub with fragrant, white, orange-blossom-like flowers.
HEIGHT: 8 ft (2.4 m)
SPREAD: 8 ft (2.4 m)

C. "Aztec Pearl"
A hybrid with more finely divided leaves composed of three to five slender leaflets, with pink-tinged, large white flowers.
HEIGHT/SPREAD:
5 ft (1.5 m)

RELIABLE PLANTS

CLEMATIS

Evergreen or deciduous climbers (a few are herbaceous perennials) with abundant flowers, often followed by silver-gray seed heads. Flowering from late winter to fall, colors include white, yellow, pink, pinkish red, reddish purple, and violet. Most clematis like fertile, well-drained soil and prefer to have their feet in the shade and their heads in the sun.

C. alpina and cultivars

Deciduous climbers with bell-shaped, white, blue or purple-pink flowers in spring, these climbers are ideal for exposed, variable weather sites.
HEIGHT: To 10 ft (3 m)

C. armandii

A vigorous, evergreen climber with star-shaped, fragrant, white flowers in early spring. Prefers a sheltered site.
HEIGHT: 15 ft (5 m)

C. montana and cultivars

Vigorous climber with masses of white or pink flowers in late spring.
HEIGHT: To 30 ft (10 m)

C. "Nelly Moser"

Compact, large-flowered climber with pinkish flowers striped with carmine in early summer.
HEIGHT: To 10 ft (3 m)

C. "The President"

Large-flowered hybrid with single, rich purple flowers in early summer.
HEIGHT: To 10 ft (3 m)

CLEMATIS FLOWER

CONVALLARIA

Lily-of-the-valley

A low-growing plant with spreading, rhizomatous roots, lily-of-the-valley makes excellent ground cover in a shady spot. However, it is only suitable for positions where its spread can be restricted as it can be invasive where conditions suit it. Good for growing as ground cover under deciduous trees.

C. majalis

Pointed, oval, mid-green leaves with clasping bases surround slender stems carrying pendent, bell-shaped white flowers arranged in open sprays. Flowers are carried in late spring and early summer, and are intensely fragrant. Several cultivars exist, but are much less commonly grown than the species. "Fortin's Giant" has larger flowers than the species and is a strong, robust grower. C. m. "Flore Pleno" has frilly, double blooms while C. m. var. rosea bears flowers of a dusky pink shade. One of the most attractive cultivars is C. m. "Variegata," whose leaves bear several narrow, golden yellow stripes down their length.
HEIGHT: 6 in (15 cm)
SPREAD: Indefinite

RELIABLE PLANTS

CORNUS
Dogwood
Mainly deciduous trees and shrubs grown for their spring flowers, foliage, and colored stems. Grow in fertile, well-drained soil in sun or partial shade.

C. alba "Sibirica"
Shrub with bright red fall leaves and winter shoots.
HEIGHT: 2 ft (1.5 m)

C. alternifolia "Argentea"
A tiered shrub or tree with white-edged leaves.
HEIGHT: 20 ft (6 m)

C. "Eddie's White Wonder"
Conical tree with masses of whitish flowers.
HEIGHT: 8 ft (2.4 m)
SPREAD: 5 ft (1.5 m)

C. stolonifera "Flaviramea"
Vigorous shrub with bright yellow-green winter shoots.
HEIGHT: 5 ft (1.5 m)

COTONEASTER
Reliable evergreen or deciduous shrubs and small trees grown mainly for their berries in fall, which follow small, creamy white, cup-shaped summer flowers. Grow in any but waterlogged soil in sun or partial shade.

C. dammeri
Prostrate evergreen shrub with white summer flowers and red berries; ideal for ground cover.
HEIGHT: 8 in (20 cm)
SPREAD: 6 ft (2 m)

C. horizontalis
Prostrate deciduous shrub that can be trained against a wall. Has pinkish flowers and red berries.
HEIGHT: 3 ft (1 cm)
SPREAD: 5 ft (1.5 m)

C. "Rothschildianus"
Semievergreen shrub with golden yellow berries.
HEIGHT/SPREAD: 15 ft (5 m)

CROCUS
Bulbs grown for their goblet-like flowers in shades of white, cream, yellow, lilac, and purple. Most flower in spring, but some emerge in late winter, and a few in fall. Grow crocuses in drifts at the front of a mixed or herbaceous border or in a lawn. They need well-drained, moderately fertile soil and full sun.

C. banaticus
Produces lilac flowers in the fall.
HEIGHT: 4 in (10 cm)
SPREAD: 2 in (5 cm)

C. cartwrightianus
Produces one to five fragrant, purple-veined, lilac or white flowers in the fall and early winter.
HEIGHT: 4 in (10 cm)
SPREAD: 1.5 in (4 cm)

C. chrysanthus
Late winter- and early spring-flowering crocus with up to four cream scented flowers. Hybrids include C. "Cream Beauty," with rich, cream flowers; C. "Snow Bunting," with white flowers; and C. "Zwanenburg Bronze," with yellow flowers, marked purplish bronze outside.
HEIGHT: 2 in (5 cm)
SPREAD: 1½ in (4 cm)

CROCUS VERNUS

RELIABLE PLANTS

DIANTHUS
Carnation, pink
Large genus of mainly summer-flowering, often fragrant, perennials. Flowers are white, pink, salmon, yellow, or mauve – sometimes contrasting colors. Compact cultivars are good in rock gardens. All have attractive foliage, usually bluish gray. Grow in a sunny site in well-drained, preferably alkaline soil.

D. armeria
Deptford pink
Bears an abundance of dense, single, bright cerise-pink flowers.
HEIGHT: 1 ft (30 cm)
SPREAD: 18 in (45 cm)

D. "Golden Cross"
Bright yellow, double carnation ideally suited for borders.
HEIGHT: 18 in (45 cm)
SPREAD: 16 in (40 cm)

D. "Gran's Favorite"
White, double, clove-scented flowers laced with pink.
HEIGHT: 10 in (25 cm)
SPREAD: 16 in (40 cm)

D. gratianopolitanus
Cheddar pink
Mat forming with pink, fragrant single flowers.
HEIGHT: 6 in (15 cm)
SPREAD: 12 in (30 cm)

ELEAGNUS
The evergreen forms of eleagnus are tough, easily grown plants that thrive in most conditions. They prefer fertile, free-draining soil and tolerate sun or shade. Variegated varieties produce their best colors in full sun.

E. pungens "Maculata"
Bushy shrub with deep green leaves, splashed bright gold. Scented, white, bell-shaped flowers appear in the fall.
HEIGHT: 10 ft (3 m)
SPREAD: 10 ft (3 m)

ERICA
Heath, heather
Mainly low-growing evergreen shrubs grown for their year-round foliage and white, pink, or purple flowers. Grow in well-drained, preferably acid soil (some tolerate alkaline soil) in full sun.

E. carnea "Ann Sparkes"
Low, spreading shrub that bears pink flowers in late winter to spring and dark golden foliage that turns crimson in cold weather.
HEIGHT: 6 in (15 cm)
SPREAD: 10 in (25 cm)

HEATHER

RELIABLE PLANTS

EUONYMUS

Deciduous and evergreen shrubs and trees; variegated evergreen varieties offer the best value for busy gardeners. Tolerate sun or light shade, and prefer free-draining soil but will grow in most soils, even chalk.

E. fortunei

A tough, hardy, evergreen species, some of which make good ground-cover plants. If supported, the plant will also grow as a self-clinging, scrambling climber. Leaves are small and oval. E. f. "Dart's Blanket" makes excellent ground cover, with purple-bronze foliage in the fall. E. f. "Emerald Gaiety" makes a low, compact hummock. Its green leaves edged with white can take on a pink tinge in the fall.
HEIGHT: 1–3 ft
(30–90 cm)
SPREAD: 2–5 ft
(60–150 cm)

E. japonicus "Ovatus Aureus"

A compact, relatively slow-growing cultivar with leaves irregularly margined with yellow; particularly bright in the winter garden. Full sun brings out the best foliage color.
HEIGHT: 4 ft (1.2 m)
SPREAD: 3 ft (90 cm)

FUCHSIA

Deciduous shrubs with showy pendulous, bell-like white, pink, red, or purple flowers over a long period from summer to fall. Hardiness varies and, depending on the size and habit, they have a range of uses from specimen shrub to bedding and hanging baskets. Grow in fertile, well-drained soil in a partially shaded site. Half-hardy and tender varieties can also be grown in sun.

F. "La Campanella"

Free flowering, trailing shrub, with bluish purple and white flowers.
HEIGHT/SPREAD: 18 in (45 cm)

F. magellanica "Variegata"

Hardy plant with red and purple flowers and leaves edged with cream.
HEIGHT/SPREAD: 2 ft (60 cm)

F. "Mrs Popple"

Hardy plant, with red and purple flowers.
HEIGHT/SPREAD: 3 ft (1 m)

F. "Swingtime"

Half-hardy, bush shrub, with large, double, red and white flowers.
HEIGHT: 2 ft (60 cm)
SPREAD: 18 in (45 cm)

F. "Thalia"

Upright, with rich orange flowers amid large, velvety leaves.
HEIGHT/SPREAD: 3 ft (1m)

FUCHSIA

RELIABLE PLANTS

GALANTHUS
Snowdrop
Perennial dwarf bulbs with appealing, nodding, bell-like flowers in late winter to early spring, usually on 6-in (15-cm) stems. The flowers are white but can be marked with other colors. Most snowdrops are vigorous and easily grown. Grow in reliably moist but well-drained soil in partial shade.

G. elwesii
Has slender bluish, honey-scented flowers in winter.
HEIGHT: 8 in (20 cm)
SPREAD: 3 in (8 cm)

G. "Ketton"
Robust with large flowers with x-shaped, dark green marks in late winter.
HEIGHT: 8 in (20 cm)
SPREAD: 3 in (8 cm)

G. nivalis "Flore Pleno"
Common snowdrop
Bears double flowers marked with green.
HEIGHT/SPREAD: 4 in (10 cm)

G. "S. Arnott"
Tall with large, fragrant flowers in late winter.
HEIGHT/SPREAD: 8 in (20 cm)

GERANIUM
Undemanding border plants, with some small varieties suited to rock gardens. Their white, pink, purple, or blue flowers appear in late spring to early summer. Grow in well-drained soil in sun or partial shade.

G. cinereum "Ballerina"
Has purplish pink flowers with dark purple veining.
HEIGHT: 6 in (15 cm)
SPREAD: 12 in (30 cm)

G. "Johnson's Blue"
Spreading perennial with blue flowers in summer.
HEIGHT/SPREAD: 12 in (30 cm)

HEBE
Evergreen, usually mound-forming shrubs with attractive leaves and spikes of summer flowers in pink, white, lilac, or purplish red. Small hebes suit rock gardens. Grow in well-drained soil in full sun.

H. cupressoides "Boughton Dome"
Dwarf, dome-shaped shrub that seldom flowers.
HEIGHT: 2 ft (60 cm)
SPREAD: 3 ft (1 m)

H. "Great Orme"
Rounded shrub with large, bright pink flowers that fade to white.
HEIGHT/SPREAD: 4 ft (1.2 m)

SPRING DISPLAY OF CONTAINERS FEATURING SNOWDROPS

RELIABLE PLANTS

HEDERA
Ivy
Evergreen, self-clinging climbers, ideal for growing against shady walls, as ground cover, or in containers. Most grow up to 15 ft (5 m) high. Grow in moist but well-drained, preferably alkaline soil in sun or partial shade.

H. algeriensis "Gloire de Marengo"
Heavily variegated yellow-green and cream leaves.

H. colchica "Dentata Variegata"
Smooth, soft green leaves margined with cream.

H. helix and cultivars
H. h. "Buttercup" has small bright golden leaves; H. h. "Glacier" has small triangular, silver-gray leaves edged with white. H. h. "Manda's Crested" has small wavy-edged leaves that turn copper in the fall.

HELLEBORUS
Hellebore
Robust perennials with cup-shaped or tubular flowers in white, cream, green, and purple in winter and spring. Grow in moist soil in sun or partial shade.

H. argutiflorus
Apple-green spring flowers above prickly leaves.
HEIGHT: 3 ft (1 m)
SPREAD: 2 ft (60 cm)

H. foetidus
Bear's foot, dungwort
Foul scented when crushed, bears bell-shaped green flowers edged with maroon in late winter.
HEIGHT: 30 in (75 cm)
SPREAD: 2 ft (60 cm)

H. orientalis
Variable, with white, pink or purple flowers, some heavily marked or spotted.
HEIGHT/SPREAD: 18 in (45 cm)

HEDERA HELIX "GOLDHEART"

RELIABLE PLANTS

HEMEROCALLIS
Daylily

Clump-forming perennials, grown for their lily-like, yellow, cream, orange, red, or pink summer flowers. These last only a day but appear in succession. Most are ideal for a mixed or herbaceous border. Grow in well-drained but moist soil in sun or partial shade.

H. "Corky"
Compact, free-flowering evergreen with clear yellow flowers. Prefers full sun.
HEIGHT: 34 in (85 cm)
SPREAD: 16 in (40 cm)

H. "Stella de Oro"
Bears circular, bright yellow flowers.
HEIGHT: 12 in (30 cm)
SPREAD: 18 in (45 cm)

HYDRANGEA
Handsome deciduous and evergreen shrubs and climbers grown for their showy, pink, blue, or white, late-summer flowers. Most grow in moist soil in sun or partial shade. They are ideal as specimen shrubs, for shrub borders, and in containers.

H. macrophylla "Ami Pasquier"
Deciduous shrub with numerous blue flowers in summer. Occasionally grown as a houseplant when young.
HEIGHT: 5 ft (1.5 m)
SPREAD: 6 ft (2 m)

H. petiolaris
Self-clinging climber with white lacecap flowers
HEIGHT/SPREAD: 50 ft (15 m)

ILEX
Holly

Slow-growing, evergreen shrubs and trees with glossy green leaves that are usually spiny and can be variegated with cream or white. Females have decorative red or yellow berries in fall and early winter. Hollies tolerate pruning to size. Grow in any well-drained soil in sun or partial shade.

I. x altaclerensis "Camelliifolia"
Large, conical female shrub with large green leaves and scarlet berries.
HEIGHT: 16 ft (5 m)
SPREAD: 10 ft (3 m)

I. x aquifolium "Golden Queen"
Male tree bearing cream stems and broad leaves margined with gold.
HEIGHT: 10 ft (3 m)
SPREAD: 4 ft (1.2 m)

I. aquifolium "Pyramidalis Fructu Luteo"
Conical female shrub bearing yellow berries.
HEIGHT: 15 ft (5 m)
SPREAD: 4 ft (1.2 m)

I. x meservae "Blue Angel"
Slow-growing with bluish leaves and red berries.
HEIGHT: 6 ft (2 m)
SPREAD: 3 ft (1 m)

HYDRANGEA

RELIABLE PLANTS

IRIS
Bulbs and rhizomes suited, according to type, to rock gardens, borders, and bog gardens. Valued for their colorful, often spectacular white, yellow, blue, or purple flowers – sometimes combining two or more colors – from late winter to summer. All irises need a sunny or partially shaded site. Grow border and rock irises in fertile, well-drained soil and bog plants in wet soil.

I. bucharica
Vigorous rhizome bearing up to six golden yellow to white flowers in spring. Suits a rock garden.
HEIGHT: 8 in (20 cm)
SPREAD: 5 in (12 cm)

I. graminea
Rhizome with fragrant, violet-purple flowers in late spring. Suits a border.
HEIGHT: 8 in (20 cm)

I. "Katharine Hodgkin"
Vigorous rhizome with blue flowers patterned with blue and yellow markings. Suits a border.
HEIGHT 5 in (12 cm)

I. laevigata
A rhizomatous bog plant that produces vivid purplish blue flowers in early summer.
HEIGHT: 32 in (80 cm)

I. pseudacorus
Vigorous bog plant with yellow flowers in mid- to late summer.
HEIGHT: 3 ft (1 m)

JUNIPERUS
Juniper
A family of conifers with many useful, easily grown species and cultivars. Their habit ranges from prostrate through wide-spreading to tall and slender; foliage colors include blue, gray, green, and gold. Their uses range from ground cover to accent plants, and they provide interest in winter.

J. communis "Compressa"
A dwarf cultivar with grayish green foliage, making a dense, erect column.
HEIGHT: To 2 ft (60 cm)
SPREAD: 4–6 in (10–15 cm)

J. pfitzeriana "Old Gold"
A spreading dwarf cultivar with bronzy gold foliage and a compact habit.
HEIGHT: 3 ft (90 cm)
SPREAD: 4 ft (1.2 m)

J. scopulorum "Skyrocket"
This slender, blue-gray conifer is ideal for adding height to rock gardens. It takes some years to reach the given dimensions.
HEIGHT: 6 ft (2 m)
SPREAD: 1 ft (30 cm)

J. squamata "Blue Star"
Compact, low, and bushy plant with spiky, steely blue leaves.
HEIGHT: 20 in (50 cm)
SPREAD: 24 in (60 cm)

Iris

RELIABLE PLANTS

LATHYRUS

Climbers grown for their scented flowers in shades of white, pink, red, and purple. Grow in fertile, well-drained soil, in sun or partial shade.

L. latifolius
Perennial pea
Perennial with white, pink, or purple flowers.
HEIGHT: 10 ft (3 m)
SPREAD: 3 ft (1 m)

L. odoratus and cultivars
Sweet pea
Annuals with fragrant flowers in late summer.
HEIGHT: 6 ft (2 m)
SPREAD: 3 ft (1 m)

LILIUM
Lily
Bulbs grown for their often heavily scented summer flowers, in all colors but blue, which can be funnel-, bowl-, or trumpet-shaped, or "turkscap" with recessed petals. Grow in fertile, well-drained soil (some need acid soil), in sun or partial shade.

L. regale
Regal lily
Medium-sized lily that produces deep red or orange-red flowers. Site in sun or partial shade.
HEIGHT: 6 ft (2 m)

LONICERA
Honeysuckle
Deciduous and evergreen shrubs and climbers, with scented, tubular summer flowers. Honeysuckles can be trained against a wall or fence and will grow in almost any, but preferably fertile, soil in sun or partial shade.

L. x americana
Deciduous twining climber with very fragrant yellow flowers in summer, followed by red berries.
HEIGHT: 22 ft (7 m)

L. nitida "Baggesen's Gold"
Golden-leaved evergreen shrub; withstands clipping.
HEIGHT: 5 ft (1.5 m)

L. x purpusii "Winter Beauty"
Semievergreen shrub with small, very fragrant white flowers in winter.
HEIGHT: 5 ft (1.5 m)

L. periclymenum "Graham Thomas"
Fragrant white flowers that turn yellow.
HEIGHT: 12 ft (4 m)

L. x tellmanniana
Woody, twining climber that produces copper-orange, unscented flowers from late spring to midsummer.
HEIGHT: 12 ft (4 m)

LATHYRUS ODORATUS

RELIABLE PLANTS

MAGNOLIA

Shrubs and small trees, which may be evergreen or deciduous, with large, waxy, showy flowers in spring. Many species are difficult to grow well, being fussy about soil, climate, and position, but these species can be recommended for the busy gardener.

M. stellata
A spreading, rounded, slow-growing shrub or small tree that makes an excellent focal point. It is a deciduous plant, whose branches are decked with a profusion of flowers in early spring before the leaves appear. The starry blooms have many narrow petals and a sweet fragrance. Several cultivars have been raised; M. s. "Royal Star" and "Waterlily" both have larger, more showy flowers than the species.
HEIGHT: 5 ft (1.5 m)
SPREAD: 6 ft (1.8 m)

M. Kosar Hybrids
Medium-sized shrubs and small trees with pink- or purple-tinged blooms. They have many of the virtues of M. stellata. Hybrids available include "Betty," "Jane," "Pinkie," and "Susan."
HEIGHT: 7 ft (2 m)
SPREAD: 4–6 ft (1.2–1.8 m)

MAHONIA

Evergreen shrubs, many with fine foliage, but mostly grown for their fragrant yellow flowers. Grow in fertile, well-drained soil in sun or partial shade.

M. argutifolius "Orange Flame"
Rust-orange young leaves turn red in winter. Makes good ground cover.
HEIGHT: 2 ft (60 cm)
SPREAD: 4 ft (1.2 m)

M. x media "Charity"
Erect shrub with bright lemon-yellow flowers.
HEIGHT: 10 ft (3 m)
SPREAD: 4 ft (1.2 m)

NARCISSUS
Daffodil

Spring-flowering bulbs, with yellow or white flowers characterized by a central, often elongated, cup or trumpet. Grow in moist, fertile, well-drained soil in sun or part shade.

N. "Actaea"
Fragrant white flowers with shallow, yellow, orange-edged cups.
HEIGHT: 18 in (45 cm)

N. "February Gold"
Vigorous daffodil with golden yellow flowers in early spring.
HEIGHT: 7 in (18 cm)

NARCISSUS "TETE-A-TETE"

RELIABLE PLANTS

OSMANTHUS
Hardy, evergreen shrubs that will grow in sun or shade and almost any soil, though well-drained soil is preferred.

O. x burkwoodii
Compact and slow growing, with leathery, dark green leaves and very fragrant white flowers in spring.
HEIGHT: 6 ft (1.8 m)
SPREAD: 4 ft (1.2 m)

O. delavayi
Rounded shrub with small, glossy, very dark green leaves and a profusion of tubular, white, fragrant flowers in spring. Prefers a reasonably sheltered spot.
HEIGHT: 6 ft (1.8 m)
SPREAD: 6 ft (1.8 m)

POPPIES IN A SILVER PLANTING

PACHYSANDRA
Japanese spurge
Dwarf, mainly evergreen, shrubs that are tolerant of deep shade. They are very useful as weed-suppressing ground-cover plants and are ideal for growing beneath trees. Moist soil is preferred, although they will tolerate dry conditions.

P. terminalis
Low-growing evergreen species with a carpet-forming habit; toothed, diamond-shaped leaves are clustered at the tips of short stems. Spikes of small, white flowers are produced during summer. P. t. "Variegata" has creamy white markings on its leaves.
HEIGHT: 6 in (15 cm)
SPREAD: 12 in (30 cm)

PAPAVER
Poppy
Annuals, biennials, and perennials with showy, bowl-shaped, white, pink, red, yellow, orange, and purple flowers in late spring and early summer. Ideal in a border; small annuals suit a rock garden. Grow in well-drained soil in full sun. Annuals thrive in poor soil.

P. orientale "Black and White"
Perennial with white flowers blotched with blackish red inside.
HEIGHT: 3 ft (1 m)
SPREAD: 2 ft (60 cm)

P. rhoeas Shirley Series
Cultivars have single or double flowers in red, yellow, pink, and orange.
HEIGHT: 36 in (90 cm)
SPREAD: 12 in (30 cm)

RELIABLE PLANTS

PELARGONIUM

Tender, shrubby, evergreen perennials that produce white, pink, or red flowers through summer. Some are grown for their scented foliage. Pelargoniums thrive in containers; trailing varieties are ideal in hanging baskets. Grow in well-drained soil in a sheltered, sunny or partially shaded site.

P. "Bird Dancer"
Dwarf pelargonium with shrimp-pink flowers. Good for bedding.
HEIGHT: 10 in (25 cm)
SPREAD: 8 in (20 cm)

P. crispum "Variegatum"
Upright with lemon-scented, yellow-edged leaves; bears clusters of pale mauve flowers.
HEIGHT: 30 in (75 cm)
SPREAD: 2 ft (60 cm)

P. "Dolly Varden"
Leaves variegated with cream; bears clusters of single scarlet flowers.
HEIGHT: 18 in (45 cm)
SPREAD: 2 ft (60 cm)

P. "L'Elégante"
Silver-green, ivylike leaves becoming variegated if kept dry, with white, star-like flowers. Trailing to 2 ft (60 cm).
HEIGHT: To 10 in (25 cm)
SPREAD: To 8 in (20 cm)

PENSTEMON

Mainly perennials with white, red, pink, or purple flowers borne in summer. Larger species can be used as border or bedding plants, while smaller plants are suitable for rock gardens. Grow in well-drained soil in a sheltered sunny or partially shaded site.

P. "Apple Blossom"
Small, tubular pink flowers from summer to early fall.
HEIGHT: 18 in (45 cm)
SPREAD: 12 in (30 cm)

P. "Stapleford Gem"
Large-leaved plant with lilac-purple flowers from midsummer to fall.
HEIGHT: 32 in (80 cm)
SPREAD: 12 in (30 cm)

PELARGONIUM

RELIABLE PLANTS

PETUNIA

Genus of erect annuals and perennials with saucer- or trumpet-shaped flowers from late spring to early fall. Flowers are a variety of colors, including pink, red, pale yellow, violet, and white. Cultivars are divided into two groups: Grandifloras have bigger flowers, are prone to rain damage, and suit sheltered hanging baskets. Multifloras have more, smaller flowers, tolerate wet weather, suit poor soil, and are ideal summer bedding.

P. Carpet Series
Multiflora spreading petunias with red and orange flowers. Ideal for ground cover.
HEIGHT: 10 in (25 cm)
SPREAD: 36 in (90 cm)

P. Flash Series
Early flowering, Grandiflora petunias with various shades of pink, red, and blue flowers. Ideal for ground cover.
HEIGHT: 16 in (40 cm)
SPREAD: 36 in (90 cm)

P. Primetime Series
One of the broadest ranges of Multiflora cultivars with 24 different flower colors and five mixtures.
HEIGHT: 14 in (35 cm)
SPREAD: 36 in (90 cm)

PHLOX

Large genus of perennials (and some annuals), some stately border plants, others trailing or cushion-forming suited for rock gardens, dry walls, and edgings. Grow in fertile, well-drained soil in sun or partial shade.

P. douglasii "Boothman's Variety"
Mound-forming evergreen that produces violet-pink flowers with dark eyes.
HEIGHT: 8 in (20 cm)
SPREAD: 12 in (30 cm)

P. maculata "Alpha"
Erect perennial bearing deep pink flowers that have dark centers.
HEIGHT: 32 in (80 cm)
SPREAD: 3 ft (1 m)

P. nana "Fujiyama"
Deciduous perennial spread by runners. Produces many pink, purple, or white flowers from summer to fall.
HEIGHT: 4 ft (1.2 m)
SPREAD: 3 ft (1 m)

POTENTILLA
Cinquefoil

Undemanding deciduous shrubs and perennials grown for their cup-shaped flowers in a range of colors including white, yellow, pink, and red. Grow in well-drained, not too fertile soil, in full sun.

P. fruticosa "Abbotswood"
Compact, bushy shrub with white flowers and dark blue-green leaves. This long-flowering plant makes an excellent shrub border or a low hedge.
HEIGHT: 30 in (75 cm)
SPREAD: 4 ft (1.2 m)

P. "Gibson's Scarlet"
Clump-forming perennial with brilliant red flowers.
HEIGHT: 18 in (45 cm)
SPREAD: 2 ft (60 cm)

P. recta
Perennial with saucer-shaped, pale yellow flowers.
HEIGHT: 24 in (60 cm)
SPREAD: 18 in (45 cm)

PETUNIA IN A HANGING BASKET

RELIABLE PLANTS

PRIMULA

Perennials grown for their appealing flowers with a variety of garden uses: some early-flowering types make good bedding, while others can be used in rock gardens and as bog plants. The following all flower in spring and early summer and require moist, neutral to acid soil in sun or partial shade.

P. denticulata
Drumstick primula
Rosette-forming perennial with upright stems and spherical heads of purple flowers. Needs acid soil.
HEIGHT/SPREAD: 18 in
(45 cm)

P. florindae
Giant cowslip
Rosette-forming perennial with white, sulfur-yellow flowers.
HEIGHT: 4 ft (1.2 m)
SPREAD: 3 ft (1 m)

P. "Inverewe"
Rosette-forming perennial with clusters of bright red flowers. Needs acid soil.
HEIGHT: 30 in (75 cm)
SPREAD: 24 in (60 cm)

P. "Wanda"
Vigorous, long-flowering evergreen. Produces clusters of solitary claret-red flowers. Thrives in both sun and shade.
HEIGHT: 4 in (10 cm)
SPREAD: 12 in (30 cm)

PRUNUS

Deciduous and evergreen trees and shrubs grown mainly for their flowers (usually produced in spring). Some members of the *Prunus* family are notable for their leaves and bark, and make excellent specimen trees. Evergreens withstand clipping. Grow in fertile, moist, well-drained soil in sun or partial shade.

EVERGREENS:
P. laurocerasus "Otto Luyken"
Dense, compact shrub with leathery leaves and candle-like white flowers.
HEIGHT: 3 ft (1 m)
SPREAD: 5 ft (1.5 m)

P. lusitanica
Portugal laurel
Dense shrub with oval leaves and cup-shaped, fragrant white flowers.
HEIGHT: 25 ft (8 m)
SPREAD: 30 ft (10 m)

DECIDUOUS:
P. "Amanogawa"
Upright tree bearing dense clusters of saucer-shaped, shell-pink flowers.
HEIGHT: 25 ft (8 m)
SPREAD: 12 ft (4 m)

P. "Shirofugen"
Spreading tree with clusters of double, scented white flowers, turning pink in fall.
HEIGHT: 25 ft (8 m)
SPREAD: 30 ft (10 m)

PYRACANTHA
Firethorn
Evergreen shrubs with thorny branches, valued for their foliage, flowers, and fruits. Often grown as wall plants, they also make rounded, free-standing shrubs. Look for disease-resistant cultivars.

P. "Navaho"
Small or medium-sized shrub with frothy, creamy white flowers in spring. Its dense clusters of orange berries deepen in color as they ripen.
HEIGHT: 10 ft (3 m)
SPREAD: 5 ft (1.5 m)

P. "Sapho Red"
Vigorous variety with white flowers, followed by brilliant red berries.
HEIGHT: 10 ft (3 m)
SPREAD: 5 ft (1.5 m)

P. "Shawnee"
Medium-sized, spreading shrub with good disease-resistance. A profusion of white flowers in spring are followed by yellow or pale orange, long-lasting berries.
HEIGHT: 15 ft (4.5 m)
SPREAD: 12 ft (4 m)

P. "Teton"
Vigorous, upright-growing shrub with small, glossy leaves and yellow or orange berries.
HEIGHT: 15 ft (4.5 m)
SPREAD: 10 ft (3 m)

RELIABLE PLANTS

ROSA
Rose

Deciduous shrubs and climbers, with colorful, often scented, single or double flowers in summer. Most grown in gardens are hybrids. According to habit, roses can be used as specimen plants, as hedges, in mixed borders, or to scramble over walls and trees (see pp. 342–3).

R. "Orange Sunblaze"
Miniature bush rose with bright orange-red flowers.
HEIGHT/SPREAD: 12 in (30 cm)

R. "Sweet Dream"
Bush rose with clusters of peach-apricot flowers.
HEIGHT/SPREAD: 16 in (40 cm)

ROSA "SWEET DREAM"

R. "Ballerina"
Robust, repeat-flowering shrub rose with a neat compact habit. Clusters of soft pink flowers with white centers are borne in profusion.
HEIGHT/SPREAD: 4 ft (1.2 m)

R. "Golden Showers"
Upright, branching climber producing clusters of numerous fragrant, deep yellow flowers that fade to creamy yellow.
HEIGHT/SPREAD: 8 ft (2.4 m)

ROSA "ORANGE SUNBLAZE"

RELIABLE PLANTS

SEDUM
Stonecrop
Perennials grown for their fleshy, succulent leaves and attractive flowers. Hardy species can be grown in a rock garden, while frost-prone species should be grown as houseplants. Grow in well-drained soil in sun.

S. "Autumn Joy"
Produces flat heads of star-shaped brick-red flowers in fall.
HEIGHT/SPREAD: 2 ft (60 cm)

S. spathulifolium "Purpureum"
Mat-forming with purple-flushed leaves and yellow flowers in summer. Tolerates light shade.
HEIGHT: 4 in (10 cm)
SPREAD: 2 ft (60 cm)

SYRINGA
Lilac
Deciduous shrubs with spikes of scented white, pink, lilac, or purple flowers in spring. Lilacs grow well as specimens or in a shrub border. Site in well-drained, preferably alkaline, soil in sun.

S. meyeri "Palibin"
Slow-growing, with small, lavender-pink flowers.
HEIGHT/SPREAD: 4 ft (1.2 m)

S. vulgaris "Charles Joly"
Bears double, deep purple flowers.
HEIGHT/SPREAD: 12 ft (3.5 m)

S. vulgaris "Mme Lemoine"
Bears compact, double white flowers.
HEIGHT/SPREAD: 12 ft (3.5 m)

TULIPA
Tulip
Spring-flowering bulbs grown for their colorful, goblet-like flowers in a wide range of shades. Excellent for beds and borders. Grow in well-drained soil in full sun.

T. "Giuseppe Verdi"
A red and yellow garden hybrid suitable for rock gardens.
HEIGHT: 8 in (20 cm)

T. praestans "Fusilier"
This species is good for naturalizing in lawns, with bright red flowers.
HEIGHT: 12 in (30 cm)

T. tarda
A low-growing species, with star-shaped, white green-tinged flowers.
HEIGHT: 4 in (10 cm)

TULIPS IN CONTAINERS

RELIABLE PLANTS

VIBURNUM

Deciduous and evergreen shrubs, some of which have fragrant flowers and/or decorative berries. Most viburnums suit a shrub border or woodland garden. Evergreens can be pruned. Grow in a fertile, well-drained soil in sun or partial shade.

V. x bodnantense **"Dawn"**
Deciduous, heavily fragrant pink winter flowers.
HEIGHT: 10 ft (3 m)
SPREAD: 6 ft (2 m)

V. x burkwoodii **"Anne Russell"**
Produces sweetly scented white spring flowers.
HEIGHT: 3 ft (1 m)
SPREAD: 4 ft (1.2 m)

VIOLAS

VINCA
Periwinkle

Vigorous, evergreen sub-shrubs that are ideal as ground cover. Periwinkles are tolerant of shade or sun and almost any soil. They can be invasive, as their trailing stems root at the tips as they grow.

V. major
Glossy, deep green, pointed leaves offset the brilliant blue flowers produced from spring until midsummer.
HEIGHT: 12 in (30 cm)
SPREAD: Indefinite

V. minor
The many cultivars of lesser periwinkle offer varying flower color and leaf variegation.
HEIGHT: 6 in (15 cm)
SPREAD: Indefinite

VIOLA

Annual pansies and perennials grown for their flowers. Ideal for containers, rock gardens, and borders. They need moist, well-drained soil and sun or part shade.

V. cornuta
Spreading perennial with violet spring flowers.
HEIGHT: 6 in (15 cm)
SPREAD: 16 in (40 cm)

V. **"Jackanapes"**
Bears yellow and brown flowers.
HEIGHT: 5 in (12 cm)
SPREAD: 12 in (30 cm)

V. riviniana **"Purpurea"**
Perennial with purple-flushed leaves and small violet flowers.
HEIGHT: 3 in (8 cm)
SPREAD: 12 in (30 cm)

INDEX

ACKNOWLEDGMENTS

p. 14 Steven Wooster/designer Geoffrey Whiten; p. 17 Steven Wooster/designer Aldermaston and Wasing Hort. Society; p. 26 Steven Wooster/designer James Alexander-Sinclair; p. 28 Steven Wooster/designer David Edmonds; p. 30 Steven Wooster/designer Geoffrey Whiten; p. 31 Steven Wooster; p. 36, p. 37, p. 44, p. 47 Steven Wooster; p. 54 Peter McHoy; p. 58a Steven Wooster; p. 58b, p. 60, p. 61 Peter McHoy; p. 65 Steven Wooster/designer Cherida Seago; p. 66, p. 67, p. 69, p. 70, p. 71, p. 74, p. 76, p. 77, p. 78, p. 79, p. 80, p. 81, p. 85, p. 86, p. 87, p. 88, p. 89, p. 90, p. 91, p. 92, p. 93 Peter McHoy; p. 103 Steven Wooster/designer Michael Balston; p. 105 Steven Wooster/designer Geoffrey Whiten; p. 106 Clive Nichols/designer Julian Treyer-Evans; p. 107 Andrew Lawson; p. 110 Steven Wooster/Chris Gregory; p. 111 Steven Wooster/designer Myles Challis; p. 129 Andrew Lawson; p. 153 Steven Wooster/designer Michael Balston; p. 168 John Glover; p. 181 Andrew Lawson; p. 190 Andrew Lawson; p. 191 S&O Mathews; p. 192 Clive Nichols; p. 209 Jerry Harpur/designer Helen Yemem; p. 215 Jerry Harpur/designer Lisette Pleasance, London; p. 216 Steven Wooster/designer Geoffrey Whiten; p. 219 Jerry Harpur/designer Isabelle Green, California;p. 221 Steven Wooster/designer Terence Conran; p. 224 Andrew Lawson/designer Anthony Noel; p. 230 Steven Wooster/designer Carol Klein; p. 231 Steven Wooster/designer Terence Conran; p. 233 Steven Wooster/designer Carol Klein; p. 234 John Glover; p. 236, p. 237 Steven Wooster/deisgner Terence Conran; p. 239 Steven Wooster/designer Chris Gregory; p. 257 Jerry Harpur/designer Anne Alexander-Sinclair; p. 258 Andrew Lawson; p. 263 Jerry Harpur/designer Edwina von Gal, New York City; p. 270 Andrew Lawson; p. 274 Steven Wooster/designer Carol Klein; p. 290 Marcus Harpur/designer Susan Rowley; p. 291 Marcus Harpur/designer Susan Rowley; p. 305 John Glover; p. 306 John Glover; p. 325 Steven Wooster/Alan Sargent; p. 327, p. 328 Can O Worms composter, Wiggly Wigglers; p. 330 Hayter Ltd; p. 334 Jerry Harpur/Chiff Chaffs, Dorset; p. 344 S&O Mathews; p. 346 John Glover; p. 351, p. 353 Andrew Lawson/Rofford Manor, Oxford; p. 360 Steven Wooster/Jacquie Gordon; p. 365 Steven Wooster/Terence Conran; p. 370 Jerry Harpur/designer Helen Yemem; p. 377 Jerry Harpur/designer Lisette Pleasance, London; p. 378 Steven Wooster/designer Geoffrey Whiten; p. 384 Steven Wooster/Fairweather Sculpture; p. 387 Jerry Harpur/designer Isabelle Green, California; p. 389 Steven Wooster/designer Terence Conran; p. 380 Andrew Lawson/designer Anthony Noel; p. 392 Jerry Harpur/designer Bob Dash, Long Island; p. 393 S&O Mathews; p. 394 Peter McHoy; p. 396 Clive Nichols; p. 397, p. 399 John Glover; p. 403 Andrew Lawson; p. 404 John Glover; p. 410 S&O Mathews.
Special photography by Peter Anderson/Steven Wooster.
Thanks to Tim Stansfield; Country Gardens, Tring; Jane Haley-Pursey and staff at Solesbridge Mill Water Gardens, Chorleywood; and Spear and Jackson.

Cover: Peter Anderson/Steven Wooster.